Teaching and Learning
in the Elementary School

Eighth Edition

JOHN JAROLIMEK
Professor Emeritus, University of Washington, Seattle

CLIFFORD D. FOSTER, SR.
Professor Emeritus (deceased),
University of Washington, Seattle

RICHARD D. KELLOUGH
Professor Emeritus, California State University,
Sacramento

PEARSON

Merrill
Prentice Hall

Upper Saddle River, New Jersey
Columbus, Ohio

Library of Congress Cataloging-in-Publication Data

Jarolimek, John.
    Teaching and learning in the elementary school / John Jarolimek, Clifford D. Foster, Sr., Richard D. Kellough.—8th ed.
        p. cm.
Includes bibliographical references and index.
    ISBN 0-13-114684-X
    1. Elementary school teaching. 2. Lesson planning. I. Foster, Clifford Donald II. Kellough, Richard D. (Richard Dean) III. Title.
    LB1555.J34 2005
    372.1102—dc22

                                                                    2003020847

Vice President and Executive Publisher: Jeffery W. Johnston
Executive Editor: Debra A. Stollenwerk
Associate Editor: Ben Stephen
Editorial Assistant: Mary Morrill
Production Editor: Kris Robinson-Roach
Production Coordination: *The GTS Companies*/York, PA Campus
Photo Coordination: Lori Whitley
Design Coordinator: Diane C. Lorenzo
Cover Designer: Ali Mohrman
Cover Image: Corbis
Production Manager: Susan Hannahs
Director of Marketing: Ann Castel Davis
Marketing Manager: Darcy Betts Prybella
Marketing Coordinator: Tyra Poole

This book was set in Dutch 823 by *The GTS Companies*/York, PA Campus. It was printed and bound by R. R. Donnelley & Sons Company. The cover was printed by Coral Graphic Services, Inc.

Photo Credits: Scott Cunningham/Merrill, pp. 61, 76, 79, 112, 158; Larry Hamill/Merrill, p. 194; Anthony Magnacca/Merrill, pp. 46, 68, 102, 152, 242, 271, 314; Major Morris/PHCollege, p. 157; Barbara Schwartz/Merrill, pp. xx, 81, 136, 171; Anne Vega/Merrill, pp. 257, 278, 290, 324; Tom Watson/Merrill, p. 37; Todd Yarrington/Merrill, pp. 9, 215.

Pearson Education Ltd.
Pearson Education Singapore Pte. Ltd.
Pearson Education Canada, Ltd.
Pearson Education—Japan

Pearson Education Australia Pty. Limited
Pearson Education North Asia Ltd.
Pearson Educación de Mexico, S.A. de C.V.
Pearson Education Malaysia Pte. Ltd.

10 9 8 7 6 5 4 3 2
ISBN: 0-13-114684-X

In addition to our continued emphasis on the social importance of the elementary school teacher, with this eighth edition we have strengthened the research base and emphasis on the professional skills and strategies necessary to becoming an exemplary elementary school teacher. Amid the social unrest swirling around them—families falling apart, communities in conflict over local issues, children suffering from neglect and abuse, bad economic times, social unrest and threats of war, domestic violence, and battered mothers—stand elementary school teachers, each Monday through Friday during the school year, teaching their charges the three Rs, how to think critically and creatively, how to live with one another, what it means to be an American, and a whole lot more! For countless numbers of children, only their teacher stands between them and the abyss of ignorance and anomie. Accordingly, in this text we paint a realistic picture of what it means to be an elementary school teacher today.

Thus, to accomplish our goals for this eighth edition, two important themes permeate this book: that elementary school teaching is basically a call to the service of humanity, and that the most effective elementary school teaching involves continual, thoughtful, and reflective decision making. This means that you must understand that teaching is a profession and, among other things, that there is no "magical bag of tricks" that can be passed from one person to another that will work for every teacher in every situation in every classroom with every group of children.

Children need teachers who care deeply about them and who can inspire them with the confidence they need to face their future. To motivate, to encourage, to stimulate, to build strong self-esteem, to provide an island of calm in what in the bigger world for many children is a sea of confusion and turmoil, and perhaps most important, to care—these descriptors really define the most important work that a teacher does with elementary school children. Saying this in no way diminishes the importance of the teacher's responsibility to teach essential subject matter.

The fundamental teaching skills presented in this text—centered around the categories of establishing and maintaining an effective learning environment, planning for instruction, assessing student learning, selecting appropriate strategies, and grouping children for instruction—have been derived from the best and most current research and practice. We list **anticipated learning outcomes** at the beginning of each chapter as mental organizers for your study.

In Memory of Clifford D. Foster, Sr.
1923–2002

Additionally, in this edition, for your guidance, at the start of each chapter regarding the content of that chapter we show the relevant principles from the Interstate New Teacher Assessment and Support Consortium (INTASC), which are, in turn, modeled on the National Board for Professional Teaching Standards (NBPTS), also shown. Model standards describing what prospective teachers should know and be able to do in order to receive a teaching license were prepared and released in 1992 by INTASC, a project of the Council of Chief State School Officers (CCSSO), in a document titled *Model Standards for Beginning Teacher Licensing and Development*. Representatives of at least 36 states and professional organizations—including the National Education Association (NEA), the American Federation of Teachers (AFT), the American Association of Colleges for Teacher Education (AACTE), and the National Council for the Accreditation of Teacher Education (NCATE)— make up the group. For information about NBPTS, see the website at http://www.NBPTS.org.

We also show relevant PRAXIS III domains from the Educational Testing Service (ETS). We include these because they represent *performance assessment criteria* that are with increasing frequency used by programs of teacher education as the basis of the development of working portfolios by students during preservice teacher training. (See Activity 2.4 in Chapter 2.) This is useful training for the graduates who are likely to continue their working portfolios during their induction year of teaching and who pursue National Board Certification. For information about PRAXIS, see http://www.ets.org and http://www.bgsu.edu/colleges/edhd/programs/MentorNet/pathprax.html.

The treatment of fundamental teaching skills in this book does not substitute for content-specific teaching methodologies. You will acquire specific teaching skills that apply to reading, mathematics, social studies, science, and the other subjects and skills of the elementary school curriculum by enrolling in special methods courses and studying the texts for those specific disciplines.

Throughout this text you will find learning activities, "verbal snapshots" of situations that a teacher might encounter. Based on real incidents, these provide provocative springboards for thinking and class discussion about teaching. Teaching involves decision making, and good teaching is the result of making wise decisions at appropriate times. Additional study questions, activities, and a list of references for further study appear at the end of each chapter and a glossary appears at the end of the book.

Subject to further directions from your course instructor, you will develop two **major performance outcomes** from your study of this book: (1) the first draft of your personal plan for a classroom management system (see Chapter 4), and (2) a unit plan of instruction for use in your teaching. The unit plan will help you connect the essence of content from one chapter to the next, especially in Chapters 6 through 9, which specifically incorporate this assignment. Both performance outcomes provide meaningful and useful performance exhibits of your study.

Besides the introductory references to INTASC principles, NBPTS standards, and PRAXIS III domains at the start of each chapter, we have strengthened the text's research base and emphasis on professional skills and strategies for teaching. To accomplish these changes, we reordered some content and reduced the number of chapters to nine.

Chapter 1 is an introductory chapter about the influences and challenges of elementary school teaching today (principally a marriage and condensation of former Chapters 1 and 2). Chapter 2 is about the professional responsibilities of being an elementary school teacher (from former Chapter 4). Chapter 3 is about teaching for thinking and questioning (former Chapter 10). Chapter 4 is about creating and managing an effective classroom learning environment (former Chapter 5). Chapter 5 is about the elementary school curriculum and selecting and establishing content standards (selected content from former Chapters 3 and 7). Chapter 6, as with former Chapter 6, is about planning the instruction. Chapter 7 is about assessing and evaluating student learning (former Chapter 11). Chapter 8, as with former Chapter 8, is about selecting the strategies of instruction, and the final chapter of the book, Chapter 9, is, as was former Chapter 9, about grouping children for instruction.

NEW TO THIS EIGHTH EDITION

- The total number of chapters is 9 as opposed to 11 chapters in the previous edition.
- There is a significant reordering of content, perhaps the most important of which is the repositioning of "Developing Skills in Thinking and Questioning" from former Chapter 10 to new Chapter 3, "Managing the Classroom Learning Environment" from former Chapter 5 to new Chapter 4, and "Assessing and Evaluating Student Performance" from former Chapter 11 to new Chapter 7.
- At the start of each chapter, a display is presented of the relevant INTASC principles, NBPTS standards, and PRAXIS III domains.
- Learning activities have been added in each chapter, providing more than 30 items in this edition.
- Throughout the book, there is a strengthened research base and emphasis on the professional skills and strategies necessary to becoming an exemplary elementary school teacher.
- Rather than concentrating on one theme as in the previous edition, two themes now form the basis of the book: that elementary school teaching is basically a call to the service of humanity, and that the most effective elementary school teaching involves continual, thoughtful, and reflective decision making.

PEOPLE WE THANK

The preparation of this eighth edition has resulted in a strong research-based book that we hope you find useful now and for at least the first several years of your professional career. We appreciate the help we have received from others who have shared their ideas and successes and who have permitted us to include their names in the book, from authors and publishers who have graciously permitted us to reprint their materials, and from chapter and man-uscript reviewers who have helped us immensely to avoid errors and improve the book's flow and content. As always, though, we assume full responsibility for any errors or shortcomings that slipped through the several screenings the manuscript received.

We are deeply grateful for the important contributions of the following reviewers: Jioanna Carjuzaa, Linfield College; Karen Moore, California State University, Sacramento; Linda F. Quinn, University of Nevada, Las Vegas; Mar-ilyn S. Howe, Clarion University of Pennsylvania; Melinda Schoenfeldt, Ball State University; Pam Whitmore, Upper Iowa University; and Sue R. Abegglen, Culver-Stockton College.

We express our continued appreciation to the efficacious professionals at Merrill, with whom we have had a long, productive, and satisfying profes-sional relationship.

Merrill Education and the Association for Supervision and Curriculum Development (ASCD) invite you to take advantage of a new online resource, one that provides access to the top research and proven strategies associated with ASCD and Merrill—the Educator Learning Center.

At **www.EducatorLearningCenter.com** you will find resources that will enhance your students' understanding of course topics and of current educational issues, in addition to being invaluable for further research.

HOW THE EDUCATOR LEARNING CENTER WILL HELP YOUR STUDENTS BECOME BETTER TEACHERS

With the combined resources of Merrill Education and ASCD, you and your students will find a wealth of tools and materials to better prepare them for the classroom.

Research

- More than 600 articles from the ASCD journal *Educational Leadership* discuss everyday issues faced by practicing teachers.
- A direct link on the site to Research Navigator™ gives students access to many of the leading education journals, as well as extensive content detailing the research process.
- Excerpts from Merrill Education texts give your students insights on important topics of instructional methods, diverse populations, assessment, classroom management, technology, and refining classroom practice.

Classroom Practice

- Hundreds of lesson plans and teaching strategies are categorized by content area and age range.
- Case studies and classroom video footage provide virtual field experience for student reflection.

- Computer simulations and other electronic tools keep your students abreast of today's classrooms and current technologies.

LOOK INTO THE VALUE OF EDUCATOR LEARNING CENTER YOURSELF

Preview the value of this educational environment by visiting **www.EducatorLearningCenter.com** and clicking on "Demo." For a free 4-month subscription to the Educator Learning Center in conjunction with this text, simply contact your Merrill/Prentice Hall sales representative.

Brief Contents

Chapter 1
Elementary School Teaching Today: An Overview of
Influences and Challenges   1

Chapter 2
The Teacher's Professional Responsibilities   47

Chapter 3
Developing Skills in Thinking and Questioning   77

Chapter 4
Managing the Classroom Learning Environment   103

Chapter 5
The Curriculum: Selecting and Setting Learning
Expectations   137

Chapter 6
Planning the Instruction   195

Chapter 7
Assessing and Evaluating Student Performance   243

Chapter 8
Modes of Teaching: Selecting the Strategies   279

Chapter 9
Organizing and Guiding Children's Learning in Groups   315

Glossary   347

Index   353

Contents

Chapter 1
Elementary School Teaching Today:
An Overview of Influences and Challenges   1

ANTICIPATED OUTCOMES   3

FUNDAMENTAL PURPOSES OF ELEMENTARY EDUCATION   3

Literacy   •   Citizenship Education   •   Personal Development   •
Quality Education for Each Child

DIVERSITY IN THE CLASSROOM   8

FAMILY LIFE   11

SOCIOECONOMIC INFLUENCES   14

EQUALITY OF EDUCATIONAL OPPORTUNITY   15

Student Rights

Activity 1.1 Teach but Don't Touch   17

Learning Styles   •   Race and Racism   •   Gender Equity   •   Inclusion   •
Newcomers to the English Language   •   School Choice and Organizational Change

CURRICULUM STANDARDS AND ACHIEVEMENT TESTING   29

Preparing Students for High-Stakes Achievement Testing

SOCIAL TRAGEDIES   31

Acquired Immune Deficiency Syndrome (AIDS)   •   Illicit Drug Use   •
Child Abuse and Neglect   •   Youth Gangs   •   Bullying and Violence

PARENTS, GUARDIANS, AND THE COMMUNITY   35

Activity 1.2 Neighborhood Violence   36

SUMMARY   38

STUDY QUESTIONS AND ADDITIONAL ACTIVITIES   39

NOTES   40

FOR FURTHER PROFESSIONAL STUDY   43

Chapter 2
The Teacher's Professional Responsibilities   47

Activity 2.1 Is This a Typical Day for an Elementary School Teacher?   48

ANTICIPATED OUTCOMES   49

THE TEACHER AS A REFLECTIVE DECISION MAKER   50

   Decision-Making Phases of Instruction

COMMITMENT AND PROFESSIONALISM   51

IDENTIFYING AND BUILDING YOUR INSTRUCTIONAL COMPETENCIES   51

   Facilitating Behaviors and Instructional Strategies: A Clarification   •   Structuring the
   Learning Environment   •   Accepting and Sharing Instructional Accountability   •
   Demonstrating Withitness and Overlapping   •   Providing a Variety of Motivating
   and Challenging Activities   •   Modeling Appropriate Behaviors   •   Facilitating Student
   Acquisition of Data   •   Creating a Psychologically Safe Environment   •
   Clarifying Whenever Necessary   •   Using Periods of Silence   •   Questioning
   Thoughtfully

CHARACTERISTICS OF THE COMPETENT CLASSROOM TEACHER:
   AN ANNOTATED LIST   59

   *Activity 2.2 Are Teachers Prepared to Deal with the Severe Social and
      Emotional Problems Many Children Bring to School? If Not, Who Is?*   64

THE AGE OF INFORMATION TECHNOLOGY   64

   *Activity 2.3 Is Technology Changing the Role of the Classroom
      Teacher?*   65

SELECTING AND USING INSTRUCTIONAL MEDIA AND OTHER RESOURCES   65

   The Internet   •   Computers and Computer-Based Instructional Tools

SUMMARY   70

   Activity 2.4 Developing Your Professional Portfolio   71

STUDY QUESTIONS AND ADDITIONAL ACTIVITIES   72

NOTES   72

FOR FURTHER PROFESSIONAL STUDY   73

Chapter 3
Developing Skills in Thinking and Questioning   77

ANTICIPATED OUTCOMES   78

TEACHING THINKING   79

   Characteristics of Intelligent Behavior   •   Direct Teaching for Thinking and Intelligent
   Behavior   •   Direct Teaching of Skills Used in Thinking

DEVELOPING SKILL IN USING QUESTIONS   83

   Framing and Stating Questions   •   Sequencing Questions   •   Pacing Questions

HANDLING STUDENT RESPONSES TO QUESTIONS   86

   Activity 3.1 Create a Story   86

   Passive Acceptance Responses   •   Evaluative (Judgmental) Responses

Activity 3.2 How Would You Say It? 87

Restating and Clarifying • Probing • Cueing

SOCRATIC QUESTIONING 89

QUESTIONS THAT FOCUS ON SPECIFIC PURPOSES 90

Procedural Questions • Questions That Check Literal Comprehension • Reflective or "Thought" Questions

QUESTIONS FROM STUDENTS 94

Activity 3.3 And Then You Said. . . . 95

Activity 3.4 And Elliot Eisner Said. . . . 96

The Question-Driven Classroom • Questioning: The Cornerstone of Critical Thinking, Real-World Problem Solving, and Meaningful Learning

Activity 3.5 Think Time and the Art of Questioning 97

SUMMARY 98

STUDY QUESTIONS AND ADDITIONAL ACTIVITIES 98

NOTES 99

FOR FURTHER PROFESSIONAL STUDY 100

Chapter 4
Managing the Classroom Learning Environment 103

ANTICIPATED OUTCOMES 105

A VALUES-BASED MANAGEMENT PLAN 106

A CLARIFICATION OF TERMS 106

Classroom Management: Contributions of Leading Experts

CHARACTERISTICS OF EFFECTIVE CLASSROOM MANAGEMENT 112

Enhancing Mental and Social Development

FACILITATING THE ACHIEVEMENT OF INSTRUCTIONAL GOALS 113

Providing Boundaries of Intellectual and Physical Freedom • Thinking in Terms of Procedures Rather Than Rules; Consequences Rather Than Punishment • Developing Skills of Self-Direction and Responsible Involvement • Working Toward Warm Human Relations

SERIOUSNESS OF PROBLEMS 116

Goofing Off • Disruptions to Learning • Defiance, Cheating, Lying, and Stealing • Violence

Activity 4.1 Shouldn't Punishment Fit the Crime? 118

CONFLICT RESOLUTION 119

Minimizing Conflict and Encouraging Harmonious Social Relations • Resolving Conflicts Immediately, with a Plan for Longer-Range Solutions • Providing Instruction on Conflict and Conflict Resolution

ORGANIZATIONAL ASPECTS OF CLASSROOM MANAGEMENT   122

    Starting the School Term Well

    Activity 4.2 My Emerging Plan for Classroom Management   *124*

    Schedule and Routines

    Activity 4.3 Ms. Badger's Effort to Empower Children   *126*

    Clarity of Directions and Goals   •   Physical Arrangements

    Activity 4.4 First Day of Spring—What Would You Have Done?   *127*

    Transitions

    Activity 4.5 What's Wrong Here?   *129*

SUMMARY   130

STUDY QUESTIONS AND ADDITIONAL ACTIVITIES   130

NOTES   132

FOR FURTHER PROFESSIONAL STUDY   133

Chapter 5
The Curriculum: Selecting and Setting
Learning Expectations   137

ANTICIPATED OUTCOMES   139

THE ELEMENTARY SCHOOL CURRICULUM   140

    Activity 5.1 What Really Is Being Learned?   *141*

ENGLISH AND THE LANGUAGE ARTS   141

    Reading   •   Spelling   •   Handwriting   •   Language Conventions

MATHEMATICS   149

SCIENCE   151

SOCIAL STUDIES   153

HEALTH AND PHYSICAL EDUCATION   154

    Health Education   •   Physical Education

THE EXPRESSIVE ARTS   158

SKILLS IN THE CURRICULUM   160

    Skill Areas   •   Study Skills   •   Critical-Thinking Skills   •   Social Skills

FOREIGN LANGUAGE STUDY   166

DOCUMENTS THAT INFLUENCE THE CURRICULUM   167

    National Curriculum Standards   •   State Curriculum Standards

GOALS AND OBJECTIVES   169

    Activity 5.2 Examining Curriculum Documents and Standards   *169*

Results-Driven Education   •   Using Instructional Objectives

Activity 5.3 Identifying Action Verbs   173

COGNITIVE DOMAIN HIERARCHY   179

Knowledge   •   Comprehension   •   Application   •   Analysis   •
Synthesis   •   Evaluation

AFFECTIVE DOMAIN HIERARCHY   181

Receiving   •   Responding   •   Valuing   •   Organizing   •
Internalizing

EDUCATION IN THE AFFECTIVE DOMAIN   182

Activity 5.4 What Can You Do About It?   184

PSYCHOMOTOR DOMAIN HIERARCHY   184

Moving   •   Manipulating   •   Communicating   •   Creating

SEQUENCING OBJECTIVES   185

SUMMARY   186

Activity 5.5 Try Your Hand at Preparing Objectives   187

STUDY QUESTIONS AND ADDITIONAL ACTIVITIES   188

NOTES   189

FOR FURTHER PROFESSIONAL STUDY   191

Chapter 6
Planning the Instruction   195

ANTICIPATED OUTCOMES   196

RATIONALE FOR WRITTEN LESSON PLANS   197

Written Plans Are *Not* Irrevocable   •   Making Adjustments as Needed

Activity 6.1 Was This Lesson "Set in Concrete"?   199

TASKS THAT REQUIRE SPECIAL PLANNING   199

INTRODUCING TEACHERS ELLEN BAXTER AND JIM BOND   199

GETTING ACQUAINTED WITH A SCHOOL   200

Making an Onsite Visit

Activity 6.2 What Is the Bottom Line?   202

PLANNING FOR INSTRUCTION: FIRST FEW DAYS AND BEYOND   203

Perusing Permanent Records: Do So Cautiously

CONSIDERING LEARNING STYLES, LEARNING CAPACITIES, AND
INDIVIDUAL DIFFERENCES   205

Recognizing and Working with Students of Diversity and Differences   •   Recognizing and
Working with Students Who Have Special Needs   •   Recognizing and Working with
Students Who Are Gifted   •   Understanding and Working with Students Who May Be
at Risk

MS. BAXTER AND MR. BOND FACE THE REALITIES OF TEACHING   215

Ms. Baxter Established Priorities • Ms. Baxter Planned a Daily Schedule •
Ms. Baxter Planned the Learning Environment • Ms. Baxter Planned Learning Activities
for the First Few Days • Mr. Bond Established Priorities • Mr. Bond Planned a Daily
Schedule • Mr. Bond Planned the Learning Environment • Mr. Bond Planned
Learning Activities for the First Few Days

SKETCH PLAN   222

Activity 6.3 Mr. Wills Seems to Have a Problem   223

LESSON PLANNING   223

THE INSTRUCTIONAL UNIT   231

Types of Instructional Units • Planning and Developing Any Unit of Instruction •
Unit Format, Inclusive Elements, and Duration

PREPARING FOR AND DEALING WITH CONTROVERSY   235

SUMMARY   237

STUDY QUESTIONS AND ADDITIONAL ACTIVITIES   237

NOTES   238

FOR FURTHER PROFESSIONAL STUDY   239

Chapter 7
Assessing and Evaluating Student Performance   243

ANTICIPATED OUTCOMES   244

THE LANGUAGE OF ASSESSMENT   245

Evaluation, Assessment, and Measurement • Authentic and Performance
Assessment • Formative and Summative Assessment • Norm-Referenced and
Criterion-Referenced Tests • Readiness Testing • Validity and Reliability

ASSESSMENT IN THE CONTEXT OF INSTRUCTION   250

Activity 7.1 Make It Right, Write!   254

ASSESSMENT IN THE CLASSROOM   254

STUDENT PARTICIPATION IN ASSESSMENT   256

Using Student Portfolios • Using Checklists and Scoring Rubrics • Guidelines for
Using Portfolios for Instruction and Assessment

DIAGNOSTIC ASSESSMENT AND CORRECTIVE INSTRUCTION   260

The Teacher as Diagnostician • Avoid Labeling • Diagnostic and Corrective
Procedures • What Evidence Is There That a Learning Problem Exists?

Activity 7.2 Selecting the Right One   262

What Specific Learning Difficulty Is the Child Encountering? • What Level of Corrective
Work Is Required?

GRADING AND MARKING   265

Determining Grades • Assessment and Grading: Not Synonymous Terms

REPORTING STUDENT PROGRESS IN ACHIEVEMENT   267

Planning for the First Student-Progress Report   •   Establishing Parent and Guardian Contacts   •   Ms. Baxter Prepares for Her First Parent/Guardian Conference   •   Mr. Bond Prepares for His First Student-Progress Report

SUMMARY   272

STUDY QUESTIONS AND ADDITIONAL ACTIVITIES   272

NOTES   273

FOR FURTHER PROFESSIONAL STUDY   274

Chapter 8
Modes of Teaching: Selecting the Strategies   279

ANTICIPATED OUTCOMES   280

THEORETICAL CONSIDERATIONS WHEN SELECTING INSTRUCTIONAL STRATEGIES   281

Direct and Indirect Instruction: A Clarification of Terms   •   Degrees of Directness   •   Direct Versus Indirect Instructional Modes: Strengths and Weaknesses of Each   •   Selecting Developmentally Appropriate Learning Activities   •   The Learning Experiences Ladder   •   Direct, Simulated, and Vicarious Experiences Help Connect Student Learning

EXPOSITORY TEACHING   287

Assumptions   •   Major Purposes   •   Role of the Teacher   •   Role of the Learner   •   Use of Instructional Resources   •   Method of Assessment

INQUIRY TEACHING   291

Inquiry Versus Discovery

Activity 8.1 Does It Really Matter What It's Called?   294

The Critical Thinking Skills of Discovery and Inquiry   •   Assumptions   •   Major Purposes   •   Role of the Teacher   •   Role of the Learner   •   Use of Instructional Resources   •   Method of Assessment

Activity 8.2 But How Do You Do It, Really?   298

THE DEMONSTRATION   299

Assumptions   •   Major Purposes   •   Role of the Teacher   •   Role of the Learner   •   Use of Instructional Resources   •   Method of Assessment

SKILLS INSTRUCTION   301

Meaningfulness   •   Learner Involvement   •   Practice   •   Feedback   •   Application   •   Maintenance

BASIC SKILLS—THE THREE Rs   305

Developing a Structured, Systematic, and Sequential Program   •   Making the Program Interesting and Stimulating   •   Conducting Frequent Assessments   •   Personalizing the Program

Activity 8.3 What Went Wrong for Antoine?   308

Using Methods and Materials That Stress Purposeful and Functional Use of Skills • Encouraging Habits of Independence

SUMMARY   309

Activity 8.4 Is There a Preferred Way?   310

STUDY QUESTIONS AND ADDITIONAL ACTIVITIES   310

NOTES   311

FOR FURTHER PROFESSIONAL STUDY   311

Chapter 9
Organizing and Guiding Children's Learning in Groups   315

ANTICIPATED OUTCOMES   316

GROUP PROCESS SKILLS   317

QUALITY LEARNING AND PERSONALIZED INSTRUCTION   318

Today's Emphasis: Quality Learning for Each Child • Assumptions About Quality Learning • Components of Any Quality Learning Model • Selected Strategies for Personalizing Instruction for Quality Learning

LEARNING ALONE   321

LEARNING IN PAIRS (PAIRED TEAM LEARNING)   322

THE CLASSROOM LEARNING CENTER   322

LEARNING IN SMALL GROUPS   325

Purposes for Using Small Groups

COOPERATIVE LEARNING   325

The Cooperative Learning Group (CLG) • The Theory and Use of Cooperative Learning • Roles Within the Cooperative Learning Group • What Students and the Teacher Do When Using Cooperative Learning Groups • When to Use Cooperative Learning Groups • Outcomes of Using Cooperative Learning Groups • Cooperative Group Learning, Assessment, and Grading • Why Some Teachers Have Difficulty Using CLGs

LARGE-GROUP INSTRUCTION   328

EXAMPLES OF LARGE- AND SMALL-GROUP INSTRUCTION   329

Large- and Small-Group Instruction: Primary Grades • Ms. Baxter's First Group Discussion

Activity 9.1 Laughter and Love in the Classroom   330

Making Provisions for Variability in Reading Levels • Ms. Baxter's Culminating Activities • Large- and Small-Group Instruction: Intermediate Grades • Mr. Bond's First Social Studies Lesson • Making Provisions for Variability in Reading Levels • Providing Additional Opportunities to Gather Information • Mr. Bond's Culminating Activities

LEARNING FROM ASSIGNMENTS AND HOMEWORK   339

Strategies for Student Recovery

SUMMARY   342

STUDY QUESTIONS AND ADDITIONAL ACTIVITIES   343

NOTES   344

FOR FURTHER PROFESSIONAL STUDY   345

Glossary   347

Index   353

Note: Every effort has been made to provide accurate and current Internet information in this book. However, the Internet and information posted on it are constantly changing; it is inevitable that some of the Internet addresses listed in this textbook will change.

INTASC Principles	PRAXIS III Domains	NBPTS Standards
• The teacher fosters relationships with colleagues, parents, and agencies in the community to support students' learning and well-being. (Principle 10) • The teacher plans instruction based upon knowledge of subject matter, students, community, and curriculum goals. (Principle 7)	• Teacher Professionalism (Domain D) • Organizing Content Knowledge for Student Learning (Domain A)	• Respect for Diversity • Family Involvement

Nearly a century ago the author H. G. Wells described the teacher as that "sower of unseen harvests" because the results of what the teacher sows in students' young minds may not be apparent until long after the teacher is gone, or perhaps even forgotten. But good teachers are rarely forgotten. They put their imprint on the students they teach just as surely as artists put their unique mark on their work. Your great challenge as an elementary school teacher, therefore, lies precisely in determining the kind of imprint you will leave on the character, sensitivity, curiosity, love of learning, and moral values of the children whom you are given the privilege and responsibility of teaching. Regardless of the long-term and positive imprint you leave on your students, however, there is today considerable pressure on teachers and schools for more immediate and measurable results to determine how well children are learning.

Welcome to the exciting, ever-changing world of elementary school teaching. In most teacher education programs students become familiar with the various techniques and strategies needed to conduct classroom instruction—how to teach reading, mathematics, science, social studies, and other subjects and skills. All of that is important to know if you are to become a competent professional, and we deal with some of these fundamentals in this text. More important, however, at this early point in your professional development, you should be thinking seriously about what it means to be an elementary school teacher, and about the kinds of responsibilities associated with the profession. You should be formulating intellectually some vision of the future for the children you will teach. As the Greek philosopher Aristotle noted, "The character of the speaker is more important than the content of his speech." The same may be said about the elementary school teacher. Your character is a critical variable in determining the kinds of "unseen harvests" that your teaching is likely to produce.

In all of society, no other professionals are given as much wide-ranging responsibility for shaping the development of young citizens as are elementary school teachers. Only parents and legal guardians spend more time with children between the ages of 5 and 12 than do teachers. Unfortunately, for some children the teacher is the *only* adult whose behavior has any possibility of affecting their lives in a positive way. Far too often, home and neighborhood influences are working at cross-purposes with what schools are attempting to achieve. Today's efforts with such positive approaches as forging home–school–community partnerships and mentoring programs hopefully are correcting that reality. Still, and regrettably, teachers and other school personnel have little to no control over many of the social forces that directly affect their work.

Despite the plethora of blue-ribbon commissions, authors, and politicians who doggedly vilify what they perceive as the failures of America's public schools, thousands of committed teachers, administrators, parents, guardians, and community members struggle daily, year after year, to provide young people with a quality education. In this chapter we focus your attention on contemporary influences and challenges that often are central to the concerns held by educators, parents and guardians, and the public about their schools.

ANTICIPATED OUTCOMES

After completing this chapter, you should be able to do the following:

1. Explain why the authors refer to the teaching profession as a "call to social service."
2. Describe today's concept of *literacy* as a purpose of formal education in this country.
3. Describe today's concept of *citizenship education* as a purpose of formal education in this country.
4. Describe today's concept of *personal development* as a purpose of formal education in this country.
5. Describe today's concept of *quality education for each child* as a purpose of formal education in this country.
6. Identify factors in and out of school that affect children's achievement in school.
7. Discuss specific ways in which elementary schools are attempting to help each child succeed in school.
8. Describe variations common to elementary-school grade organization in this country.
9. Identify arguments for and against the *graded school* concept.
10. Describe the concepts of "school choice" and "school restructuring" and the extent to which each most likely affects the work of today's elementary-school classroom teacher.
11. Describe appropriate steps a classroom teacher should take when suspecting child abuse, illicit drug use, or gang involvement.
12. Describe the status of bilingual education and English as a second language education in elementary schools.
13. Describe efforts made by today's schools to involve parents, guardians, and the community in the children's education.
14. Describe the concept of *student rights* and how the concept affects your work as an elementary school classroom teacher.
15. Describe the basic principles of the *No Child Left Behind Act* of 2001 and how that act is likely to affect your work as a classroom teacher.

FUNDAMENTAL PURPOSES OF ELEMENTARY EDUCATION

We begin with an examination of the fundamental purposes that are central to the elementary school educational enterprise: literacy, citizenship education, personal development, and quality education for each and every child.

Literacy

At its most basic, to be *literate* is to be able to read and write. Since colonial times, schools have had the responsibility of developing basic literacy in children. Colonial schools often were little more than schools for reading, a skill taught mainly for religious purposes. Reading has been an important component of the elementary school curriculum throughout our nation's history. Indeed, at the early levels, more time is spent on teaching reading than on anything else.

Dissatisfaction with school programs often focuses on what has come to be called "the basics." Used in this context, "the basics" refer to fundamental academic skills—reading, writing, and mathematical operations, also called the "three Rs." These skills are considered *basic* in the sense that without them individuals would be handicapped in being able to learn other things. They are *tools for learning*, and without them we are stymied in learning how to learn. Without command of these basic skills, adults would also be handicapped in ordinary living in a society that relies so heavily on written communication and quantitative operations.

Although the three Rs are basic to literacy, these alone cannot be considered adequate for life in our society today. When people have attended school, we assume that they have gained a general background of information about the world and its inhabitants, that they are familiar with basic scientific information, and that they have a modicum of cultural awareness. Beyond that, functional literacy is to some degree situation specific. Thus, educators today speak of "cultural literacy," "language literacy," "prose literacy," "economic literacy," "scientific literacy," "computer literacy," "quantitative literacy," "media literacy," and so on. Functional literacy does not mean the same thing for everyone, nor is it the same in all circumstances. The job of the elementary school is to focus on those aspects of literacy that are a part of the common culture and presumed to be a part of the intellectual background of all citizens.

Citizenship Education

A second purpose of elementary education, also having a long tradition in our nation's schools, is citizenship education. Education for intelligent and loyal citizenship was introduced in the school curriculum early in the nation's history to ensure self-government at an enlightened level. Citizenship education was to take place through the formal study of such subjects as history, government (civics), and geography and through the indoctrination of such values as freedom, human dignity, responsibility, independence, individualism, democracy, respect for others, and love of country. Informally, citizenship education was promoted through an educational setting that included learners from a broad social and economic spectrum of society. Unlike its European counterparts, the American dream of the "common" school was to provide an institution that would serve all the children of all the people. Although that ideal has not been reached completely, it comes close to being realized in the elementary school. Today, the mix of schoolchildren includes members of many cultural, racial, and ethnic groups. Teachers are thus challenged, perhaps as never before, to prepare children for citizenship in a dynamic multicultural society whose economic and political involvement is international in scope and global in influence.

Citizenship education in elementary school should include developing affective attachments to this nation and its democratic heritage. Pageants, plays, creative stories, poems, and creative dramatics, under the direction of an imaginative and stimulating teacher, can make the struggle for freedom and the history of the United States' development unforgettable experiences for young children. It is through activities of this type that the social values of classroom life are realized. These are powerful tools in building appreciations, ideals, and values. When sensibly used, the folklore and legends associated with the development of this nation are important and valuable vehicles for teaching citizenship. When not overly depended on, and when not a substitute for more thoughtful approaches to citizenship education, a certain amount of symbolism, such as saluting the flag and reciting the Pledge of Allegiance, is an important component of citizenship education, especially in engendering feelings of fidelity.

Today's citizenship education focuses on citizens as thinking, decision-making individuals. In a democracy, citizens are, on one hand, expected to be loyal, faithful, and law-abiding members of the community, state, and nation. On the other hand, citizens are expected to think independently and to be thoughtful critics of the system itself. Moreover, the charge of citizenship goes beyond being critical; it includes responsibility for taking action to improve the system. It is through the actions of responsible citizens, as individuals or with others, that we have seen the blessings of liberty and the privileges of democracy extended to increasing numbers of people. With each new generation of citizens the process continues.

Personal Development

The personal growth of individual children, concern about each individual's potential for development, and the inclusion of school goals to include emotional, social, and physical growth as well as intellectual development are seen as major purposes of elementary education. The nation expects its elementary schools to be concerned about *individual* children, to help children develop a sense of self-identity, to learn to feel good about themselves, to learn what their individual talents are, and to be able to set attainable goals for themselves. Out of necessity, schools must teach aggregates of children in what we call classes, but as a teacher your concern is and must always be the individual human beings within those groups.

The dimension of personal development that *has* had a long tradition in elementary education is something that might be called *character education* or *moral education*. Wynne and Ryan refer to this as "the great tradition" in education, meaning that the transmission of moral values has been and is a high-priority educational goal of most cultures of the world.[1]

Elementary schools are not simply information supermarkets—they are shapers of human beings. The earliest schools in this country recognized this reality; schools for young children were to extend and reinforce the moral and character education begun in the family's home and religious life. As schools became public, secular institutions, moral and character education became

Basic School Network at www.jmu.edu/basicschool

Character Counts Coalition at www.charactercounts.org

Character Education Partnership at www.character.org/resources/search

Educators for Social Responsibility at www.esrnational.org/about-rccp.html

Northeast Foundation for Children at www.responsiveclassroom.org/Rcinfo.htm

FIGURE 1.1
Internet resources on character education

separated from religious orientation. Schools, nonetheless, were expected to continue to concern themselves with principles of right and wrong under the assumption that such knowledge would serve the betterment of society. Teachers continue to create classroom settings that encourage children to develop a sense of fair play, do what is right, live up to verbal agreements, show consideration and respect for others, and be trustworthy. The fact is that a society cannot survive unless a majority of its people internalize common values and live their lives in accordance with them.

Reminiscent of the 1930s and the late 1960s, in the 1990s a resurgence of interest began in the development of students' values, especially those of honesty, kindness, respect, and responsibility. Stimulated perhaps by a perceived need to act to reduce students' antisocial behaviors and to produce more respectful and responsible citizens, many schools and districts today have developed or are developing curricula in character education with the ultimate goal of "developing mature adults capable of responsible citizenship and moral action."[2] A report by the late Ernest L. Boyer, president of the Carnegie Foundation for the Advancement of Teaching, entitled *The Basic School: A Community of Learning*, lists commitment to character as one of the four key priorities for a model elementary school. (The other three priorities are The School as Community, A Curriculum with Coherence, and A Climate for Learning.) In promoting character, the report suggests, schools should affirm the following virtues: honesty, respect, responsibility, compassion, self-discipline, perseverance, and giving.[3] See Figure 1.1 for Internet resources on character education.

Quality Education for Each Child

School organization has a direct effect on what students learn; if it didn't, educators wouldn't be spending so much valuable time trying to organize and reorganize their schools to effect the most productive (and cost-effective) delivery of the curriculum. Exemplary schools establish and maintain a climate of constant modification in a continual process of inquiry, reflection, and change.

Organizational changes are often referred to as *school restructuring*, a term with a variety of connotations, including site-based management, collaborative decision making, school choice, personalized learning, integrated curricula, and collegial staffing. School restructuring has been defined as "activities that change fundamental assumptions, practices, and relationships, both within the organization and between the organization and the outside world, in ways leading to improved learning outcomes."[4] No matter how it is defined, educators agree on the following point: The design and functions of schools should reflect the needs of young people of the 21st century rather than embodying a 19th century factory model.[5]

The movement to year-round operation and the redesigning of schools into smaller cohorts or "houses" represents an increasingly common movement across the country. The intention of this redesign is that schools will better address the needs and capabilities of each unique student, that is, to provide a quality education for every child so no child is left behind. (See Highlights of the No Child Left Behind Act of 2001, shown in Figure 1.2.) Undoubtedly, you will be involved with and will help accomplish many of these changes.

The No Child Left Behind Act of 2001 embodies several key principles, including

- Stronger accountability to schools for results
- Greater flexibility for states, school districts and schools in the use of federal funds
- More options for parents of children from disadvantaged backgrounds
- Emphasis on children learning to read by grade 3
- Emphasis on children learning English
- Emphasis on using teaching methods that have been demonstrated to be effective in improving learning and student achievement
- Emphasis on the provision of programs that prevent drug use and violence among youth

The act requires states to

- Develop performance and measurement standards for schools
- Create annual assessments that measure what children know and can do in reading and math in grades 3 through 8
- Upgrade certification requirements for teachers
- Issue regular progress reports to the community
- Report on school safety on a school-by-school basis

Schools failing to show adequate progress for two consecutive years will be required to

- Offer remedial instruction
- Restructure and allow parents to move their children into better-performing public schools, including public charter schools within their district; for those children the district must provide transportation

Students from low-income families in schools that fail to meet state standards for at least three years are eligible to receive supplemental educational services—including tutoring, after-school services, and summer school.

FIGURE 1.2

Highlights of the No Child Left Behind Act of 2001

Source: No Child Left Behind: A Desktop Reference to the NCLB Act of 2001, retrieved on February 22, 2003; from http://www.ed.gov/offices.OESE/reference.

Today's elementary school reforms used alone or in varying combinations and with varying degrees of success, include the following:

1. *Alternative Schools*—charter schools, theme or magnet schools,[6] Montessori schools, year-round schools.
2. *Looping*—also referred to as multiyear grouping, multiyear instruction, multiyear placement, and teacher–student progression. Looping is when a cohort of students and teachers remain together as a group for several or all of the years the students are at that school.[7]
3. *Multiage classrooms*—use of nongraded classrooms with mixed-age children, known also as continuous promotion, open education, and heterogeneous grouping.[8]
4. *School-within-a-school* (SWAS) concept, also called the "small school," "house," "village," "pod," "academy," "family," or sometimes just plain "team" concept, where a teaching team is assigned each day to the same cohort of students for a common block of time.[9]

Self-Contained Classroom

The most common arrangement for at least the K–3 level organization is the self-contained classroom. A *self-contained classroom* is one in which one teacher is assigned to a group of children of approximately the same age for an academic year, and that teacher has primary responsibility for implementing the program of instruction for those children. She or he is the teacher of record for those children for an entire school year, even though other teachers of special subjects, such as music, art, physical education, or computers, may work with them part of the time. Within the self-contained classroom, we can find incorporated many if not all the characteristics common to research findings on exemplary teaching:

- Classrooms rich in materials for children to experience choices, challenges, social interaction, and success
- Classrooms with provisions for a variety of types of group settings, including one-on-one, dyad, small group, and large-group instruction
- Climate of community, respect, and cooperation
- Climate of expectations for work and achievement
- Emphasis on skill development
- Instructional experiences designed to foster the construction of meaning
- Interdisciplinary thematic instruction
- Multilevel (differentiated) instruction
- Opportunities for peer tutoring and cross-age mentoring

DIVERSITY IN THE CLASSROOM

The bell rings, and your students enter your classroom, a kaleidoscope of personalities, all peerless and idiosyncratic, each a packet of energy with different focuses, experiences, dispositions, and learning capacities, differing proficiencies in the English language—each one a different challenge. And what a challenge this is—to understand and to teach 20 or more unique individuals, all at once, and to do it for 6 hours a day, 5 days a week, 180 days a year! What a challenge, indeed, it is to be a public elementary school classroom teacher. To succeed, you must become familiar with the diverse characteristics and needs of childhood, for the quality of children's academic achievement will depend on how well you understand and satisfy their other developmental needs.

Starting with kindergarten, teachers are challenged by the variety of needs of children who are not only demographically but also developmentally diverse. Kindergarten teachers must maintain the interest and promote the growth of children who have already demonstrated signs of early literacy and numeracy while simultaneously encouraging the emergence of basic skills in children who have not yet acquired them. In like fashion, as with all teachers, they must meet the needs of children with learning difficulties while reserving sufficient attention and effort for those with few or no difficulties and for those others who have in some way or another shown signs of giftedness.

Elementary school teachers must be prepared not only to teach several subjects, but also to do it effectively with students of different cultural backgrounds, diverse linguistic abilities, and different learning styles, and also with children who have educationally relevant differences: for example, students with disabilities, students who live in extreme poverty, and those who are significantly influenced by variations in religion or gender.

Children differ in physical characteristics, interests, home life, intellectual ability, learning capacities, motor ability, social skills, aptitudes and talents, language skills, experience, ideals, attitudes, needs, ambitions, hopes, and dreams. Furthermore, for a variety of reasons (e.g., learning styles and learning capacities, modality preferences, information-processing habits, motivational factors, physiological factors) all people learn in their own ways and at their own rates. Interests, background, innate and acquired abilities, and myriad other influences shape how and what a person will learn. From any particular learning experience no two persons ever learn exactly the same thing. But all can learn!

The variety of individual differences among students requires that teachers use teaching strategies and tactics that accommodate those differences. To most effectively teach children who are different from you, you must develop skills in the following areas:

- Establishing a classroom climate in which *all* children feel welcome, that they can learn, and that you support them in doing so
- Using techniques that emphasize cooperative and social-interactive learning
- Building on students' individual experiences, conceptions, learning styles, learning capacities, and learning modalities
- Using techniques that have proven successful for students of specific differences

The process of building your skills in these categories begins now and will continue throughout your professional career. As stated elsewhere, "Figuring out what a student needs in order to succeed is not all that difficult. Providing the appropriate type of education and amount of learning time is the hard part."[10]

A wealth of information is available to help you meet this challenge. As a professional you are expected to know it all, or at least to know where you can find all necessary information—and to review it when needed. Certain information you have stored in memory will surface and become useful at the most unexpected times. Although you are concerned about all students' safety and physical well-being, you will want to remain sensitive to each student's attitudes, values, social adjustment, emotional well-being, and cognitive development. You must be prepared not only to teach several subjects but also to do it effectively with students of different cultural backgrounds, diverse linguistic abilities, and different learning styles, as well as with children who have other educationally relevant differences, such as students with disabilities, students who live in extreme poverty, and those who are significantly influenced by variations in religion or gender. It is, indeed, a challenge, as the following statistics make even clearer.

Approximately one quarter of today's children in the United States live in poverty. Approximately one half of the children in the United States will spend some years being raised by a single parent. Between one third and one fourth of U.S. children go home after school to places devoid of any adult supervision. And, on any given day, it is estimated that 120,000 children have no place at all to call home.[11] In fact, there are now about 40 schools operating that are designed especially for homeless children.[12]

It is predicted that by the middle of this century one half of the school age population in the United States will be members of ethnic minorities, and a steady increase in interracial marriages and childbirths may challenge today's conceptions of multiculturalism and race.[13]

The United States truly is a multilingual, multiethnic, multicultural country—perhaps the most diverse nation in the world. Of kindergarten-age children, ages 5–7, approximately one of six speaks a language other than English at home. In many large school districts, as many as 100 languages are represented, with as many as 20 or more different primary languages found in some classrooms. Increasing ethnic, cultural, and linguistic diversity is affecting schools across the country, not only in large urban areas but also in traditionally homogeneous suburbs and small rural communities.

The overall picture that emerges is of a rapidly changing, diverse student population that challenges teaching skills. Teachers who traditionally have used direct instruction (discussed in Chapter 8) as their dominant mode of instruction have done so on the assumption that their students were relatively homogeneous in terms of experience, background, knowledge, motivation, way of learning, and facility with English. However, no such assumption can be made today in classrooms of such cultural, ethnic, and linguistic diversity. *As a classroom teacher today, you must be knowledgeable and skilled in using teaching strategies that recognize, celebrate, and build on that diversity.* In a nutshell, this is your challenge. Some guidelines are provided in Figure 1.3. Additional guidelines are found throughout this book.

These are the realities that confront beginning teachers in varying degrees of intensity in virtually every school district in the United States. To succeed, you must perceive these realities as challenges and opportunities. Your challenges lie in seeing that every child succeeds in school, so no child is left behind. Your opportunities can be found in making sure that the lives of *all* children are enriched through contact with classmates whose cultural and ethnic backgrounds may be quite different from their own. Responding to these challenges and grasping these opportunities underscore the idea that the teaching profession is basically a call to social service.

FAMILY LIFE

Before children have formal contact with school, they have, of course, been receiving early education from their families. There can be little doubt that these family experiences are among the most powerful and pervasive influences on human development. A family that is doing its childrearing job properly will help children learn some of the most important, fundamental things they need to know in life. Children learn language and basic linguistic skills in the home. Here, too, children learn to give and receive emotional support. The family

---

Supporting Multiracial Children and Countering Racism

- Address directly the history of and reasons for racism against groups of people, including the multiracial population.
- Among the toys for younger children, include dolls with multiracial characteristics.
- Celebrate many different heritages, stressing their interplay in life and the ways that different cultures have similar commemorations.
- Demonstrate how people in the United States have successfully mixed languages, cultures, and religions throughout the nation's history, and how the country has always been a home to multiethnic people (for example, early settlers whose parents comprised different European heritages).
- Discuss the current status of multiracial people around the world, such as Mestizos, Creoles, and Brazilians.
- Encourage the development and sharing of family trees.
- Facilitate age-appropriate discussions that foster open and supportive questioning about race in ways that build student self-concepts and educates the questioner.
- Identify multiracial historical heroes such as Frederick Douglass and James Audubon, and cultural figures like ballerina Maria Tallchief and singer Paula Abdul.
- Include curriculum study units in art, music, and literature that transcend ethnic boundaries instead of focusing on specific groups, such as "Indians."
- Include multiracial persons as role models when selecting assembly speakers and other resource persons.
- Provide children with information and pictures of people of many racial and ethnic groups, including those of mixed heritage.
- Study monoracial groups to promote an understanding of the role of race in society by exploring why some people need to belong to an exclusive group or need to feel superior to others, and what the societal and personal consequences of such attitudes are.
- Use children's books that depict multiracialism.

FIGURE 1.3
Suggestions for teachers and schools to support multiracial children and to counter racism
Source: W. Schwartz, *The Schooling of Multiracial Students,* ERIC/CUE Digest, Number 138 (New York: ERIC Clearinghouse on Urban Education, 1998).

should provide security and reassurance, thereby supplying the psychological support needed to face life and to function confidently and competently. In the process, children develop feelings of personal worth and positive self-concept. It is in the family that children first learn what is right and wrong, what things are prized and valued, and what standards of conduct are expected. Lifetime ambitions and aspirations are planted and germinate in early family life. The extent to which the family has responded to these responsibilities will reflect itself in children's life in school. For example, a child reared in a linguistically rich home environment where elaborative language is used daily is bound to have many advantages in learning language-related skills in school.

Extended families have obvious advantages in terms of bringing up children within the expectations of a family. Children have more contact with closely related adults and consequently have available a greater range of adult role models. Similarly, concerned and caring adults can more closely and constantly monitor child behavior. There is also likely to be a more elaborate family culture or set of rituals that provides emotional stability and roots for growing children, such as the gathering of the entire family for holidays, anniversaries, birthdays, and other special events. In structures of this type, children are hardly ever out of range of the supervision of some member of the immediate family.

Many factors have contributed to changes in the traditional extended-family pattern. People tend to move in the direction of increased economic opportunity. Thus, a young couple may locate hundreds of miles away from many of their relatives. Children growing up in such nuclear families today may hardly know relatives other than their parents. Babysitters replace grandparents in part-time care of children. Neighbors and friends may help supervise children in the neighborhood. Preschool children may spend the better part of their waking hours in a daycare center.

Student mobility, that is, students moving from one school to another, is common in the United States. Whether frequent movement is a symptom or a cause of poor school performance is not known, but studies indicate that children who move three or more times during elementary-school years have a greater tendency for lower achievement and diminished prospects for high-school graduation than do students who are less mobile.[14]

Undoubtedly, the most common exception to the conventional family arrangement is the one-parent family (which includes both unmarried and previously married individuals).[15] Death, separation, and, most commonly, divorce not only dissolve a marriage but leave one or the other of the partners with the responsibility of carrying on as a family. Even though joint custody arrangements are becoming more common, the custody of children is usually given to the mother in the case of divorce, and the one-parent family for the most part means a mother and her children. Divorce rates in the United States have continued to rise for the past century, after having peaked during the years immediately following World War II, receded during the 1950s and early 1960s, risen sharply again in the 1970s, and continued at a high level through the 1990s.

The problem of children left unattended and unsupervised after school continues to be a serious one. The behavior problems or low achievement of children from one-parent families is explained away on the basis of their being products of "broken homes." This, of course, ignores the fact that many children from one-parent families achieve at high levels and present no behavior problem in school, and that many from so-called intact families are low achievers and do present behavior problem. It also ignores the psychological and emotional damage to a young child that results from growing up in a dysfunctional family of whatever structure, one filled with conflict, hostility, and abuse.

Dramatic changes are occurring within family lifestyles. With increasing numbers of parents and guardians employed outside the home, greater numbers of children are enrolled in daycare centers, are placed in the care of persons other than parents for several hours each day, or are "latchkey kids" who are on their own before and after school. When compared with young children of previous generations, children today are more accustomed to being away from home much of the day and to spending much of the day with peers, and are more aware of the world around them. In many communities those factors have led to full-day kindergarten[16] and, to a lesser extent, *full-service schools*, which offer quality education and comprehensive social services under one roof.[17]

SOCIOECONOMIC INFLUENCES

Social stratification occurs because others rank individuals as being higher or lower on some standard of preference. When a segment of society is set apart as having characteristics different from others, we have the beginning of a social class. If a group of individuals has particular characteristics a society values, the group so identified will enjoy high status. The reverse is also true. In time, a hierarchy of groups develops in accordance with societal preferences, and a social-class structure emerges, one that usually correlates with socioeconomic status.

There can be no question that one variable separating the "haves" from the "have nots" in this or any other society is level of education. Those who are the decision makers, who have good jobs, who contribute in significant ways to the health and welfare of their fellow citizens, and who have power and wealth are almost always better educated than the balance of the population. It is patently clear from research, as well as from the personal experiences of countless thousands of individuals, that limited education forecloses many social and economic options and thereby severely restricts opportunity for upward social mobility. It does not follow, of course, that improved education will alleviate all socioeconomically related problems. Restricted or foreshortened education, for whatever reason, simply means limited opportunities to exercise alternatives and options for self-development.

Evidence abounds that the largest number of educational casualties comes from the lower socioeconomic levels. These children often come from educationally impoverished environments, and such an atmosphere conditions nearly every aspect of their lives. Today, these members of our school population are referred to as *at-risk children* because they are the most likely candidates for school failure and for facing multiple social and/or personal problems. Their family lifestyles contribute to the perpetuation of educational deprivation. Traditional school programs simply have not been able to deal successfully with the educational needs of these socioeconomically disadvantaged children. We are likely to have large numbers of miseducated children until we as a society hold the highest expectations for *all* students and commit ourselves to eradicating those underlying conditions that produce children for whom the school experience is meaningless. The education of children who are at risk is discussed more fully in Chapter 6.

EQUALITY OF EDUCATIONAL OPPORTUNITY

> *Equity is the approach. Equality is the goal.*
>
> —Enid Lee

Equality of educational opportunity has traditionally been interpreted to mean equal *access* to education, and the nation has made a substantial effort to make schooling available to all of its children. No area of the country is so remote as to preclude the opportunity for children who live there to go to school. Children of all racial and ethnic groups, children of migrants, children of the poor, children with physical or mental disabilities—all of these are not only encouraged but required to attend school. But does school attendance in itself ensure equality of educational opportunity? Many think not, because there are social, psychological, and economic inequities that both condition the quality of schooling provided from place to place and also affect individuals' abilities to take full advantage of what is offered.

Inequities in educational opportunity do exist in this country. Educational inequity is usually thought of in terms of differences in the dollar amounts spent on education from one place to another. Because communities differ in both their *ability* and their *willingness* to support education, the average amount spent per student varies significantly from one district to another, even within the same state.

Variations in educational spending do not, however, fully explain prevailing inequities in educational opportunity. The quality of education tends to follow the pattern of power and wealth in a community. Those parents and guardians who are reasonably well educated themselves and who have average or above-average incomes, regardless of ethnic identity, most often choose to reside in areas that provide well for their children's education. Poorly educated, low-income families, whose range of choice is much more limited, tend to live in areas that provide less well for children's education. It is not so much a matter of actual dollars spent on education in the more favored areas, as it is a combination of economic and social forces that coalesce to produce better-quality education.

Education, and most especially early education, must be concerned with the way it either opens or forecloses subsequent opportunities for learning. Teachers and schools should be greatly concerned about children who do not learn to read because this deficiency severely limits their later options. Similarly, children who grow to dislike school or to dislike particular subjects create self-imposed limiting conditions on their continued educational achievement. Any experience that children have that discourages or terminates their continued ability or motivation for further learning restricts equality of educational opportunity. This is why early intervention programs are so important for those children who are products of poverty and impoverished environments. The documented success of the Head Start program is a case in point. Children who come from low-socioeconomic-status families face a high risk of failure in school unless steps are taken very early to counteract the profound effects of poverty on their education. To the maximum extent possible, teachers and schools must accommodate learner needs whatever their background may be.

Student Rights

You probably already know that as a result of legislation of more than a quarter-century ago (Federal law Title IX of the Education Act Amendments of 1972, PL 92–318) a teacher is prohibited from discriminating among children on the basis of gender. In all aspects of school, male and female students must be treated the same. This means, for example, that a teacher must not pit males against females in a subject content quiz game—or for any other activity or reason. Further, no teacher, student, administrator, or other school employee should make sexual advances toward a student (i.e., touching or speaking in a sexual manner).

Each school or district should have a clearly delineated statement of steps to follow in the process of protecting students' rights. Many schools provide students (or parents and guardians) with a publication of these rights. Figure 1.4 presents additional resources.

D. R. Coy, *Bullying,* ERIC/CASS Digest, ED459405, available ERIC Counseling and Student Services Clearinghouse, University of North Carolina at Greensboro, 201 Ferguson Building, P.O. Box 26171, Greensboro, NC 27402-6171.

M. L. Yell and A. Katsiyannis, "Legal Issues: Student-on-Student Sexual Harassment: What Are Schools' Responsibilities?" *Preventing School Failure* 44(3): 130–132 (2000).

W. Schwartz, *Preventing Student Sexual Harassment,* ERIC Digest Number 160, ED448248, available ERIC Clearinghouse on Urban Education, Institute for Urban and Minority Education, Box 40, Teacher College, Columbia University, New York, NY 10027. Online at http://wric-web.tc.columbia.edu.

S. L. Wessler, "Sticks and Stones," *Educational Leadership* 58(4): 28–33 (December 2000–January 2001).

FIGURE 1.4
Resources on sexual harassment in schools

Activity 1.1: Teach but Don't Touch

Manley Blake, attorney for the local teachers' professional association, is addressing the teachers at their fall preschool meeting:

"Last year in this country, we had an alarming number of cases of parents and school officials taking teachers to court for touching children in ways thought to be inappropriate. In Arizona, a music teacher with 16 years' experience faced charges of sexual harassment and unprofessional conduct and a recommendation of dismissal because of a hugging incident. For the past three decades, this society has given social approval to hugging and other forms of physical contact for purposes of comfort and support. We say to people in distress, 'Is there anything I can do?' And the reply could very well be, 'I need a warm and fuzzy hug.'

"On Sunday in church you might hug your neighbor and her 10-year-old daughter and wish them 'peace,' but don't try it the next day in school without putting yourself in jeopardy! My advice to you is to teach but don't touch. Don't hug kids. Don't put your arms around them. Don't hold hands with them on the playground. Don't pat them on the back. Don't have any physical contact with them in any way. Period."

1. Do you think this attorney's advice is sound or extreme?
2. Can elementary school teachers do their jobs without having *any* physical contact with children?
3. How can teachers project feelings of affection and genuine caring without touching children?
4. Research shows that physical contact with other human beings is a critical requirement for children's normal development. If children are caressed neither at home nor at school, how can we expect them to develop normally? Is this a teacher's responsibility?
5. Using a selected specific occurrence, discuss this issue with others in your class in terms of *context* variables such as the following: (1) the age of the student; (2) the sex of the teacher and the child; (3) whether the contact is in a public, open place with others around or in an isolated area; (4) whether the contact is a pattern of the teacher's behavior; and (5) the *intent* of the teacher's behavior.

Learning Styles

Although some children may begin to learn a new idea in the abstract (e.g., through visual or verbal symbolization), most need to begin concretely (e.g., learning by actually doing it). Many children prosper while working in groups, while others prefer to work alone. Some are quick in their studies, whereas others are slow, methodical, cautious, and meticulous. Some can sustain attention on a single topic, becoming more absorbed in their study as time passes. Others are slower starters and more casual in their pursuits but are capable of shifting with ease from subject to subject. Some can study in the midst of music, noise, or movement, whereas others need quiet, solitude, and a desk or table. The point is this: *Children vary not only in their skills and preferences in the way they receive information, but also in how they mentally process that information once they receive it.* This mental processing is a person's style of learning. The topic is discussed more fully in Chapter 6. For now, the point is this: We must teach children in ways they learn best.

Race and Racism

It is perfectly obvious that human beings differ in their physical characteristics. Some are fair skinned; others are dark. Some have curly hair and others straight hair, which may be light or dark. Through the centuries, groups of people who occupied certain geographical areas of the world and who have some physical traits in common have been identified as subgroups of *Homo sapiens* and have been called *races*. These physical traits are inherited, but because their presence or absence varies so greatly *within* these groups, it is sometimes impossible to assign an individual to any one group on the basis of unique characteristics. Consequently, anthropologists and sociologists have not found the use of race to be a meaningful way of grouping human beings, preferring instead the concept of *ethnicity*, which describes people on the basis of their *cultural identity* and may include geographical and physical components. Be that as it may, the fact that groups of human beings have differing physical characteristics and that we designate these groups as races does not *in itself* give rise to social and educational problems.

Problems of race arise when nonphysical, social, or cultural qualities are assigned to individuals only because they are members of such a group. When this happens, race becomes defined socially. *Racism* is the practice of associating significant (usually pejorative) cultural abilities and/or characteristics with groups that are defined socially as races. Racism becomes institutionalized when these associations, whether overt or subtle, are given legitimacy and social approval.

Racism, particularly institutionalized racism, is difficult to deal with because of the tendency to associate it with overt and conscious acts of prejudice. It has been referred to as the "disease of hate." Thus, individuals who generally have humanitarian attitudes toward others may be shocked and outraged if accused of racist behavior. The practices may have become so thoroughly institutionalized that awareness of their racist dimensions has been hidden.

Institutionalized racism consists of practices that have been *legitimized* by society and that result in *systematic* discrimination against members of *specific* groups. Practices that have been legitimized are accepted. Few question them. Until recently, even those against whom the discrimination was directed have accepted these practices. The word *systematic* in this definition is also important. This means that the discrimination is not a random occurrence; the discrimination is practiced with consistency and regularity, rather than being whimsical or capricious. It is directed against specific groups (perhaps not even by design) because members of those groups have certain characteristics or qualities.

Following are examples of practices that would qualify as institutionalized racism, some of which are often so subtle they go undetected:

1. Unnecessary and irrelevant references, especially in social studies and current events, to an individual's or group's racial or ethnic identity, such as "the black mayor of . . . ," "the Hispanic candidate from . . . ," "Asian parents gathered . . . ," or "the driver, an Indian from Forks, was charged with drunken driving." Such references are almost never used when the individual or group is white.

2. Use of dual test norms (standards), one for minority students and another for whites. The standards applied to minority students are almost invariably lower, which implies that ethnic minorities are not able to achieve as well as whites.

3. Optional "free choice" educational programs that require one to have a certain level of affluence to be able to participate. For example, attending a particular magnet school or participating in enrichment opportunities (music, dance, sports, art, clubs) may depend on one's ability to afford transportation, supplies, or other expenses. Such demands have a disproportionate adverse affect on low-income families, many of whom are members of ethnic minorities.

4. Homogeneous grouping. This practice discriminates against ethnic minorities because it often results in their being placed in low-achieving groups.

5. Expectations that children of color are more likely to misbehave, combined with harsher and more frequent punishment for those children when they misbehave.

6. Social acceptance of a higher incidence of failure and a higher dropout rate among certain minorities.

7. Curriculum content unrelated to the life and culture of certain groups. This circumstance discriminates against those who are not represented in the subject matter of the school.

8. Curriculum content that places certain groups in a negative light, for example, introducing such study topics as "Indians as savages during the Westward Expansion" or "Pancho Villa as an outlaw."

9. Neglecting or ignoring the contributions of individuals of color to humankind in social studies, mathematics, and science classes, or wherever else it is relevant.

10. Accepting implicitly the assumption that nonwhites are less capable than whites in any field of study or endeavor or, conversely, that nonwhites have specific aptitudes but are limited to those areas of achievement.

11. Bias against the use of a language other than English or against a child who speaks a dialect of English or with a non-English accent.

12. References that portray black as bad and white as good.

Gender Equity

Just as racism is the practice of ascribing certain abilities and characteristics to individuals on the basis of their identification with groups socially defined as races, *sexism*, or *gender bias*, does the same thing on the basis of one's gender.[18] Historically, female roles tended to be stereotyped along the lines of domestic and childrearing responsibilities, whereas male roles were stereotyped in the world of work outside the home. Also, women frequently were portrayed in art and literature in subservient roles, roles in which they served, waited on, picked up after, and took orders from men.

There can be little doubt that such stereotyping works to the disadvantage of women by restricting their range of significant opportunities for self-development (perhaps less obviously, it has a similar restrictive influence on men). Additionally, it has led to manifestly unfair discrimination against women. Changing attitudes, the growing independence of women, and legislative reforms have aided in combating the invidious distinctions between males and females that result from sex-role stereotyping.

Educational programs, particularly the part that teachers play in them, are vitally important in shaping young children's images of gender roles.[19] If children always see males rather than females in preferred, prestigious occupational and social roles, they are bound to conclude that the male is superior: Because these positions are obviously not available to women, women must not be capable of holding them. It hardly seems necessary to add that when gender roles are presented this way, both boys *and* girls come to believe them, which does grave disservice to *all* children.

Some of the more common teacher behaviors that violate the concept of gender equity are these:

1. Consistently using generic terms such as *man, mankind, early man,* and *common man* when the reference is to humanity. It is always better to substitute inclusive terms such as *people, human beings, ordinary people, humankind,* and *early people.*

2. Exaggerating the emphasis on the socialization of children into traditional gender roles: neatness, conformity, docility, and fastidiousness for females; competitiveness, aggressiveness, and physical activity and strength for males. It is important to maintain a balanced emphasis.

3. Segregating children on the basis of gender, such as in the seating arrangement in the classroom, in playground games, and in classroom learning activities.

4. Allowing or ignoring humor that ridicules one gender or the other, such as that directed toward the behavior of "nonmacho" males or women drivers.

5. Neglecting or ignoring the contributions of women to humankind in social studies, mathematics, and science classes, or wherever else it is relevant.

6. Accepting implicitly the assumption that females are less capable than males in such fields as mathematics, science, and athletics and, conversely, that males have less aptitude for art, literature, music, and dance.

7. Expressing a preference for teaching either males or females.

8. Displaying charts or graphs that compare the achievement of individuals according to gender.

9. Identifying certain leadership positions or specific activities in the classroom as being solely for one gender or the other.

10. Making light of, ignoring, or even ridiculing social movements or individuals associated with movements to secure equity for women.

11. Administering harsher consequences to males than to females for the same rule infraction.

12. Interacting more with males than with females in class discussions.

If the social goal of gender equity is to be achieved, we must present a range of role models to young children as a part of their formal education. Children must learn that it is just as appropriate for a woman to be a business executive, judge, mayor, senator, astronaut, bus driver, carpenter, or any of a variety of occupations as it is for a man. They also must learn that it is equally appropriate for a man to take care of and feed his young children, to do household duties or secretarial work, to be a nurse or a dancer, or to engage in any tasks or occupations traditionally associated with women.

What is important is that, as a teacher, you must present gender-role models in ways that provide your students with maximum opportunity for choice. Perhaps many will want to conduct their lives according to more or less traditional gender role definitions. Some may wish to exercise other choices, and they should not be prevented from or handicapped in doing so because of prejudicial attitudes or ridicule. Removing gender barriers should create almost unlimited opportunity for choice.

Inclusion

During the last half of the 20th century, the Congress of the United States passed only a few statutes pertaining to education, with none perhaps as powerful an agent for change as Public Law 94–142, the Education for All Handicapped Children Act (EAHCA) of 1975. Passage of that legislation marked the beginning of free and appropriate public education services to all schoolage children and youth, regardless of disability.[20] PL 94–142 mandates that all children have the right to such educational services, as well as to nondiscriminatory assessment. (The law was amended in 1986 by PL 99–457; in 1990 by PL 101–476, at which time its name was changed to the Individuals with Disabilities Education Act— IDEA; and again in 1997 by PL 105–17.) Emphasizing normalizing the educational environment for students with disabilities, this legislation requires provision of the "least restrictive environment" (LRE) for these students. A *least restrictive environment* is one that offers the fewest restrictions and the greatest opportunities in the context of a particular disability or limiting condition.

Students with disabilities (referred to also as "exceptional" and "special needs" students) include those with disabling conditions or impairments in any one or more of the following categories: mental retardation, hearing, speech or language, visual, emotional, orthopedic, autism, traumatic brain injury, other health impairment, or specific learning disabilities. To the extent possible, students with special needs must be educated with their peers in the regular classroom.

Students identified as having special needs may be placed in the regular classroom for the entire school day, called *full inclusion* (as is the trend).[21] Those students may also be in a regular classroom the greater part of the school day, called *partial inclusion*, or only for designated periods. Although there is no single, universally accepted definition of the term *inclusion*, it is generally understood to mean that students with disabilities should be integrated into general education classrooms regardless of whether they can meet traditional academic standards.[22] Indications are that when students with disabilities are integrated into general education classrooms, as opposed to pulled out into segregated special education classrooms, they earn higher grades, achieve higher or comparable standardized test scores, attend more days of school, and draw fewer discipline referrals.[23] Inclusion has largely replaced the earlier, similar term *mainstreaming*.

As a classroom teacher you will need information and skills specific to teaching children with special needs who are included in your classroom. The law does provide for help to the regular classroom teacher in the form of paraprofessionals and aides in addition to special education teachers, although the degree of assistance and support varies widely among districts and states. Generally speaking, teaching children who have special needs requires more care, better diagnosis, greater skill, more attention to individual needs, and an even greater understanding of the children. The challenges of teaching children with special needs in the regular classroom are great enough that to do it well you need specialized training, which you are likely to receive at some point in your teacher preparation.

It is unlikely that there will ever be one model of inclusion that is the solution for all children. It is enough to say that when a child with special needs is placed in your classroom, your task is to deal directly with the differences between this child and your other students. To do this, you should develop an understanding of the general characteristics of different types of special-needs learners, identify the child's unique needs relative to your classroom, and design lessons that teach to different needs at the same time. Remember also that because a person has been identified as having one or more special needs, this does not preclude that person from being gifted or talented. As a matter of fact, often left unidentified is the cognitive giftedness of a student who has a disabling condition because the focus and attention is given to accommodating the child's disability.[24]

Congress stipulated in PL 94–142 that an Individualized Educational Program (IEP) be devised annually for each special-needs child. According to that law, an IEP is developed for each student each year by a team that includes special education teachers, the child's parents or guardians, and the classroom teachers. The IEP contains a statement of the student's present educational levels, the educational goals for the year, specifications for the services to be provided and the extent to which the student will be expected to take part in the regular education program, and the evaluative criteria for the services to be provided. Consultation by special and skilled support personnel is essential in all IEP models. A consultant works directly with teachers or with students and parents. As a classroom teacher, you may play an active role in preparing the specifications for the special-needs children assigned to your classroom, as well as a major responsibility for implementing the program.

Newcomers to the English Language

From early colonial America to the present, people from every ethnic and cultural group of the world have arrived at the borders of this nation and, of course, brought their languages with them. Often, they have settled in communities inhabited by immigrants from the same part of the world. Consequently, throughout the United States are geographic locations in which people commonly speak a language other than English.

By the early 1900s, the use of languages other than English was so widespread that in some cases those languages were used for instructional purposes in public schools. All of this changed, however, in the period during and after World War I, when adverse feelings toward immigrant groups in general and German-speaking people in particular were so great that several states passed legislation prohibiting instruction in languages other than English in public schools. At the federal level, legislation was enacted to severely restrict immigration from southern and eastern Europe and from Asia. The suppressive legislation at the state and federal levels was destructive of foreign-language learning in America. Adverse feelings were so widespread that to speak in a language other than English was considered by many to be un-American. This attitude persists today.

There have been some positive changes in attitudes and practices in recent years, in part as a result of a growing ethnic awareness, multicultural enlightenment, and our increasing global interdependency. However, the movement to legitimize bilingual education as a part of the curriculum of the public schools has been only partially successful.[25]

One argument against bilingual education has been the observation that people have succeeded without it. However, such people are usually those who have had the advantages of good early education in their country of origin. Children who arrive in the United States with a good education in their primary language have already gained two objectives of a good bilingual education program: literacy and subject matter development. Research indicates that the ability to read transfers across languages, even when the writing systems are different.

Although there are many variations, bilingual education programs can be grouped into four categories: (1) transitional, (2) immersion, (3) English as a second language (ESL), and (4) bilingual/bicultural. A fifth category, submersion, is when non-English-speaking (NES) and limited-English-speaking (LES) children are placed directly in all English-speaking classes without any sort of special help whatsoever. Submersion is simply a sink-or-swim situation and is not a bilingual program at all.[26]

Transitional bilingual education, less widely used today than it used to be, provides instruction for some subjects in the students' language but with some time each day spent on developing English skills. Classes are made up of students who share the same native language.

Immersion involves teaching English to children by a teacher who is proficient in the learners' primary language, although the teacher uses only English for instruction. The English used for instruction is simplified so the children learn English and the academic subject content. Maintaining children's primary language is not an objective of either transitional or immersion programs.

Unlike transitional and immersion programs, teaching *English as a second language* (ESL) involves placing English-language learners (ELLs) with NES and LES children in all-English-speaking classes that are taught by instructors who have special training in ESL methods, but who may or may not have second-language proficiency. ESL programs are usually transitional, but may also be used as bilingual maintenance programs.

Bilingual/bicultural programs, which are sometimes called *maintenance* programs and may also be the same as immersion, are those in which the bilingual instruction continues for several years in an effort to maintain students' fluent command of both languages. Advocates of maintenance programs argue that it makes no sense to allow the knowledge of an alternate language, already partially mastered, to deteriorate. Many experts now are encouraging the use of *two-way programs*, where both language groups, the monolingual and the bilingual students, remain together throughout the school day, serving as peer tutors for each other. Research studies indicate that after 5 or 6 years in a two-way program, English learners can demonstrate both English and native-language proficiency and also outperform monolingual students on academic tests.[27] The two-way approach is also sometimes called *dual-immersion* or *dual-language* and is one of the fastest growing in elementary education, where children are placed in dual-language classrooms starting with kindergarten with the goal to have them completely bilingual by the time they reach at least the sixth grade.[28]

Regardless, as the debates continue and we await further research evidence, certain facts stand out as significant requirements for the successful application of any program for English-language learners. At a minimum, for these students in particular, teachers must be committed to (1) holding and instilling high expectations, (2) fostering a sense of community identity, and (3) seeking and holding strong parental involvement and support.

School Choice and Organizational Change

Traditionally, elementary school children in the public schools were required to attend their local neighborhood school. It was often difficult for parents and guardians to get school district permission to send children to a public school outside the designated attendance area. To attend school in another district meant that parents had to pay the tuition cost required by the host district. Parents could, of course, send their children to a private or parochial school but also at additional cost. In recent years, however, many of these policies regarding attendance have changed. The federal courts called for a racial balance in schools, and that required the movement of some children to schools outside their neighborhood school attendance area. This had the effect of making school district administrations less rigid with respect to the specific schools children could attend. This trend may, however, be once again in the process of reversing.

There is a feeling among many that the public school system has a monopoly on the education of the nation's children and that this condition works to the detriment of quality education. The business community, oriented to the concept of competition, believes that better school programs would result if individual schools had to rely on the quality of their programs for their students. This idea has also been attractive to some governors and federal officials. Some go so far as to suggest that parents or guardians should be able to select *any* school, public or private, for their children through the use of tax credits or *vouchers* to cover at least partial tuition costs. The basic idea is that schools, much like business institutions, should obtain their "clients" (i.e., students) on a competitive basis. The most effective schools would initially have the most students, whereas the least effective schools would be forced to improve their effectiveness in order to become and remain competitive.

One of the strongest arguments against this plan is that it discriminates against the very students that it is intended to help—low-income students. It might be that parents and guardians can choose any school in the district for their children, but the children still have to be able to get to the school. Low-income parents/guardians often cannot afford the transportation costs involved. Thus, more affluent parents and guardians will select the best schools for their children, whereas lower-income families will tend to keep their children in local schools. Because income, socioeconomic level, and school achievement are such closely related variables, this usually means that the local schools in low socioeconomic areas will have a disproportionate number of low-achieving children, just as they do now.

The concept of a "charter school" is another option on the menu of school choices. A *charter school* is "an autonomous educational entity operating under a charter, or contract, that has been negotiated between the organizers, who create and operate the school, and a sponsor, who oversees the provisions of the charter."[29] Once a school is granted a charter, it qualifies for state and local funding on the same basis and at the same formula-based rate as regular public schools. Since the first in Minnesota in 1991, charter school legislation has been passed in at least 40 states, the District of Columbia, and Puerto Rico, reflecting a general dissatisfaction with centralized state or district control, bureaucratic inflexibility, and uneven progress in student performance. As stated in *A Study of Charter Schools: First-Year Report*,

> The charter school movement grew out of a belief that a carefully developed competition among existing public schools and new kinds of schools developed by local educators, parents, community members, school boards and other sponsors could provide both new models of schooling and the incentive to improve the current system of public education.[30]

Charter schools are a blend of elements of both private and public schools.[31]

There can be no doubt that school choice motivates school faculties to be concerned about the quality of their programs. The idea has certainly proved to be effective in the private-school sector. Moreover, choice encourages schools to provide enrichment programs that are attractive to children with special abilities in the academic areas, music, art, drama, or physical education. Such *magnet schools* within the public school system have an enthusiastic clientele in several large school districts across the nation. The North Dade Center for Modern Languages (Miami, FL), for example, is a public elementary magnet school that focuses on international studies and provides students with the opportunity to become bilingual, biliterate, and multicultural. Chollas Elementary School (San Diego, CA) is a math/science magnet school. Some schools, such as Paul Revere Charter/LEARN Middle School (Los Angeles, CA), are both charter and magnet schools.

Efficiency and *standardization,* two concepts from the industrial world, have had a profound effect on education in recent years. In their name the number of school districts has been reduced from more than 100,000 in 1940 to fewer than 15,000 today. These large school districts can have central curriculum personnel to plan programs for the entire district and can purchase books and materials in huge quantities, and thus at discounted prices. Record keeping, payrolls, and school maintenance can be performed more efficiently because the procedures are standardized and centralized. But, of course, what also happens is that much significant decision making concerning students, the curriculum, teachers, and the learning process takes place farther and farther away from the classroom. Accountability for students' progress, or lack of it, however, remains with the individual teacher at the classroom level. Charter schools are designed to combat some of the limitations of a large, centralized system.

With school redesigns and other trends, shown in Figure 1.5, the purpose is to better address the needs and capabilities of each unique student. As a

---

- Dividing the student body and faculty into smaller cohorts, the school-within-a school concept, and using nontraditional scheduling
- Encouraging the practices of reflective thinking and self-discipline
- Establishing and maintaining high expectations for all students by establishing goal or target standards and then assessing the achievement of each student against those standards
- Facilitating students' social skills as they interact, relate to one another, solve meaningful problems, develop skills in conflict resolution, and foster peaceful relationships and friendships
- Facilitating the developing of students' values as related to their families, the school and community, and the nation
- Focusing on the use of strategies that have been proven to work, such as heterogeneous small-group learning, peer coaching, and cross-age tutoring
- Integrating the curriculum
- Involving parents/guardians and communities in the schools
- Involving students in self-assessment
- Making multicultural education work for all children
- Movement away from the traditional "agrarian school calendar" to a 45/15 or similar year-round calendar to reduce the effect of the loss of skills and content knowledge due to the nearly 3-month summer layoff
- Providing students with the time and opportunity to think and be creative, rather than simply memorizing and repeating information
- Redefining giftedness to include nonacademic as well as traditional academic abilities
- Teaching and assessing for higher-order thinking skills
- Using the Internet in the classroom as a communication tool and learning resource

---

FIGURE 1.5
Key trends and practices in today's elementary schools

teacher in the 21st century, you will undoubtedly help accomplish many of these changes.

Grade-Level Organization

The elementary school usually enrolls children between the ages of 5 and 11 (Figure 1.6); converting these ages to grades, we get kindergarten (K) through 6. In some places, the elementary school is a primary school, with grades K–4, followed by a 4-year middle school, and then a high school. In some places, the elementary school grade ranges are K through 8, an arrangement in which there is a rekindled interest in the United States.[32] The K–8 elementary schools ordinarily are followed by a 4-year high school (K–8–4). The K–6 elementary schools are usually followed by a 3-year junior high school, or a middle school, followed by a 3-year senior high school (K–6–3–3).

Age 5	Age 6	Age 7	Age 8
Arkansas	Arizona	Alabama	Pennsylvania
Delaware	California	Alaska	Washington
Maryland	Florida	Connecticut	
New Mexico	Georgia	Idaho	
Oklahoma	Hawaii	Illinois	
South Carolina	Iowa	Indiana	
Virginia	Kentucky	Kansas	
	Massachusetts	Louisiana	
	Michigan	Maine	
	Mississippi	Minnesota	
	New Hampshire	Missouri	
	New Jersey	Montana	
	New York	Nebraska	
	Ohio	Nevada	
	Rhode Island	North Carolina	
	South Dakota	North Dakota	
	Tennessee	Oregon	
	Texas	Vermont	
	Utah		
	West Virginia		
	Wisconsin		
	Wyoming		

FIGURE 1.6

Age by state for beginning compulsory school attendance. For Colorado and District of Columbia, no ages were listed on this table, but earlier data from 1996 listed the compulsory ages at 7.

Source: Digest of Education Statistics, 2001 (Washington, DC: National Center for Education Statistics, 2001), retrieved from the Internet (http://nces.ed.gov//pubs2002/digest2001/tables/dt151.asp) on February 21, 2003.

However, a K–6 elementary school with a 2-year middle school and a 4-year high school is not uncommon.[33]

The Graded School Concept

Schools in colonial America and those of the early national period did not use the age-sorting system we call *grades*. Children of varying ages were assigned to a single teacher, who tutored them individually or taught them in small cross-age groups. It was not until the middle of the 19th century that the practice of grouping children according to age (i.e., age grading) became widespread. This practice was developed in Germany in the 8-year *Volkschule*. It appealed to American educators as an efficient way of managing the teaching of a large number of children.

Following the Civil War, there was rapid acceptance of the practice of grouping children of a similar age and keeping those groups intact from one year to the next as they progressed through school. Schools were therefore "graded" by age, and communities and states used that term in curriculum documents and school regulations and names. Even today, it is possible to find etched into the stonework of some remaining old school buildings such names as "Frederic Graded School." The expression "grade school" is common parlance when speaking of the elementary school.

Proponents of the graded school concept argue the following:

- It reduces variability within instructional groups by keeping the age of children constant within the groups.
- It equalizes educational opportunity by exposing all children to the same curriculum.
- Textbooks, instructional materials, and achievement tests can be constructed on the basis of age-grade norms.
- Children's social development, to some extent, relates to age, and therefore, age groups tend to be natural social groups.
- It is an efficient way to accommodate the large number of children who are required to attend school.
- It allows teachers to specialize their teaching skills in terms of the age of the children with whom they work best.
- It is possible to require set standards of achievement for the various grades.

Opponents of the graded school concept argue the following:

- It is too lock-step, encouraging teachers to disregard individual differences in children and in their developmental patterns.
- It sets unrealistic standards for children and is especially unfair to low achievers.
- It encourages mechanical teaching, analogous to assembly-line production in industry.
- It encourages traditional recitation–response teaching practices, ignoring what has been learned during the recent past about learning.

- It encourages a rigid and undifferentiated curriculum.
- The competitive and comparative system of determining grades (marks of achievement) and promotion are educationally dysfunctional and psychologically unsound.
- It encourages an authoritarian classroom atmosphere that is antagonistic to what is now known about how children best learn.

CURRICULUM STANDARDS AND ACHIEVEMENT TESTING

Curriculum standards are definitions of what students should know (content) and be able to do (process and performance) as a result of instruction. National curriculum standards did not exist in the United States until those developed and released for mathematics education in 1989. Shortly after the release of the mathematics standards, the National Governors Association supported national goals in education, and the National Council on Education Standards and Testing recommended that in addition to those for mathematics, national standards for subject matter content in K–12 education be developed for the arts, civics/social studies, English/language arts/reading, geography, history, and science. The U.S. Department of Education provided initial funding for the development of national standards. In 1994 the United States Congress passed the *Goals 2000: Educate America Act*, amended in 1996 with an Appropriations Act, encouraging states to set standards. Long before this, however, national organizations were defining standards, as the National Council for Teachers of Mathematics had already done for mathematics.

The national standards for a given discipline represent the best thinking by expert panels, including teachers from the discipline, about what are the essential elements of a basic core of subject knowledge that all students should acquire. They serve not as national mandates but rather as voluntary guidelines to encourage curriculum development to promote higher student achievement. State and local curriculum developers may decide the extent to which they use the standards. Strongly influenced by the national standards, nearly all 50 states have completed or are presently developing state standards for the various disciplines. The topic of curriculum standards is discussed more fully in Chapter 5.

Preparing Students for High-Stakes Achievement Testing

The adoption of tougher K–12 learning standards throughout the United States coupled with an emphasis on increased high-stakes competency testing to assess how schools and teachers are doing with respect to helping their students meet those standards has provoked considerable debate, actions, and reactions among educators, parents/guardians, politicians, and people from the world of business. Some argue that this renewed emphasis on testing means too much "teaching to the test" at the expense of more meaningful learning, and that it ignores the leverage that home, community, and larger societal influences have over the education of children and young people today. For example, in the words of Lauren Sosniak,[34]

> We need to find ways to ask what our communities, corporations, media, and all of our organizations and institutions are doing to promote the development of readers, writers, historians, scientists, artists, musicians, designers and craftspersons. Schools cannot do this work alone, in the 9% of [a child's K–12 lifetime in school] allotted to them. If this is only "school work," it is hard to imagine that our students will see it as a meaningful part of their lives and their futures. . . . For too long our schools have been held accountable for too much, with too little acknowledgement of the responsibilities of the rest of society.

Nevertheless, responding to the call for increased accountability, especially although certainly not exclusively when state and federal funding may be withheld and/or jobs are on the line for schools, teachers, and administrators where students do not score well, teachers in some schools put aside the regular curriculum for several weeks in advance of the testing date and concentrate on the direct preparation of their students for the test. As stated by Carol Ann Tomlinson,

> For many teachers, curriculum has become a prescribed set of academic standards, instructional pacing has become a race against a clock to cover the standards, and the sole goal of teaching has been reduced to raising student test scores on a single test, the value of which has scarcely been questioned in the public forum.[35]

Although interest in this practice, often called "drill and kill," has been rekindled in recent years, it is certainly not new. When comparing standardized achievement testing of today with that of about half a century ago, it is probably safe to conclude (1) the purpose for statewide standardized testing remains unchanged—it is to determine how well children are learning, at least to the extent determined by the particular test instrument; (2) although alignment of tests with curriculum standards is an expensive and time-intensive challenge, test design is accomplished today with much greater precision and accuracy; but (3) today's focus on testing is taking precious time away from the most creative aspects of teaching and learning, and (4) the manner today in which test results are being used and the long-term results of that use may have ramifications considerably more serious than at any time before.

As we think about testing policies, we should remember the wisdom in the farmer's comment that weighing a pig every day won't ever make the pig any fatter. Eventually, you have to feed the pig.

—Audrey L. Amrein and David C. Berliner

Source: A. L. Amrein and D. C. Berliner, "The Effects of High-Stakes Testing on Student Motivation and Learning," *Educational Leadership* 60(5): 32–36 (2003).

SOCIAL TRAGEDIES

The discussion of professional challenges to today's schools and teachers would not be complete without some attention to HIV/AIDS, illicit drug use, child abuse, and youth gangs, but their scope extends far beyond the school and the classroom. These topics are not exhaustive of the nation's social tragedies that deeply affect youth, nor are they necessarily related to one another except that each represents a major social tragedy of our time. It is *not* the purpose of this text to provide extensive coverage of these problems. It *is* our purpose to alert you to the need to be prepared psychologically and professionally to in some way deal with these and the other social tragedies—such as eating disorders in young people,[36] youth pregnancies, and gay and lesbian taunting and bashing—that affect children and, in some way or another, activities in the classroom.

Acquired Immune Deficiency Syndrome (AIDS)

Acquired immune deficiency syndrome (AIDS), first identified in 1981, is the final stage of a viral infection caused by the human immunodeficiency virus (HIV). In the United States, AIDS is now a leading cause of death among 1- to 4-year-olds, 15- to 24-year-olds, and 25- to 44-year-olds. Most experts believe that schools and parents should begin teaching children about HIV/AIDS as early as kindergarten so that children can grow up knowing how to protect themselves from exposure to the virus. As a matter of fact, the risk of elementary school children contracting HIV is greater than many people realize because a significant number of them have sex before they finish elementary school.[37]

In addition to the question of when and how to educate children about the disease are the questions of how to educate children who have the disease and how best to work with children who do not have the disease but nevertheless are AIDS victims.

Illicit Drug Use

It is generally acknowledged that since the 1960s the United States has had a serious drug-abuse problem, one that continues to worsen. For example, the report *America's Children* indicates that the percentages of 8th-, 10th-, and 12th-graders who smoke regularly and who abuse alcohol and drugs increased during the 1990s.[38] Studies indicate that students of the sixth, seventh, and eighth grades are at a crucial age for either adopting or rejecting the use of illicit substances.[39] Such findings have sobering implications for health education programs in the preteen grades.

Most experts agree that drug education should begin by at least the third grade, perhaps even as early as kindergarten. Moreover, a number of states have had regulations calling for the teaching of "the evils of narcotics, alcohol, and tobacco" for many years. The problem is not in finding agreement concerning the *need* for such education but in the nature of the education provided. Information is important, of course, but it is clearly inadequate as an absolute deterrent to drug abuse.

Schools can educate children about drug use in at least four ways. First, schools can provide accurate information about drugs and their effects on the human mind and body. Second, schools can stress the individual's responsibility to keep her or his own body in good physical condition. Third, the school must provide a drug-free environment. There must be a *zero-tolerance attitude* for any drug use, possession, or trafficking anywhere in the school or on the playground, day or night. Fourth, teachers can be sensitive to the behavior of individual children in order to identify signs of possible illicit drug use. Teachers must be aware of and follow school policy in reporting matters of illicit drug use.

Child Abuse and Neglect

Child abuse and neglect (e.g., physical abuse, incest, malnutrition, being improperly clothed, and inadequate dental care) have become grave matters of pressing national concern. *Teachers in all states are legally mandated to report any suspicion of child abuse.* It is a serious moral issue to not report such suspicion; lawsuits have been brought against educators for negligence in not doing so. If for any reason you suspect child abuse, follow school policy or telephone toll-free 1-800-4-A-CHILD. Proof of abuse is not necessary.

Although physical abuse is the easiest to spot, other types of abuse and neglect can be just as serious. General characteristics of children who are abused or neglected are the following: below normal in height and weight; destructive behavior; hyperactive or aggressive behavior; short attention spans and lack of interest in school activities; sudden and dramatic changes in behavior; fear of everyone and everything; fear of going home after school; fear of their parents and other adults; frequently sick and absent from school; frequently tired and often fall asleep in class; smell of alcohol; unclean, smelling of body wastes; unexpected crying; unexplained lacerations and bruises; withdrawal from adult contact; and withdrawal from peer interaction.[40] A student who comes to your classroom abused or neglected needs to feel welcome and secure while there. For guidance in working with such students, contact experts from your local school district (such as your school psychologist) or from the local Children's Protective Services (CPS) agency. In addition, request guidelines from your state department of education.

Youth Gangs

Another threat to the safety and future of the nation's youth is the escalation of youth gang activity. Although children in at least the early elementary grades are not ordinarily eligible for hardcore gang membership, a considerable amount of readiness for gang life takes place during these formative years. It is therefore imperative that elementary school teachers be aware of the gang movement and have the knowledge and courage to assist in thwarting its negative effects.[41]

Associated with gang life is unrestrained violence of the most vicious kind. Drive-by shootings, assaults, maiming, robberies, burglaries, intimidation, and murder characterize gang activity. Drug trafficking, particularly of crack cocaine, is the financial lifeblood of gangs across the country. Perhaps no community today is immune to the havoc and terror of criminal youth gangs.

Why do young people join gangs? Among the reasons most often given are identification or recognition (i.e., status), protection, fellowship and brotherhood, and intimidation. From a psychological perspective, many youth find gang life attractive because it enhances their self-esteem; it gives them a level of acceptance and sense of belonging that they do not otherwise have. In other words, they find that gang life fills personal nurturing needs not met by their home, school, or other support groups in the neighborhood. Acceptance seems to be a major factor—gang members want to know that somebody cares about them.

Gangs develop their own colors, dress codes, trappings, icons, handshakes, and signals that help establish their identity. These are perceived as almost sacred rituals, and a violation of them or their appropriation by others can result in serious retribution and even death. Regrettably, many young children find these symbols attractive and may be drawn to them long before they are eligible for gang membership. For example, when a gang member walks through a neighborhood decked out in colorful gang regalia, little children may literally follow him around out of a sense of admiration. A young child may emulate some of that behavior in the classroom. When this happens, it is a clear sign of the need for intervention.

It is important to recognize the warning signs of gang activity. Teachers and parents/guardians should be suspicious of gang involvement if a *pattern of behavior* is observed that consistently includes a combination of the following: extended absences from school or home; unexplained wealth; abrupt change in personality; withdrawing from family; decline in school grades; lack of school involvement; radical change in friends; signs of alcohol or drug abuse; keeping late hours; associating with gang members; hand signals, symbolism, and graffiti; using excessive gang verbiage; change in vocabulary, especially high use of nicknames; dress code—style, color, or specific items such as a scarf; increased violence.

How should you intervene if you have reason to believe that a child is involved in gang activity? The best course of action seems to be to come down very hard at the first sign of gang involvement. Schoolteachers at all levels are in a strategic position to observe such signs and should report their sightings and suspicions to the school principal.

Bullying and Violence

In many ways, teaching is clearly different from how it used to be.

> About a decade ago, an elementary school principal calling for a security assessment of his or her school would have been the exception, not the rule. But in light of high-profile school violence in recent years, and especially since September 11th, parents have been demanding to know what principals are doing to improve their schools' security and crisis planning.[42]

More and more often today, starting as early as kindergarten, teachers are confronted with major problems that have ramifications beyond the classroom or that begin elsewhere and spill over into the classroom. If this happens, you may need to ask for help and should not hesitate to do so. As a teacher, you must remain alert. In the words of Johnson and Johnson,

> Fifty years ago, the main disciplinary problems were running in halls, talking out of turn, and chewing gum. Today's transgressions include physical and verbal violence, incivility, and in some schools, drug abuse, robbery, assault, and murder. The result is that many teachers spend an inordinate amount of time and energy managing classroom conflicts. When students poorly manage their conflicts with each other and with faculty, aggression results. Such behavior is usually punished with detentions, suspensions, and expulsions. As violence increases, pressure for safe and orderly schools increases. Schools are struggling with what to do.[43]

Today's schools are adopting a variety of types of schoolwide and classroom instructional programs designed to reduce or eliminate violent, aggressive, student behaviors and to help all students succeed in school.[44] The most effective school programs for antiviolence use four strategies. They (1) teach social competence, (2) create a positive, calm environment, (3) establish behavior standards, and (4) establish rules and regulations for responding to violence.[45]

The Violence That Surrounds Us

Shortly after beginning my career as an educator in urban schools, I realized the importance of focusing only on issues where I had a measure of control. Let's face it, the challenges that face educators and students in urban environments can be overwhelming. Perhaps the most overwhelming of all is the issue of school violence.

Too many of our children today are as callous to violence as soldiers on a battlefield. Because schools are microcosms of society, and society as a whole is becoming increasingly violent, it is no surprise that our children act violently and have a general disregard for the value of life.

People are quick to point to violent films and television as the source of the problem. But by placing the blame on the entertainment industry—something that is largely out of our control—we actually contribute to the problem by wasting time that could be spent working toward a solution.

Before we can do anything about violence in our schools, we must first take responsibility for the daily violence in our lives. Many people, both adults and children, do not realize how much violence they accept in their own behavior, or how willing they are to accept the violent behavior of others. School officials can teach nonviolent conflict resolution day in and day out, but if students receive different messages outside—like the parent who proudly told me that she instructs her son to "hit back" if struck by another student—the effort is wasted.

How many of us notice the barely suppressed violence that takes place around us when we drive to work on a crowded highway? And what about the violent language we use when angry, or the tone and volume we use to express frustration or disappointment? It is these everyday occurrences that teach children that violence is normal and acceptable.

Those who respect themselves respect others—that's what we teach children at our school. But school rules get left at school if they are not observed at home. Schools, families, and the community must work together to help make nonviolent behavior the hallmark of our society, not the exception.

The truth is that we do have some control over the issue of school violence. If each one of us can take control of the violence in our own lives, we will be teaching everyone around us—not just our children—that violence is unacceptable.

Roger Harris
Headmaster
Boston Renaissance Charter School
Boston, Massachusetts

Source: R. Harris, *Principal* 81(5): 12 (2002). By permission.

Ever since the 1999 massacre at Columbine High School in Littleton, Colorado, where two students shot and killed a dozen classmates and a teacher before taking their own lives, parents and teachers are abandoning old notions of bullying as a kind of rite of passage and, across the nation, are launching unprecedented efforts to protect children from each other, aiming not just at physical intimidation but also at more subtle forms of emotional harassment. The most successful efforts at reducing bullying, which often leads to violence on campus, begin with kindergarten and include the following:

- Establish and consistently enforce a "no taunting policy."
- Survey the children each year to find out the nature and extent of bullying.
- Establish and follow a consistent set of words used, and consequences for, taunting and bullying, and that is followed by all school personnel, from bus drivers to teachers and other adult supervisors.
- Assign as many teachers as necessary to adequately monitor halls at the beginning and end of each school day.
- Assign as many teachers and other adults as necessary to adequately monitor playground activities.
- Make regular classroom presentations about taunting and bullying.
- Reinforce the presentations in communications to parents and guardians.[46]

For example, at Seeds University Elementary School in Los Angeles, students and their parents or guardians sign contracts at the beginning of the school year acknowledging they understand it is unacceptable to ridicule, taunt, or attempt to hurt other students.[47]

PARENTS, GUARDIANS, AND THE COMMUNITY

One of the exciting recent developments in elementary education has been the increased involvement of parents and guardians as partners in their children's education. Historically, parents and guardians have been involved in

Activity 1.2: Neighborhood Violence

Maria Garcia (all names are fictional) stands watching the front door of Emeryville Elementary School, located in an inner-city neighborhood of a large midwestern city, waiting for her 6-year-old son, Emilio, to emerge. At last he appears, flashing a gap-toothed smile. The first-grader skips along the wall of waiting parents and guardians to his mother and hands her his backpack.

Garcia is here to make sure her son gets home safely. She's concerned about gang activity in the area. A recent police alert about attempted child abductions in the neighborhood also worries her, as well as a violent fight between older children that she witnessed recently one day after school.

1. What are your initial thoughts after reading this real scenario?
2. Does this scenario sound familiar or realistic to you? Discuss why or why not with your classmates.
3. Some communities have established Neighborhood Watch programs designed to protect children while traveling from home to school. [See, for example, R. M. Salcido, V. Ornelas, and J. A. Garcia, "A Neighborhood Watch Program for Innter-City School Children," *Children & Schools* 24(3): 175–187 (July 2002)]. Are similar programs operating in your geographic area?

parent–teacher associations (PTAs), parent–teacher organizations (PTOs), or parent–student–teacher organizations (PSTOs), in fundraisers for the schools, as assistants on field trips, as guests at an annual school open house, or as audiences for their children's pageants and plays. But parents and guardians have not really been centrally involved in instructional programs as knowledgeable partners with teachers, and it is this relationship that seems to be emerging today. Quite different from most parental involvement to date, this newer relationship between parents, guardians, and schools is best described as a *partnership*.

It is well known that parents' and guardians' involvement in their children's education can have a positive impact on their children's achievement at school. For example, when parents/guardians of at-risk students get involved, the children benefit with more consistent attendance at school, more positive attitudes and actions, better grades, and higher test scores.[48]

Although not all schools have a parent organization, when elementary school principals are asked to assess the influence each extant group has exerted on their school, the one likely to have the most influence is the parent–teacher organization. In recognition of the positive effect that parent and family involvement has on student achievement and success, in 1997 the National PTA published *National Standards for Parent/Family Involvement Programs*.[49]

Many schools have adopted formal policies about home and community connections. These policies usually emphasize that parents and guardians should be included as partners in the educational program, and that teachers and administrators will inform parents and guardians about their children's progress, about the school's family involvement policy, and about any programs in which family members can participate. Some schools also are members of the National Network of Partnership 2000 Schools. Efforts to

The professional responsibilities of the elementary school teacher may extend well beyond the walls of the classroom. With the growth of site-based management, teachers in many schools are becoming more centrally involved in the governance and management of their schools. Here we see, from left to right, a principal, parents, and a teacher deliberating on matters relevant to the parents' child and the school.

foster parent/guardian and community involvement are as varied as the people who participate and include the following:

- Student–teacher–parent/guardian contracts and assignment calendars, sometimes available via the school's Web site
- Home visitor programs
- Involvement of community leaders in the classroom as mentors, aides, and role models[50]
- Newsletters, workshops,[51] and electronic hardware and software for parents and guardians to help their children
- Homework hotlines
- Regular phone calls[52] and personal notes home about a student's progress
- Involvement of students in community service learning[53]

Through the last item, community service learning, children can learn and develop through active participation in thoughtfully organized, curriculum-connected experiences that meet community needs. Figure 1.7 presents resources for home–school–community partnerships.

- Alliance for Parental Involvement in Education, PO Box 59, East Chatham, NY 12060-0059 (518-392-6900)
- Center on Families, Communities, Schools & Children's Learning, 3505 N. Charles St., Baltimore, MD 21218 (410-516-8800)
- *How to Help Your Child with Homework: Every Caring Parent's Guide to Encouraging Good Study Habits and Ending the Homework Wars (For Parents of Children Ages 6–13),* by M. C. Radencich and J. S. Schumm, 1997. Free Spirit Publishing, 400 First Avenue North, Suite 616, Minneapolis, MN
- National Coalition for Parent Involvement in Education, Box 39, 1201 16th St., NW, Washington, DC 20036
- National Community Education Association, 3929 Old Lee Highway, Suite 91A, Fairfax, VA 22030-2401 (703-359-8973)
- National PTA, 330 North Wabash Ave., Ste 2100, Chicago, IL 60611-3690 (312-670-6782)
- Parents for Public Schools, PO Box 12807, Jackson, MS 39236-2807 (800-880-1222)
- T. H. Cairney, "Beyond the Classroom Walls: The Rediscovery of the Family and Community as Partners in Education," *Educational Review* 52(2): 163–174 (2000).

FIGURE 1.7
Resources for home–school partnerships

SUMMARY

Meeting the educational and developmental needs of all children in an increasingly diverse society presents challenges to teachers and schools. As never before, teachers are challenged to prepare children for citizenship in a dynamic multicultural society whose economic and political involvement is international in scope and global in influence.

American education continues to be dramatically affected by changes occurring in the lifestyles of families, pernicious attitudes of racism, economic and educational inequities, and other issues including the threats of terrorism and war. Because the elementary school is so close to the most formative years of young human beings, these matters are of special relevance to those who teach at that level. School policies and professional concerns of teachers emerge from the social context within which the school operates.

No one who was knowledgeable about the matter ever said that elementary school teaching was easy. However, the good news is that you have many valuable resources at your disposal and that your rewards are well worth the effort needed to become and to remain a knowledgeable and effective classroom teacher. Regardless of all else, in the end the dedication, commitment, and nature of the understanding of the teacher and other adults remain the decisive elements that determine whether a child succeeds in school or is left behind and drops out somewhere along the way.

As a classroom teacher you must acknowledge that your students have different ways of receiving information and different ways of processing that information—different ways of knowing and of constructing their knowledge. These differences are unique and important and are central considerations in curriculum development and instructional practice. Although you cannot cure all the woes of society, you can ensure that each child feels welcome, accepted, respected, safe, and successful while in your classroom.

Involvement of parents and guardians in the school experiences of their children is one of the few educational issues on which there is universal accord. The importance of such involvement may rival that of family income or family education as a variable contributing to children's success in school.

In beginning your plan to develop your professional competencies, you have read in this chapter an overview of some of the issues and problems that will affect both that development and your work and effectiveness as a classroom teacher. In spite of various societywide efforts to more effectively and efficiently educate children, it is still the classroom teacher, working mostly alone in a self-contained classroom, who bears responsibility for implementing the program to meet all children's educational and developmental needs. In Chapter 2, we look more closely at the teacher's professional responsibilities.

STUDY QUESTIONS AND ADDITIONAL ACTIVITIES

1. This chapter calls attention to changes in the demographics of U.S. society. What major ethnic, racial, and/or cultural groups live in the area in which you plan to teach? Have the percentages of represented groups changed in the past 25 years? What implications are there in these social realities for your work as a teacher?

2. In your opinion, should kindergarten, all day, with a more standardized curriculum, replace first grade as the official start of school? Are 5-year-olds ready for that sort of academic thrust? Some say that we are asking too much too soon for young children. Find support for your opinion and share it with members of your class.

3. Literacy, citizenship, and moral education have been important goals of education since the time of colonial America. Research and discuss the importance of the teaching methods used to achieve these goals. Speculate on how such methods have changed through the years.

4. What are your most vivid pleasant memories of your own elementary school experience? Do you think children today still enjoy similar experiences or activities?

5. In terms of today's ethnic and cultural diversity of our society, explain why you believe that goals related to the common culture are more or less important than they were a century ago.

6. Other than those discussed in this chapter, what additional social realities influence the subject matter or methods of teaching that teachers select? Are these unique to a specific geographic area or areas of the United States?

7. What opportunity costs are sacrificed when students and their parents select a school outside the usual attendance area? What might the positive or negative long-term effects of this practice be on society as a whole if it becomes widespread?

8. Some people believe that the primary function of our schools is to transmit societal values. Others believe that schools should be agents of social reform (transformation). Still others argue that schools should be agents of *both* cultural transmission and transformation. Prepare a position paper in favor of one of these positions. Present and defend your position before your classmates.

9. Some say that the ability of United States to cope with an explosion of religious, ethnic, socioeconomic, and political diversity will determine the future of the nation in much the same way as the American Revolution and the Civil War. Explain why you agree or disagree with this position. If you agree, explain what you see to be an elementary school classroom teacher's responsibility toward making the successful changes of society.

10. Express your opinion on the following statement: It is not important that a child might complete his or her elementary school education without ever having had a male or an ethnic minority teacher.

NOTES

1. E. A. Wynne and K. Ryan, *Reclaiming Our Schools: Teaching Character, Academics, and Discipline*, 2nd ed. (Upper Saddle River, NJ: Merrill/Prentice Hall, 1997).

2. K. Burrett and T. Rusnak, *Integrated Character Education*, Fastback 351 (Bloomington, IN: Phi Delta Kappa Educational Foundation, 1993), 15.

3. E. Boyer, *The Basic School: A Community for Learning* (San Francisco: Jossey-Bass, 1995).

4. D. T. Conley, "Restructuring: In Search of a Definition," *Principal* 72(3): 12 (1993).

5. See, for example, C. H. Leland and W. C. Kasten, "Literacy Education for the 21st Century: It's Time to Close the Factory," *Reading and Writing Quarterly: Overcoming Learning Difficulties* 18(1): 5–15 (2002).

6. See, for example, M. Weertz, "The Benefits of Theme Schools," *Educational Leadership* 59(7): 68–71 (2002).

7. See, for example, T. S. Little and L. P. Little, *Looping: Creating Elementary School Communities* (Bloomington, IN: Phi Delta Kappa Educational Foundation, Fastback 478, 2001), and C. McCown and S. Sherman, "Looping for Better Performance in the Middle Grades," *Middle School Journal* 33(4): 17–21 (2002).

8. See, for example, S. J. Kinsey, *Multiage Grouping and Academic Achievement*, ED448935 (Champaign, IL: ERIC Clearinghouse on Elementary and Early Childhood Education, 2001), and D. A. Domenech, "Success by Eight: A Program for 21st Century Schools," *Principal* 78(4): 26–28, 30 (1999).

9. See, T. McAndrews and W. Anderson, *Schools Within Schools*, ED461915 (Eugene, OR: ERIC Clearinghouse on Educational Management, 2002). See how one group of teachers established a school-within-a-school for grades 1–4 at Narcoossee Community School (St. Cloud, FL) in G. McGoogan, "The Bear Dean: An Elementary Teaching Team," *Educational Leadership* 59(5): 30–32 (2002).

10. J. Grant, "Differentiating for Diversity," *Principal* 82(3): 48–51 (2003).

11. Source: National Law Center on Homelessness and Poverty. Retrieved January 10, 2003, from http://www.nlchp.org/FA_HAPIA.

12. See, for example, the Web site of the Thomas J. Pappas School at http://www.tjpappasschool.org.

13. See, for example, W. Schwartz, *The Identity Development of Multiracial Youth*, ERIC/CUE Digest, Number 137 (New York: ERIC Clearinghouse on Urban Education, 1998).

14. R. W. Rumberger, *Student Mobility and Academic Achievement*, ED466314 (Champaign, IL: ERIC Clearinghouse on Elementary and Early Childhood Education, 2002).

15. The term *one-parent family* has become a euphemism that includes a multitude of living situations involving parents and children. It is impossible to provide teachers with reliable guidelines for dealing with such cases except to say that each one is unique. Specialists have reminded us that a 15-year-old child with a baby is not a one-parent family; it is a nonfamily.

16. See, for example, J. D. Weast, "Why We Need Rigorous, Full-Day Kindergarten," *Principal* 80(5): 6–9 (2001).

17. See, for example, J. G. Dryfoos, "Full-Service Community Schools: Creating New Institutions," *Phi Delta Kappan* 83(5): 393–399 (2002).

18. It is important to distinguish between *sex* and *gender*. Sex has to do with differences attributed to genetics; that is, one is born either male or female. Gender, on the other hand, has to do with the differences attributed to the roles males and females play in a society. A society defines its idealized role behavior of males and females—what is masculine and what is feminine—and these differences are properly called *gender* differences.

19. For a research-documented discussion of the part that schools and teachers play in the gender-role development of children, see J. R. Harris and R. M. Liebert, *The Child: A Contemporary View of Development*, 3rd ed. (Upper Saddle River, NJ: Prentice Hall, 1991), Chapters 10 and 12. Also see T. L. Good and J. E. Brophy, *Contemporary Educational Psychology*, 5th ed. (White Plains, NY: Longman, 1995), 571–576, and P. D. Hunsader, "Why Boys Fail—And What We Can Do About It," *Principal* 82(2): 52–54 (2002).

20. J. S. Hewit and K. S. Whittier, *Teaching Methods for Today's Schools: Collaboration and Inclusion* (Boston: Allyn & Bacon, 1997), 18.

21. See, for example, M. L. Yell, "The Legal Basis of Inclusion," *Educational Leadership* 56(2): 70–73 (1998). For education law pertaining to special education students, see the Internet (http://www.access.digex.net/~edlawinc/).

22. E. Tiegerman-Farber and C. Radziewicz, *Collaborative Decision Making: The Pathway to Inclusion* (Upper Saddle River, NJ: Merrill/Prentice Hall, 1998), 12–13.

23. See, for example, P. J. Rea, V. L. McLaughlin, and C. Walther-Thomas, "Outcomes for Students with Learning Disabilities in Inclusive and Pullout Programs," *Exceptional Children* 68(2): 203–222 (2002), and H. M. Krank, C. E. Moon, and G. F. Render, "Inclusion and Discipline Referrals," *Rural Educator* 24(1): 13–17 (2002).

24. See C. Willard-Holt, *Dual Exceptionalities*, ERIC Digest E574 (Reston, VA: ERIC Clearinghouse on Disabilities and Gifted Education, 1999).

25. For one success story see P. H. Smith et al., "Raise a Child, Not a Test Score: Perspectives on Bilingual Education at Davis Bilingual Magnet School," *Bilingual Research Journal* 26(1): 103–121 (2002).

26. Y. Pai and S. A. Adler, *Cultural Foundations of Education*, 3rd ed. (Upper Saddle River, NJ: Merrill/Prentice Hall, 2001), 77.

27. W. P. Thomas and V. P. Collier, "Two Languages Are Better Than One," *Educational Leadership* 55(4): 23–26 (December 1997–January 1998).

28. See, for example, E. J. de Jong, "Effective Bilingual Education: From Theory to Academic Achievement in a Two-Way Bilingual Program," and B. V. Kirk Senesac, "Two-Way Bilingual Immersion: A Portrait of Quality Schooling," in *Bilingual Research Journal* 26(1): 65–84 and 85–101, respectively (2002).

29. L. A. Mulholland and L. A. Bierlein, *Understanding Charter Schools*, Fastback 383 (Bloomington, IN: Phi Delta Kappa

Educational Foundation, 1995), 7. See also the special section on charter schools in the March 2002 edition (volume 83, number 7) of *Phi Delta Kappan*. For a copy of the *National Charter School Directory*, contact the Center for Education Reform (CER) at 800-521-2118, e-mail to cerdc@aol.com, or see the Internet (http://edreform.com/research/css9697.htm).

30. U.S. Department of Education, *A Study of Charter Schools: First-Year Report 1997* (Washington, DC: Office of Educational Research and Improvement, U.S. Department of Education, 1997), 1.

31. Additional information may be found at the U.S. Charter School Web site (http://www.uscharterschools.org/).

32. See, for example, P. Pardini, "Revival of the K–8 School," *School Administrator* 59(3): 6–12 (2002).

33. For a discussion of the advantages and disadvantages of various grade-span configurations, see W. S. DeJong and J. Craig, "How Should Schools Be Organized?" *School Planning & Management* 41(6): 26–32 (2002); P. M. Brunner, "Make Way for Schools Planned for 5th and 6th Grades," *School Construction News* 5(1): 15 (2002); and the several articles in *School Administrator* 59(3):24–29 (2002).

34. L. Sosniak, "The 9% Challenge: Education in School and Society," *Teachers College Record* (Online only, 2001; retrieved May 7, 2001, from http://www.tcrecord.org, ID Number: 10756).

35. C. A. Tomlinson, "Reconcilable Differences? Standards-Based Teaching and Differentiation," *Educational Leadership* 58(1): 6–11 (2000).

36. See, for example, S. Black, "Starving in Silence," *American School Board Journal* 189 (3): 334–337 (2002).

37. D. J. Schonfeld and M. Quackenbush, "Teaching Young Children About AIDS," *Principal* 79(5): 33–35 (2000).

38. Federal Interagency Forum on Child and Family Statistics, *America's Children: Key National Indicators of Well-Being, 1998*, retrieved January 5, 1999, from the World Wide Web (http://childstats.gov/ac1998/edtxt.htm).

39. J. Adair, "Tackling Teens' No. 1 Problem," *Educational Leadership* 57(6): 44–47 (2000).

40. D. G. Gil, *Violence Against Children: Physical Child Abuse in the United States* (Cambridge, MA: Rand McNally, 1970).

41. See, for example, W. M. Craig et al., "The Road to Gang Membership: Characteristics of Male Gang and Nongang Members from Ages 10 to 14," *Social Development* 11(1): 53–68 (2002), and T. W. Cadwallader and R. B. Cairns, "Developmental Influences and Gang Awareness Among African-American Inner City Youth," *Social Development* 11(2): 245–265 (2002).

42. K. S. Trump, "Be Prepared, Not Scared," *Principal* 81(5): 10–12, 14 (2002).

43. D. W. Johnson and R. T. Johnson, *Reducing School Violence Through Conflict Resolution* (Alexandria, VA: Association for Supervision and Curriculum Development, 1995), 1.

44. See, for example, J. P. Shapiro, J. D. Burgoon, C. J. Welker, and J. B. Clough, "Evaluation of the Peacemakers Program: School-Based Violence Prevention for Students in Grades Four Through Eight," *Psychology in the Schools* 39(1):87–100 (2002), and A. D. Farrell et al., "Evaluation of the RIPP-6 Violence Prevention Program at a Rural Middle School," *American Journal of Health Education* 33(3): 167–172 (2002).

45. W. Schwartz, *Preventing Violence by Elementary School Children*, (New York: ERIC/CUE Digest Number 149, ERIC Clearinghouse on Urban Education, 1999).

46. K. Samples, "Schools Battle Emotional Bullying," *The Cincinnati Enquirer*, Sunday, May 12, 2002. (Online May 12, 2002.) Adapted by permission.

47. L. Lumsden, *Preventing Bullying*, ED463563 (Eugene, OR: ERIC Clearinghouse on Educational Management, 2002).

48. National PTA, *National Standards for Parent/ Family Involvement Programs* (Chicago: Author, 1997), P. 7. See also A. M. Shartrand, H. B. Weiss, H. M. Kreider, and M. E. Lopez, *New Skills for New Schools: Preparing Teachers in Family Involvement* (Cambridge, MA: Harvard Graduate School of Education,

1997), and K. Cotton, *Lifelong Learning Skills: Tips for Parents*, booklets 1–3 (Portland, OR: Northwest Regional Educational Laboratory, 1998).

49. See P. Sullivan, "The PTA's National Standards," *Educational Leadership* 55(8): 43–44 (1998).

50. See, for example, the Hand in Hand Web site (http://www.handinhand.org).

51. See, for example, T. Whiteford, "Math for Moms and Dads," *Educational Leadership* 55(8): 64–66 (1998).

52. See, for example, C. Gustafson, "Phone Home," *Educational Leadership* 56(2): 31–32 (1998).

53. See, for example, M. H. McCarthy and L. Corbin, "The Power of Service-Learning," *Principal* 82(3): 52–54 (2003).

FOR FURTHER PROFESSIONAL STUDY

Banks, J. A., Cookson, P., Gay, G., Hawley, W. D., Irvine, J. J., Nieto, S., Schofield, J. W., and Stephan, W. G. "Diversity Within Unity: Essential Principles for Teaching and Learning in a Multicultural Society." *Phi Delta Kappan* 83(3): 196–198, 200–203 (2001).

Barker, V., Giles, H., Noels, K., Duck, J., Hecht, M., and Clement, R. "The English-Only Movement: A Communication Analysis of Changing Perceptions of Language Vitality." *Journal of Communications* 51(1): 3–37 (2001).

Black, S. "Teaching About Religion." *American School Board Journal* 190(4): 50–53 (2003).

Brice, A., and Roseberry-McKibbin, C. "Choice of Languages in Instruction: One Language or Two?" *Teaching Exceptional Children* 33(4): 10–16 (2001).

Davies, D. "The 10th School Revisited: Are School/Family/Community Partnerships on the Reform Agenda Now?" *Phi Delta Kappan* 83(5): 388–392 (2002).

DeCesare, D. "How High Are the Stakes in High-Stakes Testing?" *Principal* 81(3): 10–12 (2002).

Finn, J. D. "Small Classes in American Schools: Research, Practice, and Politics." *Mid-Western Educational Researcher* 15(1): 19–25 (2002).

Finn, K. V., Willert, H. J., and Marable, M. A. "Substance Use in Schools." *Educational Leadership* 60(6): 80–84 (2003).

Gordon, E. W. "Bridging the Minority Achievement Gap." *Principal* 79(5): 20–23 (2000).

Gould, F. "Testing Third-Graders in New Hampshire." *Phi Delta Kappan* 84(7): 507–513 (2003).

Hardin, B., and Hardin, M. "Into the Mainstream: Practical Strategies for Teaching in Inclusive Environments." *Clearing House* 75(4): 175–178 (2002).

Hofferth, S. L., and Jankuniene, Z. "Life After School." *Educational Leadership* 58(7): 19–23 (2001).

Hoffman, J. V. "The De-Democratization of Schools and Literacy in America." *The Reading Teacher* 53(8): 616–623 (2000).

Hymowitz, K. S. "Parenting: The Lost Art." *American Educator* 25(1): 4–9 (2001).

Jonsberg, S. D. "What's a (White) Teacher To Do About Black English?" *English Journal* 90(4): 51–53 (2001).

Kelly, K. "Preserving Kindergarten in a High-Stakes Environment." *Harvard Education Letter* 15(3): 4–6 (1999).

Lantieri, L. "After 9/11: Addressing Children's Fears." *Principal* 81(5): 35–36 (2002).

Lewis, D. W., and McDonald, J. A. "How One School Went to a Year-Round Calendar." *Principal* 80(3): 22–25 (2001).

Lindeman, B. "Reaching Out to Immigrant Parents." *Educational Leadership* 58(6): 62–66 (2001).

Marriott, D. M. "Ending the Silence." *Phi Delta Kappan* 84(7): 496–501 (2003).

Marzano, R. J. "In Search of the Standardized Curriculum." *Principal* 81(3): 6–9 (2002).

McClung, M. S. *Public School Purpose: The Civic Standard.* Fastback 503. Bloomington, IN: Phi Delta Kappa Educational Foundation, 2002.

Montgomery, W. "Creating Culturally Responsive, Inclusive Classrooms." *Teaching Exceptional Children* 33(4): 4–9 (2001).

Natale, J. A. "Early Learners: Are Full-Day Academic Kindergartens Too Much, Too Soon?"

American School Board Journal 188(3): 22–25 (2001).

Olweus, D. "A Profile of Bullying at School." *Educational Leadership* 60(6): 12–17 (2003).

O'Sullivan, S. *Character Education Through Children's Literature.* Fastback 494. Bloomington, IN: Phi Delta Kappa Educational Foundation, 2002.

Pai, Y., and Adler, S. A. *Cultural Foundations of Education,* 3rd ed. Upper Saddle River, NJ: Merrill/Prentice Hall, 2001.

Pastor, P. "School Discipline and the Character of Our Schools." *Phi Delta Kappan* 83(9): 658–661 (2002).

Pearson, P. D., Sapna, V., Sensale, L. M., and Kim, Y. "Making Our Way Through the Assessment and Accountability Maze: Where Do We Go Now?" *Clearing House* 74(4): 175–182 (2001).

Popham, W. J. "Teaching to the Test?" *Educational Leadership* 59(60): 16–20 (2001).

Portes, A. "English-Only Triumphs, but the Costs Are High." *Contexts* 1(1): 10–15 (2002).

Quinn, A. E. "Moving Marginalized Students Inside the Lines: Cultural Differences in Classrooms." *English Journal* 90(4): 44–50 (2001).

Rasmussen, K. "Year-Round Education: Time to Learn, Time to Grow." *Education Update* 42(2): 1, 4–5 (2000).

Ravitch, D. "The Language Police." *The Atlantic Monthly* 291(2): 82–83 (2003).

Sanders, T. "Clearing the NCLB Hurdle." *American School Board Journal* 190(9): 26–28 (2003).

Schaeffer, E. F. "Character Education Makes a Big Difference." *Principal* 82(3): 36–39 (2003).

Singh, N. "Becoming International." *Educational Leadership* 60(2): 56–60 (2002).

Wherry, J. H. "Planning Ahead for Parent Involvement." *Principal* 81(5): 53 (2002).

INTASC Principles	PRAXIS III Domains	NBPTS Standards
• The teacher is a reflective practitioner who continually evaluates the effects of his/her choices and actions on others (students, parents, and other professionals in the learning community) and who actively seeks out opportunities to grow professionally. (Principle 9) • The teacher fosters relationships with school colleagues, parents, and agencies in the larger community to support students' learning and well-being. (Principle 10) • The teacher uses knowledge of effective verbal, nonverbal, and media communication techniques to foster active inquiry, collaboration, and supportive interaction in the classroom. (Principle 6)	• Teaching Professionalism (Domain D) • Teaching for Student Learning (Domain C)	• Instructional Resources • Reflection

Why do people select teaching as a career? Why have *you* decided to become a teacher? More specifically, why did you elect to become an elementary school teacher? What responsibilities and teaching behaviors do you expect to be held accountable for? Which responsibilities and behaviors do you feel most competent about? Which do you feel least competent about?

You will be interested to know that a number of research studies have addressed precisely the question of why individuals select elementary school teaching as a career. The reasons people most frequently give are that they like working with children and they like the social service aspect of teaching.[1]

As you study this chapter, think about your own motivations for selecting elementary school teaching as a career. What are your expectations in terms of personal and material rewards? To what extent do you have a sense of social service and a desire to work with children? Your study of this chapter will guide you as you reflect on these important questions.

The primary expectation of any teacher is to facilitate student learning. As an elementary school classroom teacher, however, your professional responsibilities will extend well beyond the ability to work effectively in a classroom from approximately 8:00 a.m. until midafternoon. In this chapter, you will learn about the many responsibilities you will assume and the competencies and behaviors necessary for fulfilling them. Much has been learned in recent years about exemplary teacher behaviors. From that research we identify three categories of responsibilities and competencies, and elaborate on specific teacher behaviors that will promote your students' learning.

The three categories of professional responsibilities are (1) responsibility as a reflective decision maker, (2) commitment to children and to the profession, and (3) fundamental teaching competencies. Our presentation of these categories and competencies will guide you through the reality of these expectations as they exist for today's elementary school classroom teacher. Our discussion of strategies will enhance your teaching effectiveness by providing you with a set of tools you will find useful throughout your career.

Activity 2.1: Is This a Typical Day for an Elementary School Teacher?

Kristin is a fifth-grade teacher in a low SES school in a moderately large city of Texas. Her 34 students include 10 limited-English speakers and 10 with identified learning problems. Some of the children have reading and comprehension skills as low as first grade. In any given week, Kristin recycles newspapers and sells snacks to pay for field trips because the school and the children can't. On a typical school day recently, Kristin began her work at school at 7:00 a.m. with three parent conferences. The children arrived and school started at 8:15 and ran until 2:45 p.m. Kristin then tutored children until 3:45, conducted four more parent conferences, and entered data into her classroom desk computer before going home at 6 p.m. In the evening she planned lessons and graded papers for another 2 hours before retiring.

1. What were your immediate thoughts and feelings after reading this synopsis of Kristin's day?
2. Do you think that Kristin's day is typical for many or most elementary school teachers? Why or why not?

Finally, as a teacher you will be a learner among learners. Long after you finish the course for which you are using this book, after you have obtained your credentials and your first teaching job, you will continue to learn about teaching. Your learning will never cease; at least, it should not. You will not automatically maintain your teaching effectiveness forever; you will need constantly to work at maintaining and improving your teaching effectiveness. This moment is or should be much closer to the start of your learning about teaching than it is to the end of that learning process.

ANTICIPATED OUTCOMES

After completing this chapter, you should be able to do the following:

1. Demonstrate your understanding of the responsibilities of being an elementary school classroom teacher.
2. Describe the decision-making and thought-processing phases of instruction and the types of decisions you must make during each phase.
3. Describe the importance of the concept of "locus of control" and its relationship to your professional responsibilities.
4. Compare and contrast facilitating behaviors with instructional strategies.
5. Demonstrate your understanding of the importance of reflection to the process of constructing skills and understandings, including to becoming a competent teacher.
6. Compare and contrast *minds-on* and *hands-on* learning.
7. Compare and contrast the teacher's use of *praise* versus *encouragement*.
8. Identify and describe the results of the exemplary execution of the basic teacher behaviors described in this chapter.
9. Describe how one can determine the effectiveness with which a teacher executes the basic teacher behaviors.
10. Describe with examples how a teacher's incongruent behavior would send children a negative message via the covert curriculum.
11. Identify and describe four ways computers are used professionally by today's elementary school classroom teachers.
12. Begin the development of your professional portfolio.
13. Demonstrate an understanding of the importance of helping children develop impulse control, and of ways of doing it.

> *Teachers who consistently get results with all groups of students have strong content knowledge, an array of effective strategies, draw on prior knowledge of their students, see the range of student abilities and differentiate instruction, and constantly examine their own attitudes about race, class, and culture.*
> —Ellen Moir

THE TEACHER AS A REFLECTIVE DECISION MAKER

During any single school day you will make hundreds, perhaps thousands, of decisions. You will make some decisions prior to meeting your students for instruction, others during instructional activities, and still others later as you reflect on the day's instruction. Let's now consider further the decision-making and thought-processing phases of instruction.

You Can Be the Reason

You can be the reason some student gets up and comes to school when his life is tough. You can be the reason some student "keeps on keeping on" even though her parents are telling her that she can't succeed. You can inspire your at-risk students. Remember that as long as you are a teacher, even on your worst day on the job, you are still some student's best hope.

—**Larry I. Bell**

Source: L. I. Bell, "Strategies That Close the Gap," *Educational Leadership* 60(4): 34 (December 2002/January 2003).

Decision-Making Phases of Instruction

Instruction can be divided into four decision-making and thought-processing phases: (1) the planning or *preactive phase*, (2) the teaching or *interactive phase*, (3) the analyzing and evaluating or *reflective phase*, and (4) the application or *projective phase*.[2]

The preactive phase consists of all those intellectual functions and decisions you will make prior to actual instruction. This includes decisions about goals and objectives, homework assignments, what children already know and can do, appropriate learning activities, questions to ask (and possible answers), and selecting and preparing instructional materials.

The interactive phase includes all decisions made during the immediacy and spontaneity of your actual teaching. This includes maintaining student attention, asking questions, types of feedback given, and ongoing adjustments to the lesson plan. As noted before, decisions made during this phase are likely to be more intuitive, unconscious, and routine than those made during planning.

The reflective phase is the time you will take to reflect on, analyze, and judge the decisions and behavior that occurred during the interactive phase. It is during reflection that you make decisions about student learning, student grades, feedback given to parents and guardians, and adjustments on what to teach next.

As a result of this reflection, you decide how to use in your subsequent teaching what students have learned. At this point, you are in the projective phase, abstracting from your reflection and projecting your analysis into subsequent teaching behaviors.

During your reflective phase, you have a choice: Do you assume full responsibility for all instructional outcomes, or do you assume responsibility for only those positive outcomes of your planned instruction while placing the blame for negative outcomes on outside forces (e.g., parents and guardians or society in general, peers, other teachers, administrators, textbooks)? Where you place responsibility is referred to as *locus of control*. Teachers who are mature, intrinsically motivated, and competent individuals tend to assume full responsibility for both positive and negative instructional outcomes.

COMMITMENT AND PROFESSIONALISM

Our second category of professional responsibility is that of commitment and professionalism. As an elementary school teacher you are expected to demonstrate commitment to the personal as well as the intellectual development of all students. Not only do the most effective teachers expect, demand, and receive positive results in learning from their students while in the classroom, they are also interested and involved in their students' activities outside the classroom, and willing to sacrifice personal time to give them attention and guidance.

IDENTIFYING AND BUILDING YOUR INSTRUCTIONAL COMPETENCIES

A major purpose of this book is to assist you in understanding and beginning to build your instructional competencies. We begin with the identification of specific teacher behaviors that have been identified from years of research that clearly promote student learning. You will continue to reflect and build on these competencies through your study of the remaining chapters of this book and throughout your professional career.

Your ability to perform your instructional responsibilities effectively directly depends on your knowledge of students and how they best learn and on your knowledge of and the *quality* of your teaching skills. As we frequently state, development of your strategy repertoire along with your skills in using specific strategies should be ongoing throughout your teaching career. To be most effective, you need a large repertoire from which to select a specific strategy for a particular goal with a distinctive group of children. In addition, you need skill in using that strategy. As with intelligences, teaching style is neither absolutely inherited nor fixed, but continues to develop and emerge throughout one's professional career. This section is designed to help you begin building your specific strategies repertoire and to develop your skills in using these strategies.

The concept of building a strategies repertoire rests on three fundamental assumptions. First, you must know why you have selected a particular strategy. An unknowing teacher is likely to use the teaching strategy most common in college classes—the lecture. However, as many student teachers have discovered the hard way, lecturing is seldom an effective or appropriate way to instruct elementary-school children. As a rule, unlike many college and university students, not many K–6 students are strong auditory learners by preference and by adeptness. Learning by sitting and listening is difficult. Instead, they learn best when physically (*hands-on*) and intellectually (*minds-on*) active—that is, when using tactile and kinesthetic experiences, touching objects, feeling shapes and textures, moving objects, and when talking about and sharing what they are learning.

Second, basic teacher behaviors create the conditions needed to enable students to think and to learn, whether the learning is a further understanding of concepts, internalizing attitudes and values, developing cognitive processes, or actuating the most complex behaviors. These basic behaviors are those that produce the following results: (1) students are physically and mentally engaged in learning activities, (2) instructional time is efficiently used, and (3) classroom distractions and interruptions are minimal. Your choice of a particular *strategy* in a given situation will in part be determined by what particular *behaviors* will, in that situation, produce these results.

Third, one can measure the effectiveness of a teacher's basic behaviors and choice of strategies by how well students learn (the topic of Chapter 7).

In the remainder of this section we discuss the following basic teacher behaviors and strategies to facilitate student learning: (1) structuring the learning environment; (2) accepting and sharing instructional accountability; (3) demonstrating withitness and overlapping; (4) providing a variety of motivating and challenging activities; (5) modeling appropriate behaviors; (6) facilitating student acquisition of data; (7) creating a psychologically safe environment; (8) clarifying whenever necessary; (9) using periods of silence; and (10) questioning thoughtfully.

Facilitating Behaviors and Instructional Strategies: A Clarification

Clearly at least some of these 10 "behaviors" are also instructional "strategies"—questioning, for example. The difference is that while behaviors must be in place for the most effective teaching to occur, strategies are more or less discretionary—that is, they are pedagogical techniques from which you may select but may not be obligated to use. For example, questioning and the use of silence are fundamental teaching behaviors, whereas giving demonstrations and showing videos are not. So, you see, your task is twofold: (1) to develop your awareness of and skills in using fundamental teaching behaviors, and (2) to develop your repertoire of and skills in selecting and using appropriate instructional strategies.

Starting now and continuing throughout your teaching career, you will want to evaluate your developing competency for each of the 10 fundamental facilitating behaviors and work to improve in those areas in which you need help. Consider the following descriptions and examples, and discuss them in your class.

Structuring the Learning Environment

Structuring the learning environment means establishing an intellectual, psychological, and physical environment that enables all students to act and react productively. Specifically, you

• Attend to the organization of the classroom as a learning laboratory to establish a positive, safe, and efficient environment for student learning.

• Establish and maintain clearly understood classroom procedures, definitions, instructions, and expectations. Help students clarify learning expectations and establish clearly understood learning objectives.

• Help students assume tasks and responsibilities, thereby empowering them in their learning.

• Organize students, helping them to organize their learning. Help students in identifying and understanding time and resource constraints. Provide instructional scaffolds, such as building bridges to learning by helping students connect what they are learning with what they already know or think they know and have experienced.

• Plan and implement techniques for schema building, such as providing content and process outlines, visual diagrams, and opportunities for concept mapping.

• Use techniques for students' metacognitive development, such as *think–pair–share*, in which students are asked to think about an idea, share thoughts about it with a partner, and then share the pair's thoughts with the entire class.

• Plan units and lessons that have clear and concise beginnings and endings. Do at least some planning collaboratively with students.

• Provide frequent summary reviews, often by using student self-assessment of what they are learning. Structure and facilitate ongoing formal and informal discussion based on a shared understanding of the rules of discourse.

Accepting and Sharing Instructional Accountability

While holding students accountable for their learning, you must be willing to be held accountable for the effectiveness of the learning process and outcomes (the "locus of control" discussed earlier in this chapter). Specifically, you

• Assume a responsibility for professional decision making, and the risks associated with that responsibility. Share some responsibility for decision making and risk taking with students. A primary goal in the education of K–12 students must be to see that they become accountable for themselves as learners and as citizens. To some degree, then, you are advised to work with students as *partners* in their learning and development. One dimension of the partnership is sharing accountability; one effective way of doing this is by using student portfolios (discussed in Chapter 7).

• Communicate clearly to parents, guardians, administrators, and colleagues.

- Communicate to students that they share with you the responsibility for accomplishing learning goals and objectives.
- Plan exploratory activities that engage students in learning.
- Provide continuous cues for desired learning behaviors, and incentives contingent on desired performance, such as grades, points, rewards, and privileges; also establish a clearly understood and continuous program of assessment that includes reflection and self-assessment.
- Provide opportunities for students to demonstrate their learning, to refine and explore their questions, and to share their thinking and results.

Demonstrating Withitness and Overlapping

In *School Begins at Two* (New York: New Republic, 1936), Harriet Johnson wrote of the early childhood educator's need to be "with it," by which she was referring to the teacher's awareness of each child's emotions and needs as well as those of the whole group. Years later, in 1970, Jacob Kounin wrote of another kind of teacher withitness. As described by Kounin, withitness and overlapping are two separate but closely related behaviors.[3] *Withitness* is your awareness of the whole group. *Overlapping* is your ability to attend to several matters simultaneously. Specifically, you

- Attend to the entire class while working with one student or with a small group of students, communicating this awareness with eye contact, hand gestures, body position and language, and clear but private verbal cues.
- Continually and simultaneously monitor all classroom activities to keep students at their tasks and to provide them with assistance and resources.
- Continue monitoring the class during any distraction, such as when a visitor enters the classroom or while students are on a field trip.
- Demonstrate understanding of when comprehension checks and instructional transitions are appropriate or needed.
- Dwell on one topic only as long as necessary for students' understanding.
- Quickly intervene and redirect potentially undesirable student behavior (see Chapter 4).
- Refocus or shift activities for a student or students when their attention begins to fade.

Providing a Variety of Motivating and Challenging Activities

The effective teacher uses a variety of activities that motivate and challenge all students to work to the utmost of their abilities, and that engage and challenge the preferred learning styles and learning capacities of more of the students more of the time. Specifically, you

- Demonstrate optimism toward each child's ability.

• Demonstrate an unwavering expectation that all students will work to the best of their ability.

• Demonstrate pride, optimism, and enthusiasm in learning, thinking, and teaching.

• View teaching and learning as an organic and reciprocal process that extends well beyond the traditional "2 by 4 by 6 curriculum"—that is, a curriculum bound by the two covers of the textbook, the four walls of the classroom, and the six hours of the school day.

• Plan exciting and interesting learning activities with students, including those that engage their natural interest in the mysterious and the novel.

Modeling Appropriate Behaviors

As said earlier, effective teachers model the very behaviors expected of their students. Specifically, you

• Arrive promptly in the classroom and demonstrate on-task behaviors for the entire class meeting just as you expect the children to demonstrate.

• Demonstrate respect for all students. For example, do not interrupt when a student is showing rational thinking, even though you may disagree with the direction of the thinking.

• Demonstrate that making "errors" is a natural event in learning and during problem solving, and readily admit and correct any mistakes you may make.

• Promptly return student papers and offer comments that provide positive, instructive, and encouraging feedback.

• Model and emphasize the skills, attitudes, and values of higher-order intellectual processes. Demonstrate rational problem-solving skills and explain to students the processes involved.[4]

• Model professionalism by spelling correctly, using proper grammar, and printing or writing clearly and legibly.

• Practice communication that is clear, precise, and to the point. For example, use "I" when you mean "I"; "we" when you mean "we."

• Practice moments of silence (see "Using Periods of Silence" later in this section), thus modeling thoughtfulness, reflectiveness, and restraint of impulsiveness.

• Realize that children are also models for other children. Reinforce appropriate student behaviors, and promptly intervene when behaviors are inappropriate.

Facilitating Student Acquisition of Data

The teacher makes sure that data are accessible to students as input that they can process. Specifically, you

• Ensure that sources of information are readily available to students for their use. Select books, media, and materials that facilitate student learning. Ensure that equipment and materials are readily available for students to use. Identify and use resources beyond the classroom walls and the boundaries of the school campus.

• Create a responsive classroom environment with a variety of direct learning experiences.

• Ensure that major ideas receive proper attention and emphasis.

• Provide clear and specific instructions.

• Provide feedback about each child's performance and progress. Encourage students to organize and maintain devices, such as learning portfolios, to self-monitor their progress in learning and thinking.

• Select and display anchoring examples that help learners bridge what they are learning with what they already know and have experienced.

• Serve as a resource person, and use cooperative learning and peer tutoring, thus regarding your students as resources, too.

Creating a Psychologically Safe Environment

To encourage positive development of student self-esteem, to provide a psychologically safe learning environment, and to encourage the most creative thought and behavior, the teacher provides an attractive and materials-rich classroom environment and makes appropriate nonevaluative and nonjudgmental responses. Specifically, you

• Avoid negative criticism. Criticism is often a negative value judgment, and "when a teacher responds to a student's ideas or actions with such negative words as 'poor,' 'incorrect,' or 'wrong,' the response tends to signal inadequacy or disapproval and ends the student's thinking about the task."[5]

• Frequently use minimal reinforcement (that is, nonjudgmental acceptance behaviors, such as nodding your head, writing a student's response on the board, or saying "I understand"). Whereas elaborate or strong praise is generally unrelated to student achievement, using minimal reinforcement, saying such words as "right," "okay," "good," "uh-huh," and "thank you," does correlate with achievement.

However, be careful with too-frequent and thereby ineffective and even damaging use of the single word "good" following student contributions during class discussion. Use the word only when the contribution was truly good; better yet, say not only "good" but tell what specifically *was* good about the contribution. This provides a more powerful reinforcement by demonstrating that you truly heard and understood the student's contribution.

• Be sparing with your use of elaborate or strong praise, especially with older children. By the time students are beyond the primary grades, teacher praise (a positive value judgment) has little or no value as a form of positive reinforcement.[6] In fact, the use of strong praise can be counterproductive to your intent. Especially when teaching children of grade 4 and above, praise should be mild, private, and for student accomplishment, rather than for effort, and for each child you should gradually reduce the frequency with which you use praise. When praise is reduced, a more diffused sociometric pattern develops, that is, more children become directly and productively involved in learning. As emphasized by Good and Brophy, praise should be simple and direct, delivered in a natural voice without dramatizing.[7] Students see overly done theatrics as insincere.

Let us take pause to consider this point. Probably no statement in this textbook raises more eyebrows than the statement that praise for most children beyond primary years especially has little or no value as a form of positive reinforcement. After all, praise may well motivate some people. However, at what cost? Praise and encouragement (sometimes referred to as "effective praise")[8] are often confused and considered to be the same, but they are not, and they do not have the same long-term results. This is explained as follows:

> For many years there has been a great campaign for the virtues of praise in helping children gain a positive self-concept and improve their behavior. This is another time when we must "beware of what works." Praise may inspire some children to improve their behavior. The problem is that they become pleasers and approval "junkies." These children (and later these adults) develop self-concepts that are totally dependent on the opinions of others. Other children resent and rebel against praise, either because they don't want to live up to the expectations of others or because they fear they can't compete with those who seem to get praise so easily. The alternative that considers long-range effects is encouragement. The long-range effect of encouragement is self-confidence. The long-range effect of praise is dependence on others.[9]

In summary, then, our advice to you is while being cautious with the use of praise, do reinforce student efforts by recognizing specific personal accomplishments (Figure 2.1).[10]

- Perceive your classroom as the place where you work, where students learn, and make that place of work and the tools available a place of pride—as stimulating and useful as possible.

Statement of Praise	Statement or Act of Encouragement
I love your drawing of a cart.	I see you have drawn a cart. What will you put in your cart?
Terrific job!	I notice you put all the crayons and scissors back in their appropriate storage bins.
I like the way you behaved on the field trip.	[nothing, as proper behavior is expected]
I love the way you have cleaned your table.	[nothing; perhaps give a smile]
You're so smart!	I see you've figured out how to turn the pieces to put that puzzle together.

FIGURE 2.1
Statements of praise versus statements or acts of encouragement

• Plan within your lessons behaviors that exhibit respect for the experiences and ideas of individual students.

• Provide positive individual student attention as often as possible. Write sincere reinforcing personalized comments on student papers. Provide incentives and rewards for student accomplishments.

• Use nonverbal cues to show awareness and acceptance of individual students. Use paraphrasing and reflective listening. Use empathic acceptance of a student's expression of feelings, that is, demonstrating by words and gestures that you understand the student's position.

Clarifying Whenever Necessary

The teacher's responding behavior seeks further elaboration from a student about that student's idea or comprehension. Specifically, you

• Help students to connect new content to that previously learned. Help students relate lesson content to their other school and nonschool experiences. Help students make learning connections among disciplines.

• Politely invite a responding student to be more specific, and to elaborate on or rephrase an idea, or to provide a concrete illustration of an idea.

• Provide frequent opportunity for summary reviews.

• Repeat or paraphrase students' responses, allowing them to correct any misinterpretations of what they said or implied.

• Select instructional strategies that help students correct their prior notions about a topic.

Using Periods of Silence

The effective teacher uses periods of silence in the classroom. Specifically, you

• Actively listen when students are talking.

• Model silence when silence and thinking are wanted. Keep silent when students are working quietly or are attending to a visual display, and maintain classroom control by using nonverbal signals and indirect intervention strategies.

• Pause while talking to allow for thinking and reflection.

• Use your silence to stimulate group discussion.

• Allow sufficient think time (also called *wait time*), longer than 2 and as long as 9 seconds, after asking a question or posing a problem.[11]

Questioning Thoughtfully

The effective teacher asks thoughtfully worded questions to induce learning and to stimulate thinking and to develop students' thinking skills. Specifically, you

- Encourage students' questioning without judging the quality or relevancy of questions. Attend to questions, and respond and encourage other students to respond, often by building on the content of a student's questions and on student responses.

- Help children to develop their own questioning skills and provide opportunities for them to explore their own ideas, to obtain data, and to find answers to their own questions and solutions to their problems.

- Plan questioning sequences that elicit a variety of thinking skills and that maneuver students to higher levels of thinking and doing. (Questioning and its relationship to thinking is discussed further in Chapter 3.)

- Use a variety of types of questions.

- Use questions to help children to explore their knowledge, to develop new understandings, and to discover ways of applying their learning.

You begin now to develop your instructional competencies and refine your basic teaching behaviors, drawing inspiration from every aspect of your professional and personal life. This development will continue throughout your professional career, as we discuss in the next section.

CHARACTERISTICS OF THE COMPETENT CLASSROOM TEACHER: AN ANNOTATED LIST

Please do not feel overwhelmed by the following list; it may well be that no teacher expertly models all the characteristics that follow. The characteristics do, however, represent an ideal to strive for.[12] We advise you that this section is well suited to frequent rereading during the next few years of your teaching career.

The teacher is knowledgeable about the subject matter content expected to be taught. You should have both historical understanding and current knowledge of the structure of those subjects you are expected to teach, and of the facts, principles, concepts, and skills needed for those subjects.

The teacher is an "educational broker." You will learn where and how to discover information about content you are expected to teach. You cannot know everything there is to know about each subject—indeed, you will not always be able to predict all that your students will learn—but you should become knowledgeable about where and how to best research it, and how to assist children in developing those same skills. Among other things, this means that you should be computer literate, that is, have the ability to understand and use computers for research and writing, paralleling reading and writing in verbal literacy.

The teacher is an active member of professional organizations, reads professional journals, confers with colleagues, maintains currency in methodology and about students, subject content, and skills to be taught. Although this book offers valuable information about teaching and learning, it is much closer to the start of your professional career than it is to the end. As a teacher you are a learner among learners; you will be perpetually learning.

The teacher understands the processes of learning. You will ensure that students understand the lesson objectives, classroom procedures, and your expectations; that they feel welcomed to your classroom and involved in learning activities; and that they have some control over the pacing of their own learning. Furthermore, when preparing your lessons, you will (1) consider the unique learning characteristics of each child; (2) present content in reasonably small doses and in a logical and coherent sequence while utilizing visual, verbal, tactile, and kinesthetic learning activities, with opportunities for guided practice and reinforcement; and (3) frequently check student comprehension to ensure they are learning.

The teacher uses effective modeling behavior. Your own behavior must be consistent with what you expect of your students. If, for example, you want children to demonstrate regular and punctual attendance, to have their work done on time, to have their learning materials each day, to demonstrate cooperative behavior and respect for others, to maintain open and inquisitive minds, to demonstrate critical thinking, and to use proper communication skills, then you must do likewise, modeling those same behaviors and attitudes for them. As a teacher, you serve as a role model for your students. Whether you realize it or not, your behavior sends important messages to students that complement curriculum content. Those messages are important components of the covert curriculum (discussed in Chapter 5). You serve your students well when you model inclusive and collaborative approaches to learning. We present specific guidelines for effective modeling later in this chapter.

The teacher is open to change, willing to take risks and to be held accountable. If there were no difference between what is and what can be, then formal schooling would be of little value. To be a competent teacher, you must not only know historical and traditional values and knowledge, but must also know the value of change and be willing to carefully plan and experiment, to move between the known and the unknown. Realizing that little of value is ever achieved without a certain amount of risk, and out of personal strength of convictions, competent teachers stand ready to be held accountable, as they undoubtedly will be, for assuming such risks. As Selma Wassermann states so succinctly, "No coward ever got the Great Teacher Award."[13]

The teacher is nonprejudiced toward gender, sexual preference, ethnicity, skin color, religion, physical disability, socioeconomic status, learning disability, and national origin. Among other things, this means making no sexual innuendoes, religious or ethnic jokes, or racial slurs. It means being cognizant of how teachers, male and female, knowingly or unknowingly, historically have mistreated female students, and of how to avoid those same errors in your own teaching. It means learning about and attending to the needs of individual students in your classroom. It means having high, not necessarily identical, expectations for all students.

The teacher organizes the classroom and plans lessons carefully. You must prepare long-range plans and daily lessons thoughtfully, and reflect on, revise, and competently implement them with creative, motivating, and effective strategies and skill.

The teacher is a capable communicator. You will learn to use thoughtfully selected words, carefully planned questions, expressive voice inflections, useful pauses, meaningful gestures, and productive and nonconfusing body language. Some of these you carefully and thoughtfully plan during the preactive phase of your instruction; others will, through practice and reflection, become second-nature skills.

The teacher can function effectively as a decision maker. The elementary school classroom is a complex place, busy with fast-paced activities. In a single day you may engage in a thousand or more interpersonal exchanges with children, to say nothing of the numerous exchanges possible with other adults. As a competent teacher you will initiate, rather than merely react, and be proactive and in control of your interactions, having learned how to manage time to analyze and develop effective interpersonal behaviors.

The elementary school classroom is a complex place, busy with fast-paced activities. In a single day you may engage in a thousand or more interpersonal exchanges with children. No wonder you may feel exhausted at the end of your teaching day!

The teacher is in a perpetual learning mode, striving to further develop a reper-toire of teaching strategies. As discussed earlier, as an effective teacher you also will be a good student, continuing your own learning by reflecting on and as-sessing your work, attending workshops, studying the work of others, and talk-ing with students, parents and guardians, and colleagues, sometimes over Internet bulletin boards.

The teacher demonstrates concern for children's safety and health. The com-petent teacher consistently models safety procedures, ensuring precautions necessary to protect the health and psychological and physical safety of all stu-dents. You must strive to maintain a comfortable room temperature with ade-quate ventilation and to prevent safety hazards in the classroom. You should encourage students who are ill to stay home and to get well. If you suspect that a student may be ill or may be suffering from neglect or abuse at home (see Chapter 1), you must appropriately and promptly act on that suspicion by re-ferring it to the school nurse or to an appropriate administrator.

The teacher demonstrates optimism for the learning of every child, while provid-ing a constructive and positive environment for learning. Both common sense and research tell us clearly that students enjoy and learn better from a teacher who is positive and optimistic, encouraging, nurturing, and happy, rather than from a teacher who is negative and pessimistic, discouraging, uninterested, and grumpy.

The teacher demonstrates confidence in each child's ability to learn. For a child, nothing at school is more satisfying than a teacher who demonstrates confidence in that student's abilities. Unfortunately, for some children, a teacher's show of confidence may be the only positive indicator that child ever receives. Each of us can recall with admiration a teacher (or other significant person) who expressed confidence in our ability to accomplish seemingly formidable tasks. As a compe-tent teacher, you will demonstrate this confidence with each and every child.

The teacher is skillful and fair in employing strategies to assess student learning. You must become knowledgeable about the importance of providing immediate intensive intervention when learning problems become apparent and of imple-menting appropriate learning assessment tools, while avoiding the abuse of power afforded by the assessment process. (Assessment of student learning is the topic of Chapter 7.)

The teacher is skillful in working with parents and guardians, colleagues, ad-ministrators, and the support staff, and maintains and nurtures friendly and ethi-cal professional relationships. Teachers, parents and guardians, administrators, cooks, custodians, secretaries, and other adults of the school community all share one common purpose, and that is to serve students' education. This, of course, happens best when everyone cooperates. An exemplary school staff and skillful teachers work together to ensure that parents or guardians are involved in their children's learning.

The teacher demonstrates continuing interest in professional responsibilities and opportunities in the learning community. Knowing that ultimately each and every school activity has an effect on the classroom, the competent teacher assumes an active interest in the school community. The purpose of the school is to serve children's education, and the classroom is the primary, but not the only, place where this occurs. Every committee meeting, school event, faculty meeting, school board meeting, office, program, and any other planned function related to school life shares in the school's ultimate purpose. Unfortunately, involved adults sometimes forget and must be reminded of that fact.

The teacher exhibits a range of interests. This includes interest in students' activities and the many aspects of the school and its surrounding community. You are interesting in part because of your interests; a variety of interests more often motivates and captures the attention of more students. If you have few interests outside your subject and classroom, you will likely seem exceedingly dull to your students.

The teacher shares a healthy sense of humor. The positive effects of appropriate humor (humor that is not self-deprecating or disrespectful of others) on learning are well established: increased immune system activity and decreased stress-producing hormones; drop in the pulse rate; reduction of feelings of anxiety, tension, and stress; activated T-cells for the immune system, antibodies that fight against harmful microorganisms, and gamma interferon, a hormone that fights viruses and regulates cell growth; and increased blood oxygen. Because of these effects, humor is a stimulant to not only healthy living, but to creativity and higher-level thinking. As they should, students appreciate and learn more from a teacher who shares a sense of humor and laughs with them. (Humor is one of the intelligent behaviors we discuss in Chapter 3.)

The teacher is quick to recognize a child who may be in need of special attention. A competent teacher is alert to recognize any child who demonstrates behaviors indicating a need for special attention. For example, patterns of increasingly poor attendance or of steadily negative attention-seeking behavior are two of the more obvious early signals of a student who is potentially at risk of dropping out of school. You must know how and where to refer such a student, and how to do so with minimal class disruption and without embarrassment to the student.

The teacher makes specific and frequent efforts to demonstrate how the subject content may relate to students' lives. With effort, you can make a potentially dry and dull topic seem significant and alive. Regardless of topic, somewhere there are competent teachers teaching that topic, and one of the significant characteristics of their effectiveness is they make the topic alive to themselves and their students, helping students make relevant connections. Time and again studies point out what should be obvious: Students don't learn much from dull, meaningless exercises and assignments. Such bland teaching may be a major cause of student disaffection with school. You may obtain ideas from professional journals, attend workshops, communicate with colleagues either personally or via electronic bulletin boards and Web sites, and use interdisciplinary thematic instruction to discover how to make a potentially dry and boring topic interesting and alive for students (and for yourself).

The teacher is reliable. The competent teacher can be relied on to fulfill professional responsibilities, promises, and commitments. If you cannot be relied on,

---

Activity 2.2: Are Teachers Prepared to Deal with the Severe Social and Emotional Problems Many Children Bring to School? If Not, Who Is?

Recently, in one metropolitan elementary school, 13 of the 20 students in a classroom had witnessed a drive-by shooting the previous day. The children could not stop talking about it, and the classroom teacher was having a difficult time settling them down. The school's full-time social worker stepped in to help counsel the children. The principal told the teacher that many of the kids at the school had seen the worst that life has to offer, including rape, physical abuse to the women in their lives, people being shot, fights, and home break-ins.

1. How available are social workers to schools in your geographic area?
2. If social workers are not readily available, are teachers then expected to make home visits to prod chronically absent children to school: to help families obtain medicine, shoes, clothing, or whatever it is that has prevented the child from coming to school?
3. What have you learned from this activity? What aspect of this problem would you like to learn more about?

---

you will quickly lose credibility with students (as well as with colleagues and administrators). Regardless of your potential for effectiveness, if you are an unreliable teacher you are an incompetent teacher. Also, teachers who are chronically absent from their teaching duties for whatever reason are "at-risk" teachers.

THE AGE OF INFORMATION TECHNOLOGY

It would be difficult to find any public school today that is not in some way making use of computers for instruction. Because today's children are the first generation to grow up in an environment saturated by digital media, many have greater familiarity with these devices than do some of their teachers. This situation, however, is rapidly changing. Teacher education programs at both the preservice and inservice levels include special courses and workshops to acquaint them with computers and the Internet as educational resources and to help them develop technological literacy.

As an elementary school classroom teacher, you need to be prepared technologically and psychologically to use computers in at least four ways. First, you will likely be expected to maintain records, such as for student attendance, and to transmit those to school and district offices and to communicate with those offices by way of a classroom computer.

Second, you may be expected to assume some responsibility for teaching children the technical skills needed to work with computers and their peripheral equipment. Sometimes a teacher who is a computer specialist provides the technical instruction, but the classroom teacher must do follow-up work on such instruction and must take responsibility for its application, including communicating, word processing, Internet browsing, making spreadsheets, and accessing databases. Imaginative teachers are encouraging students to develop computer networks that enable them to have exciting contacts with schoolchildren and adults not only in the United States but also all over the

Activity 2.3: Is Technology Changing the Role of the Classroom Teacher?

In 1922 Thomas Edison predicted that "the motion picture is destined to revolutionize our educational system and . . . in a few years it will supplant largely, if not entirely, the use of textbooks." William Levenson of the Cleveland public schools' radio station claimed in 1945 that "the time may come when a portable radio receiver will be as common in the classroom as is the blackboard." In the early 1960s B. F. Skinner believed that with the help of the new teaching machines and programmed instruction, students could learn twice as much in the same time and with the same effort as in a standard classroom. Did motion pictures, radio, programmed instruction, and television revolutionize education? Will computers become as much a part of the classroom as writing boards? What do you predict the public school classroom of the year 2050 will be like? Will the teacher's role be different in any way than it is today?

world. Increasingly, the computer is being used as a communications medium by schoolchildren as well as by the school staff.

Third, you need to know how to integrate computer-assisted instruction (CAI) into teaching the traditional subjects of mathematics, science, social studies, and language arts. Much of this work in the past consisted of "drill and practice," but today the emphasis is (or should be) on using computers to help students develop conceptual understanding and problem-solving skills. Additionally, you will need to be familiar with the computer's capabilities in the diagnosis of learning difficulties, corrective instruction, independent study, and its other potential uses as an instructional tool.

Finally, you need to have some sense of the social consequences that flow from the widespread application of computer technology. For instance, as computer-operated robots displace large numbers of workers, what do those people do to earn a living? What ethical issues are involved in storing personal, confidential information in computer banks? To what extent do or should high-tech demands determine priorities in the school curriculum? Will society place a greater value on interacting with machines than with people? What must be done to ensure adequate attention to the humanities and social studies in a global society that is increasingly dominated by computer technology? Maurer and Davidson remind us that it is perhaps not important that every child be brilliant with technology; it is, however, important that every child be brilliant in his or her own unique way.[14]

SELECTING AND USING INSTRUCTIONAL MEDIA AND OTHER RESOURCES

Important to helping students construct their understandings are the cognitive tools that are available for their use. You will be pleased to know that there is a large variety of useful and effective media, aids, and resources from which to draw as you plan your instructional experiences. On the other hand, you could also become overwhelmed by the sheer quantity of different materials available—textbooks, supplementary texts, pamphlets, anthologies, paperbacks, encyclopedias, tests, programmed instructional systems, dictionaries, reference books, classroom periodicals, newspapers, films, records and cassettes, computer software, transparencies, realia, games, filmstrips, audio- and videotapes, slides, globes, manipulatives, CD-ROMs, DVDs, and graphics. You could spend a great deal of time reviewing, sorting, selecting, and practicing with the materials and tools for your use. Although nobody can make the job easier for you, information in this section may help expedite the process.

The Internet

Originating from a Department of Defense project in 1969 (called ARPANET) to establish a computer network of military researchers, its successor, the federally funded Internet, has become an enormous, steadily expanding, worldwide system of connected computer networks. The Internet provides literally millions of resources to explore, with thousands more added nearly every day. Today you can surf the Internet and find many sources about how to use it, and you can walk into most any bookstore and find hundreds of recent titles, most of which give their authors' favorite Web sites. However, because new technologies are steadily emerging and because the Internet changes every day, with some sites and resources disappearing or not kept current, others having changed their location and undergone reconstruction, and new ones appearing, it would be superfluous for us in this book, which will be around for a few years, to make too much of sites that we personally have viewed and can recommend as teacher resources. Nevertheless, sites are mentioned and listed throughout the text (see, for example, Figures 1.1, 4.1, and 5.3, and at the ends of some of the chapters (see, for example, Chapter 5). Perhaps you have found others that you can share with your classmates.

There is such a proliferation of information today, both from printed materials and from information on the Internet—how can a person determine the validity and currency of a particular piece of information? When searching for useful and reliable information on a particular topic, how can one be protected from wasting valuable time sifting through all the information available? People need to know that just because information is published on the Internet doesn't necessarily mean that the information is accurate or current. Using a checklist, such as those found on the Internet (http://www.infopeople.org/bkmk/select.html or http://lib.nmsu.edu/instruction/eval.html), and provided with examples of materials that meet and do not meet the criteria of the checklist, students can learn how to assess materials and information found on the Internet.

Children who have Internet access at home may have an advantage over children who do not. Try to counter this by providing extra time online to children who lack access at home.

Teaching all students how to access and assess Web sites adds to their repertoire of skills for lifelong learning. Consider allowing each student or teams of students to become experts on specific sites during particular units of study. It might be useful to start a chronicle of student-recorded log entries about a particular Web site to provide comprehensive long-term data about those sites.

When students use information from the Internet, require that they print copies of sources of citations and materials so you can check for accuracy. These copies may be maintained in students' portfolios.

Student work published on the Internet should be considered as intellectual material and protected from plagiarism by others. Most school districts post a copyright notice on their home page. Usually, someone at the school or from the district office is assigned to supervise the school Web site to see that district and school policy and legal requirements are observed.

As a teacher you must be familiar with the laws about the use of copyrighted materials, printed and nonprinted, including those obtained from sources on the Internet. Remember that although on many Web pages there is no notice, the material is still copyrighted. Copyright law protects original material; that is just as true for the intellectual property created by a minor as it is for that of an adult.

Although space here prohibits inclusion of United States legal guidelines, your local school district should be able to provide a copy of current district policies for compliance with copyright laws. District policies should include guidelines for teachers and students in publishing materials on the Internet.

When preparing to make a copy, you must find out whether law under the category of "permitted use" permits the copying. If copying is not allowed under "permitted use," then you must obtain from the holder of the copyright written permission to reproduce the material. If the address of the source is not given on the material, addresses may be obtained from various references, such as *Literary Market Place*, *Audio-Visual Market Place*, and *Ulrich's International Periodicals Directory*.

Computers and Computer-Based Instructional Tools

As a teacher, you must be computer literate—you must understand and be able to use computers as well as you can read and write. The computer can be valuable to you in several ways. For example, the computer can help you manage the instruction by obtaining information, storing and preparing test materials, maintaining attendance and grade records, and preparing programs to aid in the academic development of individual students. This category of uses of the computer is referred to as *computer-managed instruction* (CMI).

The computer can also be used for instruction by employing various instructional software programs, and it can be used to teach about computers and to help students develop their metacognitive skills as well as their skills in computer use. When the computer is used to assist students in their learning, it is called *computer-assisted instruction* (CAI) or *computer-assisted learning* (CAL).

Teachers looking to make their classrooms more student-centered, collaborative, and interactive continue to increasingly turn to telecommunications networks. Webs of connected computers allow teachers and students from around the world to reach each other directly and gain access to quantities of information previously unimaginable. Students using networks learn new inquiry and

Computers are commonplace in today's elementary school classrooms. Being able to use a computer as a resource tool is one of the many skills expected of both elementary school students and their teachers.

analytical skills in a stimulating environment, and they can also gain an increased awareness of their role as world citizens.

How you use the computer for instruction is determined by several factors, including your knowledge of and skills in its use, the number of computers that you have available for instructional use, where computers are placed in the school, the software that is available, printer availability, and the telecommunications capabilities (that is, wiring and phone lines, modems, and servers).

Schools continue to purchase or to lease computers and to upgrade their telecommunications capabilities. Some school districts are beginning to purchase handheld computers. Regarding the more traditional desktop computer placement and equipment available, here are some possible scenarios and how classroom teachers work within each.

SCENARIO 1. With the assistance of a computer lab and the lab technician, computers are integrated into the whole curriculum. In collaboration with members of interdisciplinary teaching teams, in a computer lab students use computers, software, and sources on the Internet as tools to build their knowledge, to write stories with word processors, to illustrate diagrams with paint utilities, to create interactive reports with hypermedia, and to graph data they have gathered using spreadsheets.

SCENARIO 2. In some schools, students take "computer" as an elective or exploratory. Students in your classes who are simultaneously enrolled in such a course may be given special computer assignments by you that they can then share with the rest of the class.

SCENARIO 3. Some classrooms have a computer connected to a large-screen video monitor. The teacher or a student works the computer, and the entire class can see the monitor screen. As they view the screen, students can verbally respond to and interact with what is happening on the computer.

Presentation software, such as Microsoft's PowerPoint, can help teachers, and students create powerful on-screen presentations. Though PowerPoint was first developed for use in the world of business for reports at sales meetings and with clients, educators quickly became aware of the power of presentation software to display, illustrate, and elucidate information. From the world of business, presentation software made its way into university classrooms and then into K–12 classrooms; today it is not uncommon for it to be used by kindergarten children in their own presentations. When students are using modern presentation software, it is the teacher's task to ensure that students don't become so fixated on fonts and formats and other aspects of the technology that they give insufficient thought to the content of their presentations. Of course, that is no more a concern for electronic presentations than when students are using any other format to display their work, such as an interactive student-created bulletin board display.

SCENARIO 4. You may be fortunate to have one or more computers in your classroom for all or for a part of the school year, computers with Internet connections, with CD-ROM playing capabilities, a DVD player, an overhead projector, and an LCD (liquid crystal display) projection system. Coupled with the overhead projector, the LCD projection system allows you to project onto your large wall screen (and TV monitor at the same time) any image from computer software or a videodisc. With this system, all students can see and verbally interact with the multimedia instruction.

SCENARIO 5. Many classrooms have at least one computer with telecommunications capability, and some have many. When this is the case in your classroom, then you most likely will have one or two students working at the computer while others are doing other learning activities (multilevel teaching). Computers can be an integral part of a learning center and an important aid in your overall effort to personalize the instruction within your classroom.

Programs are continually being developed and enhanced to meet the new and more powerful computers being made available. For evaluating computer software programs and testing them for their compatibility with your instructional objectives, there are many forms available; forms are usually available from the local school district or from the state department of education.

With its superior sound and visual performance, the DVD may replace CDs, VCR tapes, and computer CD-ROMs. Although in appearance it resembles the CD-ROM, the DVD can store nearly 17 gigabytes of information (a minimum of seven times the amount of data stored by a CD), can provide faster retrieval of data, and can be made interactive.

You must be knowledgeable about the laws on the use of copyrighted videos and computer software materials. Although space here prohibits full inclusion of U.S. legal guidelines, your local school district undoubtedly can provide a copy of current district policies to ensure your compliance with all copyright laws. As discussed earlier, when preparing to make any copy of printed materials that are copyrighted, you must find out whether the copying is permitted by law under the category of "permitted use." If not allowed under "permitted use," then you must get written permission to reproduce the material from the holder of the copyright.

Usually, when purchasing CD-ROMs and other multimedia software packages intended for use by schools, you are also paying for a license to modify and use the contents for instructional purposes. However, not all CD-ROMs include copyright permission, so always check the copyright notice on any disk you purchase and use. Whenever in doubt, don't use it until you have asked your district media specialists about copyrights or have obtained necessary permissions from the original source.

As yet, there are no guidelines for fair use of films, filmstrips, slides, and multimedia programs. A general rule of thumb for use of any copyrighted material is to treat the work of others as you would want your own material treated were it protected by a copyright.

SUMMARY

You have reviewed the realities of the responsibilities of today's elementary school classroom teacher. Becoming and remaining a good teacher takes time, commitment, concentrated effort, and just plain hard work. Anyone who ever said that good teaching was easy work didn't know what he or she was talking about.

You have learned that your professional responsibilities as a classroom teacher will extend well beyond the four walls of the classroom, the 6 hours of the school day, the 5 days of the school week, and the 180 days of the school year. You learned of the many expectations: to demonstrate effective decision making; to be committed to young people, to the school's mission, and to the profession; to develop facilitating behaviors; and to provide effective instruction. As you have read and discussed these behaviors and responsibilities, you should have begun to fully comprehend the challenge and reality of being a competent elementary school classroom teacher.

Today, there seems to be much agreement that the essence of learning is a combined process of self-awareness, self-monitoring, and active reflection. Children learn these skills best when exposed to teachers who themselves effectively model the same behaviors. The most effective teaching and learning is interactive and involves not only learning, but also thinking about learning and learning how to learn.

Throughout your teaching career you will continue improving your knowledge and skills in all aspects of teaching and learning. Through experience, workshops, advanced coursework, coaching and training; through acquiring further knowledge by reading and study; and through collaborating with and role-modeling by significant and more experienced colleagues, you will be in a perpetual learning mode.

Now that you perceive the magnitude of the professional responsibilities of the elementary school classroom teacher, Chapter 3 focuses your attention on how to help your students develop their skills in thinking and questioning.

Activity 2.4: Developing Your Professional Portfolio

Students in teacher preparation programs find that heavy demands are placed on their time and energy, often with on-campus and off-campus commitments occurring during the same week. Preoccupation with their day-to-day responsibilities makes them less aware of the passage of time, and before they know it, they find themselves in their phase of student teaching. Then, in a matter of weeks, they will be recommended for certification and will join the ranks of teachers of the nation's children. Most are challenged by the idea; yet, the thought of the responsibilities that go with it makes them a little uneasy. We now turn to one way you should begin to be proactive—to best prepare yourself for that time. Begin preparing now how to organize and design your professional career portfolio, choosing what specifically will go into it, and setting criteria for later selections. Preparation of your professional portfolio may well be part of your teacher preparation program.

Your professional career portfolio is organized to provide clear evidence of your teaching skills and to make you professionally desirable to a hiring committee. A professional portfolio is *not* simply a collection of your accomplishments randomly tossed into a folder. It *is* a deliberate, current, and organized collection of your skills, attributes, experiences, and accomplishments. The time to begin developing your professional portfolio is *now*.

Because it would be impractical to send a complete portfolio with every application you submit, it is suggested that you have a minimum portfolio (portfolio B) that could be sent with each application, in addition to a complete portfolio (portfolio A) that you could make available on request or that you would take with you to an interview. However it is done, the actual contents of the portfolio will vary depending on the specific job being sought; you will continually add to and delete materials from your portfolio. Suggested categories and subcategories, listed in the order that they may be best presented in portfolios A and B are as follows.

1. Table of contents of portfolio (not too lengthy)—portfolio A only.
2. Your professional résumé—both portfolios.
3. Evidence of your language and communication skills (evidence of your use of English and of other languages, including American Sign Language)—portfolio A. (Also state this information briefly in your letter of application.)
   a. Your teaching philosophy, perhaps in your own handwriting to demonstrate your handwriting ability.
   b. Other evidence to support this category.
4. Evidence of teaching skills—portfolio A.
   a. For planning skills, include instructional objectives, a syllabus, and a unit plan.
   b. For teaching skills, include a sample lesson plan and a video of your actual teaching.
   c. For assessment skills, include a sample self-assessment and samples of student assessments.
5. Letters of recommendation and other documentation to support your teaching skills—both portfolios.
6. Other (for example, personal interests related to the position for which you are applying)—portfolio A.

Source: R. D. Kellough and N. G. Kellough, Teaching Young Adolescents: A Guide to Methods and Resources, 4th ed. (Upper Saddle River, NJ: Prentice Hall, 2003), 391. Reprinted by permission.

STUDY QUESTIONS AND ADDITIONAL ACTIVITIES

1. Select a teacher whom you admired when you were an elementary school student. What characteristics did this person possess? Do you see any of those qualities in yourself?

2. Describe the behavioral differences you would expect to see in a teacher who operates essentially as a reflective practitioner as opposed to one who is mainly a technician.

3. Explain the meaning of each of the following concepts and why you agree or disagree with each: (a) The teacher should hold high, although not necessarily identical, expectations for all students and never waver from those expectations. (b) The teacher should not be controlled by a concern to "cover" the content of the textbook or adopted program by the end of the school term.

4. Identify the professional teachers' organizations in your geographical area. Share what you find with others in your class. Attend a local, regional, or national meeting of a professional teachers' association, and report to your class what it was like and what you learned. Share with your classmates any free or inexpensive teaching materials you obtained.

5. Talk with experienced teachers and find out how they remain current in their teaching fields. Share your learning with others in your class.

6. Are modern learning theory and the concept of mandatory competency testing compatible ideas, or do they create a dilemma for the classroom teacher? Explain your response.

7. Distinguish the use of *praise* and of *encouragement* for student work; describe specific classroom situations in which each is more appropriate.

8. In *Educating the Reflective Practitioner* (San Francisco: Jossey-Bass, 1987), Donald Schon speaks of "reflection-on-action," "reflection-in-action," and "reflection-for-action." Read about and compare Schon's three types of reflections with the four phases of decision-making and thought processing discussed at the beginning of this chapter.

9. Refer to the section in this chapter, "Modeling Appropriate Behaviors." From the list of teacher behaviors there, identify no less than five ways a teacher's inappropriate behavior would send a negative message via the covert curriculum. What effect do you believe a teacher's incongruent behavior has on children in the classroom?

10. Explain how you feel today about being a classroom teacher—for example, are you motivated, excited, enthusiastic, befuddled, confused, depressed? Explain and discuss your current feelings with your classmates. Sort out common concerns and design avenues for dealing with any negative feelings you might have.

NOTES

1. D. R. Cruickshank, *Research That Informs Teachers and Teacher Educators* (Bloomington, IN: Phi Delta Kappa, 1990), 109.

2. See A. L. Costa, *The School as a Home for the Mind* (Palatine, IL: Skylight, 1991), 97–106.

3. J. S. Kounin, *Discipline and Group Management in Classrooms* (New York: Holt, Rinehart & Winston, 1970).

4. See, for example, R. Willey, "Writing, Reflection, and the Young Child," *Primary Voices K–6* 10(4): 8–14 (2002).

5. Costa, *The School as a Home for the Mind*, 54.

6. R. Hitz and A. Driscoll, *Praise in the Classroom* (Washington, DC: ERIC Clearinghouse on Assessment and Evaluation, 1989), ED 313108.

7. T. L. Good and J. E. Brophy, *Looking in Classrooms*, 9th ed. (New York: Addison Wesley Longman, 2003), 131.

8. R. Hitz and A. Driscoll, *Praise in the Classroom*.

9. J. Nelsen, *Positive Discipline* (New York: Ballantine Books, 1987), 103. See also L. A. Froyen, *Classroom Management: The Reflective Teacher-Leader*, 2nd ed. (Upper Saddle River, NJ: Prentice Hall, 1993), 294–298.

10. See the discussion titled "Research and theory on providing recognition," pp. 53–59 of R. J. Marzano et al., *Classroom Instruction That Works* (Alexandria, VA: Association for Supervision and Curriculum Development, 2001).

11. Studies in wait time began with the classic study by M. B. Rowe, "Wait Time and Reward as Instructional Variables, Their Influence on Language, Logic and Fate Control: Part 1. Wait Time," *Journal of Research in Science Teaching* 11(2): 81–94 (1974). See also W. Wilen, *Questioning Skills for Teachers: What Research Says to the Teacher*, 3rd ed. (Washington, DC: National Education Association, 1991).

12. The list of 22 competencies is adapted from R. D. Kellough, *A Resource Guide for Teaching: K–12*, 4th ed. (Upper Saddle River, NJ: Merrill/Prentice Hall, 2003), 85–87. You may want to identify other competencies. You may also want to compare the 22 here with the 10 common standards of practice for all beginning teachers outlined in *Model Standards for Beginning Teacher Licensing and Development: A Resource for State Dialogue*, prepared by the Interstate New Teacher Assessment and Support Consortium (INTASC), a project of the Council of Chief State School Officers (CCSSO). For copies of that document, contact CCSSO, One Massachusetts Avenue, NW, Suite 700, Washington, DC 20001, phone 202-408-5505, or see their Web site (http://www.ccsso.org). In 1997, the National Board for Professional Teaching Standards (NBPTS) released 11 categories of standards for certification as a Middle Childhood/Generalist. These standards can be accessed via the Internet (http://www.nbpts.org/nbpts.standards/mc-gen.html). Also, you may want to compare the 22 standards here with the 22 "components of professional practice" in C. Danielson, *Enhancing Professional Practice: A Framework for Teaching* (Alexandria, VA: Association for Supervision and Curriculum Development, 1996).

13. S. Wassermann, "Shazam! You're a Teacher," *Phi Delta Kappan* 80(6): 464, 466–468 (1999).

14. M. M. Maurer and G. Davidson, "Technology, Children, and the Power of the Heart," *Phi Delta Kappan* 80(6): 458–460 (1999).

FOR FURTHER PROFESSIONAL STUDY

Allen, R. "Make Me Laugh: Using Humor in the Classroom." *Education Update* 43(5): 1, 3, 7–8 (2001).

Banks, J. A., Cookson, P., Gay, G., Hawley, W. D., Irvine, J. J., Nieto, S., Schofield, J. W., and Stephan, W. G. "Diversity Within Unity: Essential Principles for Teaching and Learning in a Multicultural Society." *Phi Delta Kappan* 83(3): 196–198, 200–203 (2001).

Chamberlain, E. *Evaluating Website Content*. Fastback 492. Bloomington, IN: Phi Delta Kappa Educational Foundation, 2002.

Conn, K. *The Internet and the Law: What Educators Need to Know*. Alexandria, VA: Association for Supervision and Curriculum Development, 2002.

Corbett, D., and Wilson, B. "What Urban Students Say About Good Teaching." *Educational Leadership* 60(1): 18–22 (2002).

Daniels, D. C. "Becoming a Reflective Practitioner." *Middle School Journal* 33(5): 52–56 (2002).

Deiro, J. A. "Do Your Students Know You Care?" *Educational Leadership* 60(6): 60–62 (2003).

Freiberg, H. J. (Ed.). *Perceiving, Behaving, Becoming: Lessons Learned.* Alexandria, VA: Association for Supervision and Curriculum Development, 1999.

Hunsader, P. D. "Why Boys Fail—and What We Can Do About It." *Principal* 82(2): 52–54 (2002).

James, P. "Ideas in Practice: Fostering Metaphoric Thinking." *Journal of Developmental Education* 25(3): 26–33 (2002).

Kazemek, F. E. "Why Was the Elephant Late in Getting on the Ark? Elephant Riddles and Other Jokes in the Classroom." *Reading Teacher* 52(8): 896–898 (1999).

Kellough, R. D. *Surviving Your First Year of Teaching: Guidelines for Success.* 2nd ed. Upper Saddle River, NJ: Merrill/Prentice Hall, 2001.

Larrivee, B. "The Potential Perils of Praise in a Democratic Interactive Classroom." *Action in Teacher Education* 23(4): 77–88 (2002).

Lathrop, A., and Foss, K. *Student Cheating and Plagiarism in the Internet Era: A Wake-Up Call.* Englewood, CO: Libraries Unlimited, 2000.

Leu, D. J., Jr. "Internet Project: Preparing Students for New Literacies in a Global Village." *Reading Teacher* 54(6): 568–572 (2001).

Lifto, D. "Working in Cyberspace: What School Employees Need To Know About E-mail and the Internet." *American School Board Journal* 188(1): 36–37 (2001).

Marzano, R. J. "The Teacher-Level Factors." Chapter 8 in *What Works in Schools: Translating Research into Action.* Alexandria, VA: Association for Supervision and Curriculum Development, 2003.

McGoogan, G. "Around the World in 24 Hours." *Educational Leadership* 60(2): 44–46 (2002).

Rodgers, C. "Defining Reflection: Another Look at John Dewey and Reflective Thinking." *Teachers College Record* 104(4): 842–866 (2002).

Searson, R., and Dunn, R. "The Learning-Style Teaching Model." *Science and Children* 38(5): 22–26 (2001).

Serafini, F. "Reflective Practice and Learning." *Primary Voices K–6* 10(4): 2–7 (2002).

Simpson, C. "Copyright 101." *Educational Leadership* 59(4): 36–38 (December 2001/January 2002).

Stiggins, R. J. *Student-Involved Classroom Assessment.* 3rd. ed. Upper Saddle River, NJ: Merrill/Prentice Hall, 2001.

Weissbourd, R. "Moral Teachers, Moral Students." *Educational Leadership* 60(6): 6–11 (2003).

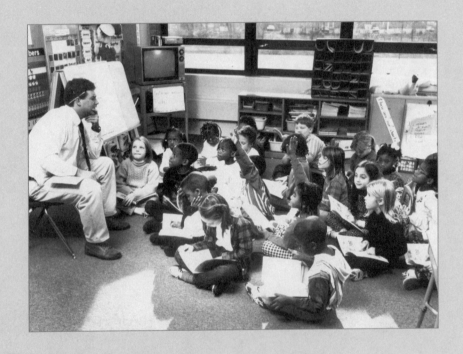

INTASC Principles	PRAXIS III Domains	NBPTS Standards
• The teacher understands the central concepts, tools of inquiry, and structures of the discipline(s) he or she teaches and can create learning experiences that make these aspects of subject matter meaningful to students. (Principle 1)	• Organizing Content Knowledge for Student Learning (Domain A)	• Knowledge of Content and Curriculum

Questioning is one of the most important of all teaching and learning strategies. You will use questioning for so many purposes that you must be skilled in its use to teach effectively. Because questioning is so important, and because it is so frequently used and abused, we devote this chapter to assisting you in developing your skills in using questioning.

ANTICIPATED OUTCOMES

After completing this chapter, you should be able to do the following:

1. Describe at least 10 characteristics of intelligent behavior.
2. Describe ways teachers can help children learn to think intelligently.
3. Identify the skills used in thinking, and identify specifically how to facilitate students' development of each skill.
4. Write a sample question for a grade of your choice for each of the types of questions discussed in this chapter.
5. Explain the need for different types and levels of questions.
6. Write a series of appropriately sequenced questions for the development of an idea for use in a grade of your choice.
7. Demonstrate ways to help students develop their metacognitive skills.
8. Explain the value of and how to use students' questions.
9. Describe when and how a teacher should and should not respond to students' questions.
10. Compare and contrast ways of thinking with levels of questions.
11. Demonstrate your ability to use questions by teaching a group of children or a peer group. The demonstration should include framing and stating questions, pacing and sequencing questions, and acknowledging learner responses.

Asking questions is a natural way to learn and to satisfy one's curiosity. When young children first become aware of their surroundings and develop the ability to speak, they ask an endless number of questions. It is a process that goes on throughout life, albeit with diminishing frequency. In fact, as you have undoubtedly heard before, when you stop asking questions, you stop learning.

Learning to think is perhaps education's highest-priority goal. To help children develop the intellectual skills associated with reflective thought, you will need to model and encourage questions that trigger their use of such skills. To this end, in this chapter we focus your attention on so-called *higher-level questions*—those that require respondents to apply knowledge and to analyze, synthesize, interpret, and evaluate information. In this context, so-called *lower-level questions*—those requiring only recall or reproduction of information—would not be appropriate. The idea of "levels" of questions comes from extensive use of Bloom's taxonomy for the cognitive domain (see Chapter 5). Although the taxonomy was designed as a way of ordering educational objectives, we can use it as well to classify and study questions and the teaching of thinking.[1] We begin this chapter with a discussion of direct teaching for thinking.

TEACHING THINKING

Pulling together what has been learned about learning and brain functioning, we encourage you to integrate explicit thinking instruction into daily lessons. In other words, help students develop their thinking skills to the point where the skills have become their disposition. In teaching for thinking, we are interested not only in what children know but also in how children behave when they don't know. Gathering evidence of the performance and growth of intelligent behavior requires watching children: observing students as they try to solve the day-to-day academic and real-life problems they encounter. By collecting anecdotes and examples of written, oral, and visual expressions, you can see students' increasingly voluntary and spontaneous performance of intelligent behaviors. We next consider the characteristics of intelligent behavior, the behaviors you will help children strive for.

Characteristics of Intelligent Behavior

As identified by others,[2] we describe in the following paragraphs 14 characteristics of intelligent behavior that you should model, teach for, and observe developing in your students.

In teaching for thinking, we are interested not only in what children know, but also in how children behave when they do not know. Gathering evidence of the performance and growth of intelligent behavior requires watching children: observing students as they try to solve the day-to-day academic and real-life problems they encounter.

Cooperative thinking—social intelligence. Humans are social beings. Real-world problem solving has become so complex that seldom can any person go it alone. Not all children come to school knowing how to work effectively in groups. They may exhibit competitiveness, narrow-mindedness, egocentrism, and ethnocentrism, and may criticize others' values, emotions, and beliefs. Listening, consensus seeking, giving up an idea to work on someone else's, empathy, compassion, group leadership, cooperative learning, knowing how to support group efforts, altruism—these behaviors indicate intelligent human beings, and children can learn them at school in the classroom.[3] Cooperative learning, for example, is more than just group work. Cooperative learning provides children opportunity to practice and develop four key thinking skills: problem solving, decision making, critical thinking, and creative thinking.[4]

Decreasing impulsiveness. Impulsive behavior can worsen conflict and can inhibit effective problem solving.[5] People who develop impulse control think before acting. You can teach children to think before beginning a project or task, and before arriving at conclusions with insufficient data. Additionally, one of several reasons that you should usually insist on a show of student hands before calling on one student to respond or question is to help them develop control over the impulsive behavior of shouting out in class.[6] (See also the guidelines given later in this chapter for practicing gender equity when questioning.)

Drawing on knowledge and applying it to new situations. A major goal of formal education is for learners to apply learned knowledge to new, real-life situations, the highest level of thinking and doing. To do this, you must give students opportunity to practice by devising classroom experiences in problem recognition, problem solving, and project-based learning.[7]

Flexibility in thinking. Sometimes referred to as *lateral thinking*, flexibility in thinking is the ability to view a problem from a new angle, using a novel approach. With your help modeling this behavior, children can learn to consider alternative points of view and to deal with several sources of information simultaneously.

Ingenuity + originality + insightfulness = creativity. All children must be encouraged to do, and be discouraged from saying "I can't." Teach your students in ways that encourage intrinsic motivation rather than reliance on extrinsic sources. (See, for example, the discussion in Chapter 2 concerning using reinforcement versus praise). You must be able to offer criticism in such a way that children understand that criticism per se is not criticism of them. In exemplary elementary school programs, students learn the value of feedback. They learn the value of their own intuition, of guessing—they learn "I can."

Listening to others with understanding and empathy. Some psychologists believe that the ability to listen to others, to empathize with and to understand their point of view, is one of the highest forms of intelligent behavior. Empathic

Children should be given many opportunities to present and discuss their learning with peers. The ability to listen to others, to empathize with and understand their point of view, is perhaps one of the highest forms of intelligent behavior.

behavior is considered an important skill for conflict resolution (discussed in Chapter 4). In class meetings, brainstorming sessions, think tanks, town meetings, advisory councils, board meetings, and in legislative bodies, people from various walks of life convene to share their thinking, to explore their ideas, and to broaden their perspectives by listening to the ideas and reactions of others. Development of this skill should begin in the earliest grades.

Metacognition. Learning to plan, monitor, assess, and reflect on one's own thinking is another characteristic of intelligent behavior. Cooperative learning groups, journals, portfolio conferences, self-assessment, and thinking aloud (as in think–pair–share dyads) are all strategies you can use to help children develop this intelligent behavior. Your own thinking aloud when solving a problem in the classroom is good modeling for your students, helping them to develop their own cognitive skills of thinking, learning, and reasoning.[8]

Persistence. Persistence is sticking to a task until it is completed. Consider the following examples:

- Amelia Earhart, born in 1898, demonstrated from the time she was a young girl that she was creative, curious, and persistent. Having learned to fly in 1920, Earhart just 8 years later became the first woman to fly the Atlantic Ocean, thereby paving the way for other women to become active in aviation.
- As the result of childhood diseases, Wilma Rudolph at the age of 10 could not walk without the aid of leg braces. At age 20, however, she won three gold medals in the 1960 World Olympics and was declared to be the fastest woman runner in the world.

Questioning and problem posing. Children are usually full of questions, and, unless discouraged, they do ask them. We want students to be alert to, and recognize, discrepancies and phenomena in their environment and to freely inquire about their causes. In exemplary elementary school classrooms, children are encouraged to ask questions and then from them to develop a problem-solving strategy to investigate their questions.

Sense of humor. The positive effects of humor on the body's physiological functions are well established: a drop in pulse rate, increased oxygen in the blood, activation of antibodies that fight against harmful microorganisms, and release of gamma interferon, a hormone that fights viruses and regulates cell growth. Humor liberates creativity and involves high-level thinking skills such as anticipation, finding novel relationships, and visual imagery. The acquisition of a sense of humor follows a developmental sequence similar to that described by Piaget[9] and Kohlberg.[10] Initially, young children may find humor in all the wrong things—human frailty, ethnic stereotypes, sacrilegious riddles, ribald profanities. Later, creative children thrive on finding incongruity and will demonstrate a whimsical frame of mind during problem solving.

Striving for accuracy and precision. You can observe children developing this intelligent behavior when they take time to check over their work, review procedures, refuse to draw conclusions with limited data, and use increasingly concise and descriptive language.

Taking risks. Encourage children to venture forth and explore their ideas. You must model risk taking and provide opportunities for children to develop this intelligent behavior, using techniques such as encouraging questions, brainstorming, exploratory investigations, student-centered projects, and cooperative learning. (Risk taking is one of the facilitating behaviors discussed earlier in Chapter 2.)

Using all the senses. Encourage children as often as is appropriate and feasible to use and develop all their sensory input channels to learn (i.e., verbal, visual, tactile, and kinesthetic). (See the Learning Experiences Ladder in Chapter 7.)

Wonderment + inquisitiveness + curiosity + the enjoyment of problem solving = a sense of efficacy as a thinker. Young children express wonderment, and this should never be stifled. Through effective teaching, children can experience that sense of wonderment as you guide them into a feeling of "I can," and to express a feeling of "I enjoy."

Strive to help your students develop these characteristics of intelligent behavior. In Chapter 2 you learned of specific teacher behaviors that aid this learning. Next, we review additional research findings that offer important considerations for student learning and developing intelligent behavior.

Direct Teaching for Thinking and Intelligent Behavior

The curriculum of any school includes developing the skills used in thinking. Because students' academic achievement increases when they are taught thinking directly, many researchers and educators concur that all students should receive direct instruction on how to think and behave intelligently.[11]

Four research perspectives have influenced the direct teaching of thinking. The *cognitive view of intelligence* asserts that intellectual ability is not fixed but can be developed. The *constructivist approach to learning* maintains that learners actively and independently construct knowledge by creating and coordinating relationships in their mental repertoire. The *social psychology view of classroom experience* focuses on learners as individuals who are members of various peer groups and of a society. The *perspective of information processing* deals with the mechanics of acquiring, elaborating on, and managing information.

Direct Teaching of Skills Used in Thinking

Rather than assuming that students have developed thinking skills (such as *classifying, comparing, concluding, generalizing,* and *inferring*), you should devote classroom time to teaching them directly. When a thinking skill is taught directly, the subject content becomes the vehicle for thinking. For example, a social studies lesson can teach children how to distinguish fact and opinion; a language arts lesson instructs students how to compare and analyze; a science lesson can teach them how to set up a problem for inquiry.

DEVELOPING SKILL IN USING QUESTIONS

Classifying questions in terms of a skill hierarchy has been useful in the effort to get teachers to focus more on questions that promote various kinds of thinking.

The terms *higher-level* and *lower-level questions* have nothing to do with how worthwhile the questions themselves are. Whether a question is good or bad depends on its purpose, how it is stated, and its suitability for the students to whom it is directed. So-called "lower-level" questions are not only good to use but are absolutely essential in assessing certain aspects of your instructional program. For example, how else could you check students' reading comprehension other than to ask specific factual questions based on the passage read? Therefore, let us dispose of any notion that there is something inherently good about higher-level questions and something inherently bad about lower-level questions, and think instead in terms of the educational purposes you serve by using each type of question.

There can be no doubt that, in general, teachers tend to overuse lower-level questions. These questions have to do with recalling and reproducing information—using such verbs as *name, locate, describe, list, identify;* they are also called "who, what, where, and when" questions. They are easy to formulate because you base them directly on the subject matter studied. If basing them on a passage students have read, you might instruct them to "put your finger on the sentence that answers the question," a practice that is fairly widespread in checking comprehension. The problem with such procedures is that they tend to exaggerate the importance of the content of the question. Your purpose may be simply to check the accuracy of students' reading, but they may be left with the idea that you are calling attention to an important piece of information.

Higher-level questions call for students to process information and to apply it in new situations. Students usually cannot answer higher-level questions directly from an information source such as the textbook or encyclopedia but must infer, surmise, or conclude from putting together pieces of information. One cannot answer a question of this type by pointing to a passage in a book. You often frame these questions evaluatively, such as by asking, "Why? How do you know? If that is true, then. . . ? What is likely to happen next? Can you summarize. . . ?" They require imaginative, creative responses linking together related bits of information into a thoughtful, logical conclusion. They are more difficult to frame, which probably is one reason teachers do not use them with greater frequency. Their purpose is mainly to give students experience in using reflective thinking processes.

There is a place for both lower- and higher-level questions in instruction. You need skill in using both types and must be sensitive to the need to balance the kinds of questions used. The questions themselves, when asked orally in class or when they appear in written form on examinations, indicate powerfully to students what you consider important for them to learn. They send out signals as surely as does anything else you do or say.

Three subskills are a part of skillful questioning: framing and stating questions, sequencing questions, and pacing questions. We discuss these subskills in the sections that follow.

Framing and Stating Questions

The first requirement for framing and stating classroom questions is that they be appropriate for the subject matter and the purpose for which you are asking them. But even if satisfactory on those counts, questions may be faulty for technical reasons. The following guidelines will help you prevent such problems:

1. The question should be grammatically correct and the syntax easy to follow. Keep the questions short and the vocabulary simple. Avoid bookish terms and expressions.
2. Express the question clearly enough that children know what you want in the way of a response.
3. Avoid embedding giveaway clues in the question.
4. If you begin the question by asking, "What do you think . . . ?" or with some similar stem that calls for the expression of an *opinion*, you must be prepared to accept *any* response from your students.
5. State questions in an encouraging tone of voice.
6. State questions in a way that stimulates children's thinking. Try not to lead them to an expected answer.

To avoid difficulties, during your preactive phase of instruction write into your lesson plan the key questions that you plan to ask during the lessons themselves. Many beginning teachers have found it helpful to make and listen to a tape recording of their teaching, or to assess their questions by asking them first to a friend.

Sequencing Questions

If you are to *develop* ideas in the course of a lesson, you must ask questions in a way that leads to a logical conclusion. Idea development means that the lesson has direction, that your questions lead somewhere. You cannot ask a series of random questions and expect ideas to build cumulatively. In the following sequence, based on a story of a young man's visit to an abandoned house, notice how each question builds on the one that precedes it.

1. Can you give an overall description of the house Charlie visited?
2. What was there about it that made Charlie uneasy?
3. When did Charlie first discover that something was out of the ordinary?
4. Why do you think Charlie did not leave at that time?
5. At what point was Charlie absolutely certain that someone else was in the house?
6. What, exactly, happened that made Charlie know he was not alone?
7. Why could Charlie not go for help then?
8. What can we learn from Charlie's experience about going into strange or unfamiliar surroundings?

Even if you are not familiar with the story, you may infer essential elements of the storyline from this sequence of questions. The same questions asked in a random order would not produce this desired effect.

Perhaps the easiest way to develop skill in asking questions sequentially is to teach a process that has a fixed sequence, such as following a product through its manufacturing process, or discussing how an item gets from where it is produced to where it is used. Science experiments that necessitate a specific sequence lend themselves well to learning how to sequence questions, as do some operations in mathematics. This aspect of questioning is much like building a sequence for a computer program. Indeed, as a classroom teacher, you *are* the programmer much of the time. Accordingly, if learning is to proceed efficiently, you should provide questions that will deal with small increments of learning in a progressively more complex sequence.

Pacing Questions

Pacing concerns the frequency with which you ask questions. Two problems are commonly associated with pacing questions. One is asking questions too rapidly one after another, with students allowed little or no time for thinking or for developing ideas associated with one question before being asked another. Such rapid-fire questioning encourages if not demands short, low-level thinking responses. The second problem has to do with the amount of thinking time (also called *wait time*) given. Too often, teachers seem to feel that unless children respond immediately, they need to restate or clarify their question, or give learners cues to the answer. Actually, when given sufficient time to think, children *will* often come forth with thoughtful responses.

Our position is that you should slow your questioning pace, and do not be hasty in providing cues, nor too quick to restate and clarify questions. The atmosphere should encourage reflection rather than quickness of response. Your questions should provoke thinking, and thinking requires time—more time for some children than for others.

You may get more thoughtful responses with older children by having them write out their answers before responding orally. This will slow the pace and also has the advantage of involving all members of the class in thinking about the questions and in writing, both of which are important for critical thinking.

HANDLING STUDENT RESPONSES TO QUESTIONS

It is important for you to know that your reply to a child's response to your question may be as important as the question itself. As a general guideline, your comments following children's responses should leave them with the

Activity 3.1: Create a Story

Using the questions in the text about Charlie's visit to the old house, have your students create a story. With children in grades 4 through 6, you might then have them try their hand at developing a set of questions that could be the basis of another story. Then show students a picture and have them frame questions and arrange them in sequential order to tell a story about it.

1. What skills are being used in this exercise?
2. How could you use this experience to enhance students' questioning skills?

perception that you both hear and accept them, and feeling that they would like to respond again to another question. Let us examine some of the ways you can deal with student responses.

Passive Acceptance Responses

There are a half dozen or so common expressions that teachers often use to acknowledge student responses, including "all right," "uh-huh," "yes," and "okay." These are noncommittal, nonevaluative (nonjudgmental), passive acceptance responses that simply recognize that a response has occurred. (Of course, these might be accompanied by nonverbal clues that carry powerful evaluative messages, such as an approving or disapproving facial expression, tone of voice, or body movement.) Passive acceptance responses are effective when you want to encourage discussion of the question. When you recognize a response in such a noncommittal way, students know that the matter is still open, and others may contribute their ideas to the discussion.

When listening to recordings of their class discussions, some teachers are surprised by how often they use the same expression, such as "okay" in acknowledging student responses. Some teachers use "okay" a hundred times a day and are not even aware of it. Rather than repeating the same verbal response, try to develop variety in your acknowledgment of students' contributions.

Evaluative (Judgmental) Responses

Some teachers seem to think that they must evaluate every response with "Yes, that's right" or "No, that's not right." Of course, you need to evaluate children's work and should not ignore incorrect responses. But there is much wrong with a procedure that necessitates such active acceptance (or nonacceptance) responses from you every time children answer a question or make a comment in class. First, you do not always *know* whether a response is right or wrong.

Activity 3.2: How Would You Say It?

The following questions are poorly stated. Identify what is wrong with each one, then restate it correctly:

1. Indian people lived how on the plains before the coming of the Europeans?
2. At what point in a musical selection does the "finale" come?
3. Can you list the steps in doing the experiment from start to finish, beginning with the last step first?
4. I don't think it was a very good idea to use those colors for the picture, do you?
5. What would happen if—but, of course, you would never want to do anything like this—you were hiking along and you suddenly stepped on a rock, twisted your ankle, and couldn't walk any farther, and you had to get help but there was no one around?
6. If you saw a hot-air balloon one day as you were playing with your beach ball, what do you think would make it stay in the air?
7. Can you add ideas to the list of suggestions offered by Jason's friend that would help his situation?

Moreover, many responses cannot be categorized as totally correct or incorrect. Also, over time you will tend to fall into the habit of asking only questions that elicit answers you can evaluate in this way, which typically represent lower-order thinking.[12] Some children will not participate in questioning of this type because they do not want their teacher to evaluate their responses negatively in front of their peers. Rather than risking such a contingency, they simply will not participate, and if called on, they will say that they do not know. Finally, evaluative statements tend to bring matters to closure. For example, if you respond to a student's answer with, "You're absolutely correct," you wouldn't seem to leave much of anything for the class to discuss.

Restating and Clarifying

You will not need to restate and clarify every response to every question, but this is good practice from time to time. It is especially appropriate when a student has responded so softly that the entire group could not hear. Also, you may know that further clarification will help to either promote continued thinking about the question or provide more precision to the response. For example, in a science lesson, you may ask, "If I have a gallon of water and I pour in a quart of oil, what happens to the oil?" A child responds by saying, "It goes to the top." You may restate and clarify, "You say it goes to the top. Do you mean that the oil will float on top of the water?" The child continues, "Yes, it separates. The oil floats on top of the water." Here, by asking another question, you are clarifying to verify that you have listened to and understood the child's response. (See also "Clarifying Whenever Necessary" in Chapter 2.)

Probing

Sometimes a student's response only partially answers your question and you want to encourage a more complete answer. You can probe for additional information by using statements such as these:

1. "Can you say a little bit more about that?"
2. "But why do you suppose he turned back?"
3. "Can you explain why it happened?"
4. "You said 'yes'; now tell why you think so."
5. "That is correct, but there is another important point you haven't mentioned."
6. "Can you give us an example?"

Sometimes you can elicit a more elaborate response by simply repeating the last word or words of the child's response, inflected in a questioning tone: "freezes?" "tree frogs?" "disease?" "four trips?" However, when probing for a more complete response, avoid pressing children so hard that they become too anxious and nervous to respond at all. Such anxiety-producing probing is counterproductive to real learning.

Cueing

It may be that your question draws a blank—a sea of empty faces, something that happens to every teacher at one time or another. It may mean that you stated the question poorly, or it may mean that the children simply did not know what you were asking. When this happens, you can give students a few leads, cues that will guide their thinking along the lines you intend. This involves more than simply repeating or rephrasing the question. In cueing, you provide small amounts of additional information, as in the following example:

Teacher: Why did the candle go out when we placed a jar over it?

Student: It doesn't get any air.

Teacher: (Probing.) Yes, but what is it in the air that the candle needs to keep burning?

Student: (No response.)

Teacher: (Cueing.) Do you remember when we learned about rust. . . ?

Student: (Picking up on the cue.) Oxygen! The candle needs oxygen to burn. It goes out when it has used up the oxygen.

Notice in this example that the teacher did not give the answer. The teacher simply provided a small hint that pointed the learner's thinking in the appropriate direction. In this case, the child was able to respond even before the teacher completed the cueing sentence.

SOCRATIC QUESTIONING

In the fifth century BCE, Socrates used the art of questioning so successfully that to this day we still hear of *Socratic questioning*.[13] What, exactly, is this method of questioning? Socrates' strategy was to ask his students a series of leading questions that gradually embroiled them to the point where they were forced to reflect on their own ideas and to think strictly for themselves. In his dialogues, Socrates tried to aid students in developing their ideas. He did not impose his own on them; rather, he encouraged them to develop their own conclusions and draw their own inferences. Of course, Socrates may have had preconceived notions about what the final learning should be and carefully aimed his questions so that students would arrive at the desired conclusions. Still, his questions were worded so as to cause *divergent* rather than *convergent* thinking. The students were free to go mentally wherever the facts and their thinking led them.

Throughout history, teachers have tried to adapt the methods of Socrates to the classroom. In some situations they have become a major mode for instruction. However, we must remember that Socrates used this method in the context of a one-to-one relationship between each student and himself. Some teachers have adapted it for whole-class direct instruction by asking questions first of one student and then of another, moving slowly about the class. Although such a strategy may work, it is difficult because the essence of the Socratic method is to build question on question in a logical fashion so that each question leads the student a step further toward the understanding sought. When you spread the questions around the classroom, you may find it difficult to build the desired sequence and to keep all students involved in the discussion. Sometimes you may be able to use the Socratic method by directing all the questions at one student—at least for several minutes—while other students watch and listen. That is how Socrates did it. But you want to avoid seeming to be picking on a student. As a rule, rather than for whole-class direct instruction, the Socratic method works best when you are working in one-on-one coaching situations or with just a small group of students.

Whether using Socratic questioning with one child, a small group, or the entire class, remember that your focus should be on the questions and on children's thinking, not on the answers. *Thinking*, then, is valued as the quintessential activity.[14] In essence, to conduct Socratic questioning, identify a problem (either student or teacher posed) and then ask children a series of probing questions designed to cause them to examine critically the problem and potential solutions to it. Plan in advance the main thrust of the questioning and your key questions so that the session will proceed logically. It is too difficult to think of quality probing questions on the spur of the moment.

QUESTIONS THAT FOCUS ON SPECIFIC PURPOSES

You must be able to select appropriate questions in terms of purposes, or the results are likely to be disappointing. For example, teachers sometimes report their inability to involve children in discussions. An examination of the kinds of questions they ask often provides clues to why they are having this problem. If they ask only low-level questions, requiring only simple yes or no answers or specific recall, there is little to discuss. The level of your questions clue children to the level of thinking and involvement expected. Questions that repeatedly require little to no thinking will elicit little to no substantive involvement.

In the following subsections we discuss questions that you may ask to achieve specific educational purposes. Before we proceed, consider the following general rules, which you should apply to all of your classroom questioning.

Practice calling on all students. Related to Rule 4 in the box, "Guidelines for Practicing Gender Equity When Questioning," you must call on not just the bright or the slow, not just boys or girls, not only on those in the front or middle of the room, but on all students. This takes concentrated effort on your part, but it is important. To help ensure calling on students equally, try this: Attach a laminated copy of the seating chart to a bright neon-colored clipboard (gives children a visual focus), and with a water-soluble marker, make a tally mark next to children's names each time you call on them. Erase the marks at the end of each day.

> **Guidelines for Practicing Gender Equity When Questioning**
>
> To practice gender equity when using questioning, follow these four rules: (1) Avoid going to a boy to bail out a girl who fails to answer a question, and (2) avoid going to a boy to improve on a girl's answer. For the first, without seeming to badger, try to give the student clues until she can answer with success. For the second, hold and demonstrate high expectations for all students. (3) Allow equal wait time regardless of student gender. (4) Call on boys and girls with equal frequency.

Give the same minimum amount of wait time (think time) to all students. This, too, will require concentrated effort on your part, but also is important. If you wait for less time when calling certain students, such as students of one gender or of some other personal characteristic, you show prejudice toward or lack of confidence in these students, both of which are detrimental when you are striving to establish for all students a positive, equal, and safe environment for classroom learning. Show confidence in all children, and never discriminate by expecting less or more from some than from others. Although some children may take longer to respond, it is not necessarily because they are not thinking or have less ability. For example, there may be cultural differences, in that some cultures simply allow more wait time than others do. It is important that you personalize, to allow children who need more time to have it. Do not vary wait time to single out students or to lead to lower expectations, but rather to allow for higher expectations.

Require students to raise their hands and be called on. This is true for teachers of kindergarten and for all teachers thereafter. When you ask questions, instead of allowing students to randomly shout out their answers, require them to raise their hands and to be called on before they respond. Establish this procedure and stick with it. This does not mean that you call only on children who have their hands raised; you can call on whomever you want. It does mean that children who want to make a contribution or ask a question must raise their hand and be acknowledged by you first. This helps to ensure that you call on all students equally, fairly distributing your interactions, and not interacting less with girls because boys tend to be more obstreperous. Even in college classrooms, male students tend to be more vociferous than female students and, when the instructor allows, tend to outtalk and to interrupt their female peers. Whether teaching kindergarten or adults or students in between, every teacher has the responsibility to guarantee a nonbiased classroom and an equal distribution of interaction time. This is impossible for you to achieve if you allow students to speak and disrespectfully interrupt others at will.

Another important reason for this advice is to aid students in learning to control their impulsiveness, to help them develop self-control. As pointed out at the beginning of this chapter, controlling one's impulsiveness is a characteristic of intelligent behavior. One of your many instructional responsibilities is to help students develop this skill.

Actively involve as many children as possible in questioning-answering discussion sessions. The traditional method of the teacher asking a question and then calling on a student to respond is essentially a one-on-one interaction. Some children, those not called on, are likely to view it as their opportunity to disengage in the lesson at hand. When calling on one child you do not likely want others to mentally disengage. There are many effective ways to keep all children engaged. Consider the following suggestions: To keep all children mentally engaged, call on students who are sitting quietly and have not raised their hands as well as on those who have, but avoid badgering or humiliating an unwilling participant. When students have no response, you might suggest they think about it and you will come back to them to make sure they eventually understand or can answer the original question. By dividing a single question into several parts, you can increase the number of students involved. For example, "What are the characteristics of animals known as insects? Who can give one characteristic?" followed by, "Who can give another?" Or, you can involve several students in answering a single question. For example, ask one student for an answer such as to the question, "What was a characteristic given in the text for animals known as insects?" Then, have a second student read the text aloud to verify the first student's answer, and perhaps ask a third to explore the reason or thinking that makes it an accepted answer.

Procedural Questions

As a teacher, you will ask many questions that have to do with classroom procedures, the clarification of directions, transitional inquiries, or rhetorical queries. Some of these questions are a necessary part of teaching, of course, but often they amount to little more than time fillers while you gather your thoughts. They may even take the form of a threat (e.g., "Do you want me to move you to another seat?"). Frequently, students will not respond; indeed, you will not expect them to. Often, teachers are usually not even fully aware of the extent of their use of questions of this type, *most of which should not even be asked*. Consider the following examples.

Examples with Suggestions for Improvement

1. "Are there any questions?" Seldom will you get the answer you want when asking this question. Sometimes you will get answers you would just as soon not have gotten. When you want to check for comprehension it is usually better to randomly check several children by asking content questions and perhaps also to search for quizzical facial expressions.

2. "Will someone review for us what we planned to do during our music period today?" This isn't the right question. A better one would be, "By a show of hands, who can review for us what we planned to do during our music period today?" To help children develop their questioning skills, you must model the same, in this instance by properly wording the question.

3. "Jaime, would you please turn off the lights?" This is not likely to cause problems unless, of course, you ask a student who might say "No." It is better, generally, to give a statement or ask for a volunteer.

4. "Do you think we can figure out a better way to return the bats and balls to the storeroom?" You probably would not want a simple "No" answer to this question. However, as worded, you must be prepared to deal with such a succinct response. Instead, think about the answer that you want, and then word your question accordingly. In this instance try, "Who can make a suggestion about how we might better return the bats and balls to the storeroom?"

5. "Is there anyone in the group who has so little to do that he or she wants me to assign additional work?" Do you suppose the teacher who asked this question really expected an answer? Such a question is really intended to be a declarative threat because the teacher is losing control. Do not confuse students by sending confusing messages. You are not employed to confuse children. Say what you intend to say, as succinctly as you can.

6. "Why don't the five of you work at the table near the window?" Again, the teacher here is giving an order, not really intending to ask a question. It is best to ask questions only when you want responses.

Questions That Check Literal Comprehension

In subject-matter fields it is necessary to know whether children are extracting the essential information presented in the required reading material. Questions used to check such literal comprehension should encourage good study habits; they should focus on important concepts and ideas rather than on inconsequential detail. For example, if you include too many low-level recall questions, children may assume that facts are all that are important in the material. It often is better to include a variety of questions—some asking students to identify important facts and ideas, others requiring understanding, and still others that make them apply, analyze, synthesize, and evaluate new knowledge. Construct your questions to help children identify the most relevant information presented in the material.

Examples of Questions That Help Children Identify Relevant Information

1. What costs are included in the price you pay for shoes?

2. After reading the passage in your science book, make a list of all the pollutants mentioned. Which ones are natural pollutants? Which are *people-made* pollutants?

3. Draw a diagram to show that you understand the number relationships in a problem of indirect measurement. Can you state two basic ideas that explain indirect measurement?

4. Which statement in each paragraph identifies the cause-and-effect relationships between the items?

5. What characteristics of the countries of the Middle East would justify grouping them together as a region?

6. Exactly what happened at each of the four stages of the experiment?

7. Can you identify five fire-danger spots in a home that were mentioned in the text?

Reflective or "Thought" Questions

Reflective questions are open ended and require higher-level thought processes. Their purpose is to stimulate learners' creative imaginations and thinking abilities. A reflective question may not have a right answer, in the sense that one and only one response is acceptable. Reflective questions are often tied to critical thinking and decision making, thereby requiring students to consider alternatives and the consequences of each. Reflective thinking requires such mental processes as application, analysis, synthesis, and evaluation.

For generations teachers have admonished their students to "think." Even today it is fairly common to hear teachers say, "Now think, boys and girls. Think real hard!" Simply telling children to think is not a satisfactory way to develop thinking abilities. You need to use activities, situations, and questions that require them to apply such intellectual skills as comparing and contrasting, noting cause and effect, considering alternatives, and drawing conclusions based on information.

Examples of Questions Encouraging Reflective Thinking

1. In the early years of our country, many people had comfortable homes and a good life in the 13 states along the Atlantic coast. Why do you suppose some chose to leave all that behind and go west, which promised a hard and often dangerous life?

2. Scientists think some chemicals are so dangerous to human health that they should not be used for insect and disease control. Can you think of conditions where they might be used even though they are dangerous? Can you think of other examples where chemicals are dangerous but still used? What criteria do people use to determine when and when not to use a dangerous chemical?

3. What businesses and what kinds of work would be in greater demand if everyone worked only 4 days a week?

4. How might the story have ended if the family had visited Aunt Sophie and Uncle Charlie one day sooner?

5. Why are some drugs sold only when prescribed by a medical doctor?

6. Do you think it would be wise to protect only those animals that are useful to human beings? Why or why not?

7. Why would the authorities want to introduce wolves from Alberta, Canada, into Yellowstone National Park and Central Idaho? Are there any groups that would be opposed to such action, and, if so, why do they oppose it?

QUESTIONS FROM STUDENTS

The kinds of questions that students ask reveal a great deal about the effectiveness of your classroom management procedures and about your conduct of instruction. For example, a preponderance of student questions that call for your reassurance and approval ("Am I doing this right?" "Is this what you want us to do?" "Is it all right if I make my picture sideways?") indicate a general feeling of insecurity, that there is considerable risk in doing things that may displease you. It could mean, too, that there is a high level of student dependence on you. It might also mean that your directions are not clear and that children do not understand precisely what you expect of them.

Sometimes you may become annoyed when children ask endless procedural and permission questions ("May I sharpen my pencil?" "Please, may I get a book?" "May I take this book home?"). Yet, you should recognize that you might be contributing to the problem. If you do not provide children opportunities to develop self-direction and to assume responsibility for a certain amount of decision-making, you may predict that they will turn to you for the authority to engage in routine procedures.

Children are likely to model their question-asking behavior on yours. As said before, from your questions children sense the level of thinking and participation you believe to be important. Thus, if you tend to ask provocative questions that enhance higher-level thinking, children in your classroom are likely to follow that example.

Activity 3.3: And Then *You* Said. . . .

Imagine that you are the teacher in the following four situations. In each, you ask a question and a student responds. The response, however, is in some way inadequate. Supply what you would say next to move the instructional sequence along.

Situation 1

Teacher: You enjoyed the poem so much yesterday that I thought we could share another one today. What was it that you liked most about the poem we read yesterday?

Student: Rhymes.

And *you* said:_____

Situation 2

Teacher: Now you notice that this line on our graph [pointing to a line showing the amount of food produced] goes up, but this other line [pointing to a line showing number of people living on farms] goes down. What does this tell us about how farming has changed?

Student: It tells us that people moved away. They got other jobs.

And *you* said:_____

Situation 3

Teacher: An electric generator produces electricity by the rotation of a coil in a magnetic field. It needs some source of energy or power to rotate the coil. Thus, we see that an electric motor uses electrical energy to produce mechanical energy. A generator, however, uses mechanical energy to produce electrical energy. What forms of mechanical energy do we use to produce electrical energy?

Student: [No response. Dead silence.]

And *you* said:_____

Situation 4

Teacher: In our social studies, we have been learning how people get the things they need to live in our community. You remember that we learned two new—and big—words. [Children respond enthusiastically, "Consumer" and "Producer."] Yes, you remembered well. Now, who can tell us something about these words?

Student: All consumers are producers.

And *you* said:_____

Activity 3.4: And Elliot Eisner Said. . . .

The kind of school we need would be staffed by teachers who are as interested in the questions students ask after a unit of study as they are in the answers students give. On the whole, schools are highly answer-oriented. Teachers have the questions, and students are to have the answers. Even with a problem-solving approach, the focus of attention is on the student's ability to solve a problem that someone else has posed. Yet the most intellectually demanding tasks lie not so much in solving problems as in posing questions.

1. Do you agree with Mr. Eisner? Why or why not?
2. What does this say to you as a classroom teacher?
3. Return to this statement and read your answers to questions 1 and 2 after you have completed your study of Chapter 8 of this book. Do you want to make any changes to your responses to the two questions? If so, describe.

Source: E. W. Eisner, "The Kind of Schools We Need," *Phi Delta Kappan* 83(8): 579 (2002).

The Question-Driven Classroom

You can and should use student questions as springboards for further questioning, discussions, and investigations. Indeed, in a constructivist learning environment, student questions often drive content.[15] Encourage students to ask questions that challenge the textbook, the process, or other persons' statements, and encourage them to seek the supporting evidence behind a statement.[16]

Questioning: The Cornerstone of Critical Thinking, Real-World Problem Solving, and Meaningful Learning

Real-world problem solving usually has no absolute right answers. Rather than "correct" answers, some simply are better than others. The person with a problem needs to learn how to (1) recognize the problem, (2) formulate a question about that problem (e.g., Should I tell Mom or not? Should I take this drug? Should the river be dammed?), (3) collect data, and (4) arrive at a temporarily acceptable answer, realizing that at some later time new data may dictate a review of this conclusion. For example, if an astronomer believes she has discovered a new planetary system, there is no textbook or teacher or any other outside authoritative source to which she may refer to inquire if she is correct. Rather, on the basis of her self-confidence in problem identification, asking questions, collecting enough data, and arriving at a tentative conclusion based on those data, she assumes that for now her conclusion is safe.

Encourage students to ask questions about content and process. Question asking often indicates that the inquirer is curious, puzzled, and uncertain; it is a sign of being engaged in thinking about a topic.[17] And, yet, in too many classrooms too few students ask questions.[18] We cannot overstate this: Encourage your students to ask questions. From children, there is no such thing as a "dumb" question. Sometimes children, like everyone else, ask questions they could just as easily have looked up or that are irrelevant or that show lack of thought or sensitivity. Those questions can consume precious class time. For a teacher, they can be frustrating. Your initial reaction may be to too quickly and

Activity 3.5: Think Time and the Art of Questioning

Role-play simulation: From your class ask for four volunteers. One volunteer will read the lines of Marcella, a second will read the one "student" line, the third reads the narrative lines about the setting (such as the one at 9:01), while the fourth volunteer uses a stopwatch to direct Marcella and the student to speak their lines at the designated times. The rest of your class will pretend to be students in Marcella's fourth-grade language arts lesson.

9:00: *Marcella*: "Think of a man whom you admire, perhaps a father figure, and write a three-sentence paragraph describing that person." Students begin their writing.

9:00:05: *Marcella*: "Only three sentences about someone you look up to. It might be your father, uncle, anyone."

9:00:07: *Student*: "Does it have to be about a man?" *Marcella*: "No, it can be a man or a woman, but someone you truly admire."

9:01: Marcella is walking the room, seeing that all children are on task.

9:01:10 *Marcella*: "Three sentences are all you need to write."

9:01:15: *Marcella*: "Think of someone you really look up to, and write three sentences in a paragraph that describes that person."

9:01:30: *Marcella*: "Someone you would like to be like."

9:02: Marcella continues walking around the room, helping children who are having difficulty. All children are on task.

9:04: *Marcella*: "Now I want you to exchange papers with your reading partner, read that person's description of the person they admire, and describe a setting that you see that person in. Write a paragraph that describes that setting."

9:04–9:05: Students exchange papers; Marcella walks around seeing that everyone has received their partner's paper and is on task.

9:05: *Marcella*: "Where do you see that person being? Below the paragraph I want you to write a new paragraph describing where you see this person, perhaps in an easy chair watching a ball game, or on a porch, in a car, in the kitchen cooking."

9:05:10: *Marcella*: "Describe a scene you see this person in."

9:05:15: *Marcella*: "After you read the description I want you to create a setting for the person described."

9:05:18: Children seem confused either about what they are reading (e.g., asking the writer what a word is or means) or what they are supposed to do.

9:05:19: *Marcella*: "Anything is fine. Use your imagination to describe the setting."

9:05:22: *Marcella*: "Describe a setting for this person."

9:09: *Marcella*: "Now I want you to exchange papers with yet someone else, and after reading the two paragraphs the two other students wrote, write a third paragraph describing a problem you think this admired person has."

Class Discussion: Following the role playing, hold a whole-class discussion or small-group discussions using the following as a springboard:

a. Describe the apparent strength or depth of Marcella's preactive phase of instruction.

b. Describe what you believe are the good points and weak points of this portion of Marcella's language arts lesson and her implementation of it.

c. Describe the apparent strength or quality of Marcella's classroom management.

d. What would you predict will happen during the next few minutes of the lesson, say from 9:10 to 9:12? Why?

mistakenly brush off this type of question with sarcasm, while assuming that the student is too lazy to look up an answer. In such instances, we advise you to think before responding and to respond kindly and professionally, although in your busy life as a classroom teacher that may not always be so easy to remember to do. However, be assured, there is a reason for every student's question, even if it is only signaling a need for recognition or simply demanding attention. When a child makes an effort to interact with you, that can be a positive sign, so without judging the quality of the child's effort gauge carefully your responses to those efforts. If a student's question is really off track, off the wall, out of order, and out of context with the content of the lesson, consider the following as a possible response: "That is an interesting question (or comment) and I would very much like to talk with you more about it. Could we meet at lunch or at some other time that is mutually convenient?"

Avoid bluffing with a question you cannot answer. Nothing will cause you to lose credibility with students faster than faking an answer. There is nothing wrong with admitting that you do not know. It helps children realize that you are human. It helps them maintain an adequate self-esteem, realizing that they are okay. What *is* important is that you know *where* and *how* to find possible answers and that you help students develop that same knowledge and those same process skills.

SUMMARY

Being able to ask questions may be more important than having right answers. Knowledge is derived from asking questions. Being able to recognize problems and knowing how to formulate questions are skills and keys to problem solving, critical-thinking skill development, and intelligent behavior. You have a responsibility to encourage students to formulate questions and to help them word their questions in such a way that they find tentative answers. This process is necessary for students to build a base of knowledge they can draw on whenever necessary to link, interpret, and explain new information in new situations. As the cornerstone to meaningful learning, thinking, communication, and real-world problem solving, you will continue to develop your skill at the art of questioning throughout your teaching career.

In Chapter 4, your attention is focused on organizing and managing your classroom.

STUDY QUESTIONS AND ADDITIONAL ACTIVITIES

1. Is there ever a time that it is okay for a teacher to bluff an answer to a student's question? Explain your response.
2. Explain why it is important to wait after asking students a content question. How long should you wait? What should you do if there is no student response after a certain amount of time?
3. To what extent should (or can) a classroom teacher allow student queries to determine content studied? To what extent should students' initial interest, or lack of interest, in a topic determine whether the topic gets taught?

4. Explain the meaning of the following statement: Rather than looking for what students can reiterate, we should look for what they can demonstrate and produce. Explain why you agree or disagree.
5. How many teachers can members of your class find during a designated period of time who actually plan and write the questions they ask children during a lesson? Discuss the results of your investigation.
6. For a subject area and a grade level of your choice, write three to five questions that would be appropriate for each of the modes of teaching discussed in Chapter 8—expository, inquiry, and demonstration. Which ones were easiest to write? Why was this so?
7. Describe the distinguishing characteristics that are associated with *higher-level* and *lower-level* questions. Using the same subject matter for each, create a higher-level and a lower-level question for a grade of your choice.
8. Explain the meaning of the concept "wait time" ("think time").
9. It is claimed that questions stimulate certain kinds of thought responses. What mental operations must students engage in to answer this question: What is the most important reason that the desert has a small population? (That is, what would the child have to know and in what sequence would they have to process the information in order to answer this question?)
10. Explain why you believe it is or is not a good idea to assign reflective questions (i.e., open-ended, "thought" questions) for homework. What research evidence can you find to support or refute your opinion?

NOTES

1. See, for example, F. P. Hunkins, *Teaching Thinking Through Effective Questioning*, 2nd ed. (Boston: Christopher-Gordon, 1995).
2. A. L. Costa, *The School as a Home for the Mind* (Palatine, IL: Skylight, 1991), 20–31. See also Armstrong's 12 qualities of genius—curiosity, playfulness, imagination, creativity, wonderment, wisdom, inventiveness, vitality, sensitivity, flexibility, humor, and joy—in T. Armstrong, *Awakening Genius in the Classroom* (Alexandria, VA: Association for Supervision and Curriculum Development, 1998), 2–15.
3. See, for example, L. Vandergrift, "'Was Nice to See That Our Predictions Were Right': Developing Metacognition in L2 Listening in Grades 4–6." *Canadian Modern Language Review* 58(4): 555–575 (2002).
4. C. Lee et al., "Cooperative Learning in the Thinking Classroom: Research and Theoretical Perspectives," paper presented at the Seventh International Conference on Thinking (Singapore, June 1–6, 1997).
5. See, for example, M. Goos and P. Galbraith, "Do It This Way! Metacognitive Strategies in Collaborative Mathematics Problem Solving," *Educational Studies in Mathematics* 30(3): 229–260 (1996).
6. For further reading about the relation of impulse control to intelligence see D. Goleman, *Emotional Intelligence: Why It Can Matter More Than IQ* (New York: Bantam, 1995); and D. Harrington-Lueker, "Emotional Intelligence," *High Strides* 9(4): 1, 4–5 (1997).
7. See, for example, L. Sherman, "Explore, Question, Ponder, and Imagine: Projects Give Kids the Chance to Delve Deeply and Find Their Own Way Through Challenging Intellectual Terrain," *Northwest Education* 7(3): 2–7 (2002).

8. See, for example, J. W. Astington, "Theory of Mind Goes to School," *Educational Leadership* 56(3): 46–48 (1998).

9. J. Piaget, *The Psychology of Intelligence* (Totowa, NJ: Littlefield Adams, 1972).

10. I. Kohlberg, *The Meaning and Measurement of Moral Development* (Worcester, MA: Clark University Press, 1981).

11. See, for example, A. Whimbey, "Test Results from Teaching Thinking," in A. L. Costa (Ed.), *Developing Minds: A Resource Book for Teaching Thinking* (Alexandria, VA: Association for Supervision and Curriculum Development, 1985), 269–271.

12. See, for example, J. W. Wimer, C. S. Ridenour, K. Thomas, and W. A. Place, "Higher Order Teaching Questioning of Boys and Girls in Elementary Mathematics Classrooms," *Journal of Educational Research* 95(1): 84–92 (2001), and R. R. Becker, "The Critical Role of Students' Questions in Literacy Development," *Educational Forum* 64(3): 261–272 (2000).

13. See, for example, V. C. Polite and A. H. Adams, *Improving Critical Thinking Through Socratic Seminars*, Spotlight on Student Success No. 110 (Philadelphia, PA: Mid-Atlantic Laboratory for Student Success, 1996).

14. B. R. Brogan and W. A. Brogan, "The Socratic Questioner: Teaching and Learning in the Dialogical Classroom," *The Educational Forum* 59(3): 288–296 (1995).

15. See how a teacher built instruction around the students' personal questions about insects in L. H. Barrow, "What Do Elementary Students Know About Insects?," *Journal of Elementary Science Education* 14(2): 53–60 (2002).

16. See, for example, I. L. Beck and M. G. McKeown, "Questioning the Author: Making Sense of Social Studies," *Educational Leadership* 60(3): 44–47 (2002).

17. See, for example, P. Fischer, "Wow! Kindergarten/First-Grade Inquiry," *Primary Voices K–6* 10(3): 9–15 (2002).

18. United States Department of Education, *Tried and True: Tested Ideas for Teaching and Learning from the Regional Educational Laboratories* (Washington, DC: Office of Educational Research and Improvement, U.S. Department of Education, 1997), 53.

FOR FURTHER PROFESSIONAL STUDY

Bartek, M. M. "Paving the Road to Critical Thinking." *Understanding Our Gifted* 14(4): 10–12 (2002).

Becker, R. R. "The Critical Role of Students' Questions in Literacy Development." *Educational Forum* 64(3): 261–272 (2000).

Bell, L. I. "Strategies That Close the Gap." *Educational Leadership* 60(4): 32–34 (2002).

Black, S. "Ask Me a Question: How Teachers Use Inquiry in a Classroom." *American School Board Journal* 188(5): 43–45 (2001).

Chin, C., Brown, D. E., and Bruce, B. C. "Student-Generated Questions: A Meaningful Aspect of Learning in Science." *International Journal of Science Education* 24(5): 521–549 (2002).

Ciardiello, A. V. "Student Questioning and Multi-dimensional Literacy in the 21st Century." *Educational Forum* 64(3): 215–222 (2000).

Edwards, J.-A., Hartnell, M., and Martin, R. "Interactive Whiteboards: Some Lessons from the Classroom." *Micromath* 18(2): 30–33 (2002).

Fischer, P. "Wow! Kindergarten/First-Grade Inquiry." *Primary Voices K-6* 10(3): 9–15 (2002).

Gauthier, L. R. "The Role of Questioning: Beyond Comprehension's Front Door." *Reading Horizons* 40(4): 239–252 (2000).

Hamm, M., and Adams, D. "Collaborative Inquiry: Working Toward Shared Goals." *Kappa Delta Pi Record* 38(3): 115–118 (2002).

Harpaz, Y., and Lefstein, A. "Communities of Thinking." *Educational Leadership* 58(3): 54–57 (2000).

Harris, R. L. "Batting 1,000: Questioning Techniques in Student-Centered Classrooms." *Clearing House* 74(1): 25–26 (2000).

Koufetta-Menicou, C., and Scaife, J. "Teachers' Questions—Types and Significance in Science Education." *School Science Review* 81(296): 79–84 (2000).

Newton, L. D. "Questions That Help Children Understanding Elementary Science." *Investigating* 18(2): 6–9 (2002).

Roberts, T. "Learn to Care, Care to Learn." *Educational Leadership* 60(1): 45–48 (2002).

Schielack, J. F., Chancellor, D., and Childs, K. M. "Designing Questions to Encourage Children's Mathematical Thinking." *Teaching Children Mathematics* 6(6): 398–402 (2000).

Shaunessy, E. "Questioning Techniques in the Gifted Classroom." *Gifted Child Today Magazine* 23(5): 14–21 (2000).

Simon, K. G. "The Blue Blood Is Bad, Right?" *Educational Leadership* 60(1): 24–28 (2002).

Tower, C. "Questions That Matter: Preparing Elementary Students for the Inquiry Process." *The Reading Teacher* 53(7): 550–557 (2000).

Whitehead, D. "'The Story Means More to Me Now': Teaching Thinking Through Guided Reading." *Reading: Literacy and Language* 36(1): 33–37 (2002).

Wilen, W. W. "Exploring Myths About Teaching Questioning in the Social Studies Classroom." *Social Studies* 92(1): 26–32 (2001).

INTASC Principles	PRAXIS III Domains	NBPTS Standards
• The teacher uses an understanding of individual and group motivation and behavior to create a learning environment that encourages positive social interaction, active engagement in learning, and self-motivation (Principle 5) • The teacher uses knowledge of effective verbal, nonverbal, and media communication techniques to foster active inquiry, collaboration, and supportive interaction in the classroom (Principle 6)	• Creating an Environment for Student Learning (Domain B)	• Learning Environment

Imagine yourself as the parent of a child about to enter elementary school. Your child will be placed in the care of an adult—your child's teacher—for approximately 5 hours each day for about 180 days each year for the next 6 or 7 years. As a parent, will you be concerned about how those teachers manage the affairs of the classrooms to which your child has been assigned? The question, of course, answers itself. You would be deeply concerned because you know that how those teachers manage their classrooms has a great deal to do with how well your child will succeed in school.

But if you are a thoughtful, caring parent, your concern will go far beyond the academic success of your child. The classrooms will doubtless have rules. If your child violates one or more of those rules, what will be the consequences? Will the teachers punish your child? How heavily will those teachers rely on punishment as a deterrent to rule infractions? Will teachers reward "good" behavior? What do those teachers perceive as "good" behavior? What system of rewards will teachers use? Do you want your child to grow up learning that one should behave properly to avoid punishment, or to get some kind of reward for good behavior? Or do you want your child to learn that one conducts oneself appropriately and responsibly because "it's the proper thing to do"? As an elementary school teacher, you can be sure that the parents and guardians of the children in your classroom will be asking themselves many of these same questions.

Managing the classroom learning environment involves much more than establishing and maintaining orderly student behavior. The classroom is really a laboratory where young human beings are shaped and socialized in accordance with the established values and mores of the community and the larger society. What happens in those elementary school classrooms for the 6 or 7 or more years that children spend in them has a great deal to do with how they will feel about themselves for years to come. A person's concept of self plays a major role in the success of that person in all aspects of life. In other words, from the dynamics of classroom living and learning, children receive many messages, both overt and covert, that help them

---

Children come to school needing to know that
• I am accepted and acceptable here just as I am.
• I am safe here—physically, emotionally, and intellectually.
• People here care about me.
• People here listen to me.
• People know how I'm doing, and it matters to them that I do well.
• People acknowledge my interests and perspectives and act upon them.

—Carol Ann Tomlinson

Source: C. A. Tomlinson, "Invitations to Learn," *Educational Leadership* 60(1): 8 (September 2002).

form images of themselves, which in turn relate directly to their school success, their social competence, and their becoming responsible, caring, problem-solving and decision-making adults. It is the purpose of this chapter to help you begin deciding how you will manage your classroom learning environment.

ANTICIPATED OUTCOMES

After completing this chapter, you should be able to do the following:

1. Describe the meaning of a *values-based management plan*.
2. Describe the contributions of leading experts regarding classroom management.
3. Describe the characteristics of a well-managed classroom learning environment.
4. Differentiate with examples between classroom procedures that are flexible and those that are inflexible.
5. Distinguish among classroom *control*, classroom *discipline*, and classroom *management*.
6. Describe characteristics of a safe, supportive, and effective classroom learning environment.
7. Distinguish between a classroom learning environment that is supportive and psychologically safe for children and one that is not.
8. Describe the advantages and disadvantages of studying children's school records to discover which ones have a history of causing trouble in the classroom.
9. With respect to classroom management, distinguish between the concepts of "consequences" and "punishment," and between "rules" and "procedures."
10. Describe specific things you can do if you want your students to develop their self-control.
11. Describe a teacher's reasonable first reaction to each of the following children: one who is aggressively violent; one who habitually lies; one who is defiant; one who tosses paper at the wastebasket; one who is sitting and doing nothing.
12. Describe steps you should take in dealing with conflict situations between children.
13. Describe steps you should take in preparing for the first few days of school.
14. Describe the meaning of and give an example of *sequenced consequences* as used for inappropriate student behavior.
15. Explain the value of using a classroom daily schedule.
16. Describe with examples how the physical arrangements of a classroom can affect learning.
17. Describe the characteristics of an effective transition.
18. Prepare the first draft of your classroom management system.

A VALUES-BASED MANAGEMENT PLAN

It should be clear from this chapter's introduction that because we live in a democratic society the foundation for your classroom management system must be a set of values consistent with such a society. There may be variation because of local community norms, but fundamentally, we are talking about a management plan based on such values as *accepting responsibility, sense of fair play, honesty,* and *respect for the rights, opinions, and possessions of others.*

As a teacher, your management system is the source of much of what children learn in school through the covert curriculum. If there are constant conflicts between children, if a general atmosphere of hostility prevails, if class morale is low, you need then to analyze the values that give direction to the management system. You also need to understand the sources of students' behavior and to reflect on your own behavior in the classroom. More often than not children inadvertently model the behaviors of the significant adults in their lives. Among the most significant adults in the life of any child are that child's parents or guardians and older family members and the child's schoolteacher.

A CLARIFICATION OF TERMS

The term *control* implies restraint, regulation, regimentation, and the direct use of power. "You have good control" is usually regarded as a compliment to a beginning teacher. One is never sure whether the meaning is intended in the broad sense (covering the larger umbrella of classroom management) or in the literal sense (meaning student behavior is so restrained that the classroom is teacher dominated). Used literally, the term *control* can easily be given unwarranted importance, becoming an end in itself rather than a means of enhancing the quality of living and learning in the classroom.

Control should not be thought of as a goal of teaching—nor should management, for that matter. You should perceive these as processes that are prerequisite for an environment conducive to teaching and learning. A negative example is a third-grade teacher who has "perfect control" of a class: the class is quiet, individuals are immobile, no one speaks out of turn, and so on. To achieve this calm, the teacher has children doing relatively meaningless busywork at their seats while she attends to other matters. These other matters may have to do with preparing lessons and materials, teaching small groups or individuals, or taking care of business relating to student accounting, reporting, or the lunch program. To achieve this level of restraint, the teacher does indeed need to control most of the physical and intellectual activities in the classroom. One must, of course, ask whether these kinds of training procedures, common to prisons and army boot training, are appropriate for the 21st-century elementary school classroom and life in a democratic society.

An objectionable aspect of the control concept is the implication that teachers are wholly responsible for maintaining orderly classrooms. This runs counter to the idea that children need to learn responsible habits of self-direction. Some of the specific strategies developed to strengthen classroom control and discipline have stressed the importance of *reducing* the reliance on power and controls imposed externally and have, instead, focused on student responsibility and student involvement. Children need to learn to control their own behavior, not to please you, the teacher, but because, in so doing, they develop greater maturity and independence. Of course, children cannot manage to do this alone. Left unguided, they are likely to become unruly and mischievous. Learning to take care of oneself should be an important outcome of the school experience. It is not likely to be achieved if you constantly control your learners' behavior. In the words of Good and Brophy,

> Teachers who approach classroom management as a process of establishing and maintaining effective learning environments tend to be more successful than teachers who place more emphasis on their roles as authority figures or disciplinarians. Teachers *are* authority figures and need to require their students to conform to certain rules and procedures. However, these rules and procedures are not ends in themselves but are means for organizing the classroom to support teaching and learning. Thus, classroom management should be designed to support instruction and to help students to gain in capacity for self-control.[1]

The term *discipline*, like *control*, may be used to mean various aspects of the larger umbrella of classroom management. "She has good discipline" usually means that the teacher maintains an orderly classroom. Discipline also connotes punishment. "Strong discipline" is used to describe teacher behavior that is rigid, firm, and unbending. There is an adversary quality to this meaning of *discipline*. When teachers say, "Anyone who gets out of their seat without permission will be disciplined," they mean that offenders will be punished. In this sense, discipline means both punishment and corrective treatment.

The modern concept of discipline is as an *intelligent behavior,* that is, in this instance, as an imposition of control on oneself to develop character, efficient work habits, proper conduct, consideration for others, orderly living, or control of one's impulses and emotions. The establishment of student *self-control* is the ultimate objective. But to develop self-control, learners must be given some independence, and the process of experimenting with such independence requires the teacher's guidance. Neither highly structured, teacher-dominated environments nor those that are completely permissive facilitate developing self-control.

Various specific approaches have been developed to help teachers understand and deal with managing student behavior and the classroom learning environment. Using the descriptors associated with them, among the best known approaches are *assertive discipline, behavior modification, control theory, logical consequences,* and *self-discipline*. Other than the brief discussion that follows, in-depth analysis of the merits and limitations of each approach is beyond the scope of this book; sources are available to those who wish to learn more about them. As a part of your professional preparation you may even be required to take a course that deals specifically with classroom management.

Used interchangeably, the terms *classroom climate, classroom environment,* and *classroom atmosphere* refer to the emotional tone and quality of the interpersonal relations that prevail. Classroom climate results from a composite of the interactions and transactions that take place in the classroom and may be described variously as relaxed, pleasant, flexible, rigid, autocratic, democratic, repressive, supportive, and so forth. Consequently, the nature of the climate of a particular classroom is cognate to the teacher's management system.

Children must be willing to cooperate with their teacher or else the teacher's management system will fail. Without their willing cooperation, an adversarial relationship develops between children and teacher. When this happens, the classroom climate becomes so tense that even the smallest issue can, and often does, become the cause of a major confrontation. If such relationships continue, the teacher becomes ineffective and will probably be forced to leave.

A teacher's procedures for classroom control reflect that teacher's philosophy about how children learn and the teacher's interpretation and commitment to the school's stated mission. In sum, those procedures represent the teacher's concept of *classroom management*. Although often eclectic in their approaches, today's teachers share a concern for selecting management techniques that enhance student self-esteem and that help children learn how to assume control of their behavior and ownership of their learning.

Effective classroom management is not a goal to achieve but a plan you have carefully thought out and skillfully implemented. That plan consists of a system of procedures and conditions that enable you and your students to attain valid educational goals and objectives. It has to do with the atmosphere of the classroom, daily procedures and routines, the deployment of students, the setting of standards of conduct, and the system of rewards and punishments that prevails. Good managers are not always good teachers, but inability to manage a classroom learning environment in ways that facilitate learning is usually a "fatal flaw" to your success as a teacher. Thus, our discussion of classroom management focuses your attention on that cluster of skills needed to plan, organize, and implement an appropriate program of instruction.

There can be little doubt that your skill in classroom management will be a major factor contributing to your teaching success. In student-teaching supervisory conferences more time is spent on classroom management than on anything else. Classroom management is the one aspect of a teacher's credentials that principals are most interested in. After all, most school administrators are probably aware that an analysis of 50 years of research studies concluded that classroom management is the single most important factor to influence student learning.[2] It is the one part of a teacher's behavior that parents and guardians are most concerned about. When a teacher is in difficulty on the job, the chances are that the problem can be traced to either (1) poor decisions the teacher made relating to classroom management, (2) inadequate attention to the preactive phase of instruction, or both. Both are related to planning. In other words, poor planning of either classroom management or of instruction is a precursor to ineffective teaching.

It is clear that management and instruction are two sides of the same coin we call teaching. Successful teaching cannot take place without both of these elements. The interaction of these two components of teaching means also that they affect each other. Skillful management facilitates the conduct of instruction. Inspired and interesting instruction reduces the likelihood of management problems.

Classroom Management: Contributions of Leading Experts

You are probably familiar with the term *behavior modification*, which describes several high-control techniques for changing behavior in an observable and predictable way; with B. F. Skinner's (1904–1990) ideas about how students learn and how behavior can be modified by using reinforcers (rewards); and with how his principles of behavior shaping have been extended by others.[3]

Behavior modification begins with four steps: (a) identify the behavior to be modified; (b) record how often and under what conditions that behavior occurs: (c) cause a change by reinforcing a desired behavior with a positive reinforcer (a reward); (d) choose the type of positive reinforcers to award— *activity or privilege reinforcers*, such as choice of playing a game, running the projection equipment for the teacher, caring for a classroom pet, decorating the classroom, choice at a classroom learning center, freed without penalty from doing an assignment or test, running an errand for the teacher; *social reinforcers*, such as verbal attention or private praise, and nonverbal such as proximity of teacher to student, and facial (such as a wink) or bodily expressions (such as a handshake or pat on the back) of approval; *graphic reinforcers*, such as numerals and symbols such as those made by rubber stamps; *tangible reinforcers*, such as candy and other edibles, badges, certificates, stickers, books; or *token reinforcers*, such as points, stars, or script or tickets that can be accumulated and cashed in later for a tangible reinforcer, such as a trip to the pizza parlor or ice cream store with the teacher.

Using an approach that emphasizes both reinforcement for appropriate behaviors and punishment or consequences for inappropriate behaviors, Lee Canter and Marlene Canter developed their *assertive discipline* model that emphasizes four major points. First, as a teacher, you have professional rights in your classroom and should expect appropriate student behavior. Second, your students have rights to choose how to behave in your classroom, and you should plan limits for inappropriate behavior. Third, an assertive discipline approach means you clearly state your expectations in a firm voice and explain the boundaries for behavior. And fourth, you should plan a system of positive consequences (e.g., positive messages home; awards and rewards; special privileges) for appropriate behavior, establish consequences (e.g., time out; withdrawal of privileges; parent/guardian conference) for inappropriate student misbehavior, and follow through in a consistent way.[4]

In his *logical consequences* approach, Rudolf Dreikurs (1897–1972) emphasized six points. First, be fair, firm, and friendly, and involve your students in developing and implementing class rules. Second, students need to clearly understand the rules and the logical consequences for misbehavior. For example, a logical consequence for a student who has painted graffiti on a school wall would be to either clean the wall or pay for a school custodian to do it. Third, allow the students to be responsible not only for their own actions but also for influencing others to maintain appropriate behavior in your classroom. Fourth, encourage students to show respect for themselves and for others, and provide each student with a sense of belonging to the classroom. Fifth, recognize and encourage student goals of belonging, gaining status, and gaining recognition. And sixth, recognize but not reinforce correlated student goals of getting attention, seeking power, and taking revenge.[5]

Continuing the work of Dreikurs, Linda Albert has developed a *cooperative discipline* model. The cooperative discipline model makes use of Dreikurs' fundamental concepts, with emphasis added on "three C's": capable, connect, and contribute.[6] Building upon the work of Dreikurs, Jane Nelsen provides guidelines for helping children develop positive feelings of self. Key points made by Nelsen are (a) use natural and logical consequences as a means to inspire a positive classroom atmosphere, (b) understand that children have goals that drive them toward misbehavior (attention, power, revenge, and assumed adequacy), (c) use kindness (student retains dignity) and firmness when administering consequences for a student's misbehavior, (d) establish a climate of mutual respect, (e) use class meetings to give students ownership in problem solving, and (f) offer encouragement as a means of inspiring self-evaluation and focusing on the student's behaviors.[7]

William Glasser developed his concept of *reality therapy* (i.e., the condition of the present, rather than of the past, contributes to inappropriate behavior) for the classroom. Glasser emphasizes that students have a responsibility to learn at school and to maintain appropriate behavior while there. He stresses that with the teacher's help, students can make appropriate choices about their behavior in school—can, in fact, learn self-control.[8] Finally, he suggests holding classroom meetings that are devoted to establishing class rules, identifying standards for student behavior, matters of misbehavior, and the consequences of misbehavior. In recent years, Glasser has expanded his message to include the student needs of belonging and love, control, freedom, and fun, asserting that if these needs are ignored and unattended at school, students are bound to fail.[9]

Today's commitment to *quality education* is largely derived from the recent work of Glasser and the corresponding concept of the *person-centered classroom* as advanced by Carl Rogers and H. Jerome Freiberg in their book

Freedom to Learn (Columbus, OH: Merrill, 1994). In schools committed to quality education and the person-centered classroom, students feel a sense of belonging, enjoy some degree of power of self-discipline, have fun learning, and experience a sense of freedom in the process.[10]

Paul Gathercoal built his *judicious discipline* model on a synthesis of professional ethics, good educational practice, and democratic principles and students' constitutional rights as outlined especially in the 1st, 4th, and 14th Amendments to the U.S. Constitution. By allowing students opportunity to experience individual freedoms and encouraging them to learn and practice the responsibilities emanating from their individual rights, students learn how to govern themselves.[11]

Haim G. Ginott (1922–1973), in his *communication model*, emphasized ways for teacher and student to communicate. He advised a teacher's sending a clear message (or messages) about situations rather than about the child. And, as we have emphasized in Chapter 2 of this book, he emphasized that teachers must model the behavior they expect from students.[12] Ginott's suggested messages are those that express feelings appropriately, acknowledge students' feelings, give appropriate direction, and invite cooperation.

Thomas Gordon emphasizes influence over control and decries use of reinforcement (i.e., rewards and punishment) as ineffective tools for achieving a positive influence over a child's behavior.[13] Rather than using reinforcements for appropriate behavior and punishment for inappropriate behaviors, Gordon advocates encouragement and development of student self-control and self-regulated behavior. To have a positive influence and to encourage self-control the teacher (and school) should provide a rich and positive learning environment, with rich and stimulating learning activities. Specific teacher behaviors include active listening, sending I-messages (rather than you-messages), shifting from I-messages to listening when there is student resistance to an I-message, clearly identifying ownership of problems to the student when such is the case (i.e., not assuming ownership if it is a student's problem), and encouraging collaborative problem solving.

Fredric Jones also promotes the idea of helping students support their own self-control, essentially, however, by way of a negative reinforcement method—rewards follow good behavior.[14] Preferred activity time (PAT), for example, is an invention derived from the Jones Model. The Jones Model makes four recommendations. First, you should properly structure your classroom so students understand the *rules* (the expectation standards for classroom behavior) and *procedures* (the means for accomplishing routine tasks). Second, you maintain control by selecting appropriate instructional strategies. Third, you build patterns of cooperative work. Finally, you develop appropriate backup methods for dealing with inappropriate student behavior.

Jacob Kounin is well known for his identification of the *ripple effect* (i.e., the effect of a teacher's response to one student's misbehavior on students whose behavior was appropriate) and of *withitness* and *overlapping ability* (discussed in Chapter 2).

CHARACTERISTICS OF EFFECTIVE CLASSROOM MANAGEMENT

Let us make this point absolutely clear: Thoughtful and thorough planning of your procedures for managing your classroom learning environment is as important a part of your preactive phase of instruction (discussed in Chapter 2) as is the preparation of units and lessons (discussed in Chapter 6). Through planning, you can anticipate and prevent problems. Let us now consider some of the characteristics of effective management: Effective management of the classroom learning environment

1. Enhances children's mental and social development.
2. Facilitates the achievement of instructional goals that suit children's developmental levels.
3. Provides intellectual and physical freedom within specified and reasonable limits.
4. Establishes procedures and consequences.
5. Allows children to develop skills of self-direction and independence.
6. Works toward a warm but firm relationship between teacher and children.

Enhancing Mental and Social Development

Establishing "control" of a class, in the sense of the teacher's ability to wield power over children, should not be much of a problem for you as an adult. You can create a situation in which you have absolute control over everything that takes place in the room. You may do this by using threats of low grades and failure, ridicule, punishment, and rigid rules and by keeping student activity controlled to the point where children cannot move or talk without permission. This may be justified on the grounds that it is the only way you can maintain order and therefore conduct instruction. But these repressive tactics can be detrimental to the mental and social development of young children. Children may conform to classroom rules, but if they have not had the rationale for the rules explained, or if they do not understand the rationale for the rules, they will resent having to obey them.

It is well known that a positive self-concept is not only important to learning but also vital to an individual's total development.[15] In the type of distrustful setting just described, children are not likely to develop positive self-images. Moreover, the pressures that build up in some children as the result of a repressive authoritarian atmosphere in school erupt, either in or outside school, in various forms of aggression, tears, withdrawal, bedwetting, nail biting, or other more serious forms of maladaptive behavior. One cannot build a positive sense of self in an atmosphere of constant negativity.

The elementary school should be a laboratory for the social growth of children. Here, children learn to give and take, to share with others, to interact with peers, and to develop a degree of responsible independence. Children learn social skills partly through instruction but mainly by having opportunities to participate with others in social situations. Programs that have children working

The joy of teaching is never more real than when children express enthusiasm and exuberance in wanting to participate in the work of the class. A well-planned and interesting instructional program is the teacher's first line of defense against student disruptive behavior and other classroom management problems.

continually on an individual basis do not provide adequately for the social dimension of their learning. One can learn social skills only in social settings.

Good management reflects itself in a classroom where children are comfortable intellectually, emotionally, and socially. Your students will recognize and respect you as an authority figure but will not fear you or perceive you as a constant threat to their self-confidence. Your classroom is a confidence-building place where children grow in their competence as human beings.

FACILITATING THE ACHIEVEMENT OF INSTRUCTIONAL GOALS

Mr. Campbell is working with a group of eight third-graders on phonetic skills in a reading lesson. Meanwhile, the remaining 20 children are moving about the room, talking loudly; occasionally, there is an altercation that necessitates Mr. Campbell's intervention. The noise level is high. The children in the reading group often ask to have things repeated because they cannot hear or are not paying attention to what is being said.

This is a serious matter because the student behavior resulting from Mr. Campbell's poor management is interfering with his instructional program. Phonetic analysis depends on fine sound discrimination; children therefore must be able to hear those sounds. This is difficult, perhaps even impossible, in the situation described. Moreover, Mr. Campbell himself cannot attend properly to the lesson because of the commotion in the room. Also, the children not in the reading group are reinforcing behavior patterns that contribute neither to good study habits nor to social skills.

To establish conditions that make it possible to conduct instruction, you must develop a systematic method of organizing classroom activities. You need to steer a course somewhere between Mr. Campbell's lack of organization and the other end of the continuum, characterized by rigidity and teacher domination. For most classrooms, you will need a schedule of daily events. These will probably not vary much from day to day. Children like this. They like to know when each of their classes is to take place. They know when there is to be quiet time and when there is activity time. This type of flexible but planned organization of the day makes it possible for you to do your job and for the children to do theirs, so that instructional goals can be achieved.

Developmental differences in children require that you select age-appropriate learning goals and presentation modes. Young children need considerably more personal teacher interaction than do older ones. Learning objectives for younger children need to be quite explicit, and you must closely monitor their work so that you can adjust it for level of difficulty.

Providing Boundaries of Intellectual and Physical Freedom

If children grew up knowing the subject matter and skills of the curriculum and were completely socialized, well mannered, and well behaved, there would be no point in sending them to school. The object of school is precisely to teach children such subject matter and skills. For children to learn them, however, they need to be in a secure environment where they can be free to try to do new things. Not only that, they should feel encouraged to do so without having to fear or be embarrassed by making mistakes.

Although children should be as free as possible to explore intellectually and should enjoy a great deal of physical freedom as well, they need also to learn that no one is totally free. There are rules, regulations, procedures, and consequences that apply in every classroom, no matter what your personal philosophy. For example, you cannot and must not allow children to do things that injure others, that are inhumane, that are disrespectful of others, or that destroy the property of others. Such behavior is simply not permitted.

When teachers have no classroom rules or fail to make them explicit, one can predict that they will have a stormy time of it. When there are no rules, no one knows what is expected. Children may run wild and in the process may injure themselves or each other. Even with explicit rules, children will test their outer edges. They seem to need to search out the limits of freedom, within which they then know they must function. When you make your procedures known, this testing will be more focused. Where rules and expected procedures are unknown, testing takes the form of trial and error—to find out your level of tolerance.

You must teach procedures and behavior expectations on a continuing basis. From time to time children need to be reminded of *why* room procedures were established in the first place. Encourage them to contribute their own ideas about how the classroom management system is working and how it might be improved. They need to be involved in classroom management to some extent in order to have some sense of investment in what goes on.

Thinking in Terms of Procedures Rather Than Rules; Consequences Rather Than Punishment

To encourage a constructive and supportive classroom environment, you may wish to think and speak in terms of "procedures" (or "standards and guidelines")[16] rather than of "rules," and of "consequences" rather than "punishment." The reason is this: When working with a cohort of children, some rules are of course necessary, but to many people, the term *rules* has a more negative connotation than does the term *procedures*. For example, a classroom rule might be, "When one person is talking we do not interrupt until that person is finished." When that rule is broken, rather than reminding children of the "rule," you may change the emphasis to a "procedure" simply by reminding students by asking, "What is our procedure (or expectation) when someone is talking?"

It is the contention of some educators that thinking in terms of and talking about "procedures" and "consequences" are more likely to contribute to a positive classroom atmosphere than referring to "rules" and "punishment." Of course, some argue that you might as well tell it like it is. Especially if your group of students is linguistically and culturally mixed, you will need to be as direct and clear as possible to avoid sending confusing or mixed signals. But remember this: As a credentialed classroom teacher you are a professional, which means that, as always, after considering what experienced others have to say, the final decision is only one of many that you must make, and that it will be influenced by your own thinking and unique situation.

Developing Skills of Self-Direction and Responsible Involvement

It is a curious fact that teachers often expect children to develop self-direction and independence without permitting them to practice the necessary skills. That seems rather like teaching them the alphabet without ever letting them put letters together to form words. Children are not likely to gain self-direction and independence in classrooms that are almost wholly teacher directed and teacher dependent. What is needed is a good balance: Provide sufficient guidance and direction on the one hand, and allow children to experiment with independence and self-direction on the other. The tendency is to be either too highly teacher directed or overly permissive. Neither provides an appropriate setting for learning.

Children should be active participants in some aspects of classroom management, thereby gaining practical experience in contributing to policy and decision-making. Such involvement *empowers* children, giving them a sense of invested ownership of the classroom. Insofar as possible, you should encourage students to feel that it is not only your room but their room as well. However, as the most mature person in the classroom and the person with the legal responsibility, you are accountable for providing the leadership and guidance to make the operation safe and effectively functional.

Working Toward Warm Human Relations

Sometimes beginning teachers, especially with older children, believe they can develop a close "buddy" relationship between the children and themselves. They encourage informality by allowing students to call them by their first name or even a nickname. Teachers who attempt to assume somewhat of a peer relationship with children remove social distance. This rarely works well; it usually means that teaching authority is compromised in the process.

At the other extreme are teachers who feel they must not "get too close," who talk in a stilted way and who cannot relax because they feel that if they did, children might take advantage of them. Remaining rather cold and distant, they are careful not to reveal much of the informal aspects of their personality.

Good teachers extend their warmth and "humanness" to children. They work with children in ways that show they enjoy young people. At the same time, they maintain the basic firmness that children need, expect, and indeed, *want*.

SERIOUSNESS OF PROBLEMS

Described next in order of increasing seriousness are categories of student misbehavior that teachers sometimes have to contend with. *Now* is the time in your career for you to begin thinking about how you will deal with such problems when they arise. Note that we didn't say "if they arise," but rather "when they arise." For no teacher, no matter how good or experienced, is exempt from these possibilities.

Goofing Off

This least-serious category includes student behaviors such as fooling around, not doing assigned tasks, daydreaming, and just generally being off task. Fortunately, in most instances, this type of behavior is momentary, and sometimes it might even be best if you pretend briefly to be unaware of it; if it persists, all it may take to get children back on task is unobtrusive (silent and private) redirection. Unobtrusive teacher behaviors include eye contact and mobility and proximity control, such as moving and standing next to children who are off task. If this doesn't work, then go to the second intervention level by rather quietly calling students by name and reminding them of the correct procedure or of what they are supposed to be doing.

Avoid asking an off-task child any question, such as a content question, knowing full well that the student is not paying attention, or asking the question, "Serena, why are you doing that?" Avoid also making a threat such as "Serena, if you don't turn around and get to work I will send you to Ms. Johnson's room for a time out." It is important you not make "mountains out of molehills," or you could cause more problems than you would resolve. Maintain Serena's focus on the lesson, that is, on the desired behavior, rather than on her off-task behavior.[17]

Examples of trivial "misbehaviors" that you need not worry about unless they become disruptive are brief whispering during a lesson and short periods of inattentiveness, perhaps accompanied by visual wandering or daydreaming. Your responses to student behavior and enforcement of procedures such as raising hands and being recognized before speaking will naturally vary depending on a number of factors, such as the particular learning activity and students' age levels (see "Guidelines for Practicing Gender Equity When Questioning" in Chapter 3).

In addition, there is sometimes a tendency among teachers when they have a problem with students goofing off and being disruptive to assume, or to act like they believe, that the entire group is being unruly, when more often it is only one, two, or three students. You must avoid giving children any impression that you believe that they all are being unruly. You may treat the group as if they all are "guilty" in an attempt to get group peer pressure to work in your favor; in fact, however, it is more likely to alienate the majority of children who are behaving properly.

Disruptions to Learning

This category includes talking out of turn, getting out of seat without permission, clowning, and tossing objects, behaviors that are more serious because they disrupt others' learning. In handling these common disruptive misbehaviors, it is important that you have explained their consequences to students, and then, following your stated procedures, promptly and consistently deal with violations. Usually a simple nonverbal reminder to disruptive children to return to the educational task at hand will suffice. Too many beginning teachers tend to ignore these class disruptions seemingly in hope that they will stop if they don't acknowledge them. You must not ignore minor infractions of this type, for if you do, they most likely will escalate beyond your worst expectations. In other words, maintain your control of classroom events, rather than become controlled by them.

Defiance, Cheating, Lying, and Stealing

When a student refuses, perhaps with hostility, to do what you say, such defiance might be worthy of temporary or permanent removal from the class. Depending on how serious you judge the situation to be you may simply give the student a time out, such as by sending the child to a nearby classroom (be sure to prearrange such moves with the teacher involved), or you may suspend the student from class until you can hold a conference about the situation, perhaps involving you, the student, the student's parent or guardian, and a school official.

Any cheating, lying, or stealing may be an isolated act, and the child may only need a one-on-one talk to find out what precipitated the incident and what might be done to prevent it ever happening again. A student who *habitually* exhibits any of these behaviors may need to be referred to a specialist. Whenever you have reason to suspect such behavior, you should follow school policy and you should discuss your concerns with appropriate colleagues or a school counselor or psychologist.

Violence

As emphasized in Chapter 1, more and more often today, even in kindergarten, teachers are confronted with major problems of misbehavior that have ramifications beyond the classroom or that begin elsewhere and spill over into the classroom. If you experience any acts of written, verbal, or overt violence, do not hesitate to ask for help. As a teacher, you must stay alert.

Activity 4.1: Shouldn't Punishment Fit the Crime?

During a physical education lesson, several of the 22 fifth-graders who made up the class were goofing around by chasing each other, punching in jest, playing leap frog, and generally ignoring the physical education teacher, who was trying to teach a lesson in basketball. Giving up trying to obtain their attention, the teacher sent for the school principal to come and assist in regaining control of the group. The principal came out to the play area and immediately ordered all 22 children into a classroom. There, as punishment, all 22 children were assigned pages to hand copy from an encyclopedia.

1. What was your first reaction on reading this case?

2. Do you believe the physical education teacher should have done something different? If so, what?

3. Do you believe the principal should have done something different? If so, what?

4. Is there ever a time when an entire class of children should be punished for the misbehavior of some of the children? Explain your answer.

5. How would you react were you the parent or guardian of one of the children who was not goofing off but who nevertheless was punished with the others?

6. Do you believe that assigning writing is ever appropriate as punishment?

CONFLICT RESOLUTION

Jason is waiting in line at the drinking fountain when Eric approaches and tries to nudge his way ahead of him. Jason tries to close the gap with his body; Eric pushes him out of the way. Jason pushes back; Eric strikes him—and the altercation has escalated into a full-blown fight. A teacher is called. The boys are separated, perhaps led off to the principal's office, and some attempt is made to resolve the matter. It may be that the issue is settled at that point or that the conflict continues, perhaps resulting in an after-school fight on the way home.

Incidents involving two children or groups of children are fairly common in schools and are usually unpleasant for all concerned. Because dominance relationships are so widespread throughout nature, including among human beings, there is really no way to avoid conflict entirely. There is rarely a social relationship in which conflict is wholly absent. This applies whether we consider national and international issues or examine social relationships on a face-to-face basis within families, in neighborhoods, or on the school playground.

You can be prepared to deal with conflict situations in the following ways: (1) establish classroom conditions that minimize the possibility of conflict and that encourage harmonious social relations; (2) resolve interpersonal conflicts immediately, but plan for longer-range solutions to problems; and (3) include instruction on conflict and conflict resolution. We discuss each briefly in the following sections.

Minimizing Conflict and Encouraging Harmonious Social Relations

Why are some classrooms characterized by a higher degree of hostility and aggression than others? To answer this question, we must examine the conditions within classrooms that give rise to such behavior.

Perhaps the most powerful force affecting classroom climate is the nature of the statements made by the teacher. A preponderance of negative and directive teacher statements will elevate the levels of tension and hostility in a classroom. This result is predictable, having been demonstrated in human-relations laboratories hundreds of times. One of the most effective ways for you to reduce hostility and aggression in groups is to increase the number of positive, constructive statements you make and to eliminate those that are negative, directive, and critical.

Hostility and aggression also escalate when children are under great pressure to work rapidly or when they are required to do more than they are able to in the time provided. We may generalize: *Any procedure that continually frustrates children is likely to reflect itself in aggression and conflict.* Those who cannot perform satisfactorily under tension-producing conditions are likely to turn on others to vent their hostilities. A conflict on the playground may be the result of frustrations built up in the classroom. A more comfortable and relaxed instructional pace, coupled with realistically achievable requirements, can go a long way in reducing the possibility of interpersonal conflicts.

Your classroom atmosphere can be more conducive to improved human relations if competitive situations are kept in proper perspective. Competition can be wholesome to the productive output of a group, provided it does not get out of hand. Children need to engage in fair competition and to learn the appropriate behavior associated with winning and losing. When children engage in competitive sports and games, the meaning of good sportsmanship is one of the important lessons they should learn. Good sportsmanship is part of the American tradition. The classroom, of course, is not a sports arena, but it can be a place where competitiveness is handled with an attitude of fairness and goodwill. When classroom competition becomes intense, with some students rudely flaunting their superiority, there is likely to be hostility leading to conflict. Cooperative group efforts by the class can do much to reduce the ill effects of competition and can teach children the values associated with consideration for others.

Resolving Conflicts Immediately, with a Plan for Longer-Range Solutions

You must intervene immediately when conflicts occur between individual children or between groups of children. Intervention may take care of a problem for the moment, but you also should undertake some type of longer-range corrective measures. A teacher who stops a fight in the lunchroom may be treating the symptoms rather than the causes of conflict. Very often, the intervening teacher begins by asking who is responsible. Of course, the children blame each other ("She hit me first," says one; "But she started it by swiping the ball," says the other). After some discussion, the children apologize to each other and shake hands, and the matter seems to be settled. When there have been hurt feelings, however, this is not a satisfactory settlement of the issue. It does little good to force an apology from a youngster or to have children shake hands unless you do something about the conditions that brought about the conflict in the first place. Exploring the conflict will often show that both children are contending for something of value, whether it is approval by classmates, peer leadership roles, positions on athletic teams, or the favor of a high-status classmate.

Providing Instruction on Conflict and Conflict Resolution

Traditionally, much of the work with conflict in the elementary school might be described as little more than moral injunctions against conflict. "Good" children do not fight, quarrel, or bully others. They show proper respect and consideration for others. They are kind to each other. They are admonished to "turn the other cheek" rather than to strike back at someone who has offended them. Although there may be some need for this kind of instruction at early levels, overall these approaches have not proved to be effective strategies for dealing with conflict. Some children and adults continue to fight, quarrel, and bully each other; they do not show respect and consideration for others—in spite of valiant efforts by the home, church, and school. We still read about ill-tempered persons who hurt or even kill others as a result of conflicts over trivial matters. The hours each week that American children spend watching television undoubtedly add little to their desire or ability to resolve conflicts rationally.

The "law of the gun" associated with life on the frontier of the Old West has become the method of choice to resolve conflicts in modern America. Dueling was outlawed as a way of settling disputes many years ago, but people in this country continue to shoot each other at an alarming rate. The frightening fact is the young age of many of the victims and perpetrators of violent acts.

One would have to conclude that powerful forces in society are causing monumental frustrations, hostility, and anger among people. Doubtless, much of this is poverty and drug related. We are not likely to see many positive changes until the societal conditions that cause the problems are adequately addressed. The physical safety of your students must be one of your priorities, as the safety of all in the school must be a schoolwide priority. Figure 4.1 presents Internet resources for maintaining school safety.

Instruction in conflict resolution involves three important elements. The first is identifying all the *facts* of the case: Who did what to whom, when, how many times, with what consequences? The second is identifying the *issues* involved: Why is there a problem? What is the source of the conflict? How and why are the facts perceived and interpreted differently? The third is defining all *possible decisions* that can be made regarding a resolution of the situation, along with the ensuing consequences of each decision. By using this model to study cases of conflict, children will learn that usually one party is not wholly wrong and the other wholly right; issues often involve value choices among options, more than one of which may be acceptable. Applying this model to the study of conflict resolution, you may devise cases, relying on children's real-life conflict experiences. Simulation games and role-playing are particularly well suited to instruction in conflict resolution.

FIGURE 4.1
Internet resources for safe schools

- Center for the Study and Prevention of Violence, http://www.colorado.edu/cspv
- National Alliance for Safe Schools, http://www.safeschools.org
- Safe Schools Coalition, http://www.thesafeschools.org
- The Safetyzone, http://www.safetyzone.org

ORGANIZATIONAL ASPECTS OF CLASSROOM MANAGEMENT

The way you organize your classroom will not, of course, eliminate management problems. But your choices can move you a long way down the road toward preventing problems and resolving them when they arise. In this regard, two principles are so important that they must precede all else said on this subject:

- The first few days of the school year are critical in setting the standard of behavior in a classroom.
- To prevent problems from arising is always easier than to correct them once they have occurred.

Starting the School Term Well

The first few days of school are a time when children are most aggressive in testing the teacher's management capability. If you are lax in establishing standards of conduct during these first few critical days, it will be almost impossible to do so later in the year. Experienced teachers know that it is easy to become more permissive as the school year progresses without compromising standards of conduct, but that it is enormously difficult to become more strict once a permissive pattern becomes the norm. Because beginning teachers want children to like them, they are sometimes reluctant to take a firm stand on student conduct for fear they will offend children. This form of indulgence is almost always a mistake. The time for firm, strict, formal (but always, of course, fair) teacher action is during the first few days of the school year. Your students will immediately respect you if you are firm but fair. Over time they may even learn to like you.

There are three important keys to getting your school term off to a good beginning. First, be *prepared* and be *fair*. Your preparation for the first day of school should include determining your classroom procedures and your basic expectations for students' behavior while they are under your supervision. Your procedures and expectations must be consistent with school policy and must seem reasonable to your students, and in enforcing them you must be a fair and consistent professional. However, being coldly consistent is not the same as being fair and professional. As a teacher, you are a professional who deals in matters of human relations and who must exercise professional judgment. You are not a robot, nor are any of your students. Human beings differ from one another, and seemingly similar situations can vary substantially because the people involved are different. Consequently, your response, or lack of response, to each of two separate but quite similar situations may differ. To be most effective, learning must be enjoyable for students; they cannot enjoy it when their teacher consistently acts like a drill sergeant. If a student breaks a rule, rather than assuming why, or seeming to not care why, or overreacting to the infraction, *find out why* before deciding your response.

Second, in preparing your classroom management system, remember that too many rules and detailed procedures at the beginning can be a source of trouble. To avoid trouble, it is best at first to present only those procedural expectations necessary for an orderly start to the school term, and then add perhaps a new one each day and reteach and reinforce each one every day.

Third, your consequences for not following established procedures must be reasonable, clearly understood, and fairly applied. In addition, apply consequences privately if at all possible, that is, without embarrassing the recipient. But remember this: Children are individuals with different needs, who behave and react differently, and each needs to be treated differently. A consequence that is fair for one child may not necessarily be fair for another. Procedures should be quite specific so that students know exactly what you do and do not expect and what the consequences are when they violate procedures. For example, "If you make a mess you clean it up"; "If you want my attention you must raise your hand and wait for me to acknowledge you."

Most teachers who are effective managers of their classroom learning environment make routine their procedures for handling inappropriate behavior and ensure that children understand the consequences for not following procedures. It is often desirable to post procedures and consequences in the classroom. Consequences will vary considerably depending on whether you are teaching kindergarten, sixth grade, or a grade level in between. Consequences might resemble the five-step model shown in Figure 4.2 (although perhaps in a more abbreviated form).

Whether offenses subsequent to the first are those that occur on the same day or within a designated period of time, such as 1 week, is one of the many decisions that you, members of a teaching team, or the entire faculty must make.

First Offense—Results in a direct but reasonably unobtrusive (nonverbal) reminder to the student. You may, for example, establish eye contact and frown.

Second Offense—Results in a private but direct verbal warning. You may, for example, lean over and whisper to the child to attend to the instructional task.

Third Offense—Results in the student being given a time out in an isolation area (one with adult supervision) followed, perhaps, by a private teacher–student conference and a phone call home.

Fourth Offense—Results in suspension from class until you can hold a student–parent/guardian–teacher conference.

Fifth Offense—Results in the student being referred to the principal or counselor's office (depending on school policy), sometimes followed by suspension or even expulsion from school.

FIGURE 4.2
Sample five-step model of consequences for inappropriate behaviors

In a way, the firmness being suggested as appropriate at the beginning of the school year is a prevention strategy. An interesting, stimulating, instructional program, combined with appropriate rewards for expected behavior, is a much more effective deterrent to disruptive student behavior than is punishment or the threat of punishment. When children know clearly what is expected, when teachers follow through on learner expectations and do not permit gradual erosion of standards of conduct, children's behavior can usually be kept within manageable limits. Of course, no classroom is totally free of behavior problems. Thus, you *should not* wait until an incident of student misbehavior has occurred to think about a management strategy to deal with it. Use the following "Emerging Plan for Classroom Management" to begin developing your own management plan, a process that will continue throughout your career.

Activity 4.2: My Emerging Plan for Classroom Management

Grade Level (or student age range) _____

Plans Before the First Day

1. Describe your classroom environment with respect to the physical room arrangement and organization, and the positive and caring classroom community that you aim to create.
2. Describe any communication you will make with your students and their families prior to the first day of school.
3. Describe characteristics of your classroom that will signal to students that it is a friendly and safe place to be.
4. Describe what you will do to help children get to know you and each other.
5. Describe how you will get to know the children.

The First Day

6. Describe how you will greet children when they arrive for the first day.
7. Describe the rules or expectations that you will have already in place and how you will present them to the children.
8. Describe how you will have children contribute to these rules and expectations.
9. Describe your classroom procedures for the following:
   - Absences, making up missed work and instruction

- Assigning helpers for classroom jobs such as taking care of pets, plants, or the calendar
- Being in the classroom before and after school, and at recess and lunch time
- Bringing toys into the classroom
- Collecting notes, money, and forms
- Distributing and collecting papers and materials
- Eating and drinking in the classroom
- Going to the bathroom
- Late arrival and early dismissal
- Movement in the halls
- Storing personal belongings
- Taking attendance
- Using the water fountain
- Using the classroom sink
- Using the pencil sharpener
- Using the teacher's desk
- Using materials and equipment
- Wearing hats and other articles of clothing in the classroom
- What to do in an emergency situation
- When a visitor comes into the classroom

10. Describe the morning opening; the day's closure.

Managing the Curriculum

11. Describe how you will help children with their organization and assignments.
12. Describe your homework expectations. Will there be any? How much and how often? Will parents

and guardians be informed? If so, how? What is their involvement to be?

13. Describe your procedure for incomplete, unacceptable, or incorrect student work.

14. Do you plan to provide comments, feedback, or corrections on student work?

15. Will you use marks of some sort—grades, value words, figures, and so forth?

16. Will you reward students for their group work? How will you assess group learning? How will you assess individual learning from group work?

17. Describe your student portfolio expectation. Where will portfolios be kept?

18. Describe your plan for communication with parents and guardians.

Maintaining Classroom Relations and Personal Behavior

19. Describe how you will bring an off-task child back on task.

20. Describe how students will know what is and what is not an appropriate level of classroom noise.

21. Describe how you will signal a need for hands and when, if ever, it is okay to call out without using hands.

22. Describe how you will support appropriate student behavior.

23. Describe how you will discourage inappropriate student behavior.

24. Describe your order of indirect and direct behavior intervention strategies.

25. Describe how you will signal your need for attention from the class, or from a distracted student.

26. Describe how you will respond when two errant behaviors are happening simultaneously but in opposing locations in the classroom.

When the Going Gets Tough

27. Describe your pattern of escalating consequences.

28. Describe how you will deal with disrespectful, inappropriate comments.

29. Describe how you will respond to remarks that are sexist or racist, or that stereotype people in cruel ways.

30. Describe how you will respond to serious and dangerous student behaviors.

Adapted from an unpublished form. Adapted by permission of Linda Current.

Schedule and Routines

Children respond best to established routines. This includes an established daily schedule of classroom events. Although the inflexibility created by clinging slavishly to a minute-by-minute schedule can hardly be condoned, this is not the same as saying there should be no schedule. By not planning and observing a daily schedule of events, you can create all sorts of management problems for yourself.

Because of the ordinary requirements imposed on teachers to attend to various areas of the curriculum, it will be possible for you to block out large periods of time to be devoted to reading, social studies, science, mathematics, language arts, expressive arts, health and physical education, and so on. Your schedule can be tentative, and you may change it from time to time during the year, if necessary. Perceive your schedule as reasonably flexible. If on some days you need a few more minutes to complete an important task, take the time. If, however, you find every lesson exceeds your budgeted time or does not require the amount of time allotted, this is evidence of weak planning, poor lesson pacing, inaccurate estimating of the time needed, or all these things.

If you make a schedule and observe it reasonably closely you will ensure that all children and all areas of the curriculum receive the attention each deserves. When you are careless about scheduling classroom events, days may go by without finding the time for some subjects. What usually happens is that your favorite subject areas get the lion's share of time; those you are less fond of, or in which you are not particularly strong, get shortchanged. Also, if you work with subgroups within the class, some groups may not get an adequate amount of your time. If this happens once in a while, it is not a serious matter, but if it occurs regularly, it cannot help but be detrimental to a well-balanced instructional program and will therefore contribute to management problems.

Closely related to schedule setting is establishing routines that regularize your day-to-day classroom activities, including entering and leaving the classroom, taking roll, moving from one grouping configuration to another, using the classroom learning centers,[18] going to the restroom, getting books and supplies, coming to order after recess, checking out athletic equipment, and so on. Routines prevent the altercations, bickering, and conflicts that are inevitable when such activities are handled ad hoc.

When your routines are reasonable and you implement them sensibly, children do not find them objectionable. As a matter of fact, they receive security from knowing what to do and how to do it.

Activity 4.3: Ms. Badger's Effort to Empower Children

Long before the opening of school, Ms. Badger had decided what behavior standards she wanted in her classroom and had constructed a set of procedures concerning student conduct. She now feels uneasy about this, however, because she remembers what one of her professors had said about children being more willing to respect and accept rules if they have a hand in formulating them. Ms. Badger resolves her dilemma in the following way.

On the first day of school, she explains to her students that she is sure that all of them want to do their best work. For this to happen, there need to be standards and procedures. If everyone does anything they please at any time, without consideration for others, no one will get anything done, and the room will not be a very pleasant place. The children, of course, understand and expect this. She goes on to explain that because standards of behavior affect everyone, the class should help her establish them. This, too, receives a favorable reaction. It is agreed

that the children will suggest procedures, and when the group accepts them, Ms. Badger will write them on the writing board.

As children make suggestions, Ms. Badger involves the class in discussing each one. She is careful not to reject any suggestion, but when one surfaces that she has already decided she wants, she says something like, "Now, that's a good idea!" By the time the period ends, the standards and procedures adopted by the class are those Ms. Badger had decided on three weeks before the opening of school, and the children seem pleased with "their" standards and procedures.

1. Do you find anything objectionable about Ms. Badger's strategy?
2. What would you predict to be the lasting effect of standards and procedures generated in this way?
3. Would you establish your procedures differently? If so, how?

Clarity of Directions and Goals

It is important that you always give clear directions. When you give directions carelessly or ambiguously, children do not know what they are to do and will consequently ask to have you clarify or repeat yourself, sometimes several times. Some teachers respond with annoyance, and may then establish a rule that they will give directions once only. This is generally a bad idea because it is patently unfair. There will be times when, for obvious reasons, directions need to be repeated. Such a teacher is then placed in the position of having to violate one of the classroom rules. If you are careful about your preactive planning, about obtaining the attention of all children before you give directions, and are skillful in giving directions clearly and completely, it is not likely that children will misunderstand you.

In addition to giving clear instructions, activities flow best when children understand their purpose. Like most of us, children are annoyed when you ask them to do things without telling them your reasons for doing them. Children in school are often assigned specific tasks without the least idea of how the task fits into the larger, long-range framework. Time you take to discuss and explain what everyone will be doing and where the activities will lead is usually time well spent.

Physical Arrangements

There is much in the arrangement of an elementary school classroom that can either contribute to or alleviate management problems. There is no one "best way" to arrange learner stations in a classroom. Most professionals agree that the arrangement should be kept flexible and that students should be deployed in the ways most suitable for accomplishing specific tasks.

Activity 4.4: First Day of Spring—What Would You Have Done?

Today is the first really warm, spring day that Middleton has had this year. In fact, it is downright hot. And the children love it! After a long cold winter and a damp and rainy spring, it seems as though summer has arrived with one big burst of sunshine, and energy that was pent up during the many dreary months has released itself like a mountain of water flowing through a broken dam! During the noon hour, the children play hard, run and yell, and have a great time in the welcomed sunshine. Now the "first" bell rings, and several hundred very reluctant children find their way into the building and to their respective classrooms, still talking loudly, perspiring profusely, and with flushed faces.

Mr. Gardner had scheduled math immediately following lunch. Today, the children are hardly ready for the concentration needed for a math lesson. Mr. Gardner sees the hopelessness of the situation confronting him and immediately decides to alter his schedule.

1. Do you think Mr. Gardner's decision was wise?
2. Can Mr. Gardner forget about math each time they have a beautiful day?
3. If this is a persistent problem, what long-term solution might Mr. Gardner find?

The guideline is simple. Just as is true with adults, when children are seated side by side, it is perfectly natural for them to talk to each other. Therefore, if your purpose is to encourage social interaction, seat children close together; if you would rather they work independently, separate them. It is unreasonable to place children in situations that encourage maximum interaction and then to admonish or berate them for whispering and talking.

You will not (or should not) be seated much of the time during the day; therefore, it matters little where your desk is located except that it is out of the way. You will move about the room, supervising, clarifying, answering questions, and providing individual instruction. In conducting instruction in small subgroups, working with individuals, or supervising seatwork, you should habitually position yourself so you can monitor children's behavior; the children should be aware of your presence.

Transitions

As long as children are at their assigned desks or work stations in the classroom, busily at work on a learning activity that is meaningful to them, there is usually little problem with disruptive behavior, although, in order to not disturb the learning going on in neighboring classrooms, you may need to remind the children to be "using their 6-inch voices."

But classrooms do not and cannot operate that way all of the time. Children must move about from time to time; different materials are used for different subjects and skills; group configuration changes in accordance with teaching and curriculum requirements. These breaks in the classroom work, when children move from one set of tasks to another, are referred to as *transitions*. There are many such transitions during the school day and as much as 15 percent of classroom time may be spent in shifting from one activity to another.[19]

Transitions are a most troublesome time for many beginning teachers. Transitions are less trouble when you plan them carefully during your preactive phase of instruction and write them into your lesson plan. In other words, the way to prevent management problems during transitions (or, for that matter, during any other time) is to think through the process in advance and structure the situation in such a way that the change can occur smoothly, efficiently, and with the least disruption. We suggest the following procedures, based on the experiences of teachers who are good at creating transitions:

1. Avoid delays of any kind, where children sit or stand with nothing to do.
2. Have the learning materials needed for the next task available, in sufficient quantity, and easily accessible to students.
3. Use student helpers to disseminate materials. Give children responsibilities.
4. At the close of one activity and before another is to begin, obtain students' undivided attention, and then give clear directions regarding the next task. Avoid giving the directions before you have students' complete attention.

5. Establish reasonable time limits within which to complete the transition. If you allow too little time, children are apt to rush around excitedly and bump into furniture or one another, which contributes to unnecessary commotion and potential accidents. Moves should be made expeditiously but not in a hurried or stressful way.

6. Insofar as is possible, make transitions in the same way each day. Establish a routine that becomes familiar to all children.

7. Avoid saying or doing things that raise children's excitement level. When children begin to raise their voices, are speaking rapidly, or rushing about the room, you should know the steps to take to calm the group. A short quiet-time break or a silent activity will usually reduce the stimulation. A recess break at such a time may exacerbate the problem because the freedom will additionally excite the children.

8. It is sometimes a good idea to make transitions by small groups rather than having the entire class move at one time.

9. As soon as children are engaged in the new activity, make sure that you are available to provide assistance to those children who seem to be having a problem getting on task.

Activity 4.5: What's Wrong Here?

Ms. Fox knows that if she is to succeed as a beginning teacher she must have good "control" in her classroom. She is determined, therefore, not to allow the slightest infraction of room conduct to go unnoticed. When children enter the room, she is usually seen standing at the door, where she can monitor children's behavior in the hallway and in the classroom at the same time. She likes to think of herself as a "no-nonsense" teacher who will not put up with any "foolishness" from her fifth-graders. Many of her comments to the children during the day run along this line:

"Stop running in the hall, boys."

"Now settle down quickly, boys and girls."

"Karen, what are you doing over there? Please take your seat."

"I want it quiet in here. What are you two talking about over there? Is that Billy's book you have, Cindy? Give it back to him, and get on with your own work."

"Everyone listen carefully to the directions, because I will give them only once."

"Clear everything from the top of your desks except the book we will be using. [Pause.] Mark, put that ruler away. Sally—put the pencil inside your desk! Jim, the waste paper goes in the basket."

Although the children have nicknamed her "Hawkeye," they really do not dislike Ms. Fox. But they often talk about the good times they had with Ms. James the year before, and this bothers Ms. Fox.

The classroom gives the outward appearance of orderliness, yet one senses an unnatural tenseness about the room. There is more carping and petty bickering among the children than one would expect. They comply with Ms. Fox's expectations, but there is little evidence of cooperation among them or between them and Ms. Fox. When the principal visits her classroom, she advises Ms. Fox to try to develop a more positive approach to room management but does not provide examples of what this entails.

1. If you were Ms. Fox, what would you do to implement the principal's recommendation?
2. What behavior can one expect if teacher talk is mainly directive, negative in content, and perhaps hostile in tone?
3. Do you think Ms. Fox will still be a teacher 2 years from now? Explain your answer.

SUMMARY

No doubt, individual differences make it easier for some teachers and more difficult for others to develop professional competencies. However, most can succeed at it. Professional competence can be strengthened through sound scholarship and by thorough preparation, planning, and reflection.

The teacher in the elementary school is, without question, the most influential and powerful personality in the classroom. The teacher's behavior will determine the quality of the interactions in the group. If the teacher is warm and caring, the chances are that children will model these traits. Conversely, if the teacher is domineering, arbitrary, carping, and critical, children are likely to reflect these behaviors.

You must appreciate the powerful influence of the unspoken cues teachers provide when communicating with children. Sometimes overt but more often quite subtle, these nonverbal cues may range from a gesture to a facial expression to simply the expression of a mood. As examples, a restless child may be calmed by your reassuring smile. You may place a hand on the shoulder of a child who seems to need emotional support. Or you will show sincere enthusiasm in your eyes as a child is relating an exciting experience. Or, while talking to the class you detect a student starting to show restlessness and casually move over next to the student (using proximity control), perhaps gently placing a hand on the student's shoulder to avert misbehavior. Some authors have referred to this system of communication as the "silent language" or "body language."

It may be that teachers communicate more profoundly through such nonverbal cues than in any other way. We always manipulate words to come out the way we think most appropriate. But true feelings and attitudes are laid bare by those unspoken messages that flow between human beings, messages that children, in their innocence, are so skillful in decoding. It is these signals that tell children whether a teacher is, indeed, a concerned and caring adult. These unspoken messages will have much to do with your management of the classroom and will, in the long run, be the deciding factor in whether your classroom is to be a fertile seedbed for the growth of an enlightened and sensitive humanity.

It is well known that before you can teach you must have, and you must maintain, your learners' attention. With your written plan for doing that well underway, in Chapters 5 and 6 we focus your attention on the topics of what content to teach and how to plan to teach it.

STUDY QUESTIONS AND ADDITIONAL ACTIVITIES

1. Flexibility seems to be an essential quality of elementary school classrooms. For a specified grade level, generate a list of five or six rules or procedures that you would wish to establish in your classroom. Indicate which ones you could flexibly enforce and which ones you could not. How do you determine which is which?

2. Explain to what extent you would want your students involved in the goal setting of your class? In the establishment of behavior standards or expectations? Of consequences? Explain why, and how you would involve them.

3. Interview two or three experienced teachers, preferably at different grade levels and with different years of experience. Find out what procedures they use at the beginning of the school year to establish a setting for responsible student conduct. Discuss with these teachers the specific strategies they use to obtain students' cooperation.

4. Sometimes, teachers encourage disruptive student behavior or even misbehavior by what they do or don't do, or by what they say. Teachers may not even be aware that students find their behavior irritating and that it "gets on their nerves." As you observe teachers (even college teachers will suffice), take notice of any teacher behaviors or idiosyncrasies that seem to encourage student hostility. Share what you discover with your colleagues and discuss your findings and how they relate to your own development as a teacher.

5. It has been said that good classroom managers are not necessarily good teachers. Do you agree or disagree? Why? Is the reverse true, that is, are good teachers necessarily good classroom managers? Explain why or why not.

6. A teacher punished children for tardiness by assigning them 20 additional math problems. What effect, if any, do you think such an experience might have on the children's attitude toward mathematics? Toward school? Toward that teacher? Does it matter whether punishment is logically related to the misbehavior? Discuss, and provide real experience examples to illustrate your points.

7. Debbie is a kindergarten teacher. Of the 19 children in her class, one, Hannah, is a special needs child who has multiple disabilities including Down's syndrome and severe hearing loss. On this day, Hannah's aide has failed to come to school and did not notify the school she would be absent. Debbie is the only adult in the class. Hannah needs to go to the bathroom now. What would you do were you Debbie?

8. One student hit a pregnant teacher, another exposed himself, and another stabbed a classmate with a pencil. All were suspended from school for up to 2 weeks during the 2002–3 school year. All were kindergartners. Some experts believe that the youngest school children are being suspended from school with greater frequency than ever. At schools in your geographic area, investigate and share with others in your class what you can find about the use of home suspension versus on-campus suspension. Describe what you can find about the advantages and disadvantages of each.

9. Experts say that "learning is easier and more pleasant when we are shown what *to* do rather than told what *not to* do" (T. L. Good and J. E. Brophy, *Looking in Classrooms*, 9th ed. [New York: Addison Wesley Longman, 2003], 126). What does that statement say regarding how to present

classroom rules and procedures? About a teacher's language and demeanor in general?

10. A historical review of disciplinary practices used in U.S. classrooms shows that corporal punishment has been a consistent and conspicuous part of schooling since the beginning. Many educators are concerned about the increased violence in schools, represented by possession of weapons, harassment, bullying, intimidation, gang or cult activity, arson, and the continued corporal punishment of students. They argue that schools are responsible for turning children's behavior into opportunities to teach character and self-control. When self-disciplined adults create a problem, they apologize, accept the consequences, make restitution, and learn from their mistakes. We have a responsibility for teaching children to do the same. An important characteristic of exemplary schooling is that of maintaining respect for children's dignity even when responding to their inappropriate behavior. Saturday School may be an acceptable alternative to more harmful disciplinary practices, as well as a step toward developing more internal rather than external student control methods. Are there any such programs in your geographic area? What is your opinion about using corporal punishment at any level of schooling? Hold a class debate on the issue.

NOTES

1. T. L. Good and J. E. Brophy, *Looking in Classrooms*, 9th ed. (New York: Addison Wesley Longman, 2003), 107.

2. M. C. Want, G. D. Haertel, and H. J. Walberg, "What Helps Students Learn?" *Educational Leadership* 51(4): 74–79 (December 1993–January 1994).

3. See B. F. Skinner, *The Technology of Teaching* (New York: Appleton-Century-Crofts, 1968) and *Beyond Freedom and Dignity* (New York: Knopf, 1971).

4. See L. Canter and M. Canter, *Assertive Discipline: Positive Behavior Management for Today's Schools*, rev. ed. (Santa Monica, CA: Lee Canter & Associates, 1992).

5. See R. Dreikurs and P. Cassel, *Discipline Without Tears* (New York: Hawthorne Books, 1972), and R. Dreikurs, B. B. Grunwald, and F. C. Pepper, *Maintaining Sanity in the Classroom: Classroom Management Techniques*, 2nd ed. (New York: Harper & Row, 1982).

6. L. Albert, *A Teacher's Guide to Cooperative Discipline: How to Manage Your Classroom and Promote Self-Esteem* (Circle Pines, MN: American Guidance Service, 1989, revised 1996).

7. J. Nelsen, *Positive Discipline*, 2nd ed. (New York: Ballantine Books, 1987) and J. Nelsen, L. Lott, and H. S. Glenn, *Positive Discipline in the Classroom: How to Effectively Use Class Meetings and Other Positive Discipline Strategies* (Rocklin, CA: Prima Publishing, 1993).

8. See, for example, W. Glasser, "A New Look at School Failure and School Success," *Phi Delta Kappan* 78(8): 597–602 (1997).

9. See W. Glasser, *Reality Therapy: A New Approach to Psychiatry* (New York: Harper & Row, 1965), *Schools Without Failure* (New York: Harper & Row, 1969), *Control Theory in the Classroom* (New York: Harper & Row, 1986), *The Quality School* (New York: Harper & Row, 1990), and *The Quality School Teacher* (New York: HarperPerennial, 1993).

10. See H. J. Freiberg (Ed.), *Beyond Behaviorism: Changing the Classroom Management Paradigm* (Boston: Allyn & Bacon, 1997). See also H. J. Freiberg (Ed.), *Perceiving, Behaving, Becoming: Lessons Learned* (Alexandria, VA: Association for Supervision and Curriculum Development, 1999), and "Consistency Management and Cooperative Discipline," on pp. 172–173 of A. W. Jackson and G. A. Davis, *Turning Points 2000: Educating Adolescents in the 21st Century* (New York: A Report of Carnegie Corporation of New York, Teachers College Press, 2000).

11. See F. Gathercoal, *Judicious Discipline*, 4th Ed. (San Francisco, CA: Caddo Gap Press, 1997).

12. See H. G. Ginott, *Teacher and Child* (New York: Macmillan, 1971).

13. T. Gordon, *Discipline That Works: Promoting Self-Discipline in the Classroom* (New York: Penguin, 1989).

14. F. Jones, *Positive Classroom Discipline* and *Positive Classroom Instruction* (both New York: McGraw-Hill, 1987).

15. See, for example, A. W. Combs, (Ed.), *Perceiving, Behaving, Becoming: A New Focus for Education* (Alexandria, VA: Association for Supervision and Curriculum Development, 1962).

16. See J. A. Queen, B. B. Blackwelder, and L. P. Mallen, *Responsible Classroom Management for Teachers and Students* (Upper Saddle River, NJ: Merrill/Prentice Hall, 1997), especially "Standards and Guidelines versus Rules" and "Replacing Rules with Standards," 110–112.

17. See, for example, Good and Brophy, *Looking in Classrooms*, 170.

18. Note: What we refer to as a classroom learning center is not to be confused with what in some schools is a place on the campus, sometimes referred to as a Modified Learning Center, that is staffed by a paraprofessional, sometimes a social worker, where students may be sent from the regular classroom for a variety of reasons, such as to complete an assignment, as a place to calm down, because of inappropriate classroom behavior, for conflict resolution and problem solving, and as an on-campus suspension.

19. W. Doyle, "Classroom Organization and Management," in M. C. Wittrock, ed., *Handbook of Research on Teaching*, 3rd ed. (New York: Macmillan, 1986), 406.

FOR FURTHER PROFESSIONAL STUDY

Baker, W. P., Lang, M., and Lawson, A. E. "Classroom Management for Successful Student Inquiry." *Clearing House* 75(5): 248–252 (2002).

Bromfield, R. "When Nothing Works." *Phi Delta Kappan* 84(5): 399–400 (2003).

Bucher, K. T., and Manning, M. L. "Exploring the Foundations of Middle School Classroom Management." *Childhood Education* 78(2): 84–90 (Winter 2001–2002).

Burns, M. T. "The Battle for Civilized Behavior: Let's Begin with Manners." *Phi Delta Kappan* 84(7): 546–549 (2003).

Charney, R. *Teaching Children to Care*. Greenfield, MA: Northeast Foundation for Children, 2002.

Clayton, M. K., and Forton, M. B. *Classroom Spaces That Work*. Greenfield, MA: Northeast Foundation for Children, 2001.

Foster-Harrison, E. S., and Adams-Bullock, A. *Creating an Inviting Classroom Environment*. Fastback 422. Bloomington, IN: Phi Delta Kappa Educational Foundation, 1998.

Freiberg, H. J. "Essential Skills for New Teachers." *Educational Leadership* 59(6): 56–60 (2002).

Greer-Chase, M., Rhodes, W. A., and Kellam, S. G. "Why the Prevention of Aggressive Disruptive Behaviors in Middle School Must Begin in Elementary School." *Clearing House* 75(5): 242–245 (2002).

Herschell, A. D., Greco, L. A., Filcheck, H. A., and McNeil, C. B. "Who Is Testing Whom? Ten Suggestions for Managing the Disruptive Behavior of Young Children During Testing." *Intervention in School and Clinic* 37(3): 140–148 (2002).

Hunsader, P. D. "Why Boys Fail—and What We Can Do About It." *Principal* 82(2): 52–54 (2002).

Marzano, R. J. "Classroom Management." Chapter 10 of *What Works in Schools: Translating Research into Action*. Alexandria, VA: Association for Supervision and Curriculum Development, 2003.

Marzano, R. J. "Safe and Orderly Environment." Chapter 6 of *What Works in Schools: Translating Research into Action*. Alexandria, VA: Association for Supervision and Curriculum Development, 2003.

Metzger, M. "Learning to Discipline." *Phi Delta Kappan* 84(1): 77–84 (2002).

Montgomery, W. "Creating Culturally Responsive, Inclusive Classrooms." *Teaching Exceptional Children* 33(4): 4–9 (2001).

Purkey, W. W., and Strahan, D. B. *Inviting Positive Classroom Discipline*. Westerville, OH: National Middle School Association, 2002.

Reinoso, M. "Teacher Leadership: The Reorganization of Room 15." *Preventing School Failure* 46(2): 70–74 (2002).

Stright, A. D., and Supplee, L. H. "Children's Self-Regulatory Behaviors During Teacher-Directed, Seat-Work, and Small-Group Instructional Contexts." *Journal of Educational Research* 95(4): 235–244 (2002).

Taylor, J. A., and Baker, R. A., Jr. "Discipline and the Special Education Student." *Educational Leadership* 59(4): 28–30 (December 2001–January 2002).

Tomal, D. R. *Discipline by Negotiation: Methods for Managing Student Behavior*. Lancaster, PA: Technomic, 1999.

Tomlinson, C. A. "Learning Environments That Support Differentiated Instruction." Chapter 4 of *The Differentiated Classroom*. Alexandria, VA: Association for Supervision and Curriculum Development, 1999.

Xin, J. F., and Forrest, L. "Managing the Behavior of Children with ADD in Inclusive Classrooms: A Collaborative Approach." *Reclaiming Children and Youth* 10(4): 240–245 (2002).

Zirkel, P. A. "Written and Verbal Threats of Violence." *Principal* 81(5): 63–65 (2002).

Chapter 5

The Curriculum: Selecting and
Setting Learning Expectations

INTASC Principles	PRAXIS III Domains	NBPTS Standards
• The teacher plans instruction based upon knowledge of subject matter, students, community, and curriculum goals. (Principle 7)	• Organizing Content Knowledge for Student Learning (Domain A)	• Multiple Paths to Knowledge

O r i g i n a l l y derived from a Latin term referring to a race course for the Roman chariots, among educators the term *curriculum* still has no singularly accepted definition. We define it for this text as that which is planned and encouraged for teaching and learning. This includes school and nonschool environments, overt (formal) and covert (informal and hidden) curricula, and both broad and narrow notions of content—its development, acquisition, and consequences.

Schools are expected to serve the purposes that society has established for them. These purposes are generally represented in the school's self-prescribed mission statement, which from school to school will vary in length and detail. As reflected in the sample mission statements shown in Figures 5.1 and 5.2, schools in the United States have traditionally been expected to develop *literacy*, to provide *citizenship education*, to contribute to children's *personal development*, and to provide *quality education* for every child. Over the years, these purposes have found expression through *educational goals* that contain statements of the desired outcomes of schooling. Such statements as "to develop literacy in oral and written English," "to develop an understanding and appreciation of our cultural heritage," and "to develop a healthy self-concept" are examples of educational goals that reflect the traditional purposes of schooling. Each of these statements identifies an expected outcome of public education. *Instruction*, too, has several definitions, some that are not clearly distinguishable from curriculum. Whereas curriculum is usually associated with *what* students learn, instruction is associated with how they learn it—that is, with methods of presenting content, conveying information, and facilitating learning. Obviously, curriculum and instruction must be in tandem to affect students' learning.

We can provide only an overview here of the elementary school curriculum. A more detailed presentation will come in your subsequent teacher preparation coursework, especially with those courses that deal individually with methods of teaching in the various disciplines such as mathematics, science, language arts, and social studies.

> The mission of our school, in cooperation with the home and the community, is to prepare each student to become a confident, productive, lifelong learner by providing meaningful, educational experiences.

FIGURE 5.1
Mission statement of Taylors Elementary School (Taylors, SC).
Reprinted by permission of Taylors Elementary School, Taylors, SC.

In a developmentally appropriate environment, [it is the mission of New York Elementary School that] all children will learn skills which will empower them to make positive life choices.

FIGURE 5.2
Mission statement of New York Elementary School (Lawrence, KS).
Reprinted by permission of New York Elementary School, Lawrence, KS.

ANTICIPATED OUTCOMES

After completing this chapter, you should be able to do the following:

1. Differentiate between the terms *curriculum* and *instruction*.
2. Differentiate between the *overt* curriculum and the *covert* curriculum.
3. Describe discipline components of today's elementary school overt curriculum and the major goals of each of the components.
4. Identify and describe various documents that influence the content of the elementary school curriculum.
5. Describe effects that the covert curriculum can have on children.
6. Differentiate among *cognitive learning, affective learning,* and *psychomotor learning*.
7. Explain by example how and when a skill becomes a habit or disposition.
8. Differentiate among *study skill, critical thinking,* and *socialization skill*.
9. Distinguish the characteristics of a low-risk classroom environment from those of a high-risk environment, and which is preferred when critical thinking is desired.
10. Describe the status of foreign language study in the elementary school curriculum.
11. Define *problem solving* and identify and describe the skills involved.
12. Describe the extent of the classroom teacher's role in helping a child develop and maintain a positive self-image.
13. Describe the meaning of each of these terms: *results-driven education; aligned curriculum; higher-order thinking*.
14. Distinguish between *educational goals* and *instructional objectives*.
15. Describe the elements of a complete instructional objective.
16. Recognize instructional objectives according to their domain.
17. Write measurable instructional objectives for use in your teaching.
18. Demonstrate your ability to arrange instructional objectives in an order that will best lead to the attainment of an educational goal.
19. Demonstrate how cognitive, psychomotor, and affective learning are distinctive and how they are interrelated.
20. Describe characteristics of a classroom that enhance affective learning.

21. Describe the relationship between and among *educational goals, instructional objectives*, and *assessment practices*.

22. Describe the characteristics and value, if any, of serendipitous learning.

THE ELEMENTARY SCHOOL CURRICULUM

The classroom environment is a direct measure of the quality of human interaction that takes place there and, consequently, has an impact on how children learn. Some messages transmitted to children by the classroom environment are easily discernible: the furniture is comfortably arranged, children's work is displayed, and there is evidence of learner involvement in classroom life. Other messages are subtler; they lie beneath the surface of what comes immediately to the eye of the classroom visitor. These are the feelings that are projected from adults to children and from the children to one another. Voice inflection and statements of praise and body language also carry these messages. These covert message systems of schools have been referred to variously as the *hidden, informal,* or *unplanned curriculum.*

The covert curriculum is pervasive in a classroom and school and reflects the attitudes of both adults and children. Without saying so directly, teachers, through a combination of circumstances, convey to children much about what expectations and values are prized. Through the covert curriculum, children learn the extent to which life at school suits them and their needs. Lessons learned through informal interaction with other children may condition children's social skills and human relationships for a lifetime. Children learn, often without being told, which models of behavior are highlighted for emulation. They learn which behavior is likely to gain favor and which is not. They know a great deal about how their teacher feels toward social issues, groups, and individuals—again, without ever having been told explicitly.

This covert curriculum is seldom planned and is almost never assessed. Because it is not possible to eliminate entirely the effects of the covert curriculum, it is important for you to understand the concept and to plan for it, that is, to *make it consistent with your overt messages*, and make it as positive as possible for children. The teacher sets the emotional tone of the classroom. Because of the high social status of teachers in elementary school classrooms, children generally treat them with deference. This being the case, you are in a position of considerable power when it comes to shaping the nature of the covert curriculum. Thus, your expression of a preference, an aside comment, a statement of surprise, or even a facial expression or other body language may strongly influence young children's thoughts and actions. What teachers *do* speaks so much more loudly than what they say. And if there is a discrepancy between what you say and do, the nonverbal message will win every time.

The elementary school curriculum is designed to achieve the fundamental purposes (also known as the broad goals) of elementary education, as discussed in Chapter 1. To achieve these broad goals, the overt (formal,

Activity 5.1: What Really Is Being Learned?

Although it is almost never assessed, children do learn through the covert curriculum. What hidden message is being sent to the children by each of the following teachers? Discuss your response with your classmates.

• Ms. Wong is a first-year teacher. After visiting her fifth-grade classroom, the principal suggested that she brighten the classroom and decorate the walls with a display of student work. When the principal returned to the classroom 2 weeks later, Ms. Wong had put up a display—a chart of the homework and test records of students.

Hidden message being sent: _____

• Mr. Lever, a second-grade teacher, has decorated one wall of his classroom with pictures and stories of famous scientists, all of whom are men.

Hidden message being sent: _____

• While Ms. Gushé is talking to her fourth-grade students, the school principal walks into the room. Ms. Gushé stops her talk and walks over to greet the principal and find out what the principal wants.

Hidden message being sent: _____

• Mr. Latte is nearly always late in arriving to his classroom after lunch, seldom beginning class until at least 5 minutes past the scheduled start time.

Hidden message being sent: _____

• During sustained silent reading in Mrs. Silencia's sixth-grade reading class, Mrs. Silencia asks for everyone's attention, verbally reprimands two students for horsing around, and then writes out a referral for each of the two students.

Hidden message being sent: _____

prescribed, intended, or planned) curriculum includes several specific subjects and skills. However the elementary school curriculum is presented, it comprises the following distinctive discipline components:

English/Language arts (also known as *literacy*)—includes reading, written expression, spelling, speaking, and listening

Mathematics—includes basic arithmetic, along with other quantitative concepts and relationships

Science—includes both natural and physical science

Social studies—includes history, geography, and civics

Expressive arts—includes dance, music, theater, and the visual arts

Health and physical education—includes basic health practices and participation in physical education

In addition to the specialized skills of these disciplines, students learn other, more general, skills as components of the elementary school curriculum. These include *study skills, critical thinking skills,* and *socialization skills.*

ENGLISH AND THE LANGUAGE ARTS

Traditionally, *language arts* has been defined as encompassing the four modes of language: listening, speaking, reading, and written expression. During the past 40 or 50 years, various movements and approaches have tried to find the most successful approach to teaching English and the language arts, under names such as whole language, integrated language arts, language experience, reading and writing in the content areas, and holistic English. Today's English and language arts study is a holistic, integrated, interdisciplinary, student-centered, multicultural field that centers on the learning and use of language. Whatever the cognomen, and although methods and materials will differ, certain common elements and goals prevail.

Let's consider reading as an example. Most children enter school knowing that one of the most important things they will do there is learn to read. Children look forward to it! Learning to read is one of those rites of passage that indicate that children are growing up. When children can say proudly, "I can read!" they are proclaiming a great deal more than simply saying they can get meaning from printed symbols; in effect, they are saying, "I can do what big kids and grown-ups can do. I'm a big kid now." Conversely, for children who do not learn how to read or to do it well, the effect can be and often is detrimental psychologically and can be devastating to attitudes toward school and to subsequent school achievement. A lot rides on learning how to read.

Whatever philosophy of language learning the elementary school faculty embraces, reading—because of its central importance to *all* school learning—is given high priority. Typically, teachers move into language experiences for children as soon as the children enter school. In some instances, formal reading instruction is begun in kindergarten, and most certainly it begins in first grade. Nearly all children in the United States, at least 98 percent, today begin first grade having had kindergarten experience.[1] Focusing specifically on the effects of kindergarten attendance on later academic achievement test scores, studies have revealed a significant difference: students with kindergarten experience scored higher in reading, language, mathematics, and overall than did children who did not attend.[2]

Whether in kindergarten or first grade, once the reading program starts it continues at least through the sixth grade. The specialized reading skills needed to handle the content fields, such as social studies, science, and mathematics, have to be taught in those fields in all grades, including high school and sometimes even during the first year or two of college.

Reading

What is the best way to teach children to read? Experts have disagreed for a long time, this disagreement usually taking the form of such dichotomies as "letters, syllables, and sounds versus meaningful words," "phonics versus look-say," "phonics versus whole language," "basal text versus children's literature (storybook)."[3] Some argue that debates became too acrimonious and went on too long with too little attention to the issue of balance.[4] Consensus today seems strong that reading programs should be balanced, drawing on multiple theoretical perspectives.[5]

Although experts may favor different approaches to teaching reading and language, there are some fairly large areas of agreement.[6] Most agree about the importance of a language-rich environment as a powerful influence in language and reading development. Early contact with books and elaborative language use at the preschool level enhance language and reading growth. Any experiences children have that sensitize them to words, word sounds, word meanings, and word use are beneficial. Similarly, the examples set by parents and guardians, older siblings, and significant role models in using books, writing, and descriptive language set the stage for building children's desire to learn to use language and to read independently. Language *use* and reading are not natural developmental processes (such as walking upright), but are *learned* by each generation of children. The specifics of these complicated processes are almost entirely governed by the culture in which children are reared. Experts also agree that reading and language learning should be meaningful to children and that rote learning of letters and sounds without learning the meanings being conveyed is counterproductive.

As Duffy and Hoffman emphasize,

> There perhaps is no one "perfect method" for teaching reading to all children . . . the answer is not in the method; it is in the teacher. It has been repeatedly established that the best instruction results when combinations of methods are orchestrated by a teacher who decides what to do in light of children's needs. Hence, reading instruction effectiveness lies not with a single program or method but, rather, with a teacher who thoughtfully and analytically integrates various programs, materials, and methods as the situation demands.[7]

We discuss here the following five aspects of reading education: augmented decoding, the whole language approach, reading comprehension in the content areas, personal reading, and guided oral and corrective reading.

Augmented Decoding

We use the term *augmented* because this approach is not limited to translating printed symbols into understood language. It emphasizes reading for meaning and incorporates those practices on which experts agree. The augmented decoding approach bears a close kinship to what has traditionally been referred to as the *basal reading program*. This approach introduces and builds skills and abilities essential to reading through a systematically organized and sequentially presented program designed to help children learn decoding skills and abilities. These include but are not limited to the following abilities and skills: building phonemic awareness and a sight recognition vocabulary; learning word recognition techniques, including phonics; skimming; reading to get the general idea; reading for details; and adjusting the speed of reading to the type of material.

Although augmented decoding does not have to be built around a basic reading textbook series, most teachers take advantage of the availability of such materials. These series are actually developmental reading programs that introduce reading skills and abilities gradually and sequentially, increasing levels of complexity as children progress through the grades. Regardless of what their critics may say, reading textbooks produced today by the major school publishing houses are carefully and professionally developed teaching materials. When taught properly, most children who use them do learn to read.

Whole Language

The whole language approach to reading received a great deal of attention from the professional community during the final decades of the 1900s as an alternative to the traditional basal reading program. Philosophically, it fits well into the concept of integrated curriculum. It relies heavily on what might be called a literacy learning environment and makes liberal use of reading and writing as ways of connecting meaning to that environment. As its name suggests, this is a process-oriented approach to language learning that integrates and uses all related language abilities and skills. Indeed, children are encouraged to talk and to write their own material; in the process, they learn reading, spelling, writing, and usage skills. The emphasis is on gaining and expressing meaning. Writing and reading are used to synthesize meaning. Whole language methods stress the importance of context, or print-rich surroundings that encourage children to use language.

Advocates of the whole language approach argue that it is a more natural way to learn language skills than are more conventional methods. Moreover, they argue that phonics and language conventions are *not* omitted from the program; they are, rather, taught as needed in functional contexts. Opponents argue that whole language learning does not produce the results claimed, and that phonics and language conventions, while present, are deemphasized to the detriment of children's developing literacy.

Whether or not teachers elect to use the whole language approach in its entirety, the movement has had an impact on the teaching of reading and language in schools. It has sensitized teachers to the interrelatedness of language abilities and skills, and it has underscored the importance of *meaning* as the critical component in all communication skills.

Reading Comprehension in the Content Areas

Quite apart from how children are introduced to and are taught reading, they need specific instruction on how to read material in the various subject-matter or content areas, as each area demands some special reading skills. Each has a specialized vocabulary and, in most cases, has to be read at an appropriate rate of speed. For instance, one reads a "word problem" in mathematics differently from the way one reads a science book when searching for a specific fact. Poetry and literature are read differently from social studies content. Because reading in each subject area requires different skills and abilities, teaching children to read in each subject area must accompany instruction in the subject itself.

Personal Reading

There is no substitute for extensive personal reading as a way to develop and strengthen reading abilities and skills. As children develop skills that qualify them as independent readers, you should make an all-out effort to encourage them to read on their own time. Beginning readers should be encouraged to select and reread books on a daily basis.[8] Imaginative teachers bring to their classrooms exciting books known to spark children's interest and will review them briefly, perhaps reading selected passages. When teachers do this in a delightfully enticing way, all hands go up when they then ask if anyone wants to read the book. Children may need much encouragement to do personal reading, but the success in producing more fluent readers is richly rewarding.

Guided Oral and Corrective Reading

Regardless of your reading program, you must prepare to accommodate children who have difficulty succeeding in reading and language use. If your total language and reading programs are strong, you should have fewer reading casualties than if programs are poorly implemented. Nonetheless, some children will, for a variety of reasons, have an inordinately difficult time learning to read: neurological or visual impairments may affect their perception of printed material; psychological problems may interfere with progress. Whatever the reason may be, the remedy is often beyond the scope of the professional service you are trained to provide. Your school district must have available additional services for those children who cannot be accommodated by regular classroom instruction in reading. The International Reading Association has expressed concern that children with the greatest need of help in their literacy development should be guided by those most qualified, while, in fact, in too many schools, nonqualified or lesser-qualified paraprofessionals are being employed to provide instruction to the neediest children.[9]

Spelling

The major purpose of the spelling program is to teach children to spell those commonly used words they will need when they write. Spelling is primarily a writing skill, and this is the major objection to an oral approach to teaching spelling. Spelling bees may motivate and entertain children, but one does not generally use oral spelling when writing. Speaking, however, *does* relate to spelling, and poor pronunciation can be a cause of poor spelling (e.g., saying *reconize* for *recognize*, *Febuary* for *February*, *pitcher* for *picture*, *libary* for *library*). Thus, modern spelling programs teach children to write words, spelled correctly, and often combine teaching elements of speaking and handwriting along with spelling. Similarly, certain aspects of reading (mainly phonics and word recognition) are related to spelling. Although a modern spelling program incorporates elements from related language arts, spelling needs explicit instruction.

In addition to teaching children to spell commonly used words automatically, the spelling program should serve at least three other important purposes. First, it should develop in children the attitude of *wanting* to spell words correctly. Some have referred to this as a *spelling conscience*. Second, children should develop an awareness of the correct and incorrect spelling of words. This takes the form of consciousness raising on the teacher's part. Third, the spelling program should help children learn how to study words. Studying words includes learning about such things as prefixes and suffixes, the formation of plural variants, limited use of rules *and* their exceptions, and the use of phonics.

English is not a consistently phonetic language, and overreliance on sound as a guide to spelling will result in many errors. For example, the "sh" sound may be spelled in at least 10 different ways; consider *schtick, she, sugar, spacious, conscious, tension, nation, anxious, parachute,* and *pressure.* Phonemic awareness is an important tool in correct spelling, but children need to learn that sounding out a word is only a guide to spelling it. Also, children should learn to be sensitive to exceptions to phonetic spelling. You should call attention to such exceptions when you encounter them in your reading program.

As is true in teaching reading, many schools provide a spelling textbook series as a guide in organizing the spelling program. This has many advantages: The words are selected on the basis of research; there is provision for review; the words are introduced in small increments of increasing difficulty; study exercises are provided; the number of words learned to mastery is cumulative; and there are built-in correlations with other language arts. This approach has some limitations as well: The spelling program is often not personalized for children; it may become routine, dull, and uninteresting; children may not have an opportunity to use the words they learn to spell; and children may not learn to spell the words they need to use in other subject-matter areas.

To be successful, a spelling program must be personalized to some extent. Adapting to your students' ability the number of words you expect them to learn can do this. Many children learn to spell the required words with almost no formal instruction, whereas others require a great deal of formal teaching and close supervision. It is best to organize your spelling program on a broad base that includes (1) words from the basal spelling series, (2) personal word lists that individual children select for their own writing needs, and (3) carefully selected words encountered in the various subject-matter fields that also are pertinent to children's lives. Regarding the last, too often teachers select long or difficult words that have only short-term usefulness—like for the chapter test! That is *not* good use of spelling.

Handwriting

Handwriting is a socially important tool of communication, and it is a responsibility of the elementary school to teach children to write legibly. Handwriting has no purpose other than to communicate, and therefore should not be perceived as an end in itself. Beyond a certain level of proficiency, small improvements in handwriting quality demand a large investment of practice time. Consequently, most schools use legibility as the criterion rather than seeking perfection or uniformity of writing style.

Handwriting is a psychomotor skill that requires accurate coordination between eye and hand.[10] Consequently, children's physical maturity has a great deal to do with how and when to teach them. Young children have difficulty controlling the small muscles of their fingers used in handwriting. The sustained muscle tension required in cursive writing is especially difficult for them. Therefore, a form of manuscript writing, using individual letters, or printing, is introduced first, with the transition to cursive writing usually made in second or third grade. The form of manuscript writing used is based on circles and straight lines, modified to form lowercase letters (e.g., *o, c, d, t,* and *h*). This system, then, provides an easy transition to cursive, in which children are taught how to connect individual letters.

Manuscript and cursive styles are both legitimate forms of handwriting. Even though cursive is taught as the highest, most "adult" form of writing, manuscript writing has merit on its own, and children should maintain skill in its use. It is useful in making captions for diagrams and illustrations and for filling out forms that say "Please print." Although manuscript writing is *not* printing, it more closely resembles the print found in reading materials than does cursive. Using manuscript in the early grades means not having to introduce children to two forms of the alphabet at the same time, one for reading and another for writing.

Many teachers teach handwriting and spelling simultaneously because there is little need for spelling until one writes, and one cannot write without being able to spell. Some teachers are also combining these skills with reading instruction, thereby stressing the holistic concept of language as multifaceted communication.[11]

Children come to school knowing they will learn to write, and most want to write. Some may have already learned how to write their own names. At the early stages of handwriting, close teacher supervision is critical to prevent children from developing awkward habits that handicap later fluency. Be sure to provide for children who may be especially poorly coordinated. They may need a longer time to develop muscle maturity and will require careful direction and much encouragement. *Never* attempt to change left-handed children to writing with their right hands. You will need to make some special provision for left-handed children because most of the instruction books and paraphernalia associated with handwriting are, unfortunately, designed for right-handed persons.[12]

Language Conventions

Children have been using a language for several years before they enter school, and with most children in the United States, that language is some variant of English. Because language is learned largely through imitation, children's language will be much like that modeled by their family. This is significant to you as an elementary school teacher because it affects the kind of language arts program that will be needed. Speech patterns not only relate to oral interactions, but have a direct effect on writing as well. People tend to write as they speak, not the other way around. For that and other reasons, there is a heavy emphasis on oral language in the primary grades. These facts together suggest that there are likely to be large individual differences among children in their use of language and that much language teaching will be based on a diagnosis of individual children's needs in writing and speaking.

If a child's home language is not English, problems learning English language conventions are more severe. For instance, the usual sequence in English sentences is subject–verb–object (e.g., "Jessica ate lunch"). Children accustomed to hearing a language in which that order is not always followed (such as German or Japanese) will have to hear English spoken a long time before being comfortable with the sequence. Of course, speaking a home language other than English may contribute to articulation problems and dialect differences as well.

Language conventions are taught to ensure that children will be able to learn how to express their ideas orally and in writing and that those ideas will be clearly understood. In the primary grades, language conventions can and should be taught informally and naturally as the need occurs. Here is an example: A teacher wants to encourage her students to respond with more than a one-word answer to questions. She and her class have just come back from a short walk, and she wants the children to recall what they saw. She has them begin by saying, "On our walk, I saw—" and writes this sentence on the writing board. She reminds the children that they learned in their reading class that such a group of words is called a *sentence* and that each sentence begins with a capital letter and ends with a period. As students volunteer what they saw on their walk, she writes each sentence and punctuates it appropriately. Most of what children learn about language conventions in the primary grades is taught this way—informally, yet targeted on the specific functional use of punctuation, capitalization, grammar, and usage.

As children move into the middle grades, there is more need for writing, and the program at these grade levels tends to become more formal. This is both a strength and a limitation of language teaching. When a program becomes too formal and bookish, it loses some of its vitality. Sensible use of a language-lesson period is recommended to provide instruction on language's many elements. However, the program should never be too far removed from the way students use language in the remainder of the curriculum and in everyday life.

The language arts curriculum often differentiates between what are called *personal* and *practical* uses of language. Application of conventions is much more flexible in personal than in practical use. Informal conversations with a friend do not require the same language standards appropriate for an oral report. Likewise, a written piece of creative work that may remain private or that may be shared with a limited audience of intimates does not require the same degree of perfection needed in writing a business letter or an article for the school newspaper. Children engaged in practical writing, such as preparing reports, writing letters, filling out forms, or making captions and labels, must pay close attention to spelling, punctuation, grammar, and other conventions. They will need to write, edit, correct, and rewrite until they attain the desired level of accuracy.

Learning to write well should begin with good instruction at the elementary school level. Writing cannot be taught by having children fill in one-word blanks on study sheets and exams. Children learn to write well by writing extensively and by having those efforts carefully and sensitively critiqued, by both teachers and peers.

Until the recent explosive popularity of the Internet, with its e-mail capability, letter writing had lost its popularity with children, being supplanted by using the telephone. The good news is that children are using the modern technology to again write. The bad news is that the nature of the technology encourages *impulse writing*, which is writing without reflection and without checking for correct spelling and grammar before sending the message. When using e-mail, encourage children to make it a habit to reflect, to think, and to check before hitting the "send" command. As we discussed in Chapter 3, resisting impulsivity, that is, thinking before acting, is a time-honored characteristic of intelligent behavior. It is a behavior that children must learn.

All elements of the language arts are closely interrelated, and all should be thoroughly enmeshed in the school's total curriculum. Ninety percent or more of instruction in schools is carried on via language. Good teaching depends on good communication. Thus, it is a mistake to think of the language arts as being taught in isolated settings. Throughout the school day, children are listening, speaking, writing, and reading in all curriculum areas, both formal and informal. Language arts skills cannot and should not be separated from substance and content. Regardless of whatever else you may be teaching and regardless of grade level, you must use every opportunity to help children become effective communicators by teaching them to think reflectively, to listen attentively, to speak clearly, to write accurately, and to read with comprehension.

MATHEMATICS

Arithmetic has been ensconced in the elementary school curriculum as the third of the three Rs—readin', 'ritin', and 'rithmetic—since the early history of this nation. In modern times, however, arithmetic is viewed as only one part of a broader field of quantitative studies in that part of the school curriculum called *mathematics*. Besides arithmetic, the scope of today's elementary school mathematics curriculum includes algebra, geometry, measurement, probability, and statistics.

The K–12 mathematics *Curriculum and Evaluation Standards* document sets forth as five general goals for all students that they will do the following:

- Learn to value mathematics
- Become confident in their ability to do mathematics
- Become mathematical problem solvers
- Communicate mathematically
- Learn to reason mathematically[13]

The standards spiral through the curriculum and reoccur at increasing levels of complexity each year. The instructional resources usually include a mathematics textbook and "math manipulatives" such as attribute blocks, cubes, tiles, power-of-10 blocks, geoboards, and pattern blocks. These materials are generally consistent in their contents and in sequence with the curriculum ideas set forth in the *Standards*.

In all areas of the school curriculum, but in mathematics and science in particular, care must be taken to provide the same opportunities to both girls and boys. Both curriculum and instruction need to provide affirmative steps in reducing the possibility of children—either girls *or* boys—from developing what is referred to as *math anxiety*. As a classroom teacher you need to understand that there is no gender-linked difference in ability to learn mathematics. For young children, mathematics is natural and fun. For mathematics to continue to be so as children get older, it may be necessary for you and your teaching colleagues to continually and actively encourage all children in mathematics and to counter negative comments that children sometimes hear about the subject, including from those adults they hold in high esteem—parents or guardians, and other teachers.

There appears to be general agreement among experts that children should be introduced to computers and calculators in the early grades. Even though the National Council of Teachers of Mathematics (NCTM) encourages the use of calculators, children still must learn the special procedures needed to do calculations, called *algorithms* in the language of mathematicians. It goes without saying that learners' increased use of handheld calculators lessens the time they spend practicing paper and pencil algorithms. Teachers need to devote an appropriate amount of instructional time to teaching both the use of calculators and the conventional algorithms. Both are essential outcomes of the mathematics curriculum. It is important to emphasize that algorithms must be taught so as to help students understand conceptually the mathematical relationships involved, not simply as rote applications of the processes.

Mental arithmetic, estimation, and approximation have become more visible in today's mathematics programs. The emphasis on meaningfulness suggests that learners should know what would be a *reasonable* answer. For example, a child asked to compare the height of the Empire State Building, which is 1,472 feet tall, to a mile that comes up with an answer of 14.72 miles should be able to sense the unreasonableness of such a response. Much of our everyday use of mathematics involves approximations rather than exact, precise calculations. For instance, if we have 20 dollars to spend in a supermarket, we should be able to approximate the total cost of a few items, each of which costs 2 or 3 dollars, to know whether we have exceeded the 20-dollar limit. For such purposes, an approximation is adequate; the cashier will tell us the exact amount when we check out (although the skill of counting back change seems to have been lost in many of today's retail outlets). We are constantly making use of quantitative relationships of this type in our daily lives.

As is the case in other skill areas of the curriculum, schools must carefully monitor the progress of individual children as well as that of class groups. As is true in most areas of learning, preassessing student skills and knowledge is often the best way to begin any unit of instruction, including those in mathematics. At any time during the school year when an individual is identified whose achievement level is judged to be less than satisfactory, corrective instruction should begin immediately.

SCIENCE

During the final years of the 20th century, emphasis reawakened of the importance of children having early and continued experiences in science. As *Educating Americans for the 21st Century* states, "The basics of the twenty-first century are not only reading, writing and arithmetic [but also] include communication and higher problem-solving skills, and scientific and technological literacy."[14] At last science was legitimized as a basic discipline.

Today it is a component of the planned elementary school curriculum because (1) learning science can build important attitudes, (2) science learning attends to and nourishes children's natural curiosity about the environment, (3) science learning builds a base for important understanding, and (4) learning science develops skills necessary for survival in the real world. In actual practice, formal science instruction has sometimes been given short shrift, partly because of some teachers' feelings of anxiety about teaching it and also because of heavy emphasis on teaching the language arts and mathematics. Because teachers believe they need more time to do an adequate job of teaching reading and mathematics in particular, they have often found themselves giving less time to science and other subjects.

The goal for science in the K–12 curriculum is to promote *scientific literacy*. The publication *Science for All Americans (SFAA)* proposes the dimensions of scientific literacy—the knowledge, skills, and attitudes—that students should have as a result of their K–12 science experiences and defines the goals of scientific literacy as the following:

- Being familiar with the natural world and recognizing both its diversity and its unity
- Understanding key concepts and principles of science
- Being aware of important ways in which science, mathematics, and technology depend on one another

- Knowing that science, mathematics, and technology are human enterprises and knowing what this fact implies about their strengths and limitations
- Having a capacity for scientific ways of thinking
- Using scientific knowledge and ways of thinking for individual and social purposes[15]

Emphasizing the connectedness of knowledge from various disciplines, and perhaps also to be sure that science gets a fairer share of the time allotted to the elementary school curriculum, SFAA recommends (1) reducing the factual detail that students must try to remember—that is, learn less content but learn it better, and (2) softening the boundaries to make better connections between and among traditional subject disciplines, such as is made possible when using curriculum integration.

The *National Science Education Standards* draw extensively on, and make independent use and interpretation of, the statements of what students and teachers should know and be able to do published in *Science for All Americans*.[16] The elementary school science curriculum should be an extension of children's natural curiosity and desire to explore the physical world. The subject matter is grouped in three categories: (1) life science (living things,

A science program that provides for a heavy loading of hands-on, minds-on activities is a valuable segment of the elementary school curriculum. Notice in this photograph that the children have been provided safety eyewear to protect against accidental injury while conducting the science investigation.

aspects of health and the human body; and ecology and the environment, as these affect living things); (2) Earth and the universe (Earth, solar system, the universe; weather and climate); and (3) physical science (changes in matter and energy; friction and machines; heat, light, and sound; magnetism and electricity). Beginning as early as kindergarten, the curriculum of every grade includes units of study from each of these three broad areas. These are arranged in such a way that the central concepts or ideas and their related skills spiral upward through the grades, increasing in complexity with each advancing year. In other words, children will learn something about each of the three general categories of science each year they are in school, with topics treated in greater depth and breadth each time they are encountered.

Although the school may use a science textbook series, exemplary science programs are activity oriented, with plenty of time devoted to hands-on and minds-on experiences and the application of learning to situations that children encounter in everyday life. It is useful to relate science to social studies for children to learn to understand and appreciate the impact of science on human affairs and to provide a context for science education. The close relationship between science and society can be further emphasized by making generous use of parents and others in the community who hold expertise in some area of science. The increasing number of retired scientists, technicians, and engineers represents a valuable resource for elementary school science teachers.

SOCIAL STUDIES

In its standards document, the National Council for the Social Studies (NCSS) defines and describes *social studies* as follows:

> Social studies is the integrated study of the social sciences and humanities to promote civic competence. Within the school program, social studies provides coordinated, systematic study drawing upon such disciplines as anthropology, archaeology, economics, geography, history, law, philosophy, political science, psychology, religion,[17] and sociology, as well as appropriate content from the humanities, mathematics, and natural sciences. The primary purpose of social studies is to help young people develop the ability to make informed and reasoned decisions for the public good as citizens of a culturally diverse, democratic society in an interdependent world.[18]

History and geography are the core subject-matter fields for social studies, but economics, political science (i.e., civics, government, and law), sociology, and anthropology provide significant contributions as well. Typically, at the elementary school level, topics for study contain subject matter from more than one of the parent disciplines. These integrated studies focus on ideas and concepts that are essential to understanding the topic.

As is true for other disciplines of the curriculum, social studies textbooks are praised by some critics and condemned by others, have limitations and advantages, and are used well and poorly. Also, unfortunately, those used in the classroom too frequently are outdated. Experts agree, however, that the textbook should not be the *sole* information source in the social studies program. There is need for media, the computer and the Internet, the community with its rich resources, reference works and encyclopedias, biographies, informative fiction, poems, and other literary works that provide information on a variety of topics.

When the term *unit teaching* is used in connection with the social studies program in an elementary school, it usually has to do with a coordinated series of learning activities planned around a broad thematic topic that involves students in a comprehensive study lasting 4 to 6 weeks or even longer. Examples of unit topics are "Working Together at School" (K), "People Who Made America" (grade 1), "Traditions, Monuments, and Celebrations" (grade 2), "Living in Our Community" (grade 3), "Heroes, Folk Tales, and Legends of the World" (grade 4), "The Westward Movement" (grade 5), and "Crossroads of Three Continents" (grade 6). Teachers organize learning activities around these topics that relate to several other areas of the school curriculum, such as reading, writing, speaking, using references, doing experiments, and using mathematics. The arts may also be included, as in painting murals, learning folk dances or engaging in other musical activities related to the unit, examining relevant art and literature, or constructing models. It is clear that a great deal of work-study and social-skill building can take place in the context of unit teaching.

Some teachers prefer using social studies units as the integrating center of their curriculum because that provides students with genuine purposes for doing the learning activities. There is clearly much of value in organizing instruction in ways that help children relate the various curriculum components to each other. Under such an arrangement, learners can get a sense of the reasons for doing activities such as reading, writing, spelling, or painting. When planned and implemented thoughtfully and skillfully, the social studies unit can be a perfect model for the development of integrated learning, while at the same time offering a social studies program that meets expectations of excellence. For example, while reading about the voyages of Christopher Columbus (history, reading, and language arts), students in a second-grade class study a globe and trace his route (globe skills). They discuss how people then thought that the world was flat (history and discourse). While comparing and contrasting maps and globes (thinking skills) they discuss reasons why one is flat and the other is round (discourse skills). From a timeline that they printed earlier in the year (computer skills) they look at the time space between 1492 and 2004 and subtract the numbers to get the difference numerically (mathematics skills).[19]

HEALTH AND PHYSICAL EDUCATION

Health and physical education have long been established areas of the elementary school curriculum in terms of state regulations. In practice, however, health and physical education have not often been regarded with the same seriousness—by parents, guardians, or regular classroom teachers—as, say, have reading or mathematics. The cost of these programs, especially for physical education, can be high because of the need for space and special facilities and equipment. Indoor space costs are often justified in that elementary school gyms are used as multipurpose rooms, serving as lunchrooms and assembly areas for school and community functions.

Health Education

It is critically important that children learn to live defensively in an environment that frequently threatens their health and safety (for example, children under 18 continue to represent, as they have for years, a very large segment of the poor population; the poverty rate of children has been holding steady at about 20 percent).[20] This means helping children develop the knowledge, skills, and attitudes needed for safe living. Schools routinely provide instruction on safe street crossing; bicycle safety; playground safety; water safety; recognition of danger signs, hazards in the home, and poisons; and the potential danger in association with strangers. As children mature, the instruction is expanded to include first-aid procedures.

In addition to safety and first aid, the following topics should be included in a comprehensive and sequential health education program that deals with students' physical, mental, and emotional health requirements: nutrition, dental care, communicable diseases, substance abuse, and healthful living. As most states require teaching of all or some combination of these topics, local curriculum documents provide information concerning the recommended scope and sequence. Much health education can and should be incorporated into science and social studies programs. This is especially important in learning about the impact of modern community and industrial development on healthful living. Because topics relating to health are so often in the news, discussion of current affairs provides a way to expand information about health and to raise children's awareness of the importance of good health.

Among the most significant outcomes of health education in the elementary school are the kinds of attitudes children develop toward their own responsibility for healthful living. Children have to learn to care about how they treat their own bodies: what and how much they eat, what dangers and risks they are willing to subject themselves to, and the importance of adequate exercise and personal habits of health and hygiene. No amount of information providing or skill building will be very effective unless the individuals themselves are willing to face up to the responsibility that each one has to maintain the highest possible level of healthful living.

The School Nurse

Never in the elementary school has the role of school nurse been more important than it is today, although because of both a shortage of nurses and as

a cost-cutting measure many school districts have replaced certified
school nurses with uncertified nurses or undereducated health aides.[21] School
nurses can provide demonstrations of health or dental practices, thereby giving these procedures a greater degree of credibility because of their status as
health professionals. The school nurse should be the first stop for teachers
who have questions about students' health matters. The nurse plays a key role
among the professionals who serve the children in an elementary school.
Some schools, known as *full-service schools* (see Chapter 1), in fact go further
in supporting their students.

It is classroom teachers, however, who have daily contact with children.
Therefore, as a teacher, you must be alert to health problems that children
may be experiencing. After having lived with your students daily for a few
weeks, you will know what is "normal" behavior for each child. When there
are observable changes in a child's behavior, you should suspect a possible
physical or mental health problem and consult the school nurse in such
cases. Also, you need to be vigilant in observing children in order to identify
possible problems of vision impairment or hearing loss. Cases have been reported in which such serious problems have gone undetected for years, cases
that an observant teacher should have spotted. Daily teacher observation is
also important in detecting skin rash, which may suggest a communicable
disease; head lice; impetigo; signs of drug or alcohol use; signs of abuse or
neglect; and other abnormalities.

Physical Education

The physical education component of the elementary school curriculum contributes to children's development by providing an organized program of
experiences that (1) focuses on bodily movement, (2) emphasizes physical fitness, (3) teaches teamwork skills and attitudes, and (4) enriches children's
lives by teaching them socially relevant games and sports. These are particularly important contributions for today's children because of the lack of physical activity that tends to characterize many of their lifestyles. Additionally, a
well-designed physical education program can offer opportunities for children to practice and improve their language arts skills.[22]

A broadly based program in physical education is needed to achieve the
goals defined in the foregoing paragraph. There is sometimes a tendency to
overemphasize those dimensions of the program that relate to popular competitive team sports, such as baseball, soccer, and basketball. Although
these lead-up sports skills can be an important part of the program, they
should not be emphasized to the exclusion of any child or of other components such as physical fitness, basic movements, rhythms, and recreational
activities. Activities that stress movement and motion should be a large part
of the physical education program in the early grades, as children learn to
control their body movements through improved coordination, better

The physical education component of the elementary school curriculum contributes to children's development by providing an organized program of experiences that (1) focuses on bodily movement, (2) emphasizes physical fitness, (3) teaches teamwork skills and attitudes, and (4) enriches children's lives by teaching them socially relevant games and sports.

balance, and the use of gross-motor skills. This is an important period for children developmentally as they learn the differentiated use of their neuro-muscular systems.

The expertise of a physical education teacher is needed in some of the more specialized aspects of the physical education instructional program, such as gymnastics, stunts, tumbling, and rhythms. In schools that do not have a physical education teacher, regular classroom teachers must handle this program along with all other curriculum areas and rely on whatever assistance is provided in the way of a curriculum guide. In some schools, teachers arrange with one another to teach some of the special subjects. For instance, one teacher feels comfortable teaching music but is uneasy with physical education. A colleague across the hall knows little about teaching music but is competent in teaching physical education. These two teachers schedule their physical education and music classes at the same time and simply trade teaching assignments for that period. This arrangement usually improves the instruction in both subjects. It is a way of taking advantage of the professional expertise that is found on most faculties, and it can be used in many subjects other than music and physical education. Naturally, such arrangements must have the approval of the school principal.

THE EXPRESSIVE ARTS

The expressive arts encompass four areas—*dance, music, theater,* and the *visual arts*.

In various ways the arts are included in the daily schedule of the classroom. During the year, children should experience a balanced program of instruction in art, music, drama, and dance. It is helpful if a teacher with

When children are free to engage in an art experience, secure in knowing that those efforts will not be ridiculed, such involvement can be a powerful and positive influence in shaping their attitude not only toward the arts but also toward learning in general.

specialized preparation in the arts is available at least part of the time. But this is not often the case, and it is likely to be the classroom teacher who carries the responsibility for teaching these subjects. As noted in the previous section, it may be possible for teachers to exchange teaching duties with each other to capitalize on personal strengths or interests.

In addition to regularly scheduled instructional periods for the arts, you can do much to integrate them into other curriculum areas. For example, as children learn about the home and family, their community, or people in other lands and other times, they can express their learning through various creative art forms. Folk songs of the period can add deeper meaning and feeling to the study of the Westward Movement. Children can role play to gain insights into social relations. They can participate in folk dances from other cultures. When the emphasis is on creative expression, including the arts in social studies generally strengthens both the social studies *and* the arts program.

There is a close link between poetry, literature, and the arts. Nowhere is this more apparent than in the use of creative dramatics, where children respond to situations spontaneously without depending on script or props to keep them in role. Using a story or a poem as the basis for a dramatic episode, children can represent the moods, feelings, and actions of the principal characters. Closely related is the use of pantomime and puppets, both of which are excellent art forms for use with elementary school children.

The arts curriculum would not be complete without providing generous opportunities for children to express their thoughts and feelings through one or more of the sensory modalities. These can take the form of voluntary activities that have no purpose other than to provide an outlet for spontaneous, creative self-expression and to gain personal satisfaction from doing so. When children are free to engage in an art experience, secure in knowing that those efforts will not be ridiculed, such involvement can be a powerful and positive influence in shaping their attitudes not only toward the arts but also toward learning in general. Additionally, in such creative endeavors, children will be participating in one of the most ancient preoccupations of human beings, that of representing and communicating feelings and thoughts symbolically.

Music, painting, dramatics, dance, singing, drawing, pageants, plays, and similar activities included in the arts curriculum are longtime favorites of children. Given an appropriate setting and encouragement, children love to express their creative impulses through the manipulation of sound, form, texture, and color. In the process, they learn to perceive their environment from new and richer perspectives. Even though the arts have often been given short shrift in school programs, participation in the arts constitutes some of the most cherished elementary school memories for many adults. If, for example, you are asked to recall a memorable elementary school experience, it most likely will be one that involved you in some way in one or more of the expressive arts.

SKILLS IN THE CURRICULUM

A major portion of elementary school instructional effort deals with skill learning. This is necessary because skills are the tools of learning; they open doors to other learning. Even though it is not clear whether low school achievement is a cause or an effect of inadequately developed skills, the evidence is clear that the two are inextricably intertwined. School records of poor achievers show a consistent pattern: inability to communicate well orally, failure to learn to read and write, little or no ability to deal with simple quantitative relationships, inadequately developed work habits, and poor social relations.

School learnings are often classified as understandings (knowledge), attitudes (values), and skills. These are often discussed in terms of cognitive, affective, and psychomotor learning. These categories have merit for purposes of analysis and study but are confusing when applied to the realities of classroom teaching and learning because of the overlap among them. Not all skills involve bodily movement, as is suggested by the term *psychomotor*. Some skills are entirely intellectual, as, for example, decision making, analyzing data, or distinguishing between fact and opinion. In almost all cases, skills that are part of the school curriculum require learners to think about what they are doing when they are learning and applying them. Thus, we can conclude that most school skills have a cognitive component. Finally, skills do have an affective dimension in that individuals have feelings about how well they like or dislike what is being done. These integrated relationships can be illustrated through an example from the field of reading.

Cody is a skillful reader. As we watch, his eyes race across the page with obvious interest in what he is reading. With the exception of his eye movements and his turning the page at intervals, we see no movement. When he completes the passage, we ask him detailed questions to find out if he comprehends what he read. We find that Cody answers all of the questions correctly, and he also gives examples of applications of ideas that were not included in the passage. Finally, we ask him how he liked what he has read, and he replies, "Just great! Wow! I could read that stuff all day!" Clearly, this skill involved cognitive as well as affective components.

Skill Areas

Certain segments of the curriculum are designated as skill areas. For example, reading, spelling, handwriting, oral and written expression, and certain aspects of mathematics are usually thought of as basic skills. They are deemed to be of such importance that a special curriculum sequence is designed to ensure their development. They are "basic" in the sense that most of whatever else children do in school calls for their use. It is important, therefore, that these skills be taught in their meaningful contexts. If children cannot apply them where they are ordinarily used, they will be severely limited in the progress they can make in any field of study.

Another important group of skills is made up of those that are an integral part of the various content fields. Each subject-matter area places demands on learners to use the specialized skills associated with that field. For instance, one reads social studies content differently from the way one reads the directions for conducting a science experiment. Moreover, neither of these situations requires precisely the same reading skills needed to read a problem in mathematics. The same could be said of other skills as well. Social studies has its map and globe skills, science its special laboratory equipment, and mathematics its own special signs and symbols. Each has its own peculiar and relatively complex vocabulary. Additionally, each has its own basic study skills that require the use of particular data sources.

Although the elementary school curriculum in most cases provides a sequential program of instruction for the language arts and mathematics, the special skills related to separate subject-matter fields are ordinarily not given as much systematic attention. More often than not they are treated in a hit-or-miss fashion. This is a major limitation of the skills curriculum in many schools. The usual assumption is that the basic skills transfer directly to the content fields. Although the professional literature has consistently called attention to the importance of specialized skills, teachers continue to emphasize content mastery and to neglect content-related skills. This is unfortunate because of the ephemeral nature of content learning as compared to the rather long-lasting quality of skills. Skills are among the most permanent learning.

Complex skills such as reading, map reading, using resources, and using oral and written language consist of many component elements that are themselves subskills. Word recognition is a subskill of the larger skill we call reading. Using phonetic clues is a subskill of word recognition. Using initial consonant blends is a further refinement of the skill of using phonetic clues. When planning a skills curriculum, these component elements must be identified and then programmed to be taught at appropriate times. Performance of a larger skill may be greatly impaired because children are unable to perform adequately one or more subskills. For this reason, it is important to regularly check children's progress as they move through the skills program. Identified deficiencies require reteaching or corrective teaching. This is particularly important in the case of a child who may have been absent from school at a time when instruction was being provided in a critical subskill.

Ideally, learning experiences will be arranged sequentially in a skills curriculum, to move learners from simple variations of the skill to complex ones over a period of several years. In such sequences it is essential to provide plenty of opportunities for children to apply their newly acquired skills in authentic settings. They should use basic skills frequently, as well as those taught in the subject areas. This is the most important way in which skills are learned. You should keep in mind that, for example, in spite of many different approaches to the teaching of reading, *the best readers are always found in those classes and schools where children do a lot of reading.*[23] The implications of this statement apply to any skill. Nothing is as damaging to skills development as failure to practice and use the skill regularly. Can you imagine, for example, learning to work well with a computer without adequate time to practice? Can you imagine a basketball player learning to shoot free throws well without adequate practice time? Practicing and using the learning skills of the elementary school curriculum is no less important.

Study Skills

To develop some degree of independence as inquiring and self-instructing learners, children must be able to skillfully use various resources and procedures useful in making information searches: the skills of finding and acquiring information; reading and interpreting maps, graphs, charts, and other pictorial material; organizing information into usable structures; and following directions. These skills are essential to successful achievement in the subject-matter areas of the curriculum and are central to any type of information gathering and data processing outside school.

Variations of study skills may be spread along a continuum from simple to complex. The instructional program will introduce simple variations of these skills in the primary grades and spiral toward increasingly complex variations as children move through school. Thus, when primary-grade children are asked, "What happened first? What happened next? Then what happened?" the teacher is acquainting them with the arrangement of ideas in sequence, an important initial subskill relating to organizing material.

Critical-Thinking Skills

Today, much is said and written about *process* outcomes; often the reference is to intellectual processes—the skills of critical thinking. Children's textbooks, books on curriculum, methods-of-teaching books, and curriculum guides, especially in the fields of science and social studies, strongly emphasize inquiry and other reflective processes. Because critical thinking has been on the national agenda for better schools, it is little wonder that intellectual skills are highlighted in many programs.

Intellectual skills are involved in most of what one does when in a conscious state. As used here, however, the term applies to processes included in the application of intelligence to the solution of problems. Some authors have referred to these as *critical-thinking skills;* others call them *inquiry skills, reflective thinking, scientific thinking, creative thinking, reasoning, discovery learning,* and so forth. No matter what the cognomen, we are referring to the skills and thinking indicative of intelligent behavior.

The use of intellectual skills in problem resolution does not mean that one necessarily follows a certain number or sequence of steps. The individual who develops the habits of mind (dispositions) of curiosity and healthy skepticism will devise a system of defining and resolving problems. But if your learners are to develop any discipline in thinking, you must emphasize the importance of such processes as recognizing and defining problems, gathering and organizing data, forming intuitive hunches and stating hypotheses, testing these against the reality of data, arriving at tentative conclusions, and behaving in accordance with these conclusions until further data arrive that nullify or modify the original conclusion.

Teaching intellectual skills and encouraging a habit of mind or disposition for critical thinking require, above all, a low-risk classroom atmosphere, one that encourages and supports diversity of thought, curiosity, and skepticism. This degree of intellectual openness, coupled with an idea-rich environment, will allow for a free flow of ideas to be analyzed, discussed, verified, and rejected or accepted. An environment in which intellectual skills develop and flourish is one that values creativity, flexibility, and inventiveness. It rewards imaginative, unusual, novel responses. It supports students and encourages them to engage in risk-taking ventures, as opposed to rewarding and praising them for their search for conventional, accepted, "right" answers. Given that your classroom will have this kind of intellectual configuration, consider the following suggestions:

1. Involve children in making decisions in the classroom, dealing with such matters as methods of work, how to allocate time, classroom management procedures, and unit activities.
2. Use role playing, simulation, and games to provide a setting for first-hand experiences in problem recognition, analysis, and resolution.
3. Make generous use of if–then questions that necessitate deriving consequences from given antecedent conditions.
4. Provide frequent opportunities for choice making, keeping in mind that choice requires alternatives from which to choose.
5. Provide instruction and experience in using structured problem-solving and thinking skills (discussed in Chapter 8).
6. Encourage children's natural curiosity.
7. Provide a classroom filled with materials and ideas that provoke curiosity.
8. Make frequent use of reflective questions. (Questioning is a focus of Chapter 3.)
9. Encourage children to explore the value dimensions of decision making; that is, have them explore how feelings can affect judgment.
10. Reward generously those student efforts that show evidence of thinking flexibly to the solution of problems. (Flexible or lateral thinking is discussed in Chapter 3.)

Social Skills

When individuals learn the role behavior appropriate to social life in a culture and can satisfy their needs through social discourse and interaction with others, we say that such persons have become *socialized*. In specific terms, this means that they know how to use the language to communicate with others, behave in accordance with the culture's mores and folkways, have internalized the culture's core values and beliefs and reflect these in their behavior, and are able to modify their behavior to suit specific social settings.

There are specific applications of the socialization concept. For example, we may speak of political socialization as the process that shapes learners' political belief systems. Or we may say that children have been socialized in the life of the school, meaning that they can perform social roles satisfactorily in the school setting.

Obviously, the total school program is concerned with socializing children. Socializing begins early in children's life in the home and continues and extends in contacts in the neighborhood, the community, and most especially the school. The forces that shape children's socialization are so powerful and pervasive that the process takes place whether or not it is willed and planned. But the nature and extent of this socialization may or may not conform to the expectations of the larger society, and this may make a considerable difference with respect to children's chances for success in a school's social environment. For some children, the social environment of the home and the school may be similar; for others, the two may be vastly different. In terms of school success, children who are familiar with some of the protocols of the school culture have a great advantage. Those children who do not have a social readiness for school are likely to be identified as ones who present behavior problems when, in fact, they simply have never developed the needed social skills. It is important to understand the debilitating effect that social skill deficits can have on a child's daily life.[24] To help children develop the necessary social skills, teachers, especially of the lower grades, need to be explicit in communicating to children what is expected of them in the classroom. This usually means specific directions, close supervision, frequent reminders of social expectations, and affirmative intervention in the formation of social and work groups in the classroom.

We deal here with a limited aspect of socialization. Indeed, we are confining our discussion to only three dimensions of socialization skills because it is known that the school environment can influence these.[25] These skills are those involved in (1) social interaction, (2) conflict resolution, and (3) cooperative group efforts (discussed in Chapter 9). Clearly, these must be considered among the most important skills in life because they profoundly affect how we deal with our fellow human beings.

For one to relate effectively to other human beings, one must first of all feel good about oneself. How one feels about oneself is usually referred to as one's *self-esteem*, *self-concept*, or *self-image*. Helping children build positive self-images is probably the single most important thing a teacher can do in terms of the total development of a young human being.

There is overwhelming evidence that those children who have poor images of self are likely not only to be low achievers but also to show other evidence of maladaptive behavior. It is not altogether clear which is the cause or the effect of the other, but it is reasonable to assume that it could be either, depending on individual cases. There are many cases of improved school achievement and more constructive behavior when children's self-esteem has improved. The reverse is also true.

Unfortunately, the school itself sometimes contributes to the deterioration of children's self-esteem. A youngster may come to school from a happy home, one that has contributed to the child's positive image of self. In school, that child may be bullied or teased by other children, encounter difficulty in learning to read, or experience failure in a variety of ways.[26]

The lack of success in school feeds on itself and can permeate children's entire lives in and out of school. For example, poor academic performance may disappoint a child's parents or guardians, and this disappointment may be conveyed to the child either unintentionally or overtly. Experiences such as these can, and often do, have a devastating effect on children's sense of personal worth. Children with such a background are almost certain to have problems in social relations; indeed, it would be remarkable if they did not. The importance of successful, confidence-building experiences is stressed repeatedly in educational and psychological literature. As a classroom teacher, then, what can you do to build in children this feeling of confidence and competence that is so vital to a good self-image?

It is imperative that you plan, establish, and maintain a classroom environment in which children feel good about themselves. Healthy self-images develop in *caring* environments that help children build histories of successful experiences. Self-images are destroyed in environments in which children get the impression that no one really cares about them, and where they experience constant failure. Also, it is doubtful whether children can perceive themselves positively if they do not have a personal liking for a teacher or if they feel a teacher does not like them.

You, the teacher, therefore, set the emotional climate of your classroom, one that facilitates social interaction based on trust, respect, and integrity. Although such a climate is achieved mainly by example, children do need to have systematic instruction in social skills. This instruction would include the following:

1. Teaching ordinary conventions and courtesies associated with social discourse.
2. Instilling sensitivity to the problems and feelings of others; seeing situations from another's point of view.
3. Listening to what others have to say.
4. Developing awareness of the consequences of large- or small-group behavior on individuals; for example, the effects of cliques, pressure on individuals to conform to group norms, and excluding certain children from group activities.
5. Achieving understanding of reasons people behave the way they do.

6. Becoming aware that social interaction involves decision making and choice and that one's choices often have consequences that affect other people.
7. Teaching and demonstrating skills of cooperative learning and following this with many opportunities for children to work cooperatively in your regular program of instruction.

> *To thrive in a global economy and a multicultural society, U.S. students need fluency in at least one language other than English.*
>
> —Myriam Met

FOREIGN LANGUAGE STUDY

Although the practice of introducing a foreign language in the elementary school is widespread among modern nations of the world, it has never enjoyed general popularity in the United States.[27] Nonetheless, the elementary years are an ideal time to teach language skills and foreign language study is offered in the curriculum of some elementary schools. Linguistic habits are less firmly fixed at those early ages, and children are therefore more readily receptive to nuances of sound and speech than they will be later. Studies demonstrate that the early study of a second language provides cognitive benefits, gains in academic achievement, and positive attitudes toward diversity.[28] The choice of language offered varies, of course, depending to some extent on the community, the availability of teachers, and whether the program can be sustained for several years.[29]

Elementary school foreign language programs fall within a spectrum of types. At one end are *total immersion* programs, where all of the classroom instruction is in the target foreign language.[30] At the other end of the spectrum are *foreign language experience (FLEX)* programs, where classes may meet only a few times a week and the goal is to introduce children to one or more foreign languages and cultures rather than to develop proficiency in the use of a target foreign language. Somewhere in the middle on the spectrum are what is known as *foreign language in the elementary school (FLES)* programs, which focus mostly on cultural awareness and developing listening and speaking skills in a target foreign language. FLES programs follow the natural sequence of language learning: understanding, speaking, reading, writing. For young children a typical FLES lesson plan would include physical activities such as songs, rhymes, games, and playacting with puppets.

Many people share the concern that the United States lags behind other nations in preparing its citizens to understand other cultures and to use other languages. Perhaps as a result of the *Goals 2000* legislation designating foreign languages as part of the core curriculum—along with the traditional disciplines of language arts, mathematics, science, and social studies—and the foreign language profession's development of national standards for K–12 foreign language programs, there soon will be an increase in foreign language study as a regular offering in the overt curriculum of elementary schools.

DOCUMENTS THAT INFLUENCE THE CURRICULUM

Whether for a semester or a school year or some other period of time, when planning the content of the curriculum you should decide what is to be accomplished in that period of time. To help in setting goals, you should examine school and other resource documents for mandates and guidelines, communicate with colleagues to learn of common expectations, and probe, analyze, and translate your own convictions, knowledge, and skills into behaviors that foster the intellectual and psychological, and in some instances the physical, development of your students.

As you begin your preparation for instruction, you will examine major documents that help guide you in selecting the content of your curriculum. These are national and state curriculum standards, school or district benchmark standards, curriculum frameworks and courses of study, and school-adopted materials such as textbooks and software programs. Sources for your examination of these documents include the Internet (see Figures 5.3 and 5.6) and personnel at school district offices and schools.

National Curriculum Standards

The paragraphs on page 168 describe the national education curriculum standards for K–12 education in the United States.

FIGURE 5.3
Internet resources on national and state curriculum standards.

National Standards
- Economics http://www.ncee.org
- English/reading http://www.ncte.org
- Foreign languages http://www.actfl.org
- Mathematics http://www.nctm.org
- Music http://www.menc.org
- Physical education http://www.aahperd.org
- Science http://www.nap.edu/readingroom/books/nses/
- Social studies http://www.ncss.org
- Technology http://www.iteawww.org
- Visual arts http://www.naea-reston.org

State Standards
- http://www.statestandards.com

Arts (visual and performing). Developed jointly by the American Alliance for Theater and Education, the National Art Education Association, the National Dance Association, and the Music Educators National Conference, the National Standards for Arts Education were completed and released in 1994.

Economics. Developed by the National Council on Economic Education, standards for the study of economics were completed and released in 1997.

English/language arts/reading. Developed jointly by the International Reading Association, the National Council of Teachers of English, and the University of Illinois Center for the Study of Reading, standards for English education were completed and released in 1996.

Foreign languages. Standards for Foreign Language Learning: Preparing for the 21st Century was completed and released by the American Council on the Teaching of Foreign Languages (ACTFL) in 1996.

Geography. Developed jointly by the Association of American Geographers, the National Council for Geographic Education, and the National Geographic Society, standards for geography education were completed and released in 1994.

Health. Developed by the Joint Committee for National School Health Education Standards, *National Health Education Standards: Achieving Health Literacy* was published in 1995.

History/civics/social studies. The Center for Civic Education and the National Center for Social Studies developed standards for civics and government, and the National Center for History in the Schools developed the standards for history, all of which were completed and released in 1994.

Mathematics. In 1989 and revised in 2000, the National Council of Teachers of Mathematics (NCTM) completed and released *Curriculum and Evaluation Standards for School Mathematics.*

Physical education. In 1995, the National Association of Sport and Physical Education (NASPE) published *Moving into the Future: National Standards for Physical Education.*

Science. In 1995, with input from the American Association for the Advancement of Science and the National Science Teachers Association, the National Research Council's National Committee on Science Education Standards and Assessment published the standards for science education.

Technology. With initial funding from the National Science Foundation and the National Aeronautics and Space Administration, and in collaboration with the International Technology Education Association, National Educational Technology Standards (NETS) were released in 2000.

State Curriculum Standards

Strongly influenced by the national standards, nearly all states have completed and are implementing at least some of their own standards for the various disciplines. For example:

• For the state of Massachusetts, standards are found in seven Curriculum Frameworks: Arts, English/Language Arts, Health, Mathematics, Science and Technology, Social Studies, and World Languages.

• For the state of Montana, Content and Performance Standards are found in documents for Reading, Mathematics, Speaking and Listening, Media Literacy, Writing, Literature, Health Enhancement, Science, Technology, World Languages, Arts, Library Media, Social Studies, and Work Place Competencies.

• For the state of North Carolina, standards are available for Arts Education, Computer/Technology Skills, English/Language Arts, Healthful Living, Mathematics, Science, Second-Language Studies, Social Studies, and Work-Force Development.

• And, for the state of Texas, standards are available in the foundations areas of English Language Arts and Reading, Mathematics, Science, Social Studies, and Spanish Language Arts and English as a Second Language, and in the enrichment areas of Languages Other Than English, Fine Arts, Health, Physical Education, and Technology Applications.

Both national and state standards provide guidance to the developers of the standardized tests being used to determine student achievement.

GOALS AND OBJECTIVES

Educational goals are achieved over an extended period of time. The goals of literacy, citizenship education, and personal development would normally require several school years for their attainment, perhaps even an entire

Activity 5.2: Examining Curriculum Documents and Standards

Using Internet addresses provided in Figure 5.3, review the national and state standards that interest you. Use the following questions as a guideline for small group discussions. Following the small group discussion, share the big ideas about the standards and perceptions of your group with the rest of your class.

  Subject area _____

• Name of the standards documents reviewed, year of publication, and development agency for each document.
• Major educational goals as specified by the standards.
• Are the standards specific as to subject matter content for each level of schooling, K–12? Explain.

• Do the standards offer specific strategies for instruction? Describe.
• Do the standards offer suggestions for teaching students who are culturally different, for students with special needs, and for students who are intellectually gifted and talented? Describe.
• Do the standards offer suggestions or guidelines for dealing with controversial topics and issues? Describe.
• Do the standards documents or their accompanying materials offer suggestions for specific resources? Describe.
• Do the standards refer to assessment? Describe.

school career for some students. Educational goals, therefore, are important in providing a sense of direction for education in the United States. One finds educational goals that reflect the basic purposes of education stated in a variety of sources, such as news releases in communications media, documents prepared by local school boards and state departments of education, and policy statements of agencies, commissions, and organizations at the national level.

Goals statements and accompanying standards of performance then are used for guidance by developers and writers of curriculum materials such as textbooks and software programs. Committees of educators and teachers at the state and local levels also use them for guidance in curriculum planning.

At the classroom level, teachers focus their attention on attaining learning expectations that are appropriate for children and relevant to a lesson or unit of study. The learning expectations are written as behaviors to be demonstrated and are referred to as *standards of performance* or, simply, as *instructional objectives*. These objectives have an immediate intent. They specify the learning outcome more sharply than do educational goals. Thus, the educational goal "to develop literacy in oral and written English" when translated for instruction and assessment may include an instructional objective for children, "As a result of this lesson, students will demonstrate their knowledge of sentence structure by using subject, verb, and object correctly in oral and written expression."

Even though the terms *goals* and *objectives* are sometimes used interchangeably, this practice fails to acknowledge the proper relationship between educational goals and instructional objectives. *Educational goals* ordinarily reflect a synthesis of the expressed ideas or values of a given society or cultural group. They are usually normative in that they reflect the prevailing ideas and values of the society or group. Therefore, they do not account for the variability that teachers encounter in specific classroom situations. To be made operational, these general statements of goals must be translated into statements of measurable performance, that is, specific instructional objectives that are relevant to the particular situation. Both types of statements serve the critical purpose of providing the means for teachers to conceptualize the direction of instruction and the nature of learning activities. This chapter will help you learn how to translate goals into specific instructional objectives and teach within what is known as an *aligned curriculum*.

Results-Driven Education

The curriculum process that involves identifying expected outcomes (objectives), teaching to those outcomes, and assessing results in terms of whether the outcomes are achieved is referred to as the *aligned curriculum* and has been central to most educational reform during recent years. For example, *results-driven education (RDE)*, also known as *outcome-based education (OBE)*, utilizes a goal-driven curriculum model with instruction that

The bottom line in education is not the amount of time spent on instruction, nor the amount of dollars expended on it, nor the certification requirements of teachers. What counts in the end are the results: what children have learned, how well they have learned it, and the difference learning it has made in their lives.

focuses on constructing individual knowledge through mastery and assessing student learning against the anticipated outcomes. The basic idea behind results-driven education is that teachers should focus on the *results* (outcomes) expected from instruction, rather than on the amount of time devoted to it. Furthermore, for schools to respond to the call for greater accountability it is imperative to know what objectives were sought and with what results. Knowing the congruency of these two variables provides one with at least a beginning sense of the effectiveness of the instruction. The "bottom line" in education is not the amount of time spent on instruction, nor the amount of dollars expended on it, nor the certification requirements of teachers. What counts in the end are the results, that is, what children have learned, how well they have learned it, and what difference it has made that they have learned it.

Using Instructional Objectives

In light of the preceding discussion, it is important that you be able to prepare instructional objectives that reflect related educational goals and curriculum standards. For example, schools stress the goal, "to produce citizens who are competent in the basic skills." Such a goal requires teachers to use objectives that enable them to measure the extent to which students have achieved it. This approach reflects the emphasis on accountability in education. It is based in part on the assumption that the best criterion for evaluating a teacher's performance is whether students are learning. Educational literature frequently contains references to the "evaluation of the product," another way of emphasizing the use of measurable objectives. As a result, objectives that are easily measured are given high visibility in educational programs. However, experienced teachers realize the importance of providing children with a variety of learning experiences. Instructional objectives that restrict learning to what can be quickly and easily measured lose the richness that a variety of learning activities brings to children. Further, if teachers develop the habit of selecting instructional objectives from a ready-made list, composed in another setting, the spontaneity and the capacity to meet the needs, abilities, and interests of a particular group of children would be greatly reduced. Marzano suggests that teachers must make a clear distinction between essential and supplemental curriculum content, and that considered as essential content should be the first priority. According to Marzano's research, "only about 46 percent of the content identified in the national and state-level documents could be identified as essential." To teach that content would take about 80 percent of the available instructional time. The remaining 20 percent of the time can be devoted to content selected at the teacher's discretion.[31]

An instructional objective should state clearly what students are supposed to be able to demonstrate as a result of their learning. It provides a match between the expected learner outcome and the capacity of children to achieve it. This requires that the objective be based on the realities of the actual classroom in which the learners are located. Therefore, it is our belief that the teacher or teachers of a particular group of learners should select or prepare the majority of the instructional objectives for those learners. Furthermore, these teachers should select or design the strategies for assessing their learning as well.

Teachers are not ordinarily held accountable for outcomes not embodied in their instructional objectives. On the other hand, teachers can and should be held accountable for outcomes that are so defined. Objectives, therefore, represent your acknowledgment of your responsibility to help children achieve certain learning. Objectives need to be challenging to both you and your students but, at the same time, should be realistically achievable. They must not be simply high-sounding and well-meaning statements of ultimately immeasurable expectations. Although, as stated, you do not want to limit yourself to easily measured goals, objectives *must* be measurable to be useful. This is why it is so important that you know how to write instructional objectives well: You should not commit yourself either to tasks that fail to challenge and stimulate students or to tasks that you cannot possibly accomplish.

Activity 5.3: Identifying Action Verbs

A good verb to use in a measurable objective is one that denotes a directly observable behavior, which is overt. Circle the words in the following list that do *not* meet this criterion, that represent covert behavior. Compare those you have circled with those circled by your classmates, and discuss any differences of opinion.

To understand	To solve	To cite
To locate	To read	To define
To appreciate	To feel	To write
To compare	To name	To listen
To believe	To realize	To recall
To comprehend	To list	To know

Elements of Measurable Learning Objectives

You may write measurable instructional objectives to do more than simply state anticipated observable learner behavior; they also can describe the conditions under which behavior will be demonstrated and the level of attainment expected. The *anticipated outcomes* that appear at the beginning of each chapter of this book are examples of simply stated measurable instructional objectives. The following is an example objective containing all three elements:

> On a science quiz containing 20 examples, the student will differentiate between descriptions of physical and chemical changes with at least 80 percent accuracy.

In this example, the *expected learner behavior* is that "students will differentiate between descriptions of physical and chemical changes"; the *conditions* under which this objective is demonstrated is "on a science quiz containing 20 examples," and the *acceptable level of attainment* is "with at least 80 percent accuracy." When the acceptable level of attainment is omitted it is usually because the level expected is mastery, that is, 85 percent or higher.[32] You may write objectives as if for a single student or for the entire class, your choice. For an entire class, the previous objective would read "On a science quiz containing 20 examples, students will differentiate between descriptions of physical and chemical changes, with at least 80 percent accuracy." You then must decide if an acceptable outcome is a class average of 16 or better correct or whether you require every student to score at least 16 correct.

The following examples illustrate measurable instructional objectives:

1. After reading the story "The Tallest Tree," the student will rewrite the story in his or her own words, including a minimum of five events.
2. During class discussion, children will ask permission before speaking by raising their hands.
3. In response to a lesson on creative writing, children will produce a written product of their own choosing and design.
4. Given a spelling list of 20 words, children will write the words with 80 percent accuracy.

Learning Objectives in the Curriculum

When planning instructional objectives, it is useful to consider what have been referred to as the three domains of learning:

Cognitive domain—involves intellectual operations from the lowest level of simple recall of information to complex, high-level thinking processes

Affective domain—involves feelings, emotions, attitudes, and values, and ranges from the lower levels of acquisition to the highest level of internalization and action

Psychomotor domain—ranges from the simple manipulation of materials to the communication of ideas, and finally to the highest level of creative performance

Educators attempt to design learning experiences to meet the five areas of developmental needs of the total child: intellectual, physical, emotional/psychological, social, and moral/ethical. As a teacher, you must include objectives that address learning within each of these categories of needs. While intellectual needs are primarily within the cognitive domain and physical needs are within the psychomotor, the others mostly are within the affective domain.

Too frequently, teachers focus on the cognitive domain while assuming that the psychomotor and affective will take care of themselves. Many experts argue that teachers should do just the opposite: that when the affective is directly attended to, the psychomotor and cognitive naturally develop. In any case, you should plan your teaching to guide students from the lowest to highest levels of operation within each of the domains, separately or simultaneously.

We discuss the three developmental hierarchies in this section to guide your understanding of each of the five areas of needs. Note the illustrative verbs used within each hierarchy. These verbs help you fashion objectives when developing your unit and lesson plans. (Figure 5.4 presents a sample of goals and objectives fit into one lesson plan. Action verbs appropriate to objectives for each category in each domain are shown in Figure 5.5.) We urge caution, however, for there can be considerable overlap among the levels at which you may appropriately use some action verbs. For example, the verb "identifies" is appropriate in each of the following objectives at different levels (identified in parentheses) within the cognitive domain:

The student will identify the correct definition of the term "magnetism." (knowledge)

The student will identify examples of natural and artificial magnetism. (comprehension)

The student will identify the effect when iron filings are sprinkled on a sheet of paper placed on a bar magnet. (application)

The student will identify the effect on the iron filings when two magnetic north poles are brought close together. (analysis)

Teacher _____ Class & Grade Level: _Language Arts/Science 5–6_   Date _____
Unit: _Investigative Research & Generative Writing_
Lesson Topic: _Writing Response and Peer Assessment via Internet_
Time duration: _several days_

1. **Anticipated Learning Outcomes**
   Goals:
   1.1. One goal for this lesson is for students to collaborate and prepare response papers to peers from around the world who have shared the results of their own experimental research findings and research paper about ozone concentrations in the atmosphere.
   1.2. The ultimate goal of this unit is for students around the world to prepare and publish for worldwide dissemination a final paper about global ozone levels in the atmosphere.

   Objectives:
   Cognitive:
   a. Through cooperative group action, students will conduct experimental research to collect data about the ozone level of air in their environment. (application)
   b. In cooperative groups, students will analyze the results of their experiments. (analyze)
   c. Students will compile data and infer from their experimental data. (synthesis and evaluation)
   d. Through collaborative writing groups, the students will prepare a final paper that summarizes their research study of local atmospheric ozone levels. (evaluation)
   e. Through sharing via the Internet, students will write response papers to their peers from other locations in the world. (evaluation)
   f. From their own collaborative research and worldwide communications with their peers, the students will draw conclusions about global atmospheric ozone levels. (evaluation)

   Affective:
   a. Students will respond attentively to the response papers of their peers. (attending)
   b. Students will willingly cooperate with others during the group activities. (responding)
   c. Students will offer opinions about the atmospheric level of ozone. (valuing)
   d. Students will form judgments about local, regional, and worldwide ozone levels. (organizing)
   e. Students will communicate accurately their findings and attend diligently to the work of their worldwide peers. (internalizing)

   Psychomotor:
   a. Students will manipulate the computer so that their e-mail communications are transmitted accurately. (manipulating)
   b. In a summary to the study, students will describe their feelings about atmospheric ozone concentrations. (communicating)
   c. Students will ultimately create a proposal for worldwide dissemination. (creating)

2. **Procedure**
   Content:
   At the start of this unit, collaborative groups were established via Intercultural E-mail Classroom Connections (IECC) (http://www.stolaf.edu/network/iecc) with other classes from schools around

(Continues)

FIGURE 5.4

Lesson plan sample: Multiple-day, project-centered, interdisciplinary, and transcultural lesson using worldwide communication via the Internet.

Source: Adapted from R. D. Kellough and N. G. Kellough, _Teaching Young Adolescents,_ 4th ed. (Upper Saddle River, NJ: Merrill/ Prentice Hall, 2003), 212–213. Adapted by permission.

the world. These groups of students conducted several scientific research experiments on the ozone level of their local atmospheric air. To obtain relative measurements of ozone concentrations in the air, for example, students set up experiments that involved stretching rubber bands on a board, then observing the number of days until the bands broke. Students maintained daily journal logs of the temperature, barometric pressure, and wind speed/direction, and recorded the number of days that it took for the bands to break.* After compiling their data and preparing single-page summaries of their results, students exchanged data via the Internet with other groups. From data collected worldwide, students wrote a one-page summary as to what conditions might account for the difference in levels of ozone. Following the exchange of students' written responses and their subsequent revisions based on feedback from the worldwide peers, students are now preparing a final summary report about the world's atmospheric ozone level. The intention is to disseminate worldwide (to newspapers and via the Internet) this final report.

Activity 1: Introduction (10 minutes)
Today, in think–share pairs, you will prepare initial responses to the e-mail responses we have received from other groups from around the world. (Teacher shares the list of places from which e-mail has been received.) Any questions before we get started?

As we discussed earlier, here are the instructions: in your think–share pairs (each pair is given one response received via e-mail), prepare a written response according to the following outline: (a) note points or information you would like to incorporate in the final paper to be forwarded via the Internet; (b) comment on one aspect of the written response you like best; (c) provide questions to the sender to seek clarification or elaboration. I think you should be able to finish this in about 30 minutes, so let's try for that.

Activity 2: (30 minutes, if needed)
Preparation of dyad responses

Activity 3: (open)
Let's now hear from each response pair.

Dyad responses are shared with the whole class for discussion of inclusion in response paper to be sent via Internet.

Activity 4: (open)
Discussion, conclusion, and preparation of final drafts to be sent to each e-mail corresponder to be done by cooperative groups (the number of groups needed will be determined by the number of e-mail corresponders at this time).

Activity 5: (open)
Later, as students receive e-mail responses from other groups, the responses will be printed and reviewed. The class then responds to each using the same criteria as before and returns this response to the e-mail sender.

3. **Closure and Assessment:**

The process continues until all groups (from around the world) have agreed on and prepared the final report for dissemination.

Assessment of student learning for this lesson is formative: journals, daily checklist of student participation in groups; writing drafts

4. **Materials and Equipment Needed:**

School computers with Internet access; printers; copies of e-mail responses

5. **Reflection:**

---

*The science experiment is described in R. J. Ryder and T. Hughes, *Internet for Educators* (Upper Saddle River, NJ: Merrill/ Prentice Hall, 1997), 98.

FIGURE 5.4
Continued

Cognitive Domain

1. Knowledge

choose	describe	list	name	recognize
complete	identify	locate	outline	select
define	indicate	match	recall	state

2. Comprehension

change	describe	explain	paraphrase	summarize
classify	discuss	generalize	predict	translate
convert	estimate	infer	recognize	
defend	expand	interpret	retell	

3. Application

apply	discover	participate	predict	simulate
calculate	exhibit	perform	relate	solve
demonstrate	modify	plan	show	use
develop	operate			

4. Analysis

analyze	compare	differentiate	illustrate	relate
arrange	contrast	discover	infer	separate
break down	debate	discriminate	inquire	subdivide
categorize	deduce	group	organize	
classify	diagram	identify	outline	

5. Synthesis

arrange	create	generate	plan	summmarize
assemble	design	hypothesize	predict	synthesize
categorize	develop	imagine	produce	tell
classify	devise	invent	rearrange	transmit
combine	document	modify	reconstruct	write
compile	explain	organize	revise	
compose	formulate	originate	rewrite	

6. Evaluation

appraise	conclude	discriminate	justify	relate
argue	consider	estimate	predict	revise
assess	contrast	explain	rank	standardize
choose	criticize	interpret	rate	support
compare	decide	judge	recommend	validate

(Continues)

FIGURE 5.5
Verbs for cognitive, affective, and psychomotor objectives

Affective Domain

1. Receiving

ask	differentiate	identify	point to	reply
choose	distinguish	locate	recall	select
describe	hold	name	recognize	use

2. Responding

answer	comply	perform	read	spend
applaud	discuss	play	recite	(time in)
approve	greet	practice	report	tell
assist	help	present	select	write
command	label			

3. Valuing

argue	differentiate	initiate	propose	select
assist	explain	invite	protest	share
complete	follow	join	read	study
describe	form	justify	report	support

4. Organizing

adhere	combine	discuss	identify	organize
alter	compare	explain	integrate	prepare
arrange	defend	form	modify	relate
balance	define	generalize	order	synthesize

5. Internalizing

act	influence	perform	qualify	serve
complete	listen	practice	question	solve
display	modify	propose	revise	verify

Psychomotor Domain

1. Moving

adjust	carry	clean	grasp	jump	locate	obtain	walk

2. Manipulating

assemble	build	calibrate	connect	play	thread	turn

3. Communicating

analyze	ask	describe	draw	explain	write

4. Creating

create	design	invent

FIGURE 5.5

Continued

COGNITIVE DOMAIN HIERARCHY

In a widely accepted taxonomy of objectives, Bloom and his associates arranged cognitive objectives into classifications according to the complexity of the skills and abilities they embodied.[33] The result was a ladder ranging from the simplest to the most complex intellectual processes. Within each domain, prerequisite to a student's ability to function at one particular level of the hierarchy is the ability to function at the preceding level or levels. In other words, a student functioning at the third level of the cognitive domain is automatically also functioning at the first and second levels. In contrast to the orderly progression from simple to complex mental operations illustrated by Bloom's taxonomy, other researchers prefer an organization of cognitive abilities that ranges from simple (information storage and retrieval) through a higher level (discrimination and concept attainment) to the highest cognitive ability (recognizing and solving problems).[34]

The six major categories (or levels) in Bloom's taxonomy of cognitive objectives are (1) *knowledge*—recognizing and recalling information; (2) *comprehension*—understanding the meaning of information; (3) *application*—using information; (4) *analysis*—dissecting information into its component parts to comprehend their relationships; (5) *synthesis*—putting components together to generate new ideas; and (6) *evaluation*—judging the worth of an idea, notion, theory, thesis, proposition, information, or opinion. In this taxonomy, the top four categories or levels—application, analysis, synthesis, and evaluation—are known as the *higher-order cognitive thinking skills*.

Although space does not allow elaboration here, Bloom's taxonomy includes various subcategories within each of these six major categories. It is probably less important that an objective be absolutely classified than it is to be cognizant of hierarchies of thinking and doing and to understand the importance of attending to student intellectual behavior from lower to higher levels of operation in all three domains of learning. We discuss each of Bloom's six cognitive domain categories in the following subsections.

Knowledge

The basic level of Bloom's taxonomy concerns the acquisition of knowledge—the ability to recognize and recall information. Although this is the lowest of the six categories, the information to be learned may itself be of an extremely high level. Included here is knowledge of principles, generalizations, theories, structures, and methodology, as well as knowledge of facts and ways of dealing with facts.

The following are examples of objectives at the knowledge level. Note especially the verb (in italics) used in each example:

- From memory, the student *will recall* the letters in the English alphabet that are vowels.

- The student *will describe* the effects of magnetism.
- The student *will identify* the major parts of speech in the sentence.

The remaining five categories of Bloom's taxonomy of the cognitive domain deal with *using* knowledge. They encompass the educational objectives aimed at developing cognitive skills and abilities: comprehension, application, analysis, synthesis, and evaluation of knowledge.

Comprehension

Comprehension includes the ability to translate, explain, or interpret knowledge and to extrapolate from it to address new situations. Examples of objectives in this category are as follows:

- From a sentence, the student *will recognize* the letters that are vowels in the English alphabet.
- From a list of different materials, the student *will explain* which materials would be affected by a magnet and which would not.
- The student *will recognize* the major parts of speech in the sentence.

Application

Once learners understand information, they should be able to apply it. Examples of objectives in this category are as follows:

- The student *will use* in a sentence a word that contains at least two vowels.
- The student *will predict* which materials on the table will be affected by a magnet.
- The student *will demonstrate* in a complete sentence each of the major parts of speech.

Analysis

This category includes objectives that require learners to use analytical skills. Objectives in this category include the following:

- From a list of words, the student *will differentiate* those that contain vowels from those that do not.
- In an investigation the student *will identify* which materials are magnetic and which are not.
- The student *will analyze* a paragraph for misuse of major parts of speech.

Synthesis

This category includes objectives that involve such skills as designing a plan, proposing a set of operations, and deriving a series of abstract relations. Examples of objectives in this category are as follows:

- The student *will rearrange* a list of words into several lists according to the vowels contained in each.
- The student *will devise* a classification scheme determining which materials on the table are magnetic, from those that are permanently magnetic to those that are not magnetic at all.
- The student *will write* a paragraph that correctly uses each of the major parts of speech.

Evaluation

This, Bloom's highest category, includes offering opinions and making value judgments. Examples of objectives in this category are as follows:

- The student *will listen to and evaluate* other students' identifications of vowels from sentences written on the board.
- While observing natural materials found in the environment, the student *will justify* her interpretation that certain of the materials are naturally magnetic and others are not.
- The student *will evaluate* a paragraph written by another student for the proper use of major parts of speech.

AFFECTIVE DOMAIN HIERARCHY

Krathwohl, Bloom, and Masia developed a useful taxonomy of the affective domain.[35] The following are their major levels (or categories), from least internalized to most internalized: (1) *receiving*—being aware of the affective stimulus and beginning to have favorable feelings toward it; (2) *responding*—taking an interest in the stimulus and viewing it favorably; (3) *valuing*—showing a tentative belief in the value of the affective stimulus and becoming committed to it; (4) *organizing*—placing values into a system of dominant and supporting values; and (5) *internalizing*—demonstrating consistent beliefs and behavior that have become a way of life. Although considerable overlap occurs among categories within the affective domain, they do give a basis by which to judge the quality of objectives and the nature of learning within this area. We discuss each of the five affective categories in the following subsections.

Receiving

At this level, which is the least internalized, learners exhibit willingness to give attention to particular phenomena or stimuli, and teachers are able to arouse, sustain, and direct that attention. Examples of objectives in this category are as follows:

- The student *listens attentively* to the ideas of others.
- The student *demonstrates sensitivity* to the property and beliefs of others.

Responding

At this level, learners respond to a received stimulus. They may do so because of some external pressure, or because they find the stimulus interesting, or because responding gives them satisfaction. Examples of objectives at this level are as follows:

- The student *discusses* what others have said.
- The student *cooperates* with others during group activities.

Valuing

Objectives at the valuing level deal with learners' beliefs, attitudes, and appreciations. The simplest objectives concern the acceptance of beliefs and values; higher ones involve learning to prefer certain values and finally becoming committed to them. Objectives in this category include the following:

- The student *protests* against racial or ethnic or gender discrimination.
- The student *synthesizes* a position on cutting trees in the rainforests.

Organizing

This fourth level in the affective domain concerns building a personal value system. Here learners are conceptualizing and arranging values into a system that recognizes their relative importance. Examples of objectives in this category are as follows:

- The student *forms judgments* concerning proper behavior in the classroom, school, and community.
- The student *defends* the important values of a particular subculture.

Internalizing

This is the highest category within the affective domain, at which learners' behaviors have become consistent with their beliefs. Examples of objectives in this category are as follows:

- The student's behavior *displays* a well-defined and ethical code of conduct.
- The student *performs* independently.

EDUCATION IN THE AFFECTIVE DOMAIN

Affective education has to do with a range of learnings that focus on feelings, values, ideals, appreciation, moral and character development, and attitudes. If we might refer in a colloquial way to cognitive learnings as those that deal with the *head* and to psychomotor learnings as those that deal with the *hand*, affective learnings would be characterized as those dealing with the *heart*. To a large extent, the curriculum focuses on affective learnings through the humanities and the arts, but affective learning surrounds children throughout the school day. The fact that so many children lose their love of learning and grow to dislike school as they progress through the grades should be a matter of great concern to teachers.

The following suggestions may help you prepare objectives dealing with affective education:

1. Every topic studied presents possibilities for affective objectives. Sensitize yourself to these possibilities. What kinds of *feelings* are children developing toward the subject? Does the material illustrate an ideal or value that is embraced by this society? Does the topic afford an opportunity to expand children's vision of the human potential? What must you avoid doing that might permanently "turn off" students' interest in this subject?

2. Keep in mind that affective learning must be internalized rather than simply verbalized. When children give all the right answers in the classroom about "showing consideration for others" and then beat up each other on the playground, it is obvious that they have not attained the learning objective. State the objective in ways that encourage children to *experience* the affective learning.

3. Avoid stating affective objectives in cognitive terms. For example, notice the difference between these two objectives:
   a. To understand the hardships endured by pioneers on their westward journey.
   b. To develop an appreciation of the hardships endured by pioneers on their westward journey.

The first is an information objective, whereas the second is an affective objective. In this case, it could be argued that *both* are important because one would more than likely develop an appreciation of these hardships by acquiring more information about settlers' actual experiences.

4. As you write affective objectives, plan how you will evaluate whether students have achieved them.

The following examples of instructional objectives in art, music, and citizenship emphasize measurable affective outcomes:

- During the week following the music lesson, children will express the desire to participate in a similar musical activity.
- After listening to the teacher read excerpts from a book dealing with life on the frontier, some children will ask to read the entire book themselves.
- During free-choice time, children will choose art activities that were presented in previous lessons.
- Following the teacher's discussion of the need for assistance in caring for classroom materials and equipment, children will demonstrate their willingness to help.

Activity 5.4: What Can *You* Do About It?

To what extent do classroom situations contribute to stealing, lying, cheating, aggression, hostility, and lack of consideration for others? Many think that the contribution is substantial. Consider the following situations:

- A teacher leaves loose change lying around on his desk during the school day.
- A teacher stores her purse on the floor next to her desk in the classroom.
- Assignments are unreasonably excessive, with embarrassing consequences for noncompletion.
- Testing situations are poorly or carelessly supervised.
- Children fear drastic consequences if the teacher learns that they have been involved in any infraction of school rules.
- The classroom atmosphere is one of high tension and anxiety; children are constantly edgy and easily irritated.
- There are many competitive situations in which children are pitted against each other and enjoy excelling or "beating" their classmates.

- The teacher makes an excessive number of negative or destructively critical statements.
- There are few opportunities to relax and enjoy social interaction.
- Children carelessly store personal items and fail to establish attitudes of respect for the belongings of others, which makes it easy for them to use and take things (innocently or intentionally) that belong to others.
- The teacher seems oblivious to the fact that while the majority of the female students in his classroom wait to be called on while raising their hands, the majority of the male students impulsively speak out at will, even interrupting one another and the girls while talking.

1. What would you predict to be the consequences of each of the situations described?
2. Do such situations encourage dishonest or inconsiderate behavior even at the college level?

PSYCHOMOTOR DOMAIN HIERARCHY

Whereas educators generally agree on identification and classification within the cognitive and affective domains, there is less agreement on classification within the psychomotor domain. Originally, the goal of this domain was simply to develop and categorize proficiency in skills, particularly those dealing with gross and fine muscle control. The classification presented here follows this lead, but includes at its highest level the most creative and inventive behaviors, thus coordinating skills and knowledge from all three domains. Consequently, the objectives are in a hierarchy ranging from simple gross locomotor control to the most creative and complex, requiring originality and fine locomotor control—for example, from simply turning on a computer to designing a software program. From Harrow we offer the following taxonomy of the psychomotor domain: (1) *moving*, (2) *manipulating*, (3) *communicating*, and (4) *creating*.[36]

Moving

This level involves gross motor coordination. Example objectives for this category are as follows:

- The student *will jump* a rope ten times without missing.
- The student *will correctly grasp* the pencil.

Manipulating

This level involves fine motor coordination. Example objectives for this category are as follows:

- The student *will assemble* the lettered blocks in alphabetical order.
- The student *will connect* the dots.

Communicating

This level involves communication of ideas and feelings. Example objectives for this category are as follows:

- By *asking* appropriate questions, the student will demonstrate active listening skills.
- The student *will describe* his feelings about the clear-cutting of tropical rain forests.

Creating

Creating is the highest level of this domain, and of all domains, and represents students' coordination of thinking, learning, and behaving in all three domains. Example objectives for this category are as follows:

- The student *will design* a mural.
- The student *will create, choreograph, and perform* a dance pattern.

SEQUENCING OBJECTIVES

We have emphasized that, as a teacher, you should be able to distinguish between educational goals and instructional objectives, be able to write measurable instructional objectives, and understand the nature and interdependence of cognitive, psychomotor, and affective outcomes. Another and equally important competence consists of being able to arrange instructional objectives in the sequence most likely to enhance children's learning.

Suppose you were thinking about how to present a new topic or new skill to your students. At this early planning stage you would be identifying objectives associated with the material you will teach. Having done that, you must analyze the new material to determine what order or *sequence* you should follow in teaching it. For example, if a middle-grade class were about to study the history of the economic growth of a region, such as the South, it would be important for learners to know something about the geography of that area. Or if children are to learn to divide whole numbers by using single-digit divisors, they would first have to know how to add, subtract, and multiply whole numbers. The critical questions are these: What needs to come first in the teaching sequence? What comes next? What should come near the end? You can aid your analysis by examining the children's textbook or by studying the order of presentation used in an encyclopedia article on the topic.

What factors affect your order of presentation? One is *complexity*. Teachers usually program their instruction along a simple-to-complex continuum. Another factor is the need to *know prerequisite material*. This is especially important in learning skills that require step-by-step mastery before progressing to the next level. The strict order in which some mathematical operations must be learned provides a good example of this principle. Another factor influencing presentation sequence is the *mode of teaching*. An access mode, for instance, would more than likely use a presentation sequence quite different from a delivery mode (we discuss modes of instruction in Chapter 8). Finally, *learner characteristics* might also have some bearing on the order of presentation. Having chosen your sequence, you would arrange the instructional objectives accordingly (see the sample lesson plan in Figure 5.4).

SUMMARY

In this chapter you learned about what is defined as *curriculum* and about the components of the formal or planned curriculum of the elementary school. In addition you learned of the power of the messages sent via the covert curriculum.

Two areas of the overt curriculum that consume a major portion of instructional time are language arts and mathematics. Science, physical education, foreign language, and the expressive arts traditionally have received less attention. Perhaps under pressure to account for children's achievement through standardized competency tests, the expressive arts, for example, have become an endangered species for young children in too many schools. However, understanding the value of the expressive arts as basic to the intellectual and psychological growth of children, many teachers today are directing their efforts toward integrating the expressive arts with language arts, science, social sciences, and mathematics. In your professional teacher preparation, you will receive additional specific instruction dealing with individual areas of the curriculum.

You learned the differences between *goals* and *objectives*. Regardless of how these terms are defined, the important point is this: *Teachers must be clear about what it is they want their students to learn and about the kind of evidence needed to verify their learning, and must communicate these things so students clearly understand them.*

Many teachers do not bother to write specific and clearly measurable instructional objectives for all the learning activities in their teaching plans. However, when teachers do prepare specific objectives (by writing them themselves or by borrowing them from curriculum documents), teach toward

Activity 5.5: Try Your Hand at Preparing Objectives

Using the information presented in this chapter, try your hand at preparing measurable instructional objectives for each of the following:

- For a lesson focusing on *knowing word meanings*
- For a social studies lesson dealing with *map directions*
- For a science lesson on *living versus nonliving things*
- For an art lesson *showing perspective in a drawing*

- For a math lesson on *placeholders*

1. Compare and discuss your examples with your classmates. What makes some examples better than others?
2. Which ones did you find easier to write? Which ones were more difficult? Why?
3. Which of your objectives would be easier to assess? Which would be more difficult? Why?

them, and assess students' progress against them, student learning is enhanced; this is called *performance-based teaching* and *criterion-referenced measurement*. It is also known as an *aligned curriculum*. In schools using results-driven education mastery learning models, those models describe levels of mastery standards or rubrics for each outcome or learning target. The taxonomies are of tremendous help in schools where teachers are expected to correlate learning activities to the school's outcome standards.

As a teacher, you will be expected to (1) plan your lessons well, (2) convey specific expectations to your students, and (3) assess their learning against that specificity. However, because such performance-based teaching tends toward high objectivity, there is the danger that it could become too objective, which can have negative consequences. If children are treated as objects, then the relationship between teacher and child becomes impersonal and counterproductive to real learning. Highly specific and impersonal teaching can discourage serendipity, creativity, and the excitement of discovery, to say nothing of its possibly negative impact on the development of students' self-esteem.

Performance-based instruction works well when teaching toward mastery of basic skills, but people tend to infer from the concept of mastery learning that there is some foreseeable end to learning, an assumption that is obviously erroneous. With performance-based instruction, the source of student

Arts Education Partnership at www.aep-arts.org

Character Education Partnership at www.character.org/resources/search

Children's Music Workshop at www.childrensmusicworkshop.com

National Commission on Service Learning at www.servicelearningcommission.org

National Endowment for the Arts at www.arts.org

National Geographic Society at www.nationalgeographic.com/education

FIGURE 5.6

Additional Web sites (see also Figure 5.3) as sources of information related to the elementary school curriculum motivation tends to be extrinsic. Teacher expectations, marks and grades, society, and peer pressures are examples of extrinsic sources that drive student performance. To be a most effective teacher, your challenge is to use performance-based criteria together with a teaching style that encourages the development of intrinsic sources of student motivation and that allows for, provides for, and encourages coincidental learning—learning that goes beyond what might be considered predictable, immediately measurable, and representative of minimal expectations.

In Chapter 6, which follows, we focus your attention on preparing the plans for instruction.

STUDY QUESTIONS AND ADDITIONAL ACTIVITIES

1. A woman with 3 years of experience left teaching at age 25 to devote full time to her family. Now, when she is 50, with her three children grown, she wants to return to the classroom as a fifth-grade teacher. Which of the subject areas of the curriculum will she find has changed most and which least? Why?

2. If the elementary school in your neighborhood were to offer one total immersion foreign-language program beginning in the first grade and continuing throughout the grades, and you were asked for your input, which language would you suggest it be and why?

3. Local control of schools and local determination of curriculum are highly prized values in American education, yet striking similarity exists in the curriculum content and sequence among schools and districts throughout the 50 states. How do you account for this?

4. Explain the difference, if any, between what is a *skill* and what is a *disposition*. Give examples of each.

5. Some experts argue that assessment is enhanced when learning objectives are clearly stated in measurable terms. Do you agree with their position? Explain why you do or do not agree.

6. For a specified grade level, describe observable behaviors that would enable you to tell whether a student is thinking critically.

7. Recall your own elementary schooling. What do you remember? Most likely you remember projects, your presentations, the lengthy research you did, and your extra effort doing artwork to accompany a presentation. Maybe you remember a teacher's compliment or a pat on the back by peers. Most likely you do *not* remember the massive amount of factual content that you covered. Discuss this and your feelings about it with your classmates.

8. Should a teacher encourage serendipitous (coincidental) learning? If not, why not? If so, describe ways to do it.

9. Webster's *New Universal Dictionary of the English Language*, unabridged, provides 87 meanings for the common word label *run*. What does this suggest about having children provide one-sentence definitions of concepts?

10. It has been said that affective learnings tend to be "caught" rather than "taught." How do you feel about the statement? Provide specific suggestions about what you as a teacher can do to facilitate affective learning. Some people object to the term *indoctrination* when applied to the process of instilling values and beliefs in others. Do you think it is possible that the fear of indoctrination may mean that preferred values and beliefs are not taught at all? Where and how should children learn basic values and acts of common courtesy?

NOTES

1. *Approaching Kindergarten: A Look at Preschoolers in the United States* (Washington, DC: National Center for Education Statistics, Document 95–280, 1995).

2. J. Paterno, *Mandatory Kindergarten: Will It Make a Difference in Kentucky?* (Washington, DC: ERIC Clearinghouse on Early Childhood Education, 1984), ED 264007.

3. See, for example, M. J. Adams, "The Great Debate: Then and Now," *Annals of Dyslexia* 47: 265–276 (1997); H. Daniels, S. Zemelman, and M. Bizar, "Whole Language Works: Sixty Years of Research," *Educational Leadership* 57(2): 32–37 (1999); and K. L. Dahl and P. L. Scharer, "Phonics Teaching and Learning in Whole Language Classrooms: New Evidence from Research," *The Reading Teacher* 53(7): 584–594 (2000).

4. See, for example, B. Matson, "Whole Language or Phonics? Teachers and Researchers Find the Middle Ground Most Fertile," *Harvard Education Letter* 12(2): 1–5 (1999).

5. A. M. Duffy-Hester, "Teaching Struggling Readers in Elementary School Classrooms: A Review of Classroom Reading Programs and Principles for Instruction," *The Reading Teacher* 52(5): 480–495 (1999).

6. See, for example, M. Moustafa and E. Maldonado-Colon, "Whole-to-Parts Phonics Instruction: Building on What Children Know to Help Them Know More," *The Reading Teacher* 52(5): 448–458 (1999).

7. G. G. Duffy and J. V. Hoffman, "In Pursuit of an Illusion: The Flawed Search for a Perfect Method," *The Reading Teacher* 53(1): 10–15 (1999).

8. See, for example, P. S. Koskinen et al., "Shared Reading, Books, and Audiotapes: Supporting Diverse Students in School and at Home," *The Reading Teacher* 52(5): 430–444 (1999).

9. Anonymous, "Title I Revision: IRA's Position," *Reading Today* 16(4): 8 (1999).

10. See, for example, D. Marr, M. Windsor, and S. Cermak, "Handwriting Readiness: Locatives and Visuomotor Skills in the Kindergarten Year," *Early Childhood Research & Practice: An Internet Journal on the Development, Care, and Education of Young Children,* 3(1): (2001). Retrieved January 9, 2003, from Internet (http://ecrp.uiuc.edu/v3n1/marr.html).

11. See, for example, M. Brunn, "The Four-Square Strategy," *The Reading Teacher* 55(6): 522–525 (2002).

12. For further information, see E. B. Kelly, *Left-Handed Students: A Forgotten Minority,* Fastback 399 (Bloomington, IN: Phi Delta Kappa Educational Foundation, 1996).

13. Commission on Standards for School Mathematics, *Curriculum and Evaluation Standards for School Mathematics* (Reston, VA: National Council of Teachers of Mathematics, 1989), 5.

14. The National Science Board Commission on Precollege Education in Mathematics, Science and Technology, *Educating Americans for the 21st Century* (Washington, DC: National Science Board, 1983), v.

15. American Association for the Advancement of Science, *Science for All Americans: Project 2061 Summary* (Washington, DC: Author, 1995), 4.

16. National Research Council, *National Science Education Standards* (Washington, DC: National Academy Press, 1996), 15.

17. "Teaching About Religion in National and State Social Studies Standards" can be viewed online at www.cie.org or www.freedomforum.org.

18. National Council for the Social Studies, *Expectations of Excellence: Curriculum Standards for Social Studies* (Washington, DC: Author, 1994), 3.

19. K. Rasmussen, "Social Studies: A Laboratory for Democracy," *Curriculum Update*, 3 (1999).

20. Federal Interagency Forum on Child and Family Statistics, *America's Children: Key National Indicators of Well-Being, 1998*. Retrieved from the World Wide Web January 5, 1999 (http://childstats.gov/ac1998/edtxt.htm).

21. J. M. Cowell, "Is the School Nurse a Nurse?" *American School Board Journal* 185(2): 45–46 (1998). See also C. A. Shearer, *Success Stories: How School Health Centers Make a Difference* (Washington, DC: National Health & Education Consortium, 1997).

22. See, for example, S. L. Cone and T. P. Cone, "Language Arts and Physical Education: A Natural Connection," *Teaching Elementary Physical Education* 12(4): 14–17 (2001).

23. See, for example, S. S. Glassner, "Personalized Reading at the Beginning-to-Read State," *Teaching and Learning Literature with Children and Young Adults* 7(3): 102–104 (1998).

24. See, for example, G. M. Gut and S. P. Safran, "Cooperative Learning and Social Stories: Effective Social Skills Strategies for Reading Teachers," *Reading and Writing Quarterly: Overcoming Learning Difficulties* 18(1): 87–91 (2002), and C. K. Malecki and S. N. Elliott, "Children's Social Behaviors as Predictors of Academic Achievement: A Longitudinal Analysis," *School Psychology Quarterly* 17(1): 1–23 (2002).

25. For example, researchers have found that students in multiage classrooms form peer relationships that show more advanced socialization skills. See B. G. Greene, "Reading Instruction in the Nongraded Classroom," *Reading Psychology* 18(1): 69–76 (1997).

26. For further information and resources on bullying, see K. Vail, "Words That Wound," *American School Board Journal* 186(9): 37–40 (1999).

27. It is estimated that a foreign language is offered by about 25 percent of urban public elementary schools and by about 65 percent of suburban private elementary schools. *Source:* M. Met, "Why Language Learning Matters," *Educational Leadership* 59(2): 36–40 (2002).

28. M. H. Rosenbusch, *Guidelines for Starting an Elementary School Foreign Language Program* (Washington, DC: ERIC Clearinghouse for Assessment and Evaluation, 1995), ED 383227. See also G. C. Lipton, "Foreign Language Instruction: What Principals Should Know." *Principal* 82(3): 26–30 (2003).

29. To see how one state of Washington school added Spanish instruction for all its children grades K–5, see G. Ernst-Slavit and A. O. Pierce, "Introducing Foreign Languages in Elementary School," *Principal* 77(3): 31–33 (1998).

30. For more than three decades, Sligo Creek Elementary School in Silver Springs, MD, has been immersing about half its student body in French until fourth grade, making Sligo Creek's immersion program one of the oldest in the United States.

31. R. J. Marzano, "In Search of the Standardized Curriculum," *Principal* 81(3): 6–9 (2002).

32. In teaching for mastery, the performance-level expectation is 100 percent. In reality, however, the performance level will most likely be between 85 and 95 percent, particularly when working with a group of students rather than with an individual student. The 5 to 15 percent difference allows for human error, as can occur in using written and oral communication.

33. B. S. Bloom, (Ed.), *Taxonomy of Educational Objectives, Book 1, Cognitive Domain* (White Plains, NY: Longman, 1984).

34. See R. M. Gagné, L. J. Briggs, and W. W. Wager, *Principles of Instructional Design,*

4th ed. (New York: Holt, Rinehart & Winston, 1994).

35. D. R. Krathwohl, B. S. Bloom, and B. B. Masia, *Taxonomy of Educational Goals,* *Handbook 2, Affective Domain* (New York: David McKay, 1964).

36. A. J. Harrow, *Taxonomy of the Psychomotor Domain* (New York: Longman, 1977).

FOR FURTHER PROFESSIONAL STUDY

Allington, R. L. "What I've Learned About Effective Reading Instruction." *Phi Delta Kappan* 83(10): 740–747 (2002).

Armbruster, B., Lehr, F., and Osborn, J. *Put Reading First: The Research Building Blocks for Teaching Children to Read, Kindergarten through Grade 3.* Washington, DC: National Institute for Literacy, 2001.

Bakunas, B., and Holley, W. "Teaching Organizational Skills." *Clearing House* 74(3): 151–154 (2001).

Bergen, D. "Differentiating Curriculum with Technology-Enhanced Class Projects." *Childhood Education* 78(2): 117–118 (Winter 2001–2002).

Black, S. "Teaching About Religion." *American School Board Journal* 190(4): 50–53 (2003).

Bodrova, E., Paynter, D. E., and Leong, D. J. "Standards in the Early Childhood Classroom." *Principal* 80(5): 10–15 (2001).

Brighton, C. M. "Straddling the Fence: Implementing Best Practices in an Age of Accountability." *Gifted Child Today Magazine* 25(3): 30–33 (2002).

Cavazos, L. F. "Emphasizing Performance Goals and High-Quality Education for All Students." *Phi Delta Kappan* 83(9): 690–697 (2002).

Checkley, K. "Health Education." *Curriculum Update*, pp. 1–3, 6–8 (2000).

Cooper, J. D. *Literacy: Helping Children Construct Meaning.* 4th ed. Wilmington, MA: Houghton Mifflin, 2000.

Costante, C. C. "Healthy Learners: The Link Between Health and Student Achievement." *American School Board Journal* 189(1): 31–33 (2002).

Deasy, R. J. "Don't Axe the Arts!" *Principal* 82(3): 15–18 (2003).

Diffily, D. "Project-Based Learning: Meeting Social Studies Standards and the Needs of Gifted Learners." *Gifted Child Today Magazine* 25(3): 4–43, 59 (2002).

Douglass, S. L. "Teaching About Religion." *Educational Leadership* 60(2): 32–36 (2002).

Fagan, H., and Sherman, L. "Starting at the End: Alaska Project-Based Learning Expert Helena Fagan Insists That Good Projects Are Designed 'Backward'—That Is, What Do We Want Kids to Know When They're Done?" *Northwest Education* 7(3): 30–35 (2002).

Franks, L. "Charcoal Clouds and Weather Writing: Inviting Science to a Middle School Language Arts Classroom." *Language Arts* 78(4): 319–324 (2001).

Fredericks, A. D. "The Ins & Outs of Guided Reading." *Science and Children* 40(6): 22–27 (2003).

Gersten, R., and Geva, E. "Teaching Reading to Early Language Learners." *Educational Leadership* 60(7): 44–49 (2003).

Griffin, M. L. "Why Don't You Use Your Finger? Paired Reading in First Grade." *Reading Teacher* 55(8): 766–774 (2002).

Inlay, L. "Values: The Implicit Curriculum." *Educational Leadership* 60(6): 69–71 (2003).

Johnson, F. R. "Spelling Exceptions: Problems or Possibilities?" *The Reading Teacher* 54(4): 372–378 (December 2000/January 2001).

Juel, C., Biancarosa, G., Coker, D., and Deffes, R. "Walking with Rosie: A Cautionary Tale of Early Reading Instruction." *Educational Leadership* 60(7): 12–18 (2003).

Kapusnick, R. A., and Hauslein, C. M. "The 'Silver Cup' of Differentiated Instruction." *Kappa Delta Pi Record* 37(4): 156–159 (2001).

Krashen, S. "Defending Whole Language: The Limits of Phonics Instruction and the Efficacy of Whole Language Instruction." *Reading Improvement* 39(1): 32–42 (2002).

Lessow-Hurley, J. *Meeting the Needs of Second Language Learners: An Educator's Guide.*

Alexandria, VA: Association for Supervision and Curriculum Development, 2003.

Lipton, G. C. "Foreign Language Instruction: What Principals Should Know." *Principal* 82(3): 40–42 (2003).

Martin, B. L., and Briggs, L. J. *The Affective and Cognitive Domains*. Englewood Cliffs, NJ: Educational Technology Publications, 1986.

Marzano, R. J. "A Guaranteed and Viable Curriculum." Chapter 3 of *What Works in Schools: Translating Research into Action*. Alexandria, VA: Association for Supervision and Curriculum Development, 2003.

Marzano, R. J. "In Search of the Standardized Curriculum." *Principal* 81(3): 6–9 (2002).

McClellan, D. E., and Katz, L. G. *Assessing Young Children's Social Competence*. ED450953. Champaign, IL: ERIC Clearinghouse on Elementary and Early Childhood Education, 2001.

Met, M. "Why Language Learning Matters." *Educational Leadership* 59(2): 36–40 (2001).

Miller, H. M. "Spelling: From Invention to Strategies." *Voices from the Middle* 9(3): 33–37 (2002).

Moats, L. C. "Learning to Read." *American School Board Journal* 189(6): 22–25 (2002).

Moats, L. C. *Whole Language Lives On: The Illusion of 'Balanced' Reading Instruction*. Washington, DC: Thomas P. Fordham Foundation, 2000.

Natale, J. A. "Early Learners: Are Full-Day Academic Kindergartens Too Much, Too Soon?" *American School Board Journal* 188(3): 22–25 (2001).

Prater, M. A., and Sileo, N. M. "Using Juvenile Literature About HIV/AIDS: Ideas and Precautions for the Classroom." *Teaching Exceptional Children* 33(6): 34–45 (2001).

Protheroe, N. "Helping Struggling Readers." *Principal* 82(3): 44–47 (2003).

Ridgway, E. "Start With the Source: Using Primary Documents for Social Studies Research." *Middle Ground* 5(4): 33–36 (2002).

Schieffer, C., Marchand-Martella, N. E., Martella, R. C., Simonsen, F. L., and Waldron-Soler, K. M. "An Analysis of the Reading Mastery Program: Effective Components and Research Review." *Journal of Direct Instruction* 2(2): 87–119 (2002).

Schon, I., and Jacobson, J. "Partner Reading: An Integrative Approach to Learning English and Spanish." *The California Reader* 34(3): 34–41 (2001).

Shearer, C. "Geography Education: Learning the 'Where O Where'." *Principal* 82(3): 32–35 (2003).

Sidelnick, M. A., and Svoboda, M. L. "The Bridge Between Drawing and Writing: Hannah's Story." *The Reading Teacher* 54(2): 174–184 (2000).

Smith, A. F. "How Global Is the Curriculum?" *Educational Leadership* 60(2): 38–41 (2002).

Stevens-Smith, D. A. "Why Your School Needs a Quality Physical Education Program." *Principal* 81(5): 30–31 (2002).

Strecker, S. K. "Reading Fluency." *The California Reader* 334(3): 23–26 (2001).

Taylor, R., and Collins, V. D. *Literacy Leadership for Grades 5–12*. Alexandria, VA: Association for Supervision and Curriculum Development, 2003.

Thames, D. G., and York, K. C. "Disciplinary Border Crossing: Adopting a Broader, Richer View of Literacy." *The Reading Teacher* 56(7): 602–610 (April 2003).

Tomlinson, C. A. *Differentiation of Instruction in the Elementary Grades*. ED443572. Champaign, IL: ERIC Clearinghouse on Elementary and Early Childhood Education, 2000.

Tomlinson, C. A., and Eidson, C. C. *Differentiation in Practice: A Resource Guide for Differentiating Curriculum, Grades 5–9*. Alexandria, VA: Association for Supervision and Curriculum Development, 2003.

Victor, E., and Kellough, R. D. *Science: An Integrated Approach*. 10th ed. Upper Saddle River, NJ: Prentice Hall, 2004.

Witt, V., and Greene, L. "Reading, Writing, and Sex Education." *Principal* 81(5): 32–33 (2002).

Wooten, D. A. *Valued Voices: An Interdisciplinary Approach to Teaching and Learning*. Newark, DE: International Reading Association, 2000.

Yopp, H. K., and Yopp, R. H. "Supporting Phonemic Awareness Development in the Classroom." *The Reading Teacher* 54(2): 130–143 (2000).

Young, J. C. "Does Your P.E. Meet Today's Needs?" *Principal* 82(3): 26–30 (2003).

Young, P. G. "Don't Leave Your Students Playing the Blues." *Principal* 82(3): 20–22, 25 (2003).

INTASC Principles	PRAXIS III Domains	NBPTS Standards
• The teacher understands the central concepts, tools of inquiry, and structures of the discipline(s) he or she teaches and can create learning experiences that make these aspects of subject matter meaningful to students. (Principle 1) • The teacher understands how children learn and develop, and can provide learning opportunities that support their intellectual, social, and personal development. (Principle 2) • The teacher understands how students differ in their approaches to learning and creates instructional opportunities that are adapted to diverse learners. (Principle 3)	• Organizing Content Knowledge for Student Learning (Domain A)	• Respect for Diversity • Meaningful Applications of Knowledge • Knowledge of Integrated Content and Curriculum

People preparing to become teachers are sometimes left with a feeling of unreality when their instructors work with them on developing plans for teaching. "Do teachers *really* take this much time writing out the details of their lesson plans?" they ask skeptically. This is a reasonable concern, and the truth is that most teachers do not spend the same time and energy on the written planning of their lessons as they did during their student teaching days. Planning for teaching is really a way of thinking about what you need to do, and experienced teachers have exactly that—the advantage of experience. Teachers on the job can do much planning mentally, because they know from experience how to identify appropriate objectives, what materials they will need to teach a specific lesson, where those materials are located, where to anticipate problems, and what to look for when assessing learning. This chapter will help you understand the importance of instructional planning and introduce you to the details of a well-designed plan.

ANTICIPATED OUTCOMES

After completing this chapter, you should be able to do the following:

1. Describe specific things you would accomplish to become acquainted with a school that hires you, before meeting the children for the first time.
2. Give several reasons why, as a beginning teacher, you should prepare detailed written instructional plans.
3. Identify the major components of a written daily lesson plan and describe the purpose and extent of each.
4. Describe the role of the instructional unit in designing curriculum and implementing instruction.
5. Differentiate between the *standard instructional unit* and the *interdisciplinary thematic unit.*
6. Organize for your first few days of instruction, including making a sketch plan for at least the first full week.
7. Describe the importance of planning for contingencies during your preactive phase of instruction.
8. Describe the cyclic nature of lesson planning.
9. Explain the meaning of the concept that says "written plans are not irrevocable."
10. Describe the role and procedures for each type of assessment of student learning—*diagnostic, formative,* and *summative*—as related to instructional planning.
11. What is the meaning of a *teachable moment?* By example, tell how you would recognize one and explain what would you do when you do.
12. Describe specific ways that your instructional planning will account for individual differences of the children in your classroom.
13. Identify a curriculum topic, or an instructional activity, or an instructional material, the use of which could create controversy for you. Describe how you would prepare for and deal with the controversy.

14. Begin your design of a unit of instruction, either for a single discipline such as reading or mathematics, or for two or more disciplines (an interdisciplinary unit), to implement for a specific grade level, which by the completion of Chapter 9, will consist of a minimum of five sequential daily lesson plans.

RATIONALE FOR WRITTEN LESSON PLANS

Without the experience afforded by firsthand knowledge, beginning teachers must write out plans step by step just as they expect a lesson to proceed. Let us make crystal clear the rationale for your preparing detailed written lesson plans.

First, *carefully prepared and written lesson plans show everyone—your students, your colleagues, your administrator, and, if you are a student teacher, your college or university supervisor—that you are a committed professional.* A lesson plan is tangible evidence that you are working at your job and demonstrates your respect for students, yourself, and your profession. A written lesson plan shows that you have been proactively thinking and planning. It is unlikely that you would want just any person to treat your own child's illness or to defend you in a legal case or to repair your automobile. You would want a doctor who is well prepared; you would expect your attorney to be well prepared; you would expect the mechanic to know what she is doing. Teaching children is no less important! There is absolutely no excuse for appearing before a class without clear evidence of being prepared. Anyone who does so with any degree of frequency should be removed from the classroom.

Written lesson plans help you to be or become a reflective decision maker. Without a written plan, it is difficult or impossible to analyze after you have taught the lesson how you might have planned or implemented some aspect differently. Written lesson planning serves as a resource for the next time you teach the same or a similar lesson and is useful for teacher self-assessment and for assessing both student learning and the curriculum itself.

Written lesson plans provide an important sense of security, which is especially useful to a beginning teacher. Sometimes an event in the classroom can distract from a lesson, causing you to forget and omit an important part of the lesson. A written plan provides a road map to guide you and help keep you on course.

Written lesson plans help you organize material and search for "loopholes," "loose ends," or incomplete content. Careful and thorough planning during the preactive phase of instruction (discussed in Chapter 4) includes anticipating how lesson activities will develop as you teach. During this anticipation you will actually visualize yourself in the classroom teaching your students, using that visualization to anticipate possible problems.

Written plans help colleagues understand what you are doing and how you are doing it. This is especially important when working with an interdisciplinary teaching team. *Written lesson plans also provide substitute teachers with a guide to follow if you are absent.*

These reasons clearly express the need for detailed written lesson planning. The list is not exhaustive, however, and you may discover additional reasons why written lesson plans are crucial to your effective teaching. In summary, we must make two points: (1) lesson planning is an important and ongoing process; and (2) teachers must take time to plan, reflect, write, test, evaluate, and rewrite their plans to reach optimal performance. In short, preparing written lesson plans is important professional work.

Written Plans Are *Not* Irrevocable

Teaching plans are never "set in concrete." You soon learn that when working with groups of children, you simply cannot consider your teaching plans irrevocable. Things happen; for example, on the very day a teacher had planned a fascinating, "hands-on" map activity of desert environments, the area had the worst snowstorm of the season, and the buses were running two hours late! Incidents that are impossible to predict seem to jump out of nowhere when least expected. Teachers learn to deal with these matters either as inconveniences (rather than as major problems) or as serendipitous "teachable moments" and modify their plans accordingly. Indeed, in addition to planning their instruction, effective teachers seize any such opportunities for teachable moments.[1] Out of necessity and out of design, therefore, we expect to find some amount of emergent planning taking place in classrooms. Teachers will accommodate changing conditions by making appropriate plans on the spot, when needed. This is what is required of you; as a teacher, you are a professional decision maker.

Another reason that lesson plans are not irrevocable is that although you may have completed plans for several consecutive lessons, what actually transpires during today's lesson may necessitate last-minute adjustments to the lesson you had planned for tomorrow.

Making Adjustments as Needed

In our discussion here, we stress the importance of diagnostic approaches to planning and teaching. Effective teachers have good "sensors"—they are alert to how children are responding and make on-the-spot adjustments as needed. In this context, planning for teaching is essentially a decision-making process in which you must choose from among the options you think will lead toward your desired goals. The teacher who plans effectively follows a sequence that flows through a number of decision-making phases as were discussed in Chapter 2. Each phase provides you with an opportunity to sort out data in order to make realistic decisions before moving to the next step.

To get the most out of this chapter and to help relate the subject matter to reality, imagine facing the responsibilities of your first teaching position. Try to visualize how *you* would handle each of the planning strategies we discuss. Go

Activity 6.1: Was This Lesson "Set in Concrete"?

In a multiage classroom at Centerville Joint Unified Intermediate School, Magdalena was teaching a humanities block, a course that integrates student learning in social studies, reading, and language arts. On this particular day during a teacher-directed whole-class lecture/discussion on the topic of "manifest destiny," one student raised his hand and, when Magdalena acknowledged him, asked, "Why aren't we [the United States] still adding states? [that is, adding still more territory to the United States]." Magdalena immediately replied, "There aren't any more states to add," and then hastily continued with her planned lesson.

1. By responding so quickly, did Magdalena miss a teachable moment, one of those too-rare moments when a teacher has her students right where she wants them: where the students are thinking and asking high-order questions?

2. Regarding Magdalena's response, consider: When was Hawaii added as a state? Why hasn't Puerto Rico become a state? Or Guam? Aren't those possibilities? Why *aren't* more states or territories being added? What are the political, economic, and social ramifications today and how do they differ from those of the 1800s?

3. How else might Magdalena have responded to the student's question? (Refer to Chapter 3 for in-depth discussion on using student questions as teachable moments.)

over the procedures mentally to test how sensible they seem to you. Put yourself in the position of Ms. Baxter and Mr. Bond, the two teachers on whom we base our vignettes in this and subsequent chapters. Ask yourself if you would respond in the same way they do in the various situations described.

TASKS THAT REQUIRE SPECIAL PLANNING

In the following sections we discuss applying planning to selected instructional tasks. At least once in their career, all teachers must become familiar with a new school; periodically every school year, all teachers must organize a term's first few days and plan how to begin that term's teaching:

1. Getting acquainted with a new school
2. Organizing the first few days of instruction
3. Planning necessary to get instruction under way

INTRODUCING TEACHERS ELLEN BAXTER AND JIM BOND

We illustrate the preceding three critical instructional tasks in vignettes based on examples selected from a primary- and an intermediate-grade classroom taught by Ellen Baxter and Jim Bond, respectively. Using them as fictional prototypes of many beginning teachers throughout the nation, we present them in situations that, when modified to fit a specific locality, are typical of those found in many school districts today. Please read these vignettes for the purpose of analyzing the ideas and principles embodied in them. Throughout the remaining chapters of this book, Ms. Baxter and Mr. Bond will be responding to situations that you yourself may actually face during your teaching.

Ellen Baxter and Jim Bond responded to their teaching situations with approaches that we believe are appropriate to the philosophy of their respective schools. You will find that Ms. Baxter was free to plan in a relatively open situation, whereas Mr. Bond's situation was somewhat more structured. Each approach exemplifies a general procedure that includes elements of the planning processes presented throughout this book. Successful teachers think about what they must do in terms of available alternatives, and then select specific techniques appropriate to the given situation.

GETTING ACQUAINTED WITH A SCHOOL

Ms. Baxter was hired to teach at the primary-grade level in Westhill Elementary School, located in a city of fifty thousand people. Most of the children were from lower-middle-class homes, with only a few from well-to-do families. There was a mix of ethnic minorities in the school; indeed, Ms. Baxter was surprised at the amount of ethnic and cultural diversity. She looked forward eagerly to reporting to her first teaching assignment.

Mr. Bond was delighted to accept a teaching position in an intermediate-grade classroom at Helen Keller Elementary School. The school was located in a section of a city similar to the one in which Ms. Baxter had secured her position. The demographic makeup of the two schools was much the same. Similar socioeconomic conditions prevailed in both schools. Mr. Bond, too, anxiously waited his first day on the job.

Ms. Baxter and Mr. Bond were aware of the challenge that teachers face in organizing for a new school year. For them the challenge was even greater because they were beginning teachers embarking on their new professional career.

Making an Onsite Visit

Recalling what they had learned in their teacher preparation program about the importance of making an early (before school term begins) onsite visit, both made their respective visits.

What Ms. Baxter Found

Ms. Baxter drove through the school neighborhood, noting several possibilities for supplementing learning activities. The traffic flow was light, and the school was located away from heavily traveled streets and approaches to the freeway. This discovery pleased her because it meant she could take children on walks to various community agencies, businesses, and industries. She noted that there was apparently a community effort to keep the environment clean. Many houses and businesses had been painted recently, and several were being renovated. She noted also that there was still room for improvement, especially in the care of vacant lots and unoccupied buildings. All in all, she was pleased with what she saw during her drive through the neighborhood.

Ms. Baxter's first impression of her assignment was positive. She felt good when she saw the school building. Roomy and attractive, with an open court, the one-story structure had a warm atmosphere. She immediately thought, "What a nice place to work." When she saw her classroom, that initial impression was reinforced. The room was large, and the furniture consisted of small tables and chairs. There were ample workspaces, a sink, and much wall space available for displays. She immediately realized that she could arrange the room in whatever way would best suit her students' needs as well as her own. She noticed that the wall adjoining the next room was a moveable partition, constructed to permit the two rooms to become one large open space. There was also a door opening to a patio in the court. She was encouraged, too, to see that the school had a well-equipped computer lab.

Shortly after receiving her teaching contract, Ms. Baxter had received a letter of welcome from Ms. Ginsburg, the school principal, who congratulated her on her appointment and assured her that she would be warmly welcomed at Westhill School. Ms. Ginsburg had closed by suggesting that Ms. Baxter come in for a conference with her when she arrived in town.

The visit had been rewarding. Ms. Ginsburg welcomed Ms. Baxter enthusiastically and introduced her to Ms. Johnson, the school secretary. Ms. Baxter was impressed by the secretary's offer to assist her in any way she could. She was pleased to learn that the principal was well acquainted with her background and teacher-preparation experiences. Ms. Ginsburg made several references to the fact that Ms. Baxter's teacher-education program had a good reputation among administrators, especially because of the substantial amount of actual classroom experience it had provided.

The principal explained that she liked to see classes in which children went about their schoolwork with a sense of purpose and a feeling of happiness and belonging. Ms. Baxter noted that Ms. Ginsburg emphasized the importance of good planning and its relationship to effective classroom management. She also noted that her principal stressed the importance of strong and positive avenues of communication with parents and guardians. She concluded that the principal would look for a high level of participation by children in the planning of learning activities.

What Mr. Bond Found

On driving to Helen Keller School, Mr. Bond found it located in a rather congested area now zoned for commercial development. He assumed correctly that because the residential area had receded some distance from the school some children now must ride a bus or be driven by parents and guardians to school. He concluded that opportunities for informal excursions with students probably would be limited.

Traditional in its appearance, Helen Keller School was a large, two-story brick building several decades old. It was durable, to be sure, and had been maintained with pride and care. It was clean and, insofar as conventional equipment was concerned, it was well furnished. Mr. Bond's classroom was located on the second floor. His room had a bank of windows overlooking a narrow front lawn. There were storage cabinets under the windows, with a countertop that extended along the length of the window wall. An old-fashioned blackboard was located along the length of the opposite wall, and there were bulletin board spaces on the wall behind the teacher's desk at the front of the room. A map rack was suspended from the wall. The rear wall provided hooks and storage spaces for the children's coats. Mr. Bond was struck by the fact that the children's desks were fixed to the floor in rows facing the teacher's desk. He became aware of the humming sound of a large clock on the front wall.

Mr. Bond was impressed by the solidness of the atmosphere. It suggested strength and durability, and he reflected on the fact that teaching and learning had been occurring in this room for many years. He could not help noticing that old as the basic structure was, it housed a relatively modern educational facility with an impressive learning resources area and computer lab. As he stood behind the teacher's desk, idly spinning the class globe in its cradle, he felt that if he had the freedom to do so, he could provide children with learning experiences that would interest and challenge them.

In his meeting with Mr. Bond, Mr. Park, the school principal, emphasized the importance of school–community relations. He stated that Helen Keller School was noted for the quality of its communication with parents and guardians. He recommended that Mr. Bond review the literature relating to procedures for parental contacts, such as parent conferences and back-to-school night, and suggested that the professional library in the teachers' lounge had several helpful references. Mr. Bond made a mental note to check these out later.

During the meeting, Mr. Bond soon realized that there would be a few constraints on his selection of learning experiences. Mr. Park stressed his concern about "excellence and accountability": notions, he said, that were receiving

Activity 6.2: What Is the Bottom Line?

The concept of accountability is no stranger to business and industry, where success has always been measured by the product; it is a different matter in education, where the product is people rather than things. Few would argue that teachers should be held responsible for what they do, but they do question whether teachers can be held responsible for what their *students* do or fail to do. Some say a teacher can no more be held responsible for a student's unwillingness to do schoolwork than a physician can be held responsible for the health of a patient who fails to follow recommended therapies.

The present concern about accountability in education stresses student achievement in the basic skills. Mr. Park in our vignette is right—this is usually recognized as achievement or nonachievement. The public is demanding a return on its tax dollar. As a prospective teacher, you can expect to hear about excellence and accountability throughout your career.

1. Do you think that teachers should be held accountable for whether their students learn?
2. Should the responsibility for accountability lie with the individual classroom teacher, the school, or the entire school district?
3. What, in your opinion, *is* "the bottom line" in elementary school education?

Berkowitz, R. "Helping with Homework: A Parent's Guide to Information Problem-Solving."
   Emergency Librarian 25(4): 45–46 (1998).
Gustafson, C. "Phone Home." *Educational Leadership* 56(2): 31–32 (1998).
Jones, R. "How Parents Can Support Learning." *American School Board Journal* 188(9): 18–22 (2001).
Lueder, D. C. *Creating Partnerships with Parents: An Educator's Guide.* Lancaster, PA: Technomic, 1998.
Miller, H. M. "No More One-Legged Chairs: Sharing the Responsibility for Portfolio Assessment with
   Students, Their Peers, and Their Parents." *Middle School Journal* 28(3): 242–244 (1997).
National PTA. *National Standards for Parent/Family Involvement Programs.* Chicago: Author, 1997.
National Parent Information Network, U.S. Department of Education. http://npin.org
Partnership for Family Involvement in Education, U.S. Department of Education. http://pfie.ed.gov
Ricci, B. J. "How About Parent–Teacher–*Student* Conferences." *Principal* 79(5): 53–54 (2000).
Shartrand, A. M., Weiss, H. B., Kreider, H. M., and Lopez, M. E. *New Skills for New Schools: Preparing
   Teachers in Family Involvement.* Cambridge, MA: Harvard Graduate School of Education, 1997.
Upham, D. A., Cheney, D., and Manning, B. "What Do Teachers and Parents Want in Their
   Communication Patterns?" *Middle School Journal* 29(5): 48–55 (1998).
Wherry, J. H. "Working with 'Dysfunctional' Families." *Principal* 81(1): 54 (2001).

FIGURE 6.1
Reference items for parent/guardian involvement

overwhelming support in the community. He explained that it really meant only one thing—that the school provide evidence that children were learning the basic skills. He explained to Mr. Bond that, as long as children learned according to their potential, he did not expect to receive any criticism from their parents. "Get the parents of your students involved in their learning," Mr. Park continued. "It is our experience that when parents and guardians get involved in their child's school and school work, students learn better and earn better grades, and teachers have positive feelings about their work."

After this meeting, Mr. Bond went to the teacher's lounge and checked out the references Mr. Park had mentioned. Figure 6.1 presents those items he found that he thought might prove helpful.

PLANNING FOR INSTRUCTION: FIRST FEW DAYS AND BEYOND

The psychological impact of the first day of school on children is tremendous, as it is on a beginning teacher. A good first day, like a good opening night in the theater, goes a long way toward promoting a successful engagement. Experienced teachers have learned that they can anticipate many characteristics of a new group of children before their first encounter with them. By cautiously (see the following section) perusing children's cumulative records, it is possible to discover many important facts about their abilities, needs, and interests. If your class includes the same children as the former year, the previous teacher's anecdotal notes concerning group traits and behavioral patterns can help you plan meaningful learning activities. Your knowledge of your instructional program's goals and student learning objectives also is important. In the same vein, you must know your available human and material resources to plan effectively.

Perusing Permanent Records: Do So Cautiously

Just as you must think carefully about any written comments you intend to make about a student, you must read with caution comments others have made. It is quite possible that some anecdotal comments in students' permanent records say more about the teachers who made the comments than about the recipients. Comments made carelessly, hurriedly, or thoughtlessly can be detrimental to a student's welfare and progress in school. Teacher comments must be professional; that is, they must be diagnostically useful to the student's continued intellectual and psychological development. This is true for any comment you make or write, whether on a child's paper, on the student's permanent school record, or on a message sent to the child's home.

As an example, consider the following unprofessional comment observed in one student's permanent record, where a teacher wrote, "Timothy is lazy." Such a description could be made by anyone; it is nonproductive and is certainly not a professional diagnosis. How many times do you suppose Timothy needs to receive such negative comments before he begins to believe that he is just that—lazy—and as a result, acts that way even more often? Such written comments can also be damaging because the teacher who next has Timothy in class may read them and be led to simply perpetuate the same expectation. "Laziness" is a subjective judgment. A more professional teacher would try to analyze *why* Timothy is behaving that way, and then *prescribe* activities likely to motivate Timothy to assume more constructive charge of his own learning behavior.

For students' continued intellectual and emotional development, your comments should be useful, productive, analytical, diagnostic, and prescriptive. Professional teachers make diagnoses and prepare prescriptions; they do *not* label students as "lazy," "vulgar," "slow," "stupid," "difficult," or "dumb." Professional teachers see student behavior as being goal directed. Perhaps "lazy" Timothy found that that particular behavioral pattern won him attention. Timothy's goal, then, was attention (don't we all need attention?), and he assumed negative, perhaps even self-destructive, behavioral patterns to reach that goal. The professional task of any teacher is to facilitate the learner's understanding (perception) of a goal, and help the student identify acceptable behaviors *positively* designed to reach that goal.

What separates professional teachers from "anyone off the street" is their ability to go beyond mere description of behavior. Keep this in mind always when you write comments that students, their parents or guardians, and other teachers will read.

CONSIDERING LEARNING STYLES, LEARNING CAPACITIES, AND INDIVIDUAL DIFFERENCES

As said in Chapter 1, *learning styles* can be defined as independent forms of knowing and processing information. While some children may begin to learn a new idea in the abstract (e.g., through visual or verbal symbolization), most need to begin concretely (e.g., learning by actually doing it). Many children prosper while working in groups, whereas others prefer to work alone. Some are quick in their studies, whereas others are slow, methodical, cautious, and meticulous. Some can sustain attention on a single topic, becoming more absorbed in their study as time passes. Others are slower starters and more casual in their pursuits but are capable of shifting with ease from subject to subject. Some can study in the midst of music, noise, or movement, whereas others need quiet, solitude, and a desk or table. The point is this: *Children vary in not only their skills and preferences in the way they receive information, but also in how they mentally process that information once they receive it.* This mental processing is a person's style of learning.

In contrast to learning styles, Gardner introduced what he calls "learning capacities" exhibited by individuals in differing ways.[2] Originally and sometimes still referred to as "multiple intelligences," or even "ways of knowing," Gardner identifies the following capacities:

- *Bodily/kinesthetic:* ability to use the body skillfully and to handle objects skillfully
- *Interpersonal:* ability to understand people and relationships
- *Intrapersonal:* ability to assess one's emotional life as a means to understand oneself and others
- *Logical/mathematical:* ability to handle chains of reasoning and to recognize patterns and orders
- *Musical:* sensitivity to pitch, melody, rhythm, and tone
- *Naturalist:* ability to draw on materials and features of the natural environment to solve problems or fashion products
- *Verbal/linguistic:* sensitivity to the meaning and order of words
- *Visual/spatial:* ability to perceive the world accurately and to manipulate the nature of space, such as through architecture, mime, or sculpture

Some educators believe that many children who are at risk of not completing school are those who may be dominant in a cognitive learning style that is not in synch with traditional teaching methods. Traditional methods are largely analytic, where information is presented in a logical, linear, sequential fashion, and fit three of Gardner's types: verbal/linguistic, logical/mathematical, and intrapersonal. Consequently, to better synchronize methods of instruction with learning styles, some teachers and schools have restructured their curriculum and instruction around Gardner's learning capacities.[3] Others have restructured their programs around

Sternberg's Triarchic Theory.[4] Sternberg identifies seven metaphors for the mind and intelligence (geographic, computational, biological, epistemological, anthropological, sociological, and systems) and proposes a theory of intelligence consisting of three elements: analytical, practical, and creative.[5]

Recognizing and Working with Students of Diversity and Differences

Quickly determine the language and ethnic groups represented by the students in your classroom. A major problem for recent newcomers, as well as some ethnic groups, is learning a second (or third or fourth) language. Although in many schools it is not uncommon for more than half the students to come from homes where the spoken language is not English, standard English is a necessity in most communities of this country if a person is to become vocationally successful and enjoy a full life. Learning to communicate reasonably well in English can take an immigrant student at least a year and probably longer; some authorities say 3 to 7 years. By default, then, an increasing percentage of teachers are teachers of English language learning. Helpful to the success of teaching students who are *English language learners (ELLs)*, that is, who have limited proficiency in English language usage, are the demonstration of respect for students' cultural backgrounds, long-term teacher-student cohorts (such as in looping), and the use of active and cooperative learning.[6]

There are numerous programs specially designed for English language learners. Most use the acronym LEP (limited English proficiency) with five number levels, from LEP 1 that designates non-English-speaking, although the student may understand single sentences and speak simple words or phrases in English, to LEP 5, sometimes designated FEP (fluent English proficient), for the student who is fully fluent in English, although the student's overall academic achievement may still be less than desired because of language or cultural differences.

Some schools use a "pullout" approach, where part of the student's school time is spent in special bilingual classes and the rest of the time the student is placed in regular classrooms. In some schools, LEP students are placed in classrooms that use a simplified or "sheltered" English approach.[7] Regardless of the program, specific techniques recommended for teaching ELL students include:

- Allowing more time for learning activities than one normally would.
- Allowing time for translation by a classroom aide or by a classmate and allowing time for discussion to clarify meaning, encouraging the students to transfer into English what they already know in their native language.
- Avoiding jargon or idioms that might be misunderstood. See the scenario that follows.

> **A Humorous Scenario Related to Idioms: A Teachable Moment in a Third-Grade Classroom**
>
> While Elina was reciting she had a little difficulty with her throat (due to a cold) and stumbled over some words. The teacher jokingly commented, "That's okay Elina, you must have a frog in your throat." Quickly, Mariya, a recent immigrant from the Ukraine, asked, "How could she have a frog in her throat?" The teacher ignored Mariya's question. Missing this teachable moment, he continued with his planned lesson.

- Dividing complex or extended language discourse into smaller, more manageable units.
- Giving directions in a variety of ways.
- Giving special attention to key words that convey meaning, and writing them on the board.
- Maintaining high expectations of each learner.
- Reading written directions aloud, and then writing the directions on the board.
- Speaking clearly and naturally but at a slower than normal pace.
- Using a variety of examples and observable models.
- Using simplified vocabulary but without talking down to students.[8]

Additional Guidelines for Working with Language-Minority Children

While they are becoming literate in English language usage, LEP students can learn the same curriculum as native English-speaking students. Although the guidelines presented in the following paragraphs are important for teaching all students, they are especially important when working with language-minority children.

Present instruction that is concrete, which includes the most direct learning experiences possible. Use the most concrete (least abstract) forms of instruction.

Build upon (or connect with) what the students already have experienced and know. Building upon what students already know, or think they know, helps them connect their knowledge and construct their understandings.

Encourage student writing. One way is by using student journals.

Help children learn the vocabulary. Assist the ELL students in learning two vocabulary sets: the regular English vocabulary needed for learning and the new vocabulary introduced by the subject content. For example, while learning mathematics a student is dealing with both the regular English language vocabulary and the special vocabulary of mathematics.

To the extent possible, involve parents or guardians or older siblings. Students whose primary language is not English may have other differences about which you will also need to become knowledgeable. These differences are related to culture, customs, family life, and expectations. To be most successful in working with language minority students, you should learn as much as possible about each student. Parents (or guardians) of new immigrant children are usually truly concerned about the education of their children and may be very interested in cooperating with you in any way possible. In a study of schools recognized for their exemplary practices with language-minority students the schools were recognized for being "parent friendly," that is, for welcoming parents and guardians in a variety of innovative ways.[9]

Plan for and use all learning modalities. As with teaching young people in general, in working with language-minority students in particular you need to use multisensory approaches—learning activities that involve students in auditory, visual, tactile, and kinesthetic learning activities.

Brain research confirms that physical activity—moving, stretching, walking— can actually enhance the learning process.

—**Eric Jensen**

Use small group cooperative learning. Cooperative learning strategies are particularly effective with language-minority students because they provide opportunities for students to produce language in a setting less threatening than is speaking before the entire class.

Use the benefits afforded by modern technology. For example, computer networking allows the language-minority students to write and communicate with peers from around the world as well as participate in "publishing" their classroom work.

Little Wonder That English Is *Not* an Easy Language to Learn

Consider the paradoxes found in the following sentences.

A bass was hanging from the top of the bass violin.

Can you see what is wound around the wound?

She was too close to the door to close it.

Since there is no time like the present, we decided it was time to present the present.

The nomad decided to desert his dessert in the desert.

To lead one might need to get the lead out.

When we walked by, the dove dove into the bushes.

With a garden, one can produce produce.

Can you think of others?

How does a teacher help children to handle these discrepancies in meanings of words that are spelled identically?

Additional Guidelines for Working with Students of Diverse Backgrounds

To be compatible with, and be able to teach, students who come from backgrounds different from yours, you need to believe that, given adequate support, all students *can* learn—regardless of gender, social class, physical characteristics, language, and ethnic or cultural backgrounds. You also need to develop special skills that include those in the following guidelines, each of which is discussed in detail in other chapters. To work successfully and most effectively with students of diverse backgrounds, you should:

• Build the learning around students' individual learning styles. Personalize learning for each student, much like what is done by using the IEP with special-needs learners. Involve students in understanding and in making important decisions about their own learning, so they feel ownership (i.e., a sense of empowerment and connectedness) of that learning. Some schools report success using personalized learning plans for all students, not only those with special needs.

• Communicate positively with every student and with the student's parents or guardians, learning as much as you can about the student and the student's culture, and encouraging family members to participate in the student's learning. Involve parents, guardians, and other members of the community in the educational program so all have a sense of ownership and responsibility and feel positive about the school program.

• Establish and maintain high expectations, although not necessarily the same expectations, for each student. Both you and your students must understand intelligence is not a fixed entity, but a set of characteristics that—through a feeling of "I can" and with proper coaching—can be developed.

• Teach to individuals by using a variety of strategies to achieve an objective or by using a number of different objectives at the same time (multilevel teaching).

• Use techniques that emphasize collaborative and cooperative learning—that de-emphasize competitive learning.

Recognizing and Working with Students Who Have Special Needs

Students with disabilities (referred to also as students with *special needs* or *exceptionalities*) include those with disabling conditions or impairments in any one or more of the following categories: mental retardation, hearing, speech or language, visual, emotional, orthopedic, autism, traumatic brain injury, other health impairment, or specific learning disabilities. To receive special education services, a child must have a disability in one or more of the categories, and by reason thereof, the child needs special education and related services. In other words, not all children who have a disability need services available via special education. For example, a child with a hearing impairment would be entitled to special services when the impairment is so severe that the child cannot understand what is being said even when the child is equipped with a hearing aid.

To the extent possible, students with special needs must be educated with their peers in the regular classroom. Public Law 94-142, the Education for All Handicapped Children Act (EAHCA) of 1975, mandates all children have the right to a free and appropriate education, as well as to nondiscriminatory assessment. (Public Law 94-142 was amended in 1986 by P.L. 99-457 and in 1990 by P.L. 101-476, at which time its name was changed to Individuals with Disabilities Education Act—IDEA, and it was amended in 1997 by P.L. 105-17.) Emphasizing normalizing the educational environment for students with disabilities, this legislation requires provision of the *least-restrictive environment (LRE)* for these students. A LRE is an environment that is as normal as possible.

Teachers today know students with disabilities fall along a continuum of learner differences rather than as a separate category of student.[10] Because of their wide differences, students identified as having special needs may be placed in the regular classroom for the entire school day, called *full inclusion.*[11] Those students may also be in a regular classroom the greater part of the school day, called *partial inclusion,* or only for designated periods. Although there is no single, universally accepted definition of the term, *inclusion* is the concept that students with disabilities should be integrated into general education classrooms regardless of whether they can meet traditional academic standards.[12] (The term *inclusion* has largely replaced use of an earlier and similar term, mainstreaming.) As a classroom teacher you will need information and skills specific to teaching learners with special needs who are included in your classes.

Generally speaking, teaching children who have special needs requires more care, better diagnosis, greater skill, more attention to individual needs, and an even greater understanding of the students. The challenges of teaching students with special needs in the regular classroom are great enough that to do it well you need specialized training beyond the general guidelines presented here. At some point in your teacher preparation you should take one or more courses in working with special-needs learners in the regular classroom.

When a student with special needs is placed in your classroom, your task is to deal directly with the differences between this student and other students in your classroom. To do this, you should develop an understanding of the general characteristics of different types of special-needs learners, identify the student's unique needs relative to your classroom, and design lessons that teach to different needs at the same time, called multilevel teaching.

Remember just because a student has been identified as having one or more special needs does not preclude that child from being gifted or talented. Gifted students with disabling conditions remain a major group of poorly recognized and underattended-to youth, perhaps because focus on accommodations for their disabilities precludes adequate recognition and development of their gifts and talents.[13]

Congress stipulated in P.L. 94-142 that an Individualized Educational Program (IEP) be devised annually for each special-needs child. According to that law, an IEP is developed for each student each year by a team that includes special education teachers, the child's parents or guardians, and the classroom teachers. The IEP contains a statement of the student's present educational levels, the educational goals for the year, specifications for the services to be provided and the extent that the student should be expected to take part in the regular education program, and the evaluative criteria for the services to be provided. Consultation by special and skilled support personnel is essential in all IEP models. A consultant works directly with teachers or with students and their parents or guardians. As a classroom teacher, you will likely play an active role in preparing the specifications for the special-needs students assigned to your classroom, and assume a major responsibility for implementing the program.

Guidelines for Working with Special-Needs Students in the Regular Classroom

Although the guidelines represented by the paragraphs that follow are important for teaching all students, they are especially important for working with special-needs students.

Familiarize yourself with exactly what the special needs of each learner are. Privately ask the special-needs student whether there is anything he or she would like for you to know about that learner and what you specifically can do to facilitate his or her learning.

Adapt and modify materials and procedures to the special needs of each student. For example, a child who has extreme difficulty sitting still for more than a few minutes will need planned changes in learning activities. When establishing student seating arrangements in the classroom, give preference to students according to their special needs. Try to incorporate into lessons activities that engage all learning modalities—visual, auditory, tactile, and kinesthetic. Be flexible in your classroom procedures, perhaps even allowing some rest time.

Children believed to be affected by *attention deficit hyperactivity disorder (ADHD)*, estimated to be between 4 and 12 percent of children, the majority of them boys, are characterized by inattention, restlessness, hyperactive and impulsive behaviors.[14] Teachers are often the first to recognize these symptoms. However, evidence indicates that some children displaying these behaviors and initially thought to be suffering from ADHD may actually be suffering from sleep problems such snoring and even sleep apnea.

Provide high structure and clear expectations by defining the learning objectives in behavioral terms (discussed in Chapter 5). Teach students the correct procedures for everything (Chapter 4). Break complex learning into simpler components, moving from the most concrete to the abstract, rather than the other way around. Check frequently for student understanding of instructions and procedures, and for comprehension of content. Use computers and other self-correcting materials for drill and practice and for provision of immediate, constructive, and private feedback to the student.

Develop your withitness, which is your awareness of everything that is going on in the classroom, at all times, monitoring students for signs of restlessness, frustration, anxiety, and off-task behaviors. Be ready to reassign individual learners to different activities as the situation warrants. Established classroom learning centers can be a big help.

Have all students maintain assignments for the week or some other period of time in an assignment book or in a folder kept in their notebooks. Post assignments in a special place in the classroom (and perhaps on the school's Web site) and frequently remind students of assignments and deadlines.

Maintain consistency in your expectations and in your responses. Special-needs learners, particularly, can become frustrated when they do not understand a teacher's expectations and when they cannot depend on a teacher's reactions.

Plan interesting activities to bridge learning, activities that help the students connect what is being learned with their real world. Learning that connects what is being learned with the real world helps motivate students and keep them on task.

Plan questions and questioning sequences and write them into your lesson plans. Plan questions you ask special-needs learners so they are likely to answer them with confidence. Use signals to let students know you are likely to call on them in class (e.g., prolonged eye contact or mentioning your intention to the student before class begins). After asking a question, give the student adequate time to think and respond. Then, after the student responds, build upon the student's response to indicate the student's contribution was accepted as being important.

Provide for and teach toward student success. Offer students activities and experiences that ensure each individual student's success and mastery at some level (mastery learning is discussed further in Chapter 9). Use of student portfolios (discussed in Chapter 7) can give evidence of progress and help in building student confidence and self-esteem.

Provide scaffolded instruction, that is, give each child as much guided or coached practice as time allows. Provide time in class for students to work on assignments and projects. During this time, you can monitor the work of each student while looking for misconceptions, thus ensuring students get started on the right track.

Provide help in the organization of students' learning. For example, give instruction in the organization of notes and notebooks. Have a three-hole punch available in the classroom so students can put papers into their notebooks immediately, thus avoiding disorganization and their loss of papers. During class presentations use an overhead projector with transparencies; students who need more time can then copy material from the transparencies. Ask students to read their notes aloud to each other in small groups, thereby aiding their recall and understanding, and encouraging them to take notes for meaning rather than for rote learning. Encourage and provide for peer support, peer tutoring or coaching, and cross-age teaching. Ensure that the special-needs learner is included in all class activities to the fullest extent possible.

Recognizing and Working with Students Who Are Gifted

Historically, educators have used the term *gifted* when referring to a person with identified exceptional ability in one or more academic subjects, and *talented* when referring to a person with exceptional ability in one or more of the visual or performing arts.[15] Today, however, the terms more often are used interchangeably, which is how they are used here, that is, as if they are synonymous.

Sometimes, unfortunately, in the regular classroom gifted students are neglected.[16] At least part of the time, it is probably because there is no singularly accepted method for identification of these students. In other words, students who are gifted in some way or another may go unidentified as such. For placement in special classes or programs for the gifted and talented, school districts traditionally have used grade point averages and standard intelligence quotient (IQ) scores. On the other hand, because IQ testing measures linguistic and logical/mathematical aspects of giftedness (refer to earlier discussion in chapter, on learning capacities and the theory of multiple intelligences), it does not account for others and thus gifted students sometimes are unrecognized; they also are sometimes among the students most at risk of dropping out of school.[17]

To work most effectively with gifted learners, their talents first must be identified. This can be done not only by using tests, rating scales, and auditions but also by observations in and out of the classroom and from knowledge about the student's personal life. With those information sources in mind, indicators of superior intelligence are ability to assume adult roles and responsibilities at home or at work; ability to cope with school while living in poverty; ability to cope with school while living with dysfunctional families; ability to extrapolate knowledge to different circumstances; ability to lead others; ability to manipulate a symbol system; ability to reason by analogy; ability to retrieve and use stored knowledge to solve problems; ability to think and act independently; ability to think logically; creativity and artistic ability; a strong sense of self, pride, and worth; and understanding of one's cultural heritage.[18]

To assist you in understanding gifted children who may or may not have yet been identified as being gifted, here are some types of students and the kinds of problems to which they may be prone, that is, personal behaviors that may identify them as being gifted but academically disabled, bored, and alienated.

• *Antisocial* students, alienated by their differences from peers, may become bored and impatient troublemakers.

• *Creative, high-achieving* students often feel isolated, weird, and depressed.

• *Divergent-thinking* students can develop self-esteem problems when they provide answers that are logical to them but seem unusual and off-the-wall to their peers. They may have only a few peer friends.

• *Perfectionists* may exhibit compulsive behaviors because they feel as though their value comes from their accomplishments. When their accomplishments do not satisfy expectations—their own, their parents' or guardians', or their teachers'—anxiety and feelings of inadequacy arise. When other students do not meet the gifted student's high standards, alienation from those students is probable.

• *Sensitive* students who also are gifted may become easily depressed because they are so aware of their surroundings and of their differences.

• *Students with special needs* may be gifted. Attention deficit disorder, dyslexia, hyperactivity, and other learning disorders sometimes mask giftedness.

• *Underachieving* students can also be gifted students but fail in their studies because they learn in ways seldom or never challenged by classroom teachers. Although often expected to excel in everything they do, most gifted students can be underachievers in some areas. Having high expectations of themselves, underachievers tend to be highly critical of themselves, develop a low self-esteem, and can become indifferent and even hostile.[19]

Understanding and Working with Students Who May Be at Risk

Children may be at risk of not finishing school for many reasons, among which are the following[20]:

• *Academic failure*—exemplified by absences, low self-esteem, low grades
• *Family instability*—exemplified by moving, separation, divorce
• *Family socioeconomic situation*—exemplified by low income, negativism, lack of education
• *Family tragedy*—exemplified by parent illness or death, health problems
• *Personal pain*—exemplified by drugs, physical and/or psychological abuse, suspension from school

Researchers conclude that children who are underachieving and at risk are more likely to need the following[21]:

• Frequent opportunities for mobility in the classroom
• Informal seating, rather than wooden, steel, or plastic chairs
• Lower illumination, because bright light contributes to hyperactivity
• Options and choices with a variety of instructional resources, environments, and sociological groupings, rather than routines and patterns
• Tactile/visual introductory resources reinforced by kinesthetic (i.e., direct experiencing and whole-body activities)/visual resources, or introductory kinesthetic/visual resources reinforced by tactile/visual resources
• To begin their learning later in the morning than is usual

Today's movement to transform schools into caring and responsive learning environments has as its sole purpose helping all children to make the transitions necessary to succeed in school and in life. The secret to exemplary teaching is exemplary planning for the instruction, and that is the focus for the remainder of this chapter.

Exemplary teachers begin each school year by quickly becoming acquainted with each child in their classroom.

MS. BAXTER AND MR. BOND FACE THE REALITIES OF TEACHING

After making their initial onsite visits, it was time for Ellen Baxter and Jim Bond to begin their work.

Ms. Baxter Established Priorities

Ms. Baxter decided to set three objectives for herself: (1) to get acquainted with her students as quickly as possible, (2) to prepare an attractive and interesting room environment, and (3) to develop tentative plans for the first few days of instruction. She jotted down the following priorities for the first week of school:

1. Observe children as they work independently and as they relate to others in the group.
2. Prepare my *Learner Profile* observation recording tools.[22]
3. Establish classroom management procedures by introducing procedures and expected behaviors.
4. Provide a stimulating and provocative learning atmosphere. (She remembered this advice from her father, also a teacher: "Your classroom is your place of work; show pride in that fact.")

5. Provide incentives for children to practice responsibility and industry in a group setting.
6. Help children develop a sense of purpose for the school year.

Ms. Baxter Planned a Daily Schedule

With these priorities in mind, Ms. Baxter decided to establish a tentative daily schedule. She knew that she could easily modify this schedule as children became more efficient in helping to plan the day. She decided to stress this point with them from the start. During her student teaching, she had made notes of daily schedules in various classrooms, and she had also examined the schedule left in the previous teacher's notebook. With these resources at hand, she planned her schedule to allow as much flexibility as possible, which permitted her to unify learning from various school subjects. She decided on a schedule (Figure 6.2) and printed it on a large chart for the children.

Ms. Baxter decided that the length of each activity should be left flexible, although she was not unmindful that the state education code mandated minimum time requirements for each subject in the core curriculum. She chose a

FIGURE 6.2
Ms. Baxter's daily schedule

Our Daily Schedule

Flag Salute
Opening Activities and Planning
Reading (to include Language Arts)
Social Studies
Computer Lab

Lunch

Mathematics
Science
Expressive Arts (Art, Music, Drama)
Health and Physical Education (alternate days)
Closing Activities

30- to 90-minute range as a reasonable beginning frame of reference, knowing that later teacher–student planning would determine the actual length.

Ms. Baxter Planned the Learning Environment

Ms. Baxter's classroom provided numerous possibilities for projecting a cheerful, positive learning environment. A door opened onto a patio in the courtyard; she immediately made a mental note to check with the principal about using a small area there for a class garden where children could grow plants. The movable furniture encouraged flexible room arrangement. She decided to organize the room into subject-specific learning centers. She first established a science center around a large aquarium (they could add a terrarium later). On the wall behind the aquarium were various pictures of marine life, with captions such as, "What is my name?" For social studies, she used a community map with the caption, "Can you find Westhill School?" She arranged photographs of community occupations and industries around the map, and placed books on community life on the study table in this center. A third center contained puzzles and other manipulative materials designed to illustrate mathematics. She created a center for reading and language arts as well, complete with an attractive display of poetry, fiction, nonfiction, and reference books. She also prepared an attractive bulletin board display of local community scenes, captioned, "How many of these places have you visited?"

Because children would be grouped for various purposes during the year, Ms. Baxter prepared nametags and made a tentative seating chart based on a more or less random selection of students. She knew that quite early in the week, the children themselves would demonstrate the feasibility of her choices. Her basic concern was to work toward a positive group feeling. Groupings for specific learning would follow soon.

Ms. Baxter Planned Learning Activities for the First Few Days

Ms. Baxter organized the first few days of school with the following activities in mind for her primary-grade children: (1) introduce the various school subjects; (2) diagnose children's needs, abilities, and interests; (3) determine children's readiness for independent, small-, and large-group activities; (4) assess their level of responsibility; and (5) determine the amount of teaching necessary to establish study, work, and social skills. Her planning for the first week resulted in the following arrangements.

Reading and Language Arts

Recalling what her college instructor had said about "whole language learning," Ms. Baxter decided to involve her students in a series of activities that would familiarize her with their language-use proficiency:

- Use informal discussion activities to establish rules for speaking and listening.

- Use the social studies unit theme, "Learning About Communities" for writing activities to produce samples of children's handwriting, spelling, and composition skills.
- Read to children daily to further determine listening skills and to ascertain critical-thinking skills.

In addition, she decided that she would use reading test scores from children's cumulative records to determine tentative textbook assignments and reading groups. She planned to regroup children later based on their specific abilities or interests and on results of the fall testing program. She planned to correlate the spelling program with reading by extending word-attack skills into the study of spelling. Finally, she decided to make maximum use of sharing and planning activities to establish guidelines for effective speaking habits.

Social Studies

Planning for this subject is presented later in the chapter.

Mathematics

Ms. Baxter planned her mathematics instruction with these points in mind:

- Identify children's skill levels from their cumulative records.
- Administer diagnostic tests to determine their present reasoning and computational skills.
- Reteach as needed in those cases where students have regressed since last spring.
- Anticipate opportunities to integrate mathematics with the social studies unit.

Science

Ms. Baxter sketched this plan for science:

- Have discussions based on the aquarium in the learning center.
- Record children's questions.
- Analyze discussions by sorting children's questions and locating relevant sources for answers.
- Integrate science, when possible, with study of marine life as it relates to the social studies unit, "Learning About Communities."

Expressive Arts

Ms. Baxter decided as a general rule to keep art activities uncomplicated until she could learn more about the group's ability to work with various media. She arranged her students' arts experiences with the following considerations:

- Encourage children to suggest songs they like to sing.
- Have children discuss their interest and involvement in music.

- Provide listening experiences based on music that highlights both instrumental and vocal selections.
- Provide opportunities for students to self-select their form of expression.
- Help children develop good work habits and a concern for proper care and use of materials.
- Organize a bulletin board committee that can plan and design displays in keeping with current units of study.

Health, Safety, and Physical Education

Ms. Baxter planned health, safety, and physical education with these points in mind:

- Review good health and safety habits learned in prior years.
- Take advantage of the warm fall weather to take short walks around the neighborhood.
- Provide opportunities for group play, and make use of them to observe children's behavior. Note the leaders, the subgroups, and very active and retiring children.
- Introduce a simple group game. Integrate with social studies by relating health to the study of community.

Room Citizenship

Ms. Baxter planned her instruction in room citizenship as follows:

- Have children take turns leading the flag salute.
- Plan the day's program with children each morning.
- Begin immediately to determine, with children's assistance, a few simple rules for good citizenship as an individual and as a group member. Record these on a chart or on the writing board, and have children write them in their own notebooks. Refer to them from time to time to evaluate behavior and to reinforce the rules' importance.
- During the first few days, teach for mastery of routines pertaining to the playground, cafeteria, rest rooms, and the like.
- Conduct discussions with children on "How well we did today" in observing good playground habits and so forth.
- Use every occasion to comment on good behavior by citing examples that prompted it.
- Take time during the beginning and ending of the class period to discuss the work habits necessary for effective learning.
- Close each day with a brief discussion of the day's activities, and solicit reactions from children about "What I liked most today."

With these notes in mind, Ms. Baxter felt confident. She had developed a plan of action. Now she could plan more specifically for her students' learning needs.

Mr. Bond Established Priorities

Mr. Bond followed procedures very similar to Ms. Baxter's. Even though he was concerned about the principal's emphasis on "excellence and account-ability," Mr. Bond knew that he would accomplish very little if he failed to get children interested in what they were supposed to do. He decided to give priority to teaching the basic skills in a meaningful context. He also gave priority to the following needs:

1. Observe children to determine their study habits and their ability to work within a group.
2. Set up my observation record book.
3. Establish classroom management procedures through teacher–student collaboration.
4. Develop a positive learning atmosphere through the display of stimulating media.
5. Reinforce positive, task-oriented student behavior.
6. Assist children to develop a sense of purpose for the school year.

Mr. Bond Planned a Daily Schedule

Mr. Bond developed a tentative daily schedule (Figure 6.3) and posted it on the bulletin board. He placed the basic skills block in the beginning period, as this would permit him to use the skills instruction to prepare children for learning tasks in the following periods.

Mr. Bond Planned the Learning Environment

The physical arrangement, especially the fixed seating, in Mr. Bond's class-room created some serious limitations on his developing an appropriate learning environment for his fifth-grade class. Doing his best, however, he was able to equip one corner of the room as a reading center, with supplementary books on science, literatures, and social studies displayed on a table. He arranged on the bulletin board an attractive map and picture display designed to generate discussion on the social studies topic, "American People and Lands." He also located a table that he arranged as a science center, with materials and equipment the class would use with their study topic, "Understanding Electromagnets."

Mr. Bond Planned Learning Activities for the First Few Days

Mr. Bond consulted several sources to help him determine possible learner activities for the first week of school. He looked forward to developing a holistic program of integrated learning for his students, but at the beginning of the year, he needed some sense of their proficiency in the various subjects and skills of the fifth-grade curriculum. The teachers' guides to the various

FIGURE 6.3
Mr. Bond's daily schedule

Daily Schedule

Pledge of Allegiance
Opening Activities and Planning
Basic Skills Block (Math, Reading,
     Language Arts)
Computer Lab
Break
Basic Skills Block (continued)

Lunch

Social Studies and Literature
Science
Expressive Arts on alternate days with
     Health and Physical Education
Closing Activities

children's textbooks had numerous suggestions for introducing the subjects. His planning for the first week resulted in the following ideas.

Basic Skills Block (Mathematics, Reading, Language Arts)

In formulating basic skills instruction, Mr. Bond followed these guidelines:

Mathematics
- Use the basal series math textbook to have children demonstrate their skills in addition, subtraction, multiplication, and division.
- Ascertain their level of skill in working with fractions, and their understanding of measurements.

Reading
- Use the basal reading texts to obtain information on children's vocabulary development and their ability to use word-attack skills.
- Use oral and silent reading related to social studies activities to learn children's ability to use such comprehension skills as selecting the main idea and recalling details.

Language Arts
- Provide children with writing experiences to determine their skill in using correct word forms, capitalization and punctuation, and sentence structure.
- Check their handwriting skills with special attention to letter formation, legibility, and neatness.
- Give spelling tests that contain words taught the previous year.

Social Studies and Literature

Mr. Bond prepared the following:

- Plan social studies activities around the room bulletin board, "American People and Lands."
- Assign reading based on the social studies topic to ascertain how well children can read in a content field.

Science, Expressive Arts, Health and Physical Education

- Delay the beginning of formal learning activities in these curriculum areas until children's basic skills levels have been ascertained.
- The basic skills and social studies focus will consume most of the instructional time during the first week.
- A school library visit to obtain reading materials, group discussion on beginning a weather station, and the discussion time necessary to establish room routines will take up the remaining time.

SKETCH PLAN

Many classroom teachers have found it useful to identify, in the form of a *sketch plan*, a variety of learning activities that they can develop over a period of several days. Sometimes this is referred to as a *weekly plan*, although it need not be limited to exactly 5 school days. By planning for work to be completed over a week or two, you are able to plan learning activities on an ongoing basis and can anticipate needed instructional materials. Beginning teachers, especially, should be prepared to engage in this type of planning because school principals frequently ask them to do so. But experienced teachers also do daily lesson planning, designed to implement the learning activities contained in the sketch plan. Skill in this form of planning provides a margin of confidence that goes a long way toward ensuring a good lesson. Your sketch plan, therefore, provides your context for individual daily lesson plans. In thinking about planning in this way, you are actually rehearsing your lessons intellectually before you teach them.

Your sketch plan outlines suggestions to draw on over the course of several days. It provides flexibility for teacher–student planning because it is not locked into a day-by-day prescription of what to do. Complete attainment of

Activity 6.3: Mr. Wills Seems to Have a Problem

Mr. Wills is considered a good first-year teacher, but things rarely work well for him when he uses materials and media. Right in the middle of a lesson, he often discovers that he is missing some important piece of equipment or material he needs to complete the presentation, or a machine breaks down. Once, he was going to demonstrate how a candle extinguishes when covered with a glass jar. He had the candles and the jars all right, but he forgot to bring matches. Another time, he planned to use an overhead projector, only to find at the last minute that the electrical cord was not long enough to reach the outlet, and he did not have an extension cord. On another occasion, using slides in a demonstration, he found that he had placed them in the carousel upside down and backward. Yesterday, while he was demonstrating on the overhead screen with a computer, the computer screen froze. Such situations always seemed to happen at the worst unexpected time to surprise Mr. Wills and spoil his plans and presentations.

1. Is it possible for Mr. Wills' carelessness to result in other, more serious, problems?
2. What action could you take to avoid such unexpected occurrences?

each objective is unrealistic for many children; thus, you must evaluate carefully the extent to which individual children are succeeding. Your plan should provide activities designed to implement this evaluation.

LESSON PLANNING

Your sketch plan serves as the source of ideas and context for the detail that becomes your lesson plan. The sketch plan also helps ensure continuity in instruction from one day to the next.

Every lesson should have a purpose that children understand. In the lesson plan, this purpose is usually stated in the form of objectives that explain *what* students are to learn. Learners should also understand the *why*. Lessons that do not provide sufficient clarity of purpose tend, more often than not, to fail. Your lesson plan should also include the instructional materials necessary for teaching it. Inadequate provision of learning materials is an invitation to management problems. The lesson plan's sequence should (1) prepare students for success by ensuring that each activity is built on those preceding it, (2) specify the learning activities, (3) include a summary or closure, and (4) provide for assessment both of how you will determine whether students have reached the learning objectives and of how you believe the lesson went and how you would improve it were you to use it again.

Let us make clear that there is no one best form for a lesson plan, nor is there consensus on the level of specificity that should be included. As a general rule, use brief, directional statements rather than detailed and scripted sentences that include what you will actually say. *A lesson plan should not be a scripted narrative of what you hope to do.* However, it *should* be a step-by-step plan of action that you can easily follow while teaching the lesson. It might be described as a "trip map" through the lesson. Your lesson plan's completeness depends on your having planned for the components, as identified here.

Components of a Lesson Plan

1. *Anticipated learning outcomes:* States what students are to be able to demonstrate at completion of the lesson and thus illustrates the lesson's purpose.
2. *Procedure:* Includes preliminary readiness activities, interest building, and lesson development; specifies the work-study activities that will occur during the lesson. Some teachers also show in their plans the anticipated noise level for the lesson. Including or at least considering noise levels is useful during planning because it helps you anticipate how active and noisy students might become during the lesson, how you might prepare for that, and whether you should warn administrators or teachers of neighboring classrooms.
3. *Closure and assessment:* Indicates closing activities designed for the lesson and assessment of whether students are reaching or have reached the expected learning outcomes.
4. *Instructional materials:* Provides a list of the specific materials or media needed to teach the lesson, especially those items not normally available in the classroom.
5. *Reflections:* Beginning teachers and teachers being mentored are encouraged to also include their assessment of how the lesson went and what they would change or do differently were they to repeat it. Sample lesson plans appear in Figures 6.4 through 6.6.

It is apparent that planning specific lessons takes place within the context of overall program goals. For instance, if you were hired as a third-grade teacher, the school authorities, the community, and, especially, the parents and guardians would expect you to achieve certain goals during the year in which you are the children's teacher. *It is important that you know what those goal expectations are and that you plan in accordance with them and assess student learning in relation to them.* These goals may be made clear to you in conferences with your principal, in preschool workshops for the faculty, or in your examination of local curriculum documents. As you have read in this chapter, our two teachers, Ms. Baxter and Mr. Bond, became familiar with the goal expectations set for them.

Once you understand the goals, your planning begins with a *diagnostic assessment of learner characteristics.* This procedure enables you to examine what children are supposed to learn in terms of how ready they are to learn it. You obtain the data needed for this assessment from a variety of sources: (1) cumulative records containing test data, anecdotal records, student progress reports, and samples of schoolwork; (2) observations; (3) interviews; and (4) preassessments. Next, and equally important, is the *assessment of the group.* You must ascertain the extent of the group's cohesiveness and readiness to participate in cooperative learning activities, and identify those children who are leaders and those who are followers and which ones seem to have difficulty staying on task. This information enables you to assess children's characteristics and to plan instruction accordingly.

Now that you are familiar with overall program goals and have some sense of your students' academic strengths and limitations, you can attend to *formulating your instructional objectives.* This part of the process also entails ascertaining available instructional materials. There is no point in making teaching plans that you cannot implement because you do not have needed materials. With all of the necessary information in hand, you are ready to begin *organizing for instruction.* This means working out the details of implementing the lesson and involves making several important decisions:

1. What learning activities will you use? How does each support the objective?
2. How is the lesson to begin? What sequence will the lesson follow?
3. What questions will you ask?

Topic: Coin value

Grade: 1

Time: One class period

Anticipated Learning Outcome:

As a result of this lesson, the children will be able to

- identify the different coins and state their value
- exchange smaller coins for larger coins

Procedure:

Ask children to tell about their visits to stores, such as supermarkets, with their parents. Have them describe what people do who work in stores. Focus the discussion on the work of the cashier or salesperson who takes money for the articles purchased. Explain that in cash sales the customer usually receives *change.* Then tell them that today they will learn the value of the various coins by playing a game.

Explain how to play the game:

- Each player gets a playing board arranged in four columns.
- One player is the banker and has all the coins. Review value for each coin.
- On his/her turn, each player rolls the die and asks for the number of pennies shown on the die (e.g., "Four pennies, please"). The banker gives the player the pennies and the player places them in the right-hand column of the game board.
- The play continues clockwise. Any time a player has five pennies in his/her first column, she/he exchanges them with the banker for a nickel and places it in the second column. Any time a player has two nickels, she/he asks the banker for a dime and places it in the third column.
- A player wins by trading two dimes and a nickel with the banker for a quarter.

Divide the class into groups of four. Monitor as the students play the game. After playing through once, banker responsibilities can be passed to a new player and the game started over.

FIGURE 6.4
Lesson plan—Primary grades

Closure and Assessment:

Close the lesson by reviewing the equivalent amounts of coins:

five pennies = one nickel

two nickels = one dime

two dimes and one nickel = one quarter

Relate what has been learned to purchases in stores as discussed in "Interest Building."

Instructional Materials:

Playing boards for each child

Multiple coins (real, cardboard, or plastic)

One die for each group

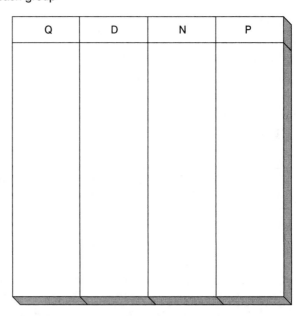

Q	D	N	P

Reflections:

FIGURE 6.4

Continued

Source: Based on a lesson prepared by Laurie L. Nelson, first-grade teacher, College Place Elementary School, Edmonds, WA.

4. How are children to get the background information they need? What books will you use? What pages will you have children read? Will you use audiovisual materials? Are they available?
5. Will you plan cooperative learning activities? If so, how will you group children? Is there something meaningful for all children to do all of the time?
6. How much time will you need to complete each part of the lesson?
7. What provisions must you make for children's different rates of learning?
8. How should you arrange the room environment to best teach the lesson?
9. How is the lesson to close? What will children do? What will you do?
10. Will you plan followup activities? If so, what are they, and how will you schedule them?

   The *implementation* phase of instruction consists of your actual teaching of the lesson and provides numerous opportunities for assessment as well. In

---

Topic: Developing observation skills

Grade: 4

Time: One class period

Anticipated Learning Outcome:

Students will refine observation skills by identifying objects, using several different senses.

Procedure:

Ask students to focus their attention on the picture you are about to show them. Then, using the overhead projector, display a photograph that shows a wide range of human activities taking place, such as a street scene at a fire, police action, or a busy outdoor market. Display the photo for 20 seconds. Then ask students to recall as many of the details of the picture as they can. Discuss their observations. Question them about agreements and disagreements in what they saw. Ask how their observations might have been made more accurate. Point out that their observations used only one sense—visual—but in this lesson, they will learn to use other senses in making observations.

Divide the class into groups of four. For the first observation, students close their eyes and try to identify sounds in the room (e.g., stapler, door opening, overhead projector screen coming down) for 60 seconds. Students record their impressions on a chart and discuss with their group. Then repeat the procedure using recorded outdoor sounds: traffic, birds, running water, wind, construction, etc.

Second observation uses sight only. Students try to identify objects displayed on the overhead projector; chalk, clear pushpins, paper clips, glue stick, rubber band, a square, a flat piece of paper, etc. Students record their observations and compare with the group.

FIGURE 6.5
Lesson plan—Intermediate grades

Third observation uses the sense of touch. Students try to determine what objects are in a bag by touch only, then record their impressions. Bag might contain such items as dry pasta shells, cuisinaire rods, Cheerios, buttons, corks, sandpaper, etc. Discuss with the group.

Then make up another type of observation using the sense of smell: perfume or cologne spray, onion, cinnamon sticks, mint, eucalyptus, etc.

Closure and Assessment:

Discuss the following questions:

- How can the different senses help us observe things that surround us?
- What senses did we not use in these observations?
- What jobs can you think of that require unusual use of some of the senses?
- What can we do to become more accurate in the use of our senses?

Instructional Materials:

Overhead projector and photographs

Cassette recorder and tape for sounds

Items for display on the overhead projector

Objects in bags

Items for sense of smell

Reflections:

FIGURE 6.5

Continued

Source: Based on a lesson plan prepared by Cynthia Magoon, third-grade teacher, Louisa May Alcott Elementary School, Lake Washington School District, Kirkland, WA, and Su Hickenbottom, teacher of gifted students, grades 4, 5, and 6, Snohomish School District, Snohomish, WA.

the event the lesson is not proceeding smoothly, you may modify it on the spot. This kind of impromptu planning is important in fine-tuning a lesson as it progresses. For instance, you may plan to have children work on tasks in small groups to accomplish a learning objective but may find that they are not able to use the time well. You must be alert to this problem, discuss it with children at that point, and perhaps decide to change to a different group configuration. Or you may find that a particular line of questioning is way over children's heads and make an adjustment immediately.

In the *assessment* phase, you conduct a comprehensive assessment of the lesson, including determining whether students have achieved the objectives.

Topic: Understanding electromagnets

Grade: 5

Time: One class period   **Anticipated noise level:** moderate

Anticipated Learning Outcomes:

As a result of this lesson, students will demonstrate their understanding that

- Electricity that passes through a wire coiled around an iron core produces a magnetic field.
- The magnetic field makes the iron core a magnet.
- The wire must form an electrical circuit if the iron core is to be a magnet.

Procedure:

Provide the children with examples (pictures or objects) of electromagnets such as electric bells and buzzers, and huge electromagnets at work moving scrap iron. Ask the children to speculate on how they work. Tell them they will demonstrate how an electromagnet works.

1. Divide the class into groups, each group having three children. Provide each group with one "D" dry-cell battery, fifteen inches of bell wire (lightweight insulated copper wire), a medium d-size nail, five paper clips, and two inches of adhesive tape.

2. Demonstrate how the wire is to be coiled around the nail. Allow a generous amount of wire on both ends. Bare one-half inch of wire at each end.

3. Have the children tape one end of the coiled wire to the bottom of the battery; then have them complete the circuit by touching the other end of the wire to the top battery terminal.

4. Have the children test the strength of their electromagnet by bringing the nail end close to the paper clips.

5. Have the children discover answers to these questions:

   - How many paper clips will the magnet pick up?
   - What happens when the wire is disconnected from the top terminal? The bottom terminal?
   - Does it make any difference which end of the wire is connected to the top and bottom of the battery terminals?
   - Will the strength of the magnet be increased if more wire is wrapped around the nail?
   - Will the strength of the magnet be increased by the use of two batteries?
   - What are the requirements for the magnet to work? Have the children record their findings.

FIGURE 6.6
Lesson Plan—Intermediate Grades

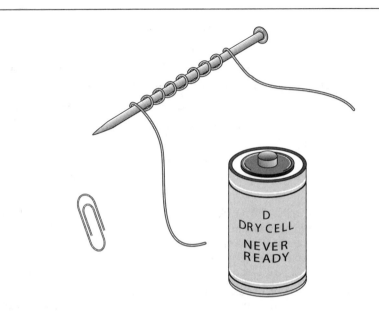

Closure and Assessment:

Have each group report their findings to the class. Discuss.

- Explain the concept *magnetic field* as it relates to the activity.

- Have the children generate concluding statements based on the activity. Through questioning, lead them toward the lesson objectives.

- Follow up by having the children read the section in their science texts that provides additional information on electromagnets.

Instructional Materials:

Supplies listed in "Procedure"; science textbook; pictures and/or objects showing how electromagnets are used.

Reflections:

FIGURE 6.6
Continued

In other words, you must determine whether they learned what they were expected to learn. You can also use this phase to assess what actually occurred during the lesson to promote or to prevent attainment of the objectives. Questions such as the following are useful in assessing a lesson:

- Did children respond with interest when I introduced the lesson?
- Did children seem to understand what was expected of them?
- Did I organize the learning environment sufficiently to reduce distractions and interruptions?
- Did I provide sufficient learning resources?
- Was there a high level of verbal and nonverbal interaction among children and between them and me?
- Did I pace the learning activities to permit adequate time for the various lesson activities?
- Did I provide children with an opportunity to evaluate what occurred and to make suggestions for the next lesson?
- Were the lesson objectives appropriate to students' abilities and interests?
- Was my planning successful in anticipating learners' reactions?
- Were my expected learner outcomes realistic?
- Did I select a teaching mode that was appropriate for achieving my desired learner outcomes?
- Do I need to follow up immediately with learning activities to address elements students either did not learn or learned insufficiently? Or should I move on to activities that allow them to extend, enrich, or apply the newly learned material?

Your responses to the foregoing questions will inform you of your lesson's effectiveness. This is called ongoing or *formative evaluation*. You may find that children did not achieve an objective because they did not have the background knowledge or skills. In the reflective and projective phases of instruction you reflect on the lesson and its results and choose steps to remediate and move forward. Some children will require followup instruction on learning how to attain the expected outcome. In any case, you are able to evaluate the lesson and decide what to do next, such as reteach it or move on to a different focus. Thus, the planning cycle begins anew (Figure 6.7).

THE INSTRUCTIONAL UNIT

An *instructional unit* is a major subdivision of a course, or of a course of study, and is made up of learning activities that are planned around a central theme, topic, issue, or problem. Organizing the content of the semester or year into units makes your teaching more manageable than when you have no plan or make only random choices.

The instructional unit is not unlike a chapter in a book, or a phase of work when undertaking a project, such as building a barn. Breaking down

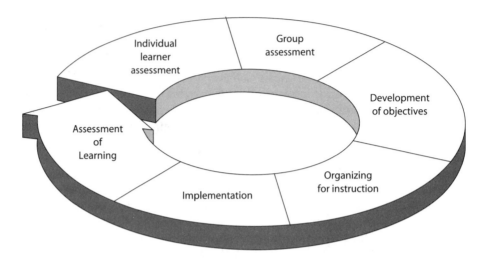

FIGURE 6.7
Planning and teaching are shown here as a set of sequential procedures, each emerging from and conditioned by the ones preceding it.

information or actions into component parts and then grouping the related parts makes sense out of learning and doing. The unit brings a sense of cohesiveness and structure to student learning and avoids the piecemeal approach that might otherwise unfold. You can learn to articulate lessons within, between, and among unit plans and focus on important elements while not ignoring tangential information of importance. Students remember "chunks" of information, especially when those chunks are related to specific units.

Types of Instructional Units

Although you may organize units in a number of ways—such as the standard unit, a contract unit, an interdisciplinary thematic unit, and a self-instructional unit—the steps for developing any type of unit are basically the same. For the purposes of this text, we consider three types—the standard unit, the thematic unit, and the interdisciplinary thematic unit—all three of which are commonly used in some fashion in elementary school teaching.

A *standard unit* (known also as a *conventional* or *traditional* unit) consists of a series of lessons centered on a topic, theme, major concept, or block of subject matter. Each lesson builds on the previous lesson by contributing additional subject matter, providing further illustrations, and supplying more practice or other added instruction, all of which are aimed at bringing about mastery of the knowledge and skills on which the unit is centered.

A standard unit focused on a central theme, such as "Flight," is referred to as a *thematic unit*. When, by design, the thematic unit integrates disciplines, such as combining science and mathematics or social studies and English/ language arts, or combining all four core (or any other) disciplines, then it is called an *integrated* (or *interdisciplinary*) *thematic unit (ITU)*, or simply an *integrated* unit.[23]

Planning and Developing *Any* Unit of Instruction

Whether for a standard, thematic, or integrated thematic unit, steps in planning and developing are the same, as described in the following list.

1. *Select a suitable theme, topic, issue, or problem.* These may be already laid out in your course of study or textbook program or already have been agreed to by members of the teaching team.
2. *Select the goals of the unit and prepare the overview.* Goals are written as an overview or rationale, covering what the unit is about and what the students are to learn. In planning the goals, you should do the following:
   a. Become as familiar as possible with the topic and materials used.
   b. Consult curriculum documents, such as courses of study, state frameworks, and resource units for ideas.
   c. Decide content and procedures (i.e., what students should learn about the topic and how you will present it to them).
   d. Write the rationale or overview, where you summarize what you expect the students will learn about the topic.
   e. Be sure your goals are congruent with those of the grade-level program.
3. *Select suitable anticipated learning outcomes/instructional objectives* (see Chapter 7). For this, you should do the following:
   a. Include understandings, skills, attitudes, appreciations, and ideals.
   b. Be specific, avoiding vagueness and generalizations.
   c. Write the objectives in measurable terms.
   d. Be as certain as possible that the objectives will contribute to the major learning described in your goals statement.
4. *Detail instructional procedures.* Include the subject content and the learning activities, established as a series of lessons. Proceed with the following steps in your initial planning of instructional procedures:
   a. By referring to curriculum documents, resource units, and colleagues as resources, gather ideas for learning activities that might be suitable for the unit.
   b. Check all activities to make sure that they will actually contribute to the learning designated in your objectives, discarding those that do not.
   c. Make sure that the activities are feasible. Can you afford the time, effort, or expense? Do you have the necessary materials and equipment? If not, can you obtain them? Are the activities suited to students' intellectual and maturity levels?
   d. Check resources available to be certain that they support the content and learning activities.

   e. Decide how to introduce the unit. Provide *introductory activities* that
      will (1) arouse student interest; (2) inform students of what the unit is
      about; (3) help you learn about your students—their interests, abilities,
      experiences, and present knowledge of the topic; (4) provide transi-
      tions that bridge this topic with those students have already learned;
      and (5) involve children in the planning.
   f. Plan *developmental activities* that will sustain student interest, provide
      for individual student differences, promote learning as cited in your
      specific objectives.
   g. Plan *culminating activities* that will summarize what students have
      learned, bring together loose ends, apply learning to new situations,
      provide students with opportunity to demonstrate their learning, and
      provide transfer to the unit that follows.
5. *Plan for preassessment and assessment of student learning.* Preassess what
   students already know or think they know. Assessing student progress in
   achieving your learning objectives (formative assessment) should permeate the entire unit (that is, as often as possible, assessment should be a
   daily component of lessons). Plan to gather information in several ways,
   including informal observations, checklist observations of student performance and portfolios, and paper and pencil tests.
6. *Provide for the materials and tools of instruction.* The unit cannot function
   without materials. Therefore, you must plan long before the unit begins
   for media equipment and materials, references, reading materials, repro-
   duced materials, and community resources. Librarians and media center
   personnel are usually more than willing to assist you in finding appropriate materials to support a unit of instruction.

Unit Format, Inclusive Elements, and Duration

In addition to the six steps listed for developing any type of unit, we must
make two general points. First, although there is no single best format for a
teaching unit, there are minimum inclusions. Particular formats may be best
for specific grade levels (kindergarten versus sixth grade, for example), topics, and types of activities. During your student teaching, your college or university program for teacher preparation and/or your cooperating teacher(s)
may have a format that you will be expected to follow. Regardless of the format, the following seven elements should be evident in any unit plan:

1. Identification of grade level, subject, topic, and duration of the unit
2. Statement of rationale and general unit goals
3. Major unit objectives
4. Identification and location of needed materials and resources
5. Sequenced lesson plans
6. Strategies for preassessment, formative assessment, and summative
   assessment

7. Statement of how the unit will attend to students' individual differences, such as reading levels, English proficiency, experiential backgrounds, and special needs

Second, there is no set duration for a unit plan, although for specific units curriculum guides will recommend certain time spans. Units may extend for a minimum of several days or, as in the case of some interdisciplinary thematic units, for several weeks. However, be aware that when standard units last more than 2 or 3 weeks they tend to lose their character as clearly identifiable units. Any unit of instruction's exact duration will be dictated by several factors, including the topic, problem, or theme; children's age, interests, and maturity; and the scope of the learning activities.

PREPARING FOR AND DEALING WITH CONTROVERSY

Regardless of the unit topic or theme and regardless of grade level, the potential for controversy is always lingering in the wings ready to threaten your work as a teacher. Although you can never completely avoid controversy, nor should you, you can prepare for the eventuality. Controversial content and issues abound in teaching, especially in certain disciplines (for example, in English/language arts, over whole language/phonics and over certain books; in social studies, over values and moral issues; in science, over biological evolution; in mathematics, over use of classroom calculators). As a general rule, if you are concerned that a particular topic or activity might create controversy, it probably will. During your teaching career, you undoubtedly must decide how you will handle such matters. Consider the following guidelines when selecting content or activities that might be controversial.

Maintain a perspective with respect to your own goal, which is at the moment to obtain your teaching credential, and then a teaching job, and then tenure. Student teaching is not a good time to become involved in controversy. If you communicate closely with your cooperating teacher and your college or university supervisor, you should be able to prevent major problems dealing with controversial issues. Sometimes a controversial subject will emerge spontaneously during normal discussion in the classroom, catching you off guard. If this happens, think before saying anything. You may wish to postpone further discussion until you have a chance to talk over the issue with more experienced colleagues or with your supervisors. Controversial topics can seem to arise from nowhere for any teacher, and this is perfectly normal. Young people are developing their moral and value systems, and they need and want to know how adults feel about issues that are important to them, particularly those adults they hold in esteem—such as their teachers. Children need to discuss issues that are important to society, and there is absolutely nothing wrong with dealing with those issues as long as you follow certain guidelines.

First, students should learn about all sides of an issue. Controversial issues are open ended and should be treated as such. They do not have "right" answers or "correct" solutions; if they did, there would be no controversy. (As used here, an "issue" differs from a "problem" in that a problem generally has a solution, whereas an issue generates many opinions and several alternative solutions.) Therefore, your focus should be on process as well as on content. A major goal is to show children how to deal with controversy and to mediate wise decisions and choices on the basis of carefully considered information. Another goal is to help children learn how to disagree without being disagreeable—how to resolve conflict. To that end children need to learn the difference between conflicts that are destructive and those that can be constructive: in other words, to see that conflict (disagreement) can be healthy, that it can have value. A third goal, of course, is to help children learn about the content of an issue so, when necessary, they can make decisions based on knowledge rather than on ignorance.

Second, as with all lesson plans, you should carefully think through potentially controversial topics during your preactive phase of instruction. You must carefully consider problem areas and prepare resources in advance. Problems are most likely to occur when you have not thoroughly thought out your plan.

Third, at some point all persons directly involved in an issue have a right to input—students, parents and guardians, community representatives, and other faculty. This does not mean, for example, that people outside the school have the right to censor your plan, but it does mean that parents or guardians and students should have the right, without penalty, to choose to not participate and to select an alternate activity. Most school districts have written policies that deal with challenges to instructional materials. As a beginning teacher, you should become aware of policies of your school district. In addition, professional associations such as the NCTE, NCSS, NBTA, and NSTA have published guidelines for dealing with controversial topics, materials, and issues.

Fourth, there is nothing wrong with children knowing your opinion about an issue as long as it is clear that students may disagree without reprisal or academic penalty. However, it is probably best to wait and give your opinion only after students have had full opportunity to study and report on facts and opinions from other sources. Sometimes it is helpful if you assist children in separating facts from opinions on a particular issue being studied by setting up on the overhead or writing board a fact–opinion table, with the issue stated at the top and two columns, one for facts and the other for related opinions.

A primary characteristic of a successful democracy is the freedom for all its people to speak out on issues. This freedom should not be excluded from public school classrooms. Teachers and students should be encouraged to express their opinions about the great issues of today, to study the issues, to suspend judgment while collecting data, and then to form and accept each other's reasoned opinions. We must understand the difference between teaching truth, values, and morals, and teaching *about* truth, values, and morals.

However, as a public elementary school teacher there *are* limits to your academic freedom, much greater than are the limits on a university professor.

You must understand this fact. The primary difference is that, because the children with whom you will be working are not adults, you must protect them from dogma and allow them the freedom to learn and to develop their values and opinions, free from coercion from those who have power and control over their learning.

SUMMARY

Many school districts have curriculum maps that incorporate state curriculum standards and the district's core of knowledge benchmarks. Teachers are held accountable for teaching these essential learnings, frequently in a specific sequence and time frame. Become very familiar with your school's curriculum expectations, preferably before students arrive for that first class meeting. Keep the standards in a place where you can refer to them quickly and often.

Some elementary school teachers in particular find themselves in a school where the curriculum in language arts or mathematics is highly scripted. If this is the situation for you, just remember that even though the curriculum is scripted, you can still apply your own instructional planning and tweaking of the lessons for your unique group of children. For example, after each daily lesson, you can tweak the lesson that follows with each of your children in mind. Regardless of the origin of a lesson, you, the teacher, will bring to the implementation of that lesson your own unique and creative self. A curriculum that is highly scripted is *not* necessarily antagonistic to student-centered and differentiated instruction. Consider championship ice-skating: Even though others may plan the moves, the ultimate decisions, skill, and art of implementation remain the property of individual skaters. Similarly, teachers who are most effective are those who have learned to modify the key variables of time, methodology, and grouping to help individual students achieve mastery of the key curriculum standards.

With this chapter you deepened your understanding of why planning is important, how lesson plans are useful pedagogical tools, how to prepare for working with specific groups of children, and how to deal with controversial topics or activities. In addition, you began preparing your first instructional unit, an activity that will continue through the rest of your study of this text. Chapter 7 will focus your attention on the assessment component of the reciprocal teaching/learning process.

STUDY QUESTIONS AND ADDITIONAL ACTIVITIES

1. Describe how teachers can support and defend the use of integrated curriculum when faced with the demands of the standards-based reform movement.
2. In this book, we present the process of planning for and implementing instruction as a systematic, cyclical process that consists of four phases, the

preactive, interactive, reflective, and projective. Create a superimposition of those phases on the diagram shown in Figure 6.7. Share and explain your creation with those of your classmates.

3. Ms. Baxter and Mr. Bond were placed in elementary schools in which the school principals had different styles of leadership. Briefly describe each style. Would you feel more comfortable teaching in one or the other? If so, explain which and why.

4. Explain the value of organizing instruction into units. In grade-level discussion groups, list and describe specific considerations you should give to child safety when preparing instructional plans. Share your lists with other groups.

5. Give at least three reasons that both a student teacher and a first-year teacher need to prepare detailed lesson plans, even when the textbook program you are using provides them.

6. Describe at least three sources that you are likely to use for ideas for learning activities.

7. Describe how, when designing unit plans, you can attend to student learning styles, learning capacities, and modality strengths.

8. Describe any merits and limitations of the practice of teachers' studying the school records of children to learn more about their potential academic strengths and weaknesses.

9. Name and describe at least three different sources of ideas for interdisciplinary themes.

10. Describe a book, topic, teaching method, or issue that could be controversial and that could create a problem for you as a classroom teacher. Share with your colleagues how you would prepare yourself to avoid problems when dealing with such a potential problem.

NOTES

1. See, for example, L. M. Morrow, D. H. Tracey, D. G. Woo, M. Pressley, and A. M. Duffy-Hester, "Characteristics of Exemplary First-Grade Literacy Instruction," *The Reading Teacher* 52(5): 462–476 (1999), especially page 468.

2. For Gardner's distinction between "learning style" and "intelligences," see: H. Gardner, "Multiple Intelligences: Myths and Messages," *International Schools Journal* 15(2): 8–22 (1996), and the many articles in the "Teaching for Multiple Intelligences" theme issue of *Educational Leadership* 55(1): (1997).

3. See, for example, T. R. Hoerr, *Becoming a Multiple Intelligences School* (Alexandria,

VA: Association for Supervision and Curriculum Development, 2000).

4. See, for example, R. J. Sternberg, "Teaching and Assessing for Successful Intelligence," and L. English, "Uncovering Students' Analytic, Practical, and Creative Intelligences: One School's Application of Sternberg's Triarchic Theory," *School Administrator* 55(1): 26–27, 30–31, and 28–29, respectively, (1998).

5. See R. J. Sternberg, "Teaching and Assessing for Successful Intelligence," *School Administrator* 55(1): 26–27, 30–31 (1998). See also R. J. Sternberg, E. L. Grigorenko, and L. Jarvin, "Improving Reading Instruction:

The Triarchic Model," *Educational Leadership* 58(6): 48–51 (2001).

6. See P. Berman et al., *School Reform and Student Diversity, Volume II: Case Studies of Exemplary Practices for LEP Students* (Berkeley, CA: National Center for Research on Cultural Diversity and Second Language Learning, 1995).

7. For a description of a variety of programs for teaching English language learners, see F. Genesee, "Teaching Linguistically Diverse Students," *Principal* 79(5): 24–27 (2000).

8. D. R. Walling, *English as a Second Language: 25 Questions and Answers*, Fastback 347 (Bloomington, IN: Phi Delta Kappa Educational Foundation, 1993), p. 26.

9. C. Minicucci et al., "School Reform and Student Diversity," *Phi Delta Kappan* 77(1): 77–80 (1995), p. 78.

10. A. Meyer and D. H. Rose, "Universal Design for Individual Differences," *Educational Leadership* 58(3): 39–43 (2000), p. 40.

11. See, for example, M. L. Yell, "The Legal Basis of Inclusion," *Educational Leadership* 56(2): 70–73 (1998).

12. E. Tiegerman-Farber and C. Radziewicz, *Collaborative Decision Making: The Pathway to Inclusion* (Upper Saddle River, NJ: Merrill/Prentice Hall, 1998), pp. 12-13.

13. C. Wilard-Holt, *Dual Exceptionalities* (Reston, VA: ERIC Digest E574, ERIC Clearinghouse on Disabilities and Gifted Education, 1999).

14. AAP Media Resource Team, *Just the Facts . . . Diagnosing ADHD*, from the American Academy of Pediatrics, retrieved March 3, 2003; from http://www.aap.org/mrt.factsda.htm.

15. See the discussion in G. Clark and E. Zimmerman, "Nurturing the Arts in Programs for Gifted and Talented Students," *Phi Delta Kappan* 79(10): 747–751 (June 1998).

16. See, for example, J. F. Feldhusen, "Programs for the Gifted Few or Talent Development for the Many?" *Phi Delta Kappan* 79(10): 735–738 (1998), and M. U. M. Gross, "Exceptionally and Profoundly Gifted Students: An Underserved Population," *Understanding Our Gifted* 12(2): 3–9 (2000).

17. C. Dixon, L. Mains, and M. J. Reeves, *Gifted and At Risk*, Fastback 398 (Bloomington, IN: Phi Delta Kappa Educational Foundation, 1996), 7.

18. S. Schwartz, *Strategies for Identifying the Talents of Diverse Students*. ERIC/CUE Digest, Number 122 (New York:ED410323, ERIC Clearinghouse on Urban Education, 1997).

19. Adapted from Dixon, Mains, and Reeves, pp. 9–12. By permission of the Phi Delta Kappa Educational Foundation.

20. P. L. Tiedt and I. M. Tiedt, *Multicultural Teaching: A Handbook of Activities, Information, and Resources*, 5th ed. (Boston: Allyn & Bacon, 1999), 35.

21. R. Dunn, *Strategies for Educating Diverse Learners*, Fastback 384 (Bloomington, IN: Phi Delta Kappa Educational Foundation, 1995), 9.

22. With modern technology, such as is afforded, for example, by the software program *Learner Profile*, a teacher can record observations electronically anywhere at any time. For information about *Learner Profile*, contact Sunburst, 101 Castleton St., P.O. Box 100, Pleasantville, NY 10570–0100, phone 1–800–321–7511.

23. See, for example, for grades K–3, H. Devona, "Whales: Incredible Ocean Mammals," *Journal of Geography* 91(4): 166–170 (1992); for fourth grade, K. Freeland and K. Smith, "A Thematic Teaching Unit on Flight," *Social Studies and the Young Learner* 5(4): 15–17 (1993); and for middle grades, L. Schiller, "Coming to America: Community from Diversity," *Language Arts* 73(1): 46–51 (1996).

FOR FURTHER PROFESSIONAL STUDY

Adams, T. L. "Helping Children Learn Mathematics Through Multiple Intelligences and Standards for School Mathematics." *Childhood Education* 77(2): 86–92 (Winter 2000–2001).

Armstrong, T. *Multiple Intelligences in the Classroom*. 2d ed. Alexandria, VA: Association for Supervision and Curriculum Development, 2000.

Armstrong, T. *The Multiple Intelligences of Reading and Writing.* Alexandria, VA: Association for Supervision and Curriculum Development, 2003.

Black, S. "Teaching About Religion." *American School Board Journal* 190(4): 50–53 (2003).

Brand, S., Dunn, R., and Greb, F. "Learning Styles of Students with Attention Deficit Hyperactivity Disorder: Who Are They and How Can We Teach Them?" *Clearing House* 75(5): 268–272 (2002).

Brown, J. *Educating African-American Children.* Fastback 486. Bloomington, IN: Phi Delta Kappa Educational Foundation, 2001.

Cade, T. and Gunter, P. L. "Teaching Students with Severe Emotional or Behavioral Disorders to Use a Musical Mnemonic Technique to Solve Basic Division Calculations." *Behavioral Disorders* 27(3): 208–214 (2002).

Callahan, C. M. "Beyond the Gifted Stereotype." *Educational Leadership* 59(3): 42–46 (2001).

Caskey, M. "A Lingering Question for Middle School: What Is the Fate of Integrated Curriculum?" *Childhood Education* 78(2): 97–99 (Winter 2001–2002).

Curtis, D. "The Power of Projects." *Educational Leadership* 60(1): 50–53 (2002).

Fagan, H., and Sherman, L. "Starting at the End: Alaska Project-Based Learning Expert Helena Fagan Insists That Good Projects Are Designed 'Backward'—That Is, What Do We Want Kids to Know When They're Done?" *Northwest Education* 7(3): 30–35 (2002).

Fasko, D., Jr. "An Analysis of Multiple Intelligences Theory and Its Use with the Gifted and Talented." *Roeper Review* 23(3): 126–130 (2001).

Franklin, J. "The Art of Differentiation." *Education Update* 44(2): 1, 3, 8 (2002).

Franks, L. "Charcoal Clouds and Weather Writing: Inviting Science to a Middle School Language Arts Classroom." *Language Arts* 78(4): 319–324 (2001).

Fredrick, L. D.; Keel, M. C.; and Neel, J. H. "Making the Most of Instructional Time: Teaching Reading at an Accelerated Rate to Students at Risk." *Journal of Direct Instruction* 2(1): 57–63 (2002).

Frykholm, J. A., and Meyer, M. R. "Integrated Instruction: Is It Science? Is It Mathematics?" *Mathematics Teaching in the Middle School* 7(9): 502–508 (2002).

Grant, J. "Differentiating for Diversity." *Principal* 82(3): 48–51 (2003).

Johns, K. M., and Torrez, N. *Helping ESL Learners Succeed.* Fastback 484. Bloomington, IN: Phi Delta Kappa Educational Foundation, 2001.

Joiner, L. L. "Where Did We Come From?" *American School Board Journal* 190(4): 30–34 (2003).

Keller, C. L. "A New Twist on Spelling Instruction for Elementary School Teachers." *Intervention in School and Clinic* 38(1): 3–7 (2002).

Kellough, R. D. *A Resource Guide for Teaching: K–12.* 4th ed. Upper Saddle River, NJ: Merrill/Prentice Hall, 2003.

Kelly, K. "Lesson Study: Can Japanese Methods Translate to U.S. Schools?" *Harvard Education Letter* 18(3): 4–7 (2002).

Little, T. S., and Little, L. P. *Looping: Creating Elementary School Communities.* Fastback 478. Bloomington, IN: Phi Delta Kappa Educational Foundation, 2001.

Marzano, R. J. "Classroom Curriculum Design." Chapter 11 of *What Works in Schools: Translating Research into Action.* Alexandria, VA: Association for Supervision and Curriculum Development, 2003.

Montgomery, W. "Creating Culturally Responsive, Inclusive Classrooms." *Teaching Exceptional Children* 33(4): 4–9 (2001).

Moore, J. N., Ed. "Geography and Generations." *English Journal* 90(4): 119–124 (2001).

Nuthall, G. "The Way Students Learn: Acquiring Knowledge from an Integrated Science and Social Studies Unit." *Elementary School Journal* 99(4): 303–341 (1999).

Ownbey, M., and Thompson, M. "Combining P.E. and Music." *Principal* 82(3): 30 (2003).

Palincsar, A. S., Magnusson, S. J., Collins, K. M., and Cutter, J. "Making Science Accessible to All: Results of a Design Experiment in Inclusive Classrooms." *Learning Disability Quarterly* 24(1): 15–32 (2001).

Posamentier, A. S. *Math Wonders to Inspire Teachers and Students.* Alexandria, VA: Association for Supervision and Curriculum Development, 2003.

Reid, J. "Publishing Their Way to Better Writing." *Principal* 80(3): 43–46 (January 2001).

Roberts, P. L., and Kellough, R. D. *A Guide for Developing an Interdisciplinary Thematic Unit.* 3rd ed. Upper Saddle River, NJ: Merrill/Prentice Hall, 2004.

Roser, N. L. and Keehn, S. "Fostering Thought, Talk, and Inquiry: Linking Literature and Social Studies." *Reading Teacher* 55(5): 416–426 (2002).

Rubado, K. "Empowering Students Through Multiple Intelligences." *Reclaiming Children and Youth* 19(4): 233–235 (2002).

Searson, R., and Dunn, R. "The Learning-Style Teaching Model." *Science and Children* 38(5): 22–26 (2001).

Slocumb, P. D., and Payne, R. K. "Identifying and Nurturing the Gifted Poor." *Principal* 79(5): 28–32 (2000).

Tomlinson, C. A. *Differentiation of Instruction in the Elementary Grades.* ED443572. Champaign, IL: ERIC Clearinghouse on Elementary and Early Childhood Education, 2000.

Vacca, D. M. "Confronting the Puzzle of Nonverbal Learning Disabilities." *Educational Leadership* 59(3): 26–31 (2001).

VanTassel-Baska, J., Zuo, L., Avery, L. D., and Little, C. A. "A Curriculum Study of Gifted-Student Learning in the Language Arts." *Gifted Child Quarterly* 46(1): 30–44 (2002).

Victor, E., and Kellough, R. D. *Science K–8: An Integrated Approach.* 10th ed. Upper Saddle River, NJ: Merrill/Prentice Hall, 2004.

Vogler, K. E. "An Integrated Curriculum Using State Standards in a High-Stakes Testing Environment." *Middle School Journal* 34(4): 5–10 (2003).

Warger, C. *Helping Students with Disabilities Succeed in State and District Writing Assessments.* ED463622. Arlington, VA: ERIC Clearinghouse on Disabilities and Gifted Education, 2002.

Winebrenner, S. "Gifted Students Need an Education, Too." *Educational Leadership* 59(1): 52–56 (2000).

Xin, J. F., and Forrest, L. "Managing the Behavior of Children with ADD in Inclusive Classrooms: A Collaborative Approach." *Reclaiming Children and Youth* 10(4): 240–245 (2002).

INTASC Principles	PRAXIS III Domains	NBPTS Standards
• The teacher understands and uses formal and informal assessment strategies to evaluate and ensure the continuous intellectual, social, and physical development of the learner. (Principle 8)	• Organizing Content Knowledge for Student Learning (Domain A)	• Assessment

H o w can we tell if children are performing at a satisfactory level of educational achievement? What standards of achievement should we expect of them? Can we provide for individual differences among learners and, at the same time, expect a minimal level of performance from *all* children? Should we promote children to the next grade if they do not attain the minimal standard of achievement for their current grade placement? What should the school do with those children who do not succeed in achieving these standards a second, third, or fourth time? Do we pass them anyway? How does the school achievement of U.S. children compare with that of other modern, industrialized nations? These questions deal with the topic of assessment of student learning; they are difficult questions that have bothered teachers, the public, and politicians for many years.

Assessment is an integral part and ongoing process in the educational arena. Curricula, buildings, materials, specific courses, teachers, supervisors, administrators, equipment—all must be periodically assessed in relation to student learning, the purpose of the school. When gaps between anticipated results and student achievement exist, those responsible try to eliminate those factors that seem to be limiting the educational output, or find some other way to improve the situation. Thus, educational progress occurs. In this book we can only begin to scratch the surface of this huge and enormously important topic of assessment of student learning.

ANTICIPATED OUTCOMES

After completing this chapter, you should be able to do the following:

1. Demonstrate your understanding of the importance of assessment in teaching and learning.
2. Describe the relationship of assessment to goals and objectives.
3. Explain the concept of "authentic assessment."
4. Explain the value of and give an example of a performance assessment that you could use at a particular grade level or discipline.
5. Explain why criterion-referenced grading is preferable to norm-referenced grading.
6. Explain how teachers use rubrics, checklists, and portfolios in assessing student learning.
7. Differentiate among *diagnostic, summative,* and *formative assessment,* giving examples of when and how to use each with a particular grade level or discipline.
8. Describe the importance of self-assessment in teaching and learning.
9. Describe the importance of involving parents and guardians in their children's education, and identify at least three ways to involve them.
10. Complete the diagnostic, formative, and summative assessment tools of the unit plan that you began working on in Chapter 6.

THE LANGUAGE OF ASSESSMENT

We first explain some of the terms and concepts associated with the process of determining whether children are achieving satisfactorily.

Evaluation, Assessment, and Measurement

Evaluation is a generic term having to do with determining the extent to which goals and objectives of teaching and learning have been attained. *Assessment* has much the same meaning, and some authors use the terms interchangeably. In the strictest sense, however, assessment has to do with gathering data used to make value judgments about student progress. Evaluation specifically refers only to the *judgment* part of this process. Some value of preference is associated with both evaluation and assessment because standards serve as the basis both for estimating and measuring performance (assessment) and then for judging its adequacy (evaluation).

Measurement has to do with using objective tests and procedures whose results can be converted into quantitative data. The data per se do not tell anything about the quality of the performance. For example, if a child obtained a score of 75 on a test, this score by itself does not indicate whether it is high or low, acceptable or unsatisfactory. If you knew that 500 children took the test, that the average score was 45, and that the second highest score was 63, you would then be inclined to say 75 was, indeed, a high score. However, if you were informed that the 500 children who took the test were all developmentally disabled (mild mental retardation), you might need to qualify your interpretation of 75 as a high score. This example illustrates how *measurement* provides data that can be useful in making an *evaluation*.

Authentic and Performance Assessment

Children's development encompasses growth in the cognitive, affective, and psychomotor domains. Traditional objective paper and pencil tests provide only a portion of the data needed to indicate student progress in these domains. Many experts today, as indeed they have in the past, question the traditional sources of data and encourage searching for, developing, and using alternative means to assess more authentically students' development of thinking and higher-level learning. Although many things are not yet clear, it is clear that you must employ various assessment techniques to determine how students work, what they are learning, and what they can produce as a result of that learning. As a teacher, you must develop a repertoire of ways to assess learner behavior and academic progress.

When assessing for student achievement, it is important that you use procedures that are compatible with the expected outcomes, that is, with your instructional objectives. This is referred to as *authentic assessment* (also called *accurate, active, aligned, alternative,* and *direct assessment*). Although some teachers call this *performance assessment*, performance assessment specifically refers to the type of student response being assessed, whereas authentic assessment refers to the assessment situation. Although not all performance assessments are authentic, assessments that *are* authentic are most assuredly performance assessments. For example, you would best measure (i.e., with the highest reliability) someone's competency to teach specific skills in physical education to second-grade students by directly observing the person doing exactly that—teaching specific skills in physical education to second-graders. Using a standardized paper and pencil test of multiple-choice items to determine a person's ability to teach specific physical education skills to second grade children is not authentic assessment.

Consider another example: "If students have been actively involved in classifying objects using multiple characteristics, it sends them a confusing message if they are then required to take a paper-and-pencil test that asks them to 'define classification' or recite a memorized list of characteristics of good classifications schemes."[1] An authentic assessment technique would be a performance item that actually involves students in classifying objects. In other words, to accurately assess students' learning, you would use a performance-based assessment procedure, that is, a procedure that requires them to produce rather than to select a response, such as in the following three examples:

1. Write a retelling of your favorite myth and create a diorama to go along with it.
2. As a culminating project (as a summative assessment tool) for a unit on sound, the teacher challenged groups of students to design and make their own musical instruments. The performance assessment instructions included the following:
   a. Play your instrument for the class.
   b. Show us the part of the instrument that makes the sound.
   c. Describe the function of other parts of your instrument.
   d. Demonstrate how you change the pitch of the sound.
   e. Share with us how you made your instrument.
3. Measure and calculate the area of our outdoor playing field to the nearest square meter.

Advantages claimed for authentic assessment include (1) the *direct* (also called *performance-based*, *criterion-referenced*, or *outcome-based*) measurement of what students should know and can do and (2) emphasis on higher-order thinking. On the other hand, disadvantages of authentic assessment include (1) a higher cost and (2) problems with validity, reliability, and comparability.

Performance testing can be difficult and time consuming to administer to a group of children. Adequate supply of materials could be a problem. Scoring may tend to be subjective. It may be difficult to give makeup tests to students who were absent. To the extent possible in your own teaching, use your creativity to design and use performance tests, as they tend to measure well

1. Specify the performance objective (anticipated outcome).
2. Specify the test conditions.
3. Establish the standards (a scoring rubric) for judging student performance.
4. Prepare directions in writing, outlining the situation, with instructions students are to follow.
5. Share the procedure with a colleague for feedback before using it with students.

FIGURE 7.1
Steps for setting up a performance assessment situation

your most important objectives. To reduce subjectivity in scoring, prepare distinct scoring guidelines (rubrics). To set up a performance assessment situation, follow the steps shown in Figure 7.1.

Formative and Summative Assessment

Teachers on the job are constantly observing children's work and behavior and making some judgment about their quality. Perhaps they supplement these observations with short progress tests or quizzes that provide feedback about how well children are learning. In terms of these observations and tests, they will modify their instruction to be certain that it remains focused on the target. This type of ongoing assessment of children's learning is referred to as *formative evaluation*.

Formative evaluation contrasts with *summative evaluation* in that the latter occurs at or near the conclusion of a unit, at the end of a school term or semester, or at the end of the year. Summative evaluation is generally used to provide an accounting of learners' achievement status—individually or as a group—rather than to fine-tune the instructional process in progress.

Norm-Referenced and Criterion-Referenced Tests

In *norm-referenced tests*, the level of achievement against which performance is judged is based on the scores obtained by hundreds, perhaps even thousands, of students of the same age and school grade who have taken the test. These test results are reported as averages, or *norms*, and you can use them to determine whether an individual student's score is less than, equal to, or greater than that of the population for which the test data were obtained. Scores for groups, such as a class or a single grade in an entire school or school district, can also be compared with the scores obtained by the norming population.

Standardized tests are norm-referenced tests available for various subjects and skills from commercial test publishers. In many states, the state departments of education have produced their own standardized tests for basic school subjects. Standardized-test results constitute a useful tool for you in revealing general strengths or weaknesses in the achievement of individuals or of an entire class. As instruments of summative evaluation, you ordinarily administer them near the end of the school year.

Standardized tests can be an objective yardstick to assess children's achievement. However, they do have limitations and have, in recent years, come under increased criticism. The following are frequently cited objections to the use of standardized tests:

1. They can be misused by teachers who believe that all children must attain the average score and by teachers who teach specifically for the test content.
2. They rely on reading skill, and therefore often do not provide good measures of concept attainment and knowledge of informational content.
3. They may be used to label children as high or low achievers, and may thereby create self-fulfilling prophecies.
4. They may have the effect of limiting or "freezing" the curriculum to the content of the tests.
5. They are not able to accommodate adequately the local variations found in the curricula of U.S. schools.
6. They test not only school achievement but life experiences and out-of-school learning of all types; that is, the tests have a sociocultural bias favoring children who come from middle and upper socioeconomic levels and whose families have a better than average formal education.
7. They focus on measuring easily identified objectives dealing with subject matter and information and often do not evaluate the broader goals of education.
8. If the test measures for traditional outcomes—as many do—their use maintains the inertia of traditional instruction, thereby impeding adoption of educational reform.
9. Tests in specific subject fields, such as mathematics, are not always consistent with the most current scientific research on what understandings should be expected of children at various grade levels.

Criterion-referenced tests are those that establish specific levels of expected performance. The best example is a learning situation in which you expect mastery. You may expect children to learn all of the spelling words, and they continue to study them until they are able to spell them all correctly. Or you may expect a certain level of quality of handwriting, and students do not complete the requirement until they meet that quality (or "criterion") level. Criterion-referenced tests are often used to evaluate the performance of motor skills, such as those associated with physical education. Any pass–fail test is an example of a criterion-referenced test. Criterion-referenced tests should always be used to assess learning in which less than an adequate performance would result in potentially disastrous consequences. Such learning includes (1) the administration of first aid; (2) fire drills or earthquake alert routines; (3) use of potentially hazardous tools, materials, or equipment; and (4) procedures, such as experiments, that could injure participants if not performed correctly.

Readiness Testing

A *readiness test* is used to determine whether learners have the prerequisite knowledge, skills, and interest to learn new material. Readiness testing is also referred to as *diagnostic assessment* or *preassessment*. Readiness may also have to do with learners' physical maturity. For example, if you expect children to learn a skill that involves complex eye–hand coordination, you would need to ascertain whether they are sufficiently mature physically to perform the task. In the area of physical education, certain learning experiences are referred to as *lead-up activities* and are intended to build the needed readiness for a forthcoming major activity, such as a team game.

Preassessment is also a way of determining students' misconceptions (naïve theories) about a topic you plan to study. At any grade level, you must determine what children already know or think they know about a subject or skill in order to set new instruction at the appropriate level of difficulty. If instruction is too simple, you are only reviewing what children already know or are proficient in doing. If too difficult, they cannot learn it successfully because it will not be linked psychologically to their existing intellectual framework. Gauging the appropriate level of difficulty for learners is an ability that good teachers are able to apply masterfully. They develop informal evaluation techniques and procedures to establish the degree of readiness. Then, they build readiness for new material by using appropriate "lead-up" or "lead-in" activities. Interest building is necessarily an important part of this process. It is critical that you make good decisions at this stage of instructional planning if new learning is to result.

Validity and Reliability

The degree to which a measuring instrument actually measures what it is intended to measure is that instrument's *validity*. For example, when we ask if a test has validity, we are asking the following key questions concerning that test: Does it adequately sample the intended content? Does it measure the cognitive, affective, and psychomotor knowledge and skills that are important to the unit of content being tested? Does it sample all the instructional objectives of that unit of content?

The accuracy with which a technique consistently measures what it is intended to measure is its *reliability*. If, for example, you know that your body weight is 135 pounds, and a scale consistently records 135 pounds when you stand on it, then that scale has reliability. However, if the same scale consistently records 200 pounds when you stand on it, we can still say the scale has reliability. By this example, then, it should be clear to you that an instrument could be reliable (it produces similar results when used again and again) although *not* necessarily valid. In this second instance, the scale is not measuring what it is supposed to measure—that is, rather than 135 pounds it is showing 200 pounds—so although it is reliable, it is not valid. Although a technique might be reliable but not valid, it *must* have reliability before it can have validity. The greater the number of test items or situations measuring for a particular content objective, the higher the reliability. The higher the reliability, the more consistently students' scores will measure their understanding of that particular objective.

ASSESSMENT IN THE CONTEXT OF INSTRUCTION

Assessment is an essential part of teaching and learning because it focuses learners' attention on their need to improve their performance. Furthermore, the more precisely assessment tells learners what they are doing well and what less well, the easier it will be for them to improve. Just as goals and objectives point students in desired directions, assessment lets them know whether and how well they are proceeding toward attaining them. Assessment helps clarify goals and objectives for students and helps define for them what you, the teacher, believe to be important. Assessment, therefore, is an inseparable part of teaching and learning, and whatever the school accepts as part of its teaching responsibility needs to be evaluated.

It is important for you to understand that the object of assessment in schools is learner *performance* and not to evaluate individuals as human beings. Often these two become confused, and we find ourselves judging the value of people on the basis of their school performance. Thus, there is the ever-present danger that children who do poorly in school may feel as a result that they are not adequate human beings. Teachers and schools must be careful not to encourage or reinforce any notion that the only worthwhile people are those who do well in school. The world is full of creative and successful people who at one time or another did not do well in school.

As we have stated several times in this book, your assessment should properly take place in terms of established goals and objectives. You must align your assessment with your anticipated outcomes. That means that (1) you must know what children are supposed to learn and (2) you must be able to identify behavior that indicates they have learned it. If you use measurable instructional objectives, as explained in Chapter 5, these two dimensions of assessment are embodied in the objective itself. Table 7.1 lists commonly used assessment procedures, along with some of the purposes each can serve.

Keeping samples and exhibits of children's work for purposes of assessing progress is something many teachers have been doing for generations. In recent years, however, students have acquired more responsibility for assembling and maintaining such samples, and the term *portfolio* is now applied to this technique. This usage derives from the adult world, where commercial artists, architects, technical writers, portrait photographers, advertising executives, and others whose careers involve developing products prepare a professional

Table 7.1 includes eight assessment procedures that elementary school teachers commonly use. These appear in the leftmost column. Notice that you may use any one of these eight procedures to assess learning that falls in the three domains discussed in Chapter 5. Because the nature of learning is different in each of the three domains you would of necessity use the assessment procedures differently. Take, for example, the first listed procedure "Group Discussion." You might be *primarily* interested in assessing one of the following:

1. How have children expanded their knowledge of the substantive content of the topic studied? (In this case, the suggestions in the column "Assessment of Cognitive Gain" would be appropriate.) *Or. . .*

2. How have children's feelings or attitudes been affected by studying the topic? (Here the suggestions in the column "Assessment of Attitude and Value Change" would apply.) *Or. . .*

3. How well have children learned certain skills associated with their study of the topic? (For this purpose, you should use the suggestions in the column "Assessment of Skill Development.")

Go through the entire table and try to visualize how you could use each of the eight assessment procedures. As you study the suggestions in the columns, notice what different kinds of learner behaviors they assess.

TABLE 7.1
Procedures commonly used by elementary school teachers to assess student progress

Procedure	Assessment of Cognitive Gain	Assessment of Attitude and Value Change	Assessment of Skill Development
Group Discussion	*Things to note:* How well do the children use the appropriate vocabulary? Are the essential concepts understood? Are the important relationships understood? Are there important concepts needing further study? Is the factual base adequate for the ideas being discussed?	*Things to note:* Extent to which the children express like or dislike of a topic. Presence or absence of comments suggesting racism, sexism, or prejudice. Extent of openness to new ideas. Evidence of responsible self-evaluation.	*Things to note:* Ability to express ideas. Contributions to discussion. Ability to use standards in evaluating work. Evidence of being informed on the topic.
Observation	*Do the children:* Talk with understanding about the topics under study? Cite examples of out-of-school applications of the ideas studied? Propose new plans of action based on the information gained?	*Do the children:* Show respect for the ideas and feelings of others? Carry a fair share of the workload? Show evidence of responsible habits of work?	*Do the children:* Use relevant skills independently when they are needed? Have apparent deficiencies in skills? Avoid using certain important and needed skills?

TABLE 7.1
Continued

Procedure	Assessment of Cognitive Gain	Assessment of Attitude and Value Change	Assessment of Skill Development
Checklists	*Used to:* Indicate mastery, as on a pass–fail performance. Record specific areas of strength or weakness in the knowledge of a subject. Report student progress, as on report cards.	*Used to:* Record observations of specific behaviors of students—such as attitudes toward class-mates, toward authority, or toward attending school.	*Used to:* Evaluate the use of a specific skill, such as giving an oral report, clarity of speaking, or use of references.
Conferences	*Used to:* Examine children orally who may not be able to read or write. Discover evidence of con-fusion or misunderstanding of ideas. Clarify the kinds of assis-tance needed by the child. Discover the nature of the needed corrective work.	*Used to:* Learn specific interest of individual children—likes, dislikes, preferred activi-ties, books, topics, and so on.	*Used to:* Diagnose specific problems. Check the proficiency of skill use on an individual basis.
Anecdotal Records	Items listed under Group Discussion and Observation are appropriate here.	Items listed under Group Discussion and Observation are appropri-ate here.	Items listed under Group Discussion and Observation are appropri-ate here.
Work Samples and Portfolios	*Used to:* Note qualitative differences in the child's work products over time: a written report, booklet, map, or a class-room test. Show ability to apply, analyze, or summarize ideas.	*Used to:* Note greater sensitivity to others in written work and artwork. Note increased concern for neatness of work; concern for punctuality in completing assigned work. Note originality and creative abilities.	*Used to:* Note qualitative differences in proficiency in use of specific skills. Illustrate student's ability to structure responses.
Diaries and Logs	*Used to:* Help the children recall what has been learned.	*Used to:* Remind the children of the gap between intentions and behavior.	*Used to:* Show improvement in skill use over time.

TABLE 7.1
Continued

Procedure	Assessment of Cognitive Gain	Assessment of Attitude and Value Change	Assessment of Skill Development
Teacher-made Tests	*Used to:* Evaluate understanding of concepts, generalizations, trends, and informational content through the use of such exercises as the following: Matching causes and effects. Arranging events in order or arranging steps in a sequence. Providing reasons or explanations for events. Selecting the best explanations from a list of options. Determining the truth or falsity of statements. Providing examples of concepts. Supplying a generalization based on given facts. Being able to use key terms correctly. Providing ends to unfinished stories or situations based on facts. Placing events on a time line.	*Used to:* Find out about likes, dislikes, interests, and preferences for activities through the use of such exercises as the following: From a list, select the things you liked best, liked least. Check what you like to do during your free time. Write ends to unfinished stories that deal with emotions, prejudice, and discrimination. Select words from a narrative that engender strong feelings.	*Used to:* Check the proficiency of skill use or to diagnose specific difficulties through the use of exercises such as the following: Locating places on a map. Reading to find the main idea. Making an outline of material read, or finishing a partially completed outline. Using an index to find information. Skimming to find specific facts. Writing an ending to a story.

portfolio they then use to document their background when they apply for new positions or seek clients. The use of student portfolios can vividly highlight both progress and deficiencies in learning. Moreover, the display of written work, creative endeavors, and science and social studies projects illustrates clearly students' progress over time and shows parents and guardians how their children are progressing. Seeing children's actual work over time is much more meaningful to most parents and guardians than is a letter grade alone. We discuss self-assessment and portfolios later in this chapter.

Activity 7.1: Make It Right, *Write!*

Megan Nalley remembered that her language arts methods instructor said, "Children who learn to write well are those who do a whole lot of writing and are provided critical feedback on their writing efforts." This made a lasting impression on Megan, and now, in her first year as a sixth-grade teacher, she has her students write one-page essays each week. Additionally, she requires them to write lengthy answers to their assigned work in their science, health, and social studies classes. She goes over these papers carefully and writes numerous comments on them. Her problem now is that she has time to do little else but read and correct children's written work. The task is overwhelming! After about 6 weeks, she complains about it to a fellow teacher who has several years of experience and asks her what she should do. The teacher offers Megan the following advice:

• Reduce the *length* of the written assignments. In many cases, a single paragraph might be adequate to build a specific writing skill.
• Teach children to edit their own papers for such items as spelling and basic punctuation.

• From time to time, have children work in pairs and edit each other's papers.
• Identify common errors that many children make, and comment to the entire class rather than writing the same comment on 25 papers.
• Divide the class into groups of four and have children read their essays aloud to each other. In the process, they also can edit their papers.
• Select specific items for evaluation rather than identifying all the errors in every paper.

1. If Megan uses some of these suggestions, will it be possible for her to attain her objective of improving the writing skills of her sixth-graders?
2. In addition to creating an impossible workload for herself, what other detrimental effects might flow from the amount of writing Megan is requiring her students to do?
3. Can you add other helpful suggestions to the six Megan's colleague offered?

ASSESSMENT IN THE CLASSROOM

If the elementary school experience is to help students achieve a range of learning goals, it follows that teachers must use a variety of assessment techniques and procedures to evaluate those outcomes. As is evident from Table 7.1, your assessment of student learning can take many forms. These are often informal techniques that rely mainly on your professional judgment and thoughtful observation of student behavior. When you become involved in the preparation of formal tests, however, it is important to ensure that such instruments are technically correct. This demands specialized knowledge usually covered in a course dealing with testing, measurement, and evaluation, a standard requirement in most teacher certification programs. It is in such a course that you, the prospective teacher, should learn about constructing and using such item types as (1) alternative response (true-false, yes-no, agree-disagree, etc.; also called *selected response*), (2) multiple choice, (3) matching, (4) short answer, (5) completion, and (6) essay. It is beyond the purpose of this text to provide detail on such topics, but we do refer you to sources in the suggested readings at the end of this chapter.[2]

Considering that elementary school students range in age from 5 to 13 years and are in the process of mastering some of the basic learning of our culture, it makes sense to use classroom assessment to measure what they can do after instruction as compared with what they could do prior to it. A few examples will clarify this point. If your class has spent 20 minutes each day for a week learning to spell 20 words, the appropriate test at the end of the week would involve having them write the words and spell them correctly. If you are teaching children how to add three-digit whole numbers, your test should require them to add some three-digit whole numbers to see if they can do it correctly. If children have been learning in social studies about causes and effects, give them a list of causes and a list of effects to see if they can correctly match the items with each other. This is the essence of authentic assessment.

Testing techniques of this type can be misused when teachers exercise poor judgment in selecting either what is to be learned or the specific testing technique. Let us return to the spelling example in the preceding paragraph. If you *only* have students memorize the words in rote fashion and write them from memory when you dictate them and do not have students use the words in purposeful written communication, one could hardly defend such a procedure as an appropriate performance test. The performance test of any skill or the application of newly learned knowledge should always take place in a context as close to the "real thing" as classroom conditions will allow. This is what the term *authentic* means with reference to evaluating learning.

The following suggestions will help you construct classroom tests for determining students' learning achievement.

1. When constructing knowledge-based tests, emphasize ideas and concepts requiring reflective thinking rather than focusing solely on recall of information. Remember that students believe that the test defines what is important for them to learn.

2. Select and state items in ways that will encourage good study habits. For example, it is *not* considered good to create test items that require children to memorize lengthy text passages.

3. Cast test items in a practical, functional context, that is, close to the "real thing." This includes spelling words. Words on spelling tests should be from the context of the unit of study, not from isolated, disconnected word lists.

4. Be sure that the test relates to what you have taught; do not teach for one set of objectives and test for another.

5. Be aware of the readability factor in *any* performance test that requires students to read. (The test may simply be a reading test rather than a test of science, social studies, current events, or literature.)

6. Do not use textbook language or quote directly from the text in constructing, for example, true-false or completion items.

7. If you require a *factual* response, do not ask for students' opinions, such as by asking "What do you think. . . ?" "Why do you suppose. . . ?" "When do you believe. . . ?"

8. Be sure the test is at the appropriate level of difficulty for students.

9. Check to see that each test item clearly states what you are asking students to do; also make sure you clearly state the test directions.

10. Avoid providing clues to answers in the statement, stem, or format of the question (e.g., grammatical clues; length of blanks to fill in; mixing names, events, and places; providing the answer to one question in the stem of another).

11. Sample a large enough portion of students' behavior to accurately draw conclusions about the adequacy of their performance.

12. To make assessment consistent with the instruction on which it is based, teach from measurable instructional objectives whenever possible, that is, from an *aligned curriculum*.

STUDENT PARTICIPATION IN ASSESSMENT

You should plan students' continuous self-assessment as an important component of your assessment program. If students are to improve their *metacognition* (their understanding of their own thinking) and continue to develop intellectually, then they must receive instruction and guidance in how to become more responsible for their own learning. You must help teach them the processes of self-understanding and self-assessment. They must experience success to achieve this self-understanding; to do this they must know how to measure their own achievement. This empowerment raises students' self-esteem and teaches them to think better of their individual capabilities.

To meet these goals, provide opportunities for students to think about what they are learning, how they are learning it, and how far they have progressed. As stated previously, one good procedure is to have students maintain portfolios of their work, using rating scales or checklists periodically to self-assess their progress.

Using Student Portfolios

Teachers use portfolios as a means of instruction, and teachers and students both use them as one means of assessing student learning. Although there is little research evidence to support or to refute the claim, educators believe that the instructional value comes from the process of assembling and maintaining

Teachers meet periodically with individual students to discuss their self-assessments to reinforce and guide student learning and development. Such individual conferences provide children with understandable and achievable short-term goals and help them develop and maintain adequate self-esteem.

a personal portfolio. During this creative process you can expect students to self-reflect, to think critically about what they are learning, and to assume some responsibility for their own learning.

Educators have invented various categories or types of portfolios, each with a unique purpose, such as *growth portfolio* (to document improvement over a period of time), *proficiency portfolio* (to document mastery of content and skills), or *showcase portfolio* (to document a student's best work over time).[3] Elementary school teachers most commonly use combined growth and proficiency portfolios, but portfolios clearly should not be simply collections of *everything* students have done over time.

Although you and your students should make jointly the final decision as to content, you must ensure that students organize their portfolios well, exhibiting their efforts, progress, and achievements in a way that clearly tracks their learning successes. Generally, portfolios should contain such items as assignment sheets, class worksheets, the results of homework, project binders, and forms for student self-assessment and reflection. As a model of a *career portfolio*, you can show students your personal professional career portfolio (see Activity 2.4 in Chapter 2).

Before using portfolios as an alternative to traditional assessment and instruction, you must carefully consider and clearly understand your reasons for doing so, and determine whether they are practical for your situation. Then decide carefully portfolio content, establish rubrics or expectation standards, anticipate grading problems, and consider and prepare for parent/guardian reactions.

Although portfolio assessment as an alternative to traditional methods of evaluating student progress has gained momentum in recent years, establishing standards has been difficult. Research on the use of portfolios for assessment indicates that validity and reliability of *teacher* evaluation are often quite low. In addition, it is not always practical for every teacher to use portfolio assessment.

Using Checklists and Scoring Rubrics

Students periodically should assess themselves and reflect on their work to maintain a basis by which to measure their progress. You will need to help them learn how to analyze these comparisons. Although students can use almost any assessment instrument for self-assessment, in some cases you may wish to construct specific instruments designed to aid students' self-understanding. These instruments should provide students with new information about their progress and growth.

Elementary school teachers often employ a series of checklists to assess children's learning. Students can maintain these checklists in their portfolios, and may thus easily compare current with previous self-assessments. Items on the checklist will vary depending on your purpose, subject, and grade level (Figure 7.2). Students indicate for each skill whether they currently can

---

Checklist: Oral Report Assessment

Student _____   Date _____

Teacher _____   Time _____

Did the student	Yes	No	Comments
1. Speak so that everyone could hear?	____	____	_____
2. Finish sentences?	____	____	_____
3. Seem comfortable in front of the group?	____	____	_____
4. Give a good introduction?	____	____	_____
5. Seem well informed about the topic?	____	____	_____
6. Explain ideas clearly?	____	____	_____
7. Stay on the topic?	____	____	_____
8. Give a good conclusion?	____	____	_____
9. Use effective visuals to make the presentation interesting?	____	____	_____
10. Give good answers to questions from the audience?	____	____	_____

FIGURE 7.2
Sample checklist: Assessing a student's oral report

demonstrate it satisfactorily by filling in the appropriate blanks. Open-ended questions allow students to provide additional information as well as to do some expressive writing. After a student has demonstrated each skill satisfactorily, you would note this next to the student's name in your gradebook.

While emphasizing your assessment criteria, rating scales and checklists provide students with means of expressing their feelings and give you still another source of assessment data. In addition, you should meet periodically with individual students and discuss their self-assessments to reinforce and guide their learning and development. Such conferences provide students with understandable and achievable short-term goals and help them develop and maintain adequate self-esteem.[4]

As you can see from the scoring rubric and checklist shown in Figure 7.3, there is little difference between a rubric and a checklist; the difference is that rubrics show degrees of satisfactory completion for the desired characteristics, whereas checklists usually show only their completion. You easily may turn a checklist into a scoring rubric or vice versa.

FIGURE 7.3

Checklist and scoring rubric compared

Sample scoring rubric for assessing a student's skill in listening.

Score Point 3—Strong listener:
- Responds immediately to oral directions
- Focuses on speaker
- Maintains appropriate attention span
- Listens to what others are saying
- Is interactive

Score Point 2—Capable listener:
- Follows oral directions
- Usually attentive to speaker and to discussions
- Listens to others without interrupting

Score Point 1—Developing listener:
- Has difficulty following directions
- Relies on repetition
- Often inattentive
- Has short attention span
- Often interrupts the speaker

Sample checklist for assessing a student's skill in map work.

Check each item if the map comes up to standard in this particular category.
_____ 1. Accuracy
_____ 2. Neatness
_____ 3. Attention to details

Guidelines for Using Portfolios for Instruction and Assessment

Use the following general guidelines when employing student portfolios to assess student learning.

1. Children should understand that the dual purpose of the portfolio is to illustrate their growth in learning and to showcase their finest work.
2. Contents of the portfolio should reflect goals and objectives.
3. Students should have some say in what goes into their portfolios.
4. Students should date everything that goes into their portfolios.
5. After determining what materials students are to keep in their portfolios, announce clearly (post schedule in room) when, how, and by what criteria you will review portfolios. Stress the word *review*. The purpose of this review is to determine growth and areas for continued focus (see item 8).
6. Students are responsible for maintaining their own portfolios.
7. Portfolios should stay in the classroom.
8. Do *not* grade or compare in any way students' portfolios with each other. They exist for student self-assessment and for showing progress in learning. For this to happen, students should keep in their portfolio all papers, or major sample papers. For grading purposes, simply record whether students are maintaining their portfolios and by checking that all required materials are present.

DIAGNOSTIC ASSESSMENT AND CORRECTIVE INSTRUCTION

The challenge of teaching is to secure a best "fit" between individual learner interests, capabilities, and learning styles and the instructional mode—and to do this in the setting of a classroom group. But no matter how well you personalize instruction and how sensitive you are to individual students' needs, learners will respond differently to presentations, and some will need corrective instruction to enable them to progress. A relatively minor learning problem or a missed lesson because of inattentiveness or absence may, if left unattended, escalate into a serious learning handicap for a child. You must, therefore, be alert and able to spot difficulties and correct them before they take on serious proportions. As a teacher, you must see yourself as being in a continuous mode of diagnostic and formative assessment.

In this discussion of diagnostic assessment and corrective instruction, we are not referring to children with special needs. We are, rather, referring to ordinary boys and girls who, for one reason or another, are not progressing as well as you expect. Such children usually respond well to corrective instruction because their learning problem is not related to serious psychological or physical impairment.

The Teacher as Diagnostician

A competent elementary school teacher is constantly assessing children's learning in terms of both specific expected outcomes and the school's overall goals, basing most of these assessments on astute observations of children's behavior. The teacher notices that a child is not able to use recently taught word-attack skills; another is unable to compute simple problems in mathematics; a third is losing interest in school. It is from these observations that the teacher forms judgments about an appropriate program of corrective instruction.

Competent teachers do not assume that children learn new concepts and skills simply because they have been taught. They teach and reteach as needed. If one presentation is not clear, good teachers will try another approach. They present complex concepts in varied settings, and they provide adequate drill and practice when teaching skills. Teachers are as much diagnosticians as presenters in the day-to-day work of the classroom. Their assessment of children's behavior is critical to the many decisions they must make each day: how to group, what materials and media to use, which children need more practice, and which ones need special help. Much of what we call effective teaching consists of diagnosing learner needs and shaping the instructional program in accordance with them. Your insight and judgment are critical in doing this well. (See as an illustration the special feature, "What Went Wrong for Antoine?" in Chapter 8.)

Avoid Labeling

In taking a diagnostic approach to teaching, you must avoid labeling children. Labels are of dubious value and often detrimental to children's learning. Quite clearly, labels mark children with stereotypical characteristics that may or may not be appropriate to specific cases. Besides, attaching a label to a behavior does not in and of itself do anything to correct it. In fact, identifying a child as being "aphasic," "dyslexic," "autistic," "mentally retarded," or "a stutterer" may contribute to the complexity of the problem. What *is* important is to know enough about any child's learning problem to be able to develop a suitable program of instruction that will enable the child to progress.

Diagnostic and Corrective Procedures

Teachers oriented to diagnostic assessment and corrective instruction are constantly monitoring children's responses and adjusting their instruction in accordance with such observations. As you become involved in more formal diagnostic work, three questions will guide you: (1) What evidence is there that a learning problem exists? (2) What is the *specific* learning difficulty the child is encountering? (3) What level of corrective work is required? Let us examine each of these questions carefully in turn.

What Evidence Is There That a Learning Problem Exists?

Assume that while examining your students' test scores you discover that, with one exception, mathematics, their scores are consistently high. Assuming the problem is not with your tests, this is, then, a clear indicator that a learning problem exists in the mathematics area. If the test results are reported as mean scores, it may be that the scores of a few low-achieving children are depressing the average for the entire group. On the other hand, most children may in fact have scored relatively lower on math than they did on the other parts of the test battery. You will need to explore this situation in detail.

Assume further that your case is different from that of another class, in which the teacher finds children's achievement scores low in *all* subjects. This teacher will need to know if this happened because the group as a whole is less capable than an average class, whether the children received poor instruction in prior years, whether the test was given under adverse conditions or at the wrong time of the year, or for some other reason. In any case, the low test scores will alert the teacher to the possibility of learning problems that seem pervasive among those children.

Standardized achievement tests are only one method—and perhaps not even the most important one—that may alert you to the presence of learning prob-

Activity 7.2: Selecting the Right One

For each listed situation, suggest a specific appropriate assessment procedure. Use Table 7.1 to help you make your suggestions.

Grade: 1
Subject: Reading
Objective: Children will be able to use the word-attack skills appropriate for first graders as defined by the curriculum guide.

Assessment:

Grade: 2
Subject: Social Skills
Objective: Children will be able to work with other children in cooperative learning assignments.

Assessment:

Grade: 3
Subject: Science
Objective: Children will learn the similarities and differences among states of matter (i.e., solid, liquid, and gas).

Assessment:

Grade: 4
Subject: Social Studies
Objective: Children will learn to origin of selected place names in their home state.

Assessment:

Grade: 5
Subject: Physical Education
Objective: Children will be able to execute safely each of the following partner and group stunts: Eskimo roll, pyramids, angel balance, and lap-sit.

Assessment:

Grade: 6
Subject: Mathematics
Objective: Children will understand the meaning and function of place value.

Assessment:

lems. Your best and most reliable tool for this purpose is skillful observation of children's behavior. To aid your observation, make careful notes, record each child's progress, and systematically keep samples of children's work. A child's progress in learning subject matter and skills is likely to progress in spurts from one week to the next. But over a period of several weeks or months, each child should show signs of improvement. Failure to do so indicates a problem affecting a child's progress. Similarly, if a child is showing no interest in schoolwork, does not pay attention, or has behavioral difficulties, you must suspect and begin a search for a lurking problem.

You should be particularly observant of children's responses when introducing skills. Skills competence is built on practice, and if children are not initially performing the skill properly, they will be practicing it incorrectly. It is not uncommon to find children in the upper grades who are handicapped in their use of skills because they are performing them inefficiently or incorrectly: simple mechanical errors in handwriting, inability to write a single complete sentence, incorrect spelling of most commonly used words, inability to do simple mathematics problems, faulty methods of work (e.g., adding when they should subtract), and so on.

What *Specific* Learning Difficulty Is the Child Encountering?

After you have identified a child's general area of learning difficulty, you must locate as precisely as possible the limitations and deficiencies that child is experiencing. It is insufficient to know that a child is a "poor reader." Anyone off the street could quickly make that determination. What separates professional teachers from "anyone off the street" is their ability to go beyond mere description of behavior, to diagnose the nature of a difficulty and to prescribe corrective instruction.

So, to provide corrective instruction for a child with a reading difficulty, for example, you must diagnose the precise nature of the problem. For example, does the child have limited word-recognition techniques? Does the child not comprehend the reading? Is the child unable to use reading aids? Does the child have a limited sight vocabulary? If children do not progress rapidly when given corrective instruction, it may be because the instruction does not focus on the precise learning problem. No amount of drill and practice on sentence comprehension, for example, is going to help a child who does not have a repertoire of word-attack skills.

What Level of Corrective Work Is Required?

After identifying the learning problem, you should try to determine its probable cause. There are many; some reside within learners, some with the classroom and school, others are external to school. You need to recognize this, without at the same time using it as an excuse to justify continued poor achievement.

Generally speaking, we may sort children's learning problems into three levels of complexity. The simplest are those that you can handle within the classroom. For instance, a child is absent from school just as you are teaching the class how to multiply fractions. When the child returns, spend some individual time with him, and he will soon be multiplying fractions as well as his classmates. Most learning difficulties are of this level of complexity. All that is required is that you be alert and observant, and that you care enough about individual children to help them overcome minor hurdles in their learning.

A second level of complexity of learning problems requires more time or more specialized instruction than you are able to provide in the classroom. Children with such specific learning difficulties have, for one reason or another, not been able to respond satisfactorily to regular classroom group instruction. For example, a child may have a vision problem, partially corrected by special lenses. Because the child has experienced the problem all her life, however, she has accumulated learning deficits she now needs to overcome. You do not have time to provide such corrective instruction in class. Thus, the child is pulled out of the regular class for special instruction targeted on the needed work. When she is able to function on a par with her classmates, the corrective work is terminated.

Occasionally, you will encounter children with learning difficulties that far exceed the complexity of the previous two types. In these cases, the learning problem is often a symptom of some deeply rooted physical, neurological, or psychological disorder. Problems of this type may often exceed the professional competence of both you and your school's remedial teacher. Intensive one-to-one tutoring is not likely to be fruitful because such instruction targets the symptoms rather than the cause of the difficulty. That is, the learning problem is a manifestation of some other, less apparent problem. Children with learning difficulties of this magnitude require the highly specialized psychological, diagnostic, and corrective services of a psychoeducation clinic.

It is your responsibility, therefore, to diagnose learning difficulties in accordance with their complexity and to act appropriately in each case. You will attend to by far the greatest number of learning difficulties in class on an ongoing basis. A few children may need more intensive corrective work than you have time or skills to provide. You would refer these children to the school remedial teacher for special tutoring for a short time each day until they have overcome their problem. If such teachers are not available, you must make some other arrangement to provide these children with the needed individual help—perhaps by contacting parents or guardians, aides, or volunteers. Your responsibility to children with the most severe learning difficulties is to see that an appropriate referral is made. This involves consulting with the principal, parents or guardians, and the person in charge of your district's special services.

Your professional judgment and competence as a reflective decision maker are always tested in sorting out the severity of learning difficulties. You cannot assume that you can attend to all learning problems in the context of your busy classroom. On the other hand, you cannot refer all children with learning problems to someone else. You develop your skills of diagnostic assessment and corrective instruction through experience, technical preparation, and maturity as a professional.

GRADING AND MARKING

If conditions were ideal (which they are not), and if teachers did their job perfectly well (which many of us do not), then all students would receive top marks (the ultimate in mastery or quality learning). Were that the case, then there would be less need to talk here about grading and marking. (Believing that letter grades do not reflect the nature of young children's developmental progress, most school districts hold off using letter grades until children are in at least the third grade or even the sixth grade, and instead favor using developmental checklists and narratives.)[5] Mastery learning implies that some end point of learning is attainable, but there probably is no end point. In any case, because conditions for teaching are never ideal and we teachers are mere humans, let us discuss this topic of grading.

The term *achievement* appears frequently throughout this text. What exactly does this term mean? Achievement means *accomplishment*, but which—accomplishment of anticipated outcomes (that is, instructional objectives) against preset standards, or simply any accomplishment? Most teachers probably choose the former, where they subjectively establish a standard students must meet to receive a certain mark or grade for an assignment, project, test, quarter, semester, or course. Such teachers, then, measure achievement by degrees of accomplishment.

Preset standards are usually expressed in percentages (degrees of accomplishment) needed for marks or A-B-C grades. If no student achieves the standard required for the top mark, an A, for example, then no student receives an A. On the other hand, if all students meet the preset standard, then all receive As. Determining student marks and grades on the basis of preset standards is referred to as *criterion-referenced grading*, and for elementary school teaching it is the *only* sensible basis by which to arrive at student marks or grades.

While criterion-referenced (or competency-based) grading is based on preset standards, norm-referenced grading measures the relative accomplishment of individuals in the group (e.g., one classroom of fourth-graders) or in a larger group (e.g., all fourth-graders) by comparing and ranking students. This is commonly known as "grading on a curve." Because it encourages competition and discourages cooperative learning, *most educators now do not recommend using norm-referenced grading* to determine student grades. Norm-referenced grading is educationally dysfunctional. For your personal interest, after several years of teaching, you can produce frequency-distribution studies of grades you have given over a period of time, but *do not* base student grades on such a curve. That you should *always* grade and report in reference to learning criteria, and never "on a curve," is well supported by research studies and authorities on the matter.[6] Tie grades for student achievement to performance levels and determine them on the basis of each student's achievement toward preset standards, that is, on your anticipated outcomes or objectives (as discussed in Chapter 5). This approach implies that effective teaching and learning result in high grades ("A"s) or marks for most students. In fact, when using a mastery concept, students must accomplish the objectives before being allowed to proceed to the next learning task (or to the next grade level). *The philosophy of teachers who favor criterion-referenced procedures recognizes individual potential.* Such teachers accept the challenge of finding learning strategies to help children progress from where they are to the next designated level. Instead of wondering how Juan compares with Sean, you instead compare what Juan could do yesterday and what he can do today and how well these performances compare to your preset standard.

Most school systems use some sort of combination of norm-referenced and criterion-referenced data. Sometimes both kinds of information are useful. For example, students' sixth-grade report cards might indicate how they are meeting certain criteria, such as mastering addition of fractions. Another entry might show that this mastery is expected, however, in the fifth grade. Both criterion- and norm-referenced data may be communicated to parents or guardians as well as to students. Use appropriate procedures: a criterion-referenced approach to show whether students can accomplish a task, and if so, to what degree, and a norm-referenced approach to show how well they perform compared to the larger group to which they belong.

Determining Grades

When determining achievement grades for student performance, you must make several important and professional decisions. Although in a few schools, and for certain classes or assignments, only marks such as E, S, and I or "pass/no pass" are used, percentages of accomplishment and letter grades are used for most intermediate grades and higher.[7] To reflect each students' progress toward meeting state curriculum standards, many elementary schools now use numeral marks (see Figure 7.4).

FIGURE 7.4
Sample rubric for numerical
reporting of grade-level standards

5 = exceeds grade-level standards proficiency expectation

4 = proficiency level expectation

3 = basic proficiency expectation

2 = below basic performance expectation

1 = far below basic performance expectation

At the start of the school term, explain your marking and grading policies *first to yourself*, then to your students, and to their parents or guardians either at "back-to-school night" or by a written explanation students take home, or both. Share sample scoring and grading rubrics with both students and parents/guardians.

Be as objective as possible when converting your interpretation of a student's accomplishments to a letter grade. For criteria for A-B-C grades (or for 1-2-3 numerical marks), select a percentage standard, such as 90 percent for an A, 80 percent for a B, 70 percent for a C, and 60 percent for a D. Cutoff percentages used are your decision, although the school may have established guidelines you are expected to follow.

Build your grading policy around degrees of accomplishment rather than failure, where students proceed from one accomplishment to the next. This is continuous promotion, not necessarily the promotion of students from one grade level to the next, but within the classroom. (However, some schools have eliminated grade-level designation and, in its place, use the concept of continuous promotion from the time students enter the school through their graduation or exit from it.)

Assessment and Grading: *Not* Synonymous Terms

Remember that "assessment" and "grading" are *not* synonymous. Assessment implies collecting information from a variety of sources, including measurement techniques and subjective observations. These data, then, become your basis for arriving at a final grade, which in effect is a final value judgment. Grades are one aspect of evaluation only and are intended to communicate educational progress to students and to their parents or guardians. To validly indicate that progress, you *must* use a variety of sources of data to determine a student's final mark or grade.

Decide beforehand your policy about makeup work. Students will be absent and will miss assignments and tests, so it is best to clearly communicate to students and to their parents or guardians your policies about late assignments and missed tests.

REPORTING STUDENT PROGRESS IN ACHIEVEMENT

One of your responsibilities as a classroom teacher is to report student progress in achievement to parents or guardians as well as to the school administration for record keeping. As stated earlier, some schools report student progress and effort as well as achievement. As described in the discussions that follow, reporting is done in at least two, and sometimes more than two, ways.

Schools periodically issue progress reports generally from four to six times a year, depending on the school, its purpose, and its type of scheduling.

Progress and grade reports may be distributed during an advisory period or may be mailed to students' homes, or parents and guardians may pick them up from the school or online. This report represents an achievement report and grade (formative assessment). The final report of the semester is also the semester grade, and for courses only one semester long it also is the final grade (summative assessment). In essence, the first and sometimes second reports are progress notices, with the semester grade being transferred to students' permanent records.

In addition to academic achievement in the various subject areas, you must report students' social behaviors (classroom conduct) while in your classroom. Whichever reporting form you use, you must separate your assessment of students' social behaviors from their academic achievement. In most instances, there may be a location on the reporting form for you to check whether students have met basic grade-level standards.

Planning for the First Student-Progress Report

We return to the professional lives of Ms. Baxter and Mr. Bond, this time to understand how they prepared for their first real-life student-progress reporting.

With the school year barely under way, Ms. Baxter and Mr. Bond were confronted with the task of preparing student-progress reports, popularly known as *report cards*. They were aware that elementary school teachers across the nation were also involved in this process, which has become almost a ritual during early November. Because a considerable amount of emphasis had been placed on the importance of reporting student progress, they were fully aware of its major purposes:

1. To inform children of their progress.
2. To provide parents and guardians with an assessment of children's learning strengths and weaknesses.
3. To serve as a two-way mode of communication between home and school.

They were also aware of the several basic types of student-progress reports used in elementary schools. The most common are numerical or alphabetical ratings, written narratives, checklists, portfolios, and parent/guardian-teacher conferences. In actual practice, most schools use a combination of all of these.

Establishing Parent and Guardian Contacts

Both Ms. Baxter and Mr. Bond were glad to have had the opportunity to meet most of their students' parents and guardians at the "Back to School" night held a month ago in their respective schools. Having had that experience makes them now feel a little less trepidation about communicating with parents and guardians about their children's progress.

Ms. Baxter Prepares for Her First Parent/Guardian Conference

The parent/guardian conference is more prevalent as a way of reporting to parents and guardians of children of grades K–3 than it is for children of grade 4 and beyond. This is partly because it is easier to explain progress in beginning reading in a conference setting than on a report card. You can do a better job of conveying to parents and guardians what their children are actually doing, what their needs are, and what the adults can do at home to assist. The conference also enables you to become aware of parents' and guardians' attitudes toward their children, the home, and the school. This information helps you establish the best possible learning program for children, and select appropriate materials for individuals.

Many primary-grade teachers conduct parent/guardian conferences during the first student-progress reporting period and write narrative reports during the remainder of the school year. Some teachers alternate parent/guardian conferences and written reports. Frequently, the first parent/guardian conference follows an "open house," when parents and guardians are invited to attend school, meet the teachers, and listen to an explanation of the school program. This was the procedure at Westhill Elementary School, where Ms. Baxter taught. The school principal began planning with the teachers early in September for the November open house and parent/guardian conferences. She stressed the importance of involving parents and guardians in their children's education. She made the following points:

1. Have children prepare and maintain a portfolio with samples of their schoolwork. Include for each subject representative products that show children's progress over time.
2. Write anecdotes that objectively describe children's behavior.
3. Interpret children's performance on readiness and achievement tests. Be sure to specify children's performance level in terms of their potential.

The principal also provided helpful hints on conducting a parent/guardian conference:

1. Begin on a positive note.
2. Try to make parents and guardians feel comfortable.
3. Emphasize children's strengths.
4. Be specific about any learning difficulties children may be experiencing.
5. Provide constructive suggestions about ways parents and guardians can assist in helping their children learn. To this end the principal ensured that relevant materials and resources for materials were available and posted in the teacher's lounge.
6. Listen to what parents and guardians have to say; be receptive to their suggestions.
7. *Never* compare one child with another.
8. Close on a positive note and with a plan of action.

Ms. Baxter discovered that her parent/guardian conferences were very rewarding. The conferences were scheduled over a period of 2 weeks, during which the children were dismissed an hour early. The open house had tested her ability to describe for parents and guardians the type of work the children would be doing that year. She began to appreciate the time she had spent in determining goals for the school year and in getting acquainted with the textbooks and other instructional resources. These early planning activities had provided her with a frame of reference that made her reporting task much easier than it otherwise would have been. As a result, she felt more secure in arranging for parents' and guardians' constructive involvement in their children's learning program.

Mr. Bond Prepares for His First Student-Progress Report

Mr. Bond received student-progress report forms early in September. The school principal emphasized that teachers should keep a work folder for every child. He also suggested that in certain instances, teachers might find it useful to schedule a parent/guardian conference to inform the parents/guardians of children's progress. The work samples would prove worthwhile in such instances.

Mr. Bond was disappointed that the form did not provide for student self-assessment. He made the decision to improvise his own system for this purpose. He developed a simple report form that would allow children to self-assess their "school habits" (Figure 7.5). He began discussing self-assessment with children as soon as they had demonstrated that they could work together as a group. He told them that he would discuss the form with each of them personally, at which time he would ask them to complete it. He prepared an enlargement of the form for a wall chart, and gave all students a copy for their notebooks.

My School Habits				
	Always	Usually	Seldom	Never
I assume responsibility.				
I contribute to the group.				
I work well with others.				
I play well with others.				
I do my best in my studies.				
I take care of materials.				
I follow school rules.				

FIGURE 7.5
Mr. Bond's form for student self-assessment

When he began to confer with the children about their self-assessments, he learned that some of them were realistic in their ratings and others were not. In each instance, Mr. Bond was able to have a candid discussion with the child about behavior that is important to personal, social, and academic development. He felt much closer to each child following the discussion. He also spent a few minutes each week discussing the student-progress report form with them. He wanted them to know ahead of time the standards on which he was evaluating them.

Mr. Bond found that the planning he had done at the beginning of the year had been of great value to him in completing the student-progress reports. He followed the advice of a colleague and began writing the reports a couple of weeks before they were due. He was very glad he had followed this advice instead of waiting until the last minute.

Mr. Bond sent the student-progress reports home on schedule and was pleasantly surprised to learn that many parents and guardians were pleased with their children's performance. He formed this conclusion on the basis of

The parent/guardian and teacher conference allows parents to ask questions of the teacher and for the teacher to convey what their children are actually doing, what their needs seem to be, and what the adults might do at home to assist. The conference also enables the teacher to become aware of the adult's attitudes toward their children, the home, and the school. Some teachers, usually later in the school year, incorporate the use of student-planned and -led three-way conferences that, as shown in the photograph, involve the student, the child's parents or guardians, and the teacher.

adults' written remarks on the returned forms. Two parents requested followup conferences; Mr. Bond scheduled them during after-school hours. He
found that these personal contacts helped him establish a closer rapport with
the parents. By the end of the year, he knew all of his students' parents or
guardians, many of them on a first-name basis. Mr. Bond made a mental note
to himself to look into the prospect for next year of having student-led three-
way (that is, student–parent/guardian–teacher) conferences.[8]

SUMMARY

Assessment of student learning is an integral and ongoing factor in teaching
and learning; consequently, in this chapter we have emphasized the importance of your including the following in your teaching:

- Use a variety of instruments to collect a body of evidence to most reliably as-
sess children's learning, focusing on their individual development.
- Involve students in assessment; keep children informed of their progress.
- Be sure to base your assessments only on material you have actually taught.
- Strive to assess all students objectively and impartially.

The exponential rate of advances taking place in technology is creating
rapid changes in assessment practices. As classroom teacher, to keep your
own program of assessment of student learning most effective and efficient
you will need to actively plan to stay abreast of the developments.

STUDY QUESTIONS AND ADDITIONAL ACTIVITIES

1. The practice of kindergarten retention seems to be increasing. Find research evidence that indicates that the retention of a child in kindergarten has any positive value. Are there options to retention? Share your
findings with others in your class. Do you believe there is value in retention of any child in any grade? Share your opinion with others.
2. During a parent/guardian conference, how would you respond to a parent
or guardian who is critical of a teacher colleague, critical of the school, or
critical of other children in your class? Or, one who is critical of you? Invite two or three experienced elementary school teachers to your class
and have them share difficult questions they have received from parents
and guardians and how they responded. Role play a parent/guardian conference with one of your classmates. Include parent/guardian questions
that challenge the teacher to provide a thoughtful, discreet response.
3. For a specific unit of study, develop the tools for the diagnostic, formative,
and summative assessment of student learning of that unit, using some of
the assessment techniques and procedures found in Table 7.1. Include at

least one tool that assesses each of the following three categories of outcomes: cognitive gain, affective change, and psychomotor development.

4. If you are now student teaching, or if you have contact with a classroom teacher, ask that teacher to explain to you the local policies regarding the use of standardized tests. Find out when they are given, which tests are used, what procedures the teacher uses in administering the tests, how they are scored, and what use is made of the results. Share your findings in your methods class.

5. You are the teacher of a child who has been achieving satisfactorily in mathematics. In correcting the child's written work, you notice that the child answered incorrectly every problem involving dividing fractions. How would you go about finding out what the difficulty is? How would your approach differ if you discovered that *all* your students answered such problems incorrectly?

6. Visit a school in your area to become familiar with the kinds of educational and psychological referral services available for children with learning problems that the classroom teachers cannot handle.

7. Should teachers' effectiveness be judged by the scores that their students obtain on standardized tests near the end of the school year? Explain why or why not.

8. Describe any student learning activities or situations that you believe should *not* be graded but should or could be used for assessment of student learning.

9. One recent study reports that 29 percent of teachers surveyed included "effort" when assigning grades, 8 percent included "behavior," 4 percent included "cooperation," and 8 percent included "attendance."[9] Explain why you believe that a teacher should or should not include these factors when determining and reporting a student's academic grades or marks.

10. Investigate various ways that schools housing some combination of grades K–6 are experimenting with assessing and reporting student achievement. Share and critique your findings with your classmates.

NOTES

1. S. J. Rakow, "Assessment: A Driving Force," *Science Scope* 15(6): 3 (1992).

2. For a discussion of the virtues of the various assessment types and the mechanics of using response item alternatives, see especially R. J. Stiggins, *Student-Involved Classroom Assessment*, 3d ed. (Upper Saddle River, NJ: Merrill/Prentice Hall, 2001).

3. See, for example, M. F. Roe and C. Vukelich, "Literacy Portfolios: Challenges That Affect Change," *Childhood Education* 74(3): 148–153 (1998).

4. For a discussion of the biological importance and educational benefits of positive feedback, student portfolios, and group learning, see R. Sylwester, "The Neurobiology of Self-Esteem and Aggression," *Educational Leadership* 54(5): 75–79 (1997).

5. K. Lake and K. Kafka, "Reporting Methods in Grades K–8," Chapter 9 in T. R. Guskey (Ed.),

Communicating Student Learning: 1996 Year-book (Alexandria, VA: Association for Supervision and Curriculum Development, 1996), 91.

6. See, for example, Guskey, *Communicating Student Learning*, 18–19; and R. J. Stiggins, *Student-Involved Classroom Assessment*, 3rd ed. (Upper Saddle River, NJ: Merrill/Prentice Hall, 2001), especially Part 4.

7. For other methods being used to report student achievement see Lake and Kafka, "Reporting Methods in Grades K–8."

8. Preferring a student-led conference, some educators argue that "placing students in charge of the conference makes them individually accountable, encourages them to take pride in their work, and encourages student–parent communication about school performance" (D. W. Johnson and R. T. Johnson, "The Role of Cooperative Learning in Assessing and Communicating Student Learning," p. 43 in Guskey, *Communicating Student Learning*). For more about student-led conferences, see the several references in the following section.

9. R. J. Marzano, "In Search of the Standardized Curriculum," *Principal* 81(3): 6–9 (2002).

FOR FURTHER PROFESSIONAL STUDY

Airasian, P. W. *Classroom Assessment: Concepts and Applications*. 4th ed. Boston: McGraw-Hill, 2001.

Allen, R. "Learning Disabilities At the Assessment Crossroads." *Curriculum Update* 1–3, 6–8 (Fall 2000).

Andrade, H. G. "Using Rubrics to Promote Thinking and Learning." *Educational Leadership* 57(5): 13–18 (2000).

Arter, J., and McTighe, J. *Scoring Rubrics in the Classroom: Using Performance Criteria for Assessing and Improving Student Performances*. Thousand Oaks, CA: Corwin Press, 2001.

Asp, E. "Assessment in Education: Where Have We Been? Where Are We Headed?" In R. S. Brandt (Ed.), *Education in a New Era* (pp. 123–157). Alexandria, VA: ASCD Yearbook, Association for Supervision and Curriculum Development, 2000.

Bailey, J. M., and Guskey, T. R. *Implementing Student-Led Conferences*. Thousand Oaks, CA: Corwin Press, 2001.

Boers, D. "Helping Parents Help Their Children Succeed in School." *Principal* 81(3): 52–53 (2002).

Bond, B. "Using Standards-Based Performance Assessment with At-Risk Students." *Middle Ground* 4(3): 36–39 (2001).

Bracey, G. W. *A Short Guide to Standardized Testing*. Fastback 459. Bloomington, IN: Phi Delta Kappa Educational Foundation, 2000.

Brookhart, S. M. *Grading*. Upper Saddle River, NJ: Merrill/Prentice Hall, 2004.

Carr, J. F., and Harris, D. E. *Succeeding with Standards: Linking Curriculum, Assessment, and Action Planning*. Alexandria, VA: Association of Supervision and Curriculum Development, 2001.

Carr, S. C. "Self-Evaluation: Involving Students in Their Own Learning." *Reading and Writing Quarterly: Overcoming Learning Difficulties* 18(2): 195–199 (2002).

Chappuis, S., and Stiggins, R. J. "Classroom Assessment for Learning." *Educational Leadership* 60(1): 40–43 (2002).

Chen, Y., and Martin, M. A. "Using Performance Assessment and Portfolio Assessment Together in the Elementary Classroom." *Reading Improvement* 37(1): 32–38 (2000).

Cleland, J. V. "We Can Charts: Building Blocks for Student-Led Conferences." *Reading Teacher* 52(6): 588–595 (1999).

Coray, G. "Rubrics Made Simple." *Science Scope* 23(6): 38–40 (2000).

Demers, C. "Beyond Paper-and-Pencil Assessment." *Science and Children* 38(2): 24–29, 60 (2000).

Farenga, S., and Joyce, B. "Preparing for Parents' Questions." *Science Scope* 23(6): 12–14 (2000).

Franklin, J. "Assessing Assessment: Are Alternative Methods Making the Grade." *Curriculum Update*, 1–3, 6, 8 (Spring 2002).

Garthwait, A. and Verrill, J. "E-Portfolios: Documenting Student Progress." *Science and Children* 40(8): 22–27 (2003).

Georgiady, N. P., and Romano, L. G. *Positive Parent-Teacher Conferences*. Fastback 491. Bloomington, IN: Phi Delta Kappa Educational Foundation, 2002.

Guskey, T. R. "How Classroom Assessments Improve Learning." *Educational Leadership* 60(5): 6–11 (2003).

Henk, W. A., Moore, J. C., Marinak, B. A., and Tomasetti, B. W. "A Reading Lesson Observation Framework for Elementary Teachers, Principals, and Literacy Supervisors." *The Reading Teacher* 53(5): 358–369 (2000).

Herschell, A. D., Greco, L. A., Filcheck, H. A., and McNeil, C. B. "Who Is Testing Whom? Ten Suggestions for Managing the Disruptive Behavior of Young Children During Testing." *Intervention in School and Clinic* 37(3): 140–148 (2002).

Jimerson, S. R., and Kaufman, A. M. "Reading, Writing, and Retention: A Primer on Grade Retention Research." *The Reading Teacher* 56(7): 622–635 (2003).

Jimerson, S. R., Anderson, G. E., and Whipple, A. D. "Winning the Battle and Losing the War: Examining the Relation Between Grade Retention and Dropping Out of High School." *Psychology in the Schools* 39(4): 441–457 (2002).

Kosmoski, G. J., and Pollack, D. R. *Managing Conversations with Hostile Adults: Strategies for Teachers*. Thousand Oaks, CA: Corwin Press, 2001.

Lawrence, K. M. "Red Light, Green Light, 1-2-3: Tasks to Prepare for Standardized Tests." *Reading Teacher* 55(6): 525–528 (2002).

Lederhouse, J. N. "The Power of One-on-One." *Educational Leadership* 60(7): 69–71 (2003).

Lipnickey, S. C. "Between Two Homes: How Schools Can Help Children of Divorce." *American School Board Journal* 18(1): 46–47, 55 (2001).

Marzano, R. J. "Challenging Goals and Effective Feedback." Chapter 4 of *What Works in Schools: Translating Research into Action*. Alexandria, VA: Association for Supervision and Curriculum Development, 2003.

Marzano, R. J. *Transforming Classroom Grading*. Alexandria, VA: Association for Supervision and Curriculum Development, 2000.

Matkins, J. J., and Sterling, D. R. "Designing Assessments." *Science and Children* 40(8): 34–37 (2003).

Montgomery, K. "Classroom Rubrics: Systematizing What Teachers Do Naturally." *Clearing House* 73(6): 324–328 (2000).

Moon, T. R. "Using Performance Assessment in the Social Studies Classroom." *Gifted Child Today Magazine* 25(3): 53–59 (2002).

Moskal, B. M. *Scoring Rubrics Part I: What and When*. ED446110. Washington, DC: Assessment and Evaluation, 2000.

Moskal, B. M. *Scoring Rubrics Part II: How?* ED446110. Washington, DC: Assessment and Evaluation, 2000.

Munk, D. D., and Bursuck, W. D. "Preliminary Findings on Personalized Grading Plans for Middle School Students with Learning Disabilities." *Exceptional Children* 67(2): 211–234 (2001).

Nitko, A. J. *Educational Assessment of Students*. 3rd ed. Upper Saddle River, NJ: Prentice Hall, 2001.

Oosterhof, A. *Classroom Applications of Educational Measurement*. 3rd. ed. Upper Saddle River, NJ: Merrill/Prentice Hall, 2001.

Owings, W. A., and Kaplan, L. S. *Alternatives to Retention and Social Promotion*. Fastback 481. Bloomington, IN: Phi Delta Kappa Educational Foundation, 2001.

Ratcliff, N. J. "Using Authentic Assessment to Document the Emerging Literacy Skills of Young Children." *Childhood Education* 78(2): 66–69 (Winter 2001–2002).

Ravitch, D. "The Language Police." *The Atlantic Monthly* 291(2): 82–83 (2003).

Reinemann, D., and Thomas, J. "New Species Found!" *Science and Children* 40(8): 28–33 (2003).

Rolheiser, C., Bower, B., and Stevahn, L. *The Portfolio Organizer: Succeeding with Portfolios in Your Classroom*. Alexandria, VA: Association for Supervision and Curriculum Development, 2000.

Ronis, D. *Brain Compatible Assessments*. Arlington Heights, IL: Skyline, 2000.

Salend, S. J., and Duhaney, L. M. G. "Grading Students in Inclusive Settings." *Teaching Exceptional Children* 34(3): 8–15 (2002).

Serafini, F. "Three Paradigms of Assessment: Measurement, Procedure, and Inquiry." *The Reading Teacher* 54(4): 384–393 (December 2000/January 2001).

Skillings, M. J., and Ferrell, R. "Student-Generated Rubrics: Bring Students into the Assessment Process." *Reading Teacher* 53(6): 452–455 (2000).

Smith, J. K., Smith, L. F., and De Lisi, R. *Natural Classroom Assessment: Designing Seamless Instruction & Assessment*. Thousand Oaks, CA: Corwin Press, 2001.

Stiggins, R. J. *Student-Involved Classroom Assessment*. 3rd ed. Upper Saddle River, NJ: Merrill/Prentice Hall, 2001.

Stodolsky, S. S., and Grossman, P. L. "Changing Student, Changing Teaching." *Teachers College Record* 102(1): 125–172 (2000).

Trumbull, E., and Farr, B. (Eds.). *Grading and Reporting Student Progress in an Age of Standards*. Norwood, MA: Christopher-Gordon, 2000.

Wang, C. "How to Grade Essay Examinations." *Performance Improvement* 39(1): 12–15 (2000).

Warger, C. *Helping Students with Disabilities Succeed in State and District Writing Assessments*. ED463622. Arlington, VA: ERIC Clearinghouse on Disabilities and Gifted Education, 2002.

INTASC Principles	PRAXIS III Domains	NBPTS Standards
• The teacher understands and uses a variety of instructional strategies to encourage students' development of critical thinking, problem solving, and performance skills. (Principle 4)	• Organizing Content Knowledge for Student Learning (Domain A)	• Multiple Paths to Knowledge

The act of teaching is so complex that no specific way of teaching is superior to other ways for all purposes, for all teachers, with all children, for all times, and in all circumstances. Although sound guidelines are available from research, individual teachers must adapt what they do to their own personality styles and to the idiosyncrasies of the situations in which they find themselves. The dynamics and flow of day-to-day work with children call for flexible and fluid teacher behavior, accommodating and adjusting to the constant unfolding of classroom circumstances. Truly good teaching is as much an art as it is a science. It is indeed a profession. This means that teachers are continually *making decisions* about when to negotiate, when to hold firm, when to intervene, and when to let events play themselves out. As previously noted, a refined decision-making ability and the judgment that goes with it undoubtedly have much to do with exemplary teaching.

Much of good teaching simply is the application of commonsense principles. For example, someone interested in a topic is more likely to want to learn than someone not interested in it. Consequently, anything you as a teacher can do to create interest will be beneficial to learning. Young children have difficulty sitting quietly for long periods of time; therefore, on a commonsense basis, you would provide a balance among activities calling for quiet time and those requiring movement. Children learn at differing rates; it therefore follows that some learners need more time and teacher assistance than do others.

More than any other creatures, to become who and what they are human beings depend *less* on instinct and *more* on learning. Most of that learning comes from other human beings who have already learned the requirements of the culture in which they live. Children reared in isolation or without intimate contact with older human beings are rarely able to function well as adults. The teaching and learning that take place during the earliest months and years are so subtle that we are hardly aware of them. Much early learning is done by observing, mimicking, trial and error, responding to signals of approval or disapproval, and so on. It is for the most part informal, spontaneous, "on-the-job" teaching and learning. This kind of subtle interaction between children and adults continues into the school years through the covert curriculum (see Chapter 5). Additionally, schools have designed a continually emerging overt curriculum that is meant to be presented and learned through some type of planned program of instruction, usually organized around instructional units. In this chapter you will learn more about selecting and implementing various modes of instruction.

ANTICIPATED OUTCOMES

After completing this chapter, you should be able to do the following:

1. Describe the specific considerations you must make when selecting an instructional strategy.
2. Distinguish between *access* and *delivery* modes of instruction.

3. Distinguish between *direct experience* and *direct instruction*.
4. Differentiate between *direct* and *indirect* instruction.
5. Describe, behaviorally, both the teacher's and learner's roles in the expository, inquiry, and demonstration modes of instruction.
6. Compare and contrast inquiry and discovery learning.
7. Describe the extent to which the elementary school curriculum consists of learning the basic skills.
8. Describe the essential factors necessary for the most effective learning of skills and how the classroom teacher can apply these factors.
9. Outline specific things the elementary school classroom teacher can plan that will make the program of instruction interesting and stimulating for children.
10. Describe the meaning and the relevance of the term *frequent assessment*.
11. Describe means by which a classroom teacher can effectively personalize instruction for each child.
12. Describe the role of feedback in meaningful learning.
13. Continue development of the daily lessons for the unit plan that you began in Chapter 6.

THEORETICAL CONSIDERATIONS WHEN SELECTING INSTRUCTIONAL STRATEGIES

As you detail your instructional plan, which you began in Chapter 6, you will be narrowing in on selecting and planning your instructional activities. In Chapter 2, you learned about specific teacher behaviors that must be in place for students to learn—structuring the learning environment; accepting and sharing instructional accountability; demonstrating withitness and overlapping; providing a variety of motivating and challenging activities; modeling appropriate behaviors; facilitating students' acquisition of data; creating a psychologically safe environment; clarifying whenever necessary; using periods of silence; and questioning thoughtfully. In the discussions that follow, you will learn more not only about how to implement some of these fundamental behaviors, but also about the large repertoire of other strategies, aids, media, and resources available to you (Figure 8.1). You will learn more about how to select and implement from this repertoire.

You must make myriad decisions to select and implement a particular teaching strategy effectively. Your selection depends in part on your decision whether to deliver information directly (direct, expository, or didactic teaching) or to provide students with access to information (indirect or facilitative teaching).

Direct and Indirect Instruction: A Clarification of Terms

You are probably well aware that professional education is replete with its own special jargon, which can confuse the neophyte. The use of the term

Assignment	Game	Problem solving
Autotutorial	Group work	Project
Brainstorming	Guest speaker	Questioning
Coaching	Homework	Reading partners
Collaborative learning	Individualized instruction	Review and practice
Cooperative learning	Inquiry	Role play
Debate	Interactive media	Self-instructional module
Demonstration	Investigation	Script writing
Diorama	Journal writing	Silent reading
Discovery	Lecture	Simulation
Drama	Library/resource center	Study guide
Drill	Metacognition	Symposium
DVD or compact disc	Mock up	Telecommunication
Dyad learning	Multimedia	Term paper
Expository	Panel discussion	Textbook
Field trip	Portfolio assessment	Think-pair-share

FIGURE 8.1
Instructional strategies

direct teaching (or its synonyms *direct instruction, expository teaching,* or *teacher-centered instruction*) and its antonym, *direct experiences,* is an example of how confusing the jargon can be. Additionally, *direct teaching* (or any of its synonyms) can have a variety of definitions, depending on who is doing the defining. For now, you should keep this distinction in mind so as not to confuse *direct instruction* with *direct experience:* the terms indicate two separate (though not incompatible) instructional modes. The dichotomy of pedagogical opposites shown in Figure 8.2 provides a useful visual distinction. While terms in one column are similar if not synonymous, they are near or exact opposites of those in the other column.

Delivery mode of instruction		Access mode of instruction
Didactic instruction		Facilitative teaching
Direct instruction		Indirect instruction
Direct teaching	versus	Direct experiencing
Expository teaching		Discovery learning
Teacher-centered instruction		Student-centered instruction

FIGURE 8.2
Pedagogical opposites

Degrees of Directness

Rather than thinking and behaving in terms of opposites, as Figure 8.2 may suggest, it is more likely that your instruction will be distinguished by "degrees of directness" or "degrees of indirectness." For example, for a unit of instruction, you may give directions for a culminating project in a direct or expository minilesson, followed by a student-designed inquiry that leads to the project itself.

Rather than focus your attention on selecting a particular model of or approach to teaching, we emphasize the importance of an eclectic approach—selecting the best from various models or approaches. As indicated by the example in the preceding paragraph, there will be times when you want to use a direct, teacher-centered (expository) approach, perhaps a minilecture and a demonstration. There will be many more times when you will want to use an indirect, student-centered, or social-interactive approach, such as the use of cooperative learning and projects. And perhaps even more often you will be doing both at the same time, such as using a teacher-centered approach with one small group of children, perhaps giving them direct instruction, while another group or several groups are working at learning stations or on their project studies (student-centered approaches). The information that follows will help you make decisions about when each approach is most appropriate and provides guidelines for their use.

Direct Versus Indirect Instructional Modes: Strengths and Weaknesses of Each

When selecting an instructional strategy, you must make a distinct choice of one of two modes: should you deliver information to students directly or should you provide students with access to information? (Refer to Figure 8.2.)

The *delivery* mode (known also as the *didactic, expository,* or *traditional* style) is used to deliver information. Knowledge is passed on from those who know (usually the teacher, with the aid of textbooks) to those who do not (the students). Within the delivery mode, traditional and time-honored strategies are textbook reading, teacher talk or lecture, questioning, and teacher-centered or teacher-planned discussions.

With the *access mode*, instead of direct delivery of information and direct control over what is learned, you provide students with access to information by working *with* them. Students collaborate on designing experiences that facilitate their building existing schemata and obtaining new knowledge and skills. Within the access mode, important instructional strategies include cooperative learning, inquiry, and investigative student-centered project learning, each of which most certainly will use questioning, although the questions more frequently will come from the students than from you or the textbook or some other source extrinsic to students. Discussions and lectures on particular topics also may be involved. But when used in the access mode, discussions and lectures occur during or after (rather than precede) students' direct, hands-on learning. In other words, rather than preceding student inquiry, discussions and teacher lectures *result* from it, and then may themselves result in further student investigation.

You are probably more experienced with the delivery mode. To be most effective as an elementary school teacher, however, you must become knowledgeable and skillful in using access strategies. Access mode strategies clearly facilitate students' positive learning and acquisition of conceptual knowledge and help build their self-confidence and self-esteem.

Figures 8.3 and 8.4 present overviews of the specific strengths and weaknesses of each mode, making it clear that the strengths and weaknesses of one mode are nearly mirror opposites of the other. As noted earlier, although as a teacher you should be skillful in using strategies from both modes, for the most developmentally appropriate teaching for most groups of K–6 learners, you should concentrate more on using access mode strategies. Strategies within that mode are more student centered, hands-on, and concrete; students interact with one another and are actually closer to doing what they are learning to do—that is, the learning is likely more *authentic*. Learning that occurs from access mode instruction is longer lasting (fixes into long-term memory). Additionally, as students interact with one another and with their learning, they develop a sense of "can do," which enhances their self-confidence and self-esteem.

FIGURE 8.3
Delivery mode: Its strengths and weaknesses

Delivery Mode

Strengths

- Much content can be covered within a short span of time, usually by formal teacher talk, which then may be followed by an experimental activity.
- The teacher is in control of what content is covered.
- The teacher is in control of time allotted to specific content coverage.
- Strategies within the delivery mode are consistent with competency-based instruction.
- Student achievement of specific content is predictable and manageable.

Potential Weaknesses

- The sources of student motivation are mostly extrinsic.
- Students have little control over the pacing of their learning.
- There may be little opportunity for divergent or creative thinking.
- Students make few important decisions about their learning.
- Student self-esteem may be inadequately served.

FIGURE 8.4
Access mode: Its strengths and weaknesses

> **Access Mode**
>
> *Strengths*
> - Students learn content, and in more depth.
> - The sources of student motivation are more likely intrinsic.
> - Students make important decisions about their own learning.
> - Students have more control over the pacing of their learning.
> - Students develop a sense of personal self-worth.
>
> *Potential Weaknesses*
> - Content coverage may be more limited.
> - Strategies are time consuming.
> - The teacher has less control over content and time.
> - The specific results of student learning are less predictable.
> - The teacher may have less control over class procedures.

Selecting Developmentally Appropriate Learning Activities

Can you imagine teaching children keyboarding skills without ever allowing them to operate a computer? Can you imagine teaching children the letters of the alphabet without ever letting them put the letters together to form words? Can you imagine teaching a child to ride a bicycle without ever allowing her to climb onto a real bike? Can you imagine teaching a child to read without ever allowing him to touch a book? Unfortunately, too many teachers do almost those exact things—they try to teach students to do something without letting the students practice doing it.

In planning and selecting developmentally appropriate learning activities, an important rule to remember is to select activities that are as close to the real thing as possible. That is learning through direct experiencing. When students are involved in direct experiences, they are using more of their sensory input channels, their learning modalities (i.e., auditory, visual, tactile, kinesthetic). And when all the senses are engaged, learning is more integrated and is most effective, meaningful, and longest lasting. This "learning by doing" is *authentic learning*—or, as referred to in Chapter 2, *hands-on/minds-on learning*.

The Learning Experiences Ladder

Figure 8.5 presents the Learning Experiences Ladder, a visual depiction of a range of kinds of learning experiences from which you may select. Hands-on/minds-on learning, the most concrete learning, is at the bottom of the ladder. At the top are abstract experiences, where learners are exposed only to symbolization (i.e., letters and numbers) and use only one or two senses (auditory or

A
B
S
T
R
A
C
T
▲
▼
C
O
N
C
R
E
T
E

Verbal Experiences
Teacher talk, written words; engaging only one sense; using the most abstract symbolization; students physically inactive. *Examples:* (1) Listening to the teacher talk about tidal pools. (2) Listening to a student report about the Grand Canyon. (3) Listening to a guest speaker talk about how the state legislature functions.

Visual Experiences
Still pictures, diagrams, charts; engaging only one sense; typically symbolic; students physically inactive. *Examples:* (1) Viewing slide photographs of tidal pools. (2) Viewing drawings and photographs of the Grand Canyon. (3) Listening to a guest speaker talk about the state legislature and show slides of it in action.

Vicarious Experiences
Laser videodisc programs; computer programs; video programs; engaging more than one sense; learner indirectly "doing"; may be some limited physical activity. *Examples:* (1) Interacting with a computer program about wave action and life in tidal pools. (2) Viewing and listening to a video program about the Grand Canyon. (3) Taking a field trip to observe the state legislature in action.

Simulated Experiences
Role-playing; experimenting; simulations; mock-up; working models; all or nearly all senses engaged; activity often integrating disciplines; closest to the real thing. *Examples:* (1) Building a classroom working model of a tidal pool. (2) Building a classroom working model of the Grand Canyon.(3) Designing a classroom role-play simulations patterned after the operating procedure of the state legislature.

Direct Experiences
Learner actually doing what is being learned; true inquiry; all senses engaged; usually integrates disciplines; the real thing. *Examples:* (1) Visiting and experiencing a tidal pool. (2) Visiting and experiencing the Grand Canyon. (3) Designing an elected representative body to oversee the operation of the school-within-the-school program and patterned after the state legislative assembly.

FIGURE 8.5

The learning experiences ladder

Source: From R. D. Kellough, *A Resource Guide in Teaching,* 4th ed. (Upper Saddle River, NJ: Merrill/Prentice Hall, 2003), 216. Reprinted by permission. (*Note:* Earlier versions of this concept were Charles F. Hoban, Sr., et al., *Visualizing the Curriculum* (New York: Dryden, 1937), 39; Jerome S. Bruner, *Toward a Theory of Instruction* (Cambridge, MA: Harvard University Press, 1966), 49; Edgar Dale, *Audio-Visual Methods in Teaching* (New York: Holt, Rinehart & Winston, 1969), 108; and Eugene C. Kim and Richard D. Kellough, *A Resource Guide for Secondary School Teaching,* 2d ed. (Englewood Cliffs, NJ: Merrill/Prentice Hall, 1978), 136.)

visual). The teacher talks while students sit and watch and hear. Visual and verbal symbolic experiences, although impossible to avoid when teaching, are less effective in ensuring that planned and meaningful learning occurs. This is especially so with young children, learners who have special needs, learners with ethnic and cultural differences, and children with limited English proficiency. Thus, when planning learning experiences and selecting instructional materials, select activities that engage children in the most direct experiences possible and that are developmentally and intellectually appropriate for your specific group.

As you may infer from the Learning Experiences Ladder, when teaching about tide pools (the first example for each step) the most effective mode is to take the children to a tide pool (direct experience), where students can see, hear, touch, smell, and perhaps even taste (if not polluted with toxins) the pool itself. The least effective mode is to merely talk about tide pools (verbal experience, the most abstract and symbolic experience), engaging one sense only—auditory.

Of course, for various reasons, such as time, matters of safety, lack of resources, or geographic location of your school, you may not be able to take your students to a tide pool. You cannot always use the most direct experience, so sometimes you must select from higher on the ladder. Self-discovery teaching is not even always appropriate. Sometimes it is more appropriate to build on what others have discovered and learned. Although learners do not need to "reinvent the wheel," the most effective and longest-lasting learning is that which engages most or all of their senses. On the Learning Experiences Ladder, those are the experiences that fall within the bottom three categories— direct, simulated, and vicarious. This is true with kindergarten children, adult learners, and students of any age group in between.

Direct, Simulated, and Vicarious Experiences Help Connect Student Learning

Another value of direct, simulated, and vicarious experiences is that they tend to be interdisciplinary; that is, they blur or bridge subject–content boundaries. That makes these experiences especially useful when you want to help children connect learning of one discipline with that of others and to bridge what students are learning with their own life experiences. Direct, simulated, and vicarious experiences are more like real life.

You must be skillful in using more than a single strategy appropriately. To do so, you need to understand the basic theory that underlies each and must also be able to use the specific teaching skills associated with each. It is important to note that you will seldom use a single strategy in isolation. For example, a demonstration may involve questioning, or an inquiry may involve discussion. In the following sections we examine three strategies—expository teaching, inquiry teaching, and demonstration—in terms of (1) the assumptions underlying each, (2) the purposes to be served, (3) the role of the teacher, (4) the role of the learner, (5) the use of instructional resources, and (6) the appropriate method of assessment.

EXPOSITORY TEACHING

The term *expository* is derived from the concept of *exposition*, which means, most simply, to exhibit or perform. In the context of teaching, exposition has to do with you, the teacher, providing facts, ideas, and other essential information to learners. You do, in fact, perform. The lecture as familiar to college students is the most representative example of the expository mode. Most often, for elementary school teaching, expository strategies are *telling* or *explaining* strategies. Suppose, for example, that you were about to present the concept *boundary line* in a social studies lesson, using an expository strategy. Displayed about the room might be maps of the local community or city, a home-state map showing the counties, a map of the United States showing the states, and one of North America showing the countries. You might also display photographs showing state-line markers and border crossings between countries, and a photograph of the sign at the entrance to your city. Perhaps you would begin the explanation by citing an analogous situation familiar to children, such as the areas assigned to different groups on the playground. You would use visual devices to explain the meaning of *boundary line*, giving children not one but many examples of the concept in a variety of settings. After your explanation, there would be some discussion, along with followup work calling for students to apply the concept to new situations. This strategy is probably quite familiar to you. In the example cited, you, the teacher, were doing the explaining, but other sources of information and data, such as books and media, are often used in expository teaching.

Expository teaching, if well done, can be an effective teaching strategy, even with children in the primary grades. Some of elementary school children's most interesting and long-remembered experiences are short and exciting explanations provided by an animated teacher. The problem is that teachers often do *too much* expository teaching, that is, too much talking and explaining, with a corresponding reduction in their use of other, more child-centered, learner-involving strategies. It is generally true that instead of balancing its use with other strategies, teachers have relied too heavily on expository teaching.

Teaching in an expository mode can easily deteriorate into an "assign–read–write–discuss" routine that becomes deadly dull for both you and your students. Expository teaching can and should involve learners, engaging them in a variety of challenging learning activities that build critical-thinking skills.

Assumptions

Teaching by exposition assumes that there is an essential body of content, skills, and values to be learned. Examples of such essential components are the basic literacy skills, information relating to cultural imperatives, and survival skills. It is assumed, further, that this learning has been pulled together into courses of study, textbooks, and other curriculum documents that form the core learning of the school curriculum. Teachers are prepared to teach this essential material. Teaching is assumed to be basically a transmission process. Teachers and instructional resources serve as conduits for moving information, skills, and values from their sources to learners. Teaching, therefore, is a variation of telling; learning is the receiving of information that has already been processed in terms of its importance and "learnability." Information and information-gathering skills are deemed important. Consequently, achievement is measured either by the amount of information students can recall or by how effectively they can use information-gathering skills.

Major Purposes

The major purpose of expository teaching is, clearly, to transmit knowledge and skills from those who know (teacher and textbook, for example) to those who don't (learners). Information deemed important relating to science, mathematics, social studies, health, safety, and so on can often be taught efficiently and effectively through an expository approach. Exposition does not necessarily concern itself with the social values of the learning experience. Its purpose is purely and simply to get across to learners what is specified by curriculum requirements. For example, you may want to teach a group of fourth-graders that the major land masses and water bodies of the earth are called *continents* and *oceans*, respectively. You might display a world map, point out the relevant information, name and label the continents and oceans, and explain that the earth's surface is divided between water and land and that these land and water bodies have names. Your students are not necessarily involved in discovering anything for themselves; the essential information they are to learn is presented to them.

Role of the Teacher

Using expository teaching, teachers direct the learning program. They *are* the programmers. They must see to it that the prescribed curriculum is covered and that children have mastered it. Teachers are an important data source and are an important component of the transmission line between instructional resources and learners. Teachers decide what books and other instructional materials to use. Their role is to guide learners to get the "right" answers—those that are a part of the required curriculum. In the expository mode, teachers' directions and explanations to learners must be crystal clear. Ambiguous questions and inconclusive explanations are a deterrent to learning. Teachers are accountable for their presentation of essential material to children and use appropriate assessment procedures to validate that students have, indeed, learned it.

Role of the Learner

With expository strategies learners are expected to meet requirements the teacher has established. These usually include reading the required material, answering assigned questions, discussing presented topics or problems, and demonstrating skills deemed to be important. Learners are not required to exercise the same degree of self-direction expected in inquiry teaching (discussed in the following section). Children do not need to go beyond the assigned tasks, although teachers sometimes encourage this by providing "extra credit" for additional work or by providing some type of extended activities for enrichment.

The learner's role in learning by exposition is often inaccurately described as "passive." Actually, learners can be and often are very active in reading, searching for answers to questions, using instructional resources, or going on field trips. Their activity, however, is directed toward externally established requirements, rather than toward those they have themselves initiated.

Use of Instructional Resources

Teaching by exposition requires that learners obtain certain prescribed information from the instructional resources used. Typically, students use instructional materials to respond to questions framed by someone *other* than themselves, that is, by teachers, textbook authors, and so forth. Rather than seeking data to make their own interpretations, children look for and learn the interpretations and summaries presented by the information sources. When using expository teaching, instructional resources are best used to summarize learning. There can be no question that teaching by exposition relies heavily on instructional materials that stress verbal learning as opposed to direct experience. It also uses instructional resources that are compartmentalized along conventional subject-matter lines: reading, mathematics, social studies, science, and so forth.

Method of Assessment

Teaching by exposition operates on the premise that children are supposed to learn a predetermined curriculum. Learners' achievements are determined by the extent to which they have acquired the subject matter and skills the teacher

If thinking is to be the central purpose of U.S. education, as many believe it should be, then teachers must devise ways to help individual children develop their thinking skills. One such way is through inquiry, where the teacher's role is to both challenge and assist learners by helping them recognize problems and questions and by guiding their inquiry.

has transmitted to them. It follows, therefore, that methods of assessing that learning will be those that assess the extent to which students have achieved this goal. Tests that assess knowledge of informational content covered in the curriculum are appropriate, as are those that measure skills. Conventional standardized tests are a good example of the evaluative devices suitable for the expository mode. Teacher-made tests designed to find out whether learners can reproduce correct answers are also consistent with learning by exposition.

INQUIRY TEACHING

To *inquire* means to ask questions, to seek information, to carry on an investigation. Inquiry strategies in teaching and learning, therefore, are those that involve learners in these processes. To a large extent, learners are responsible for providing ideas and questions to explore, proposing hypotheses to test, accumulating and organizing data to test hypotheses, and coming to tentative conclusions. Inquiry can take many forms, but the problem-solving format suggested by the prominent American educator John Dewey nearly a century ago is the one most commonly used.[1] This process involves five steps. The learner confronts a problem situation: what Dewey called a "felt need." The learner moves to resolve this need by searching for a solution. In the process, the student proposes possible solutions or hypotheses and then searches for evidence that will support or reject them. On the bases of acquired data and the results from testing proposed solutions, the learner either comes to a tentatively held conclusion or rejects the hypothesis and continues to search until finding a satisfactory resolution to the problem. These five steps—(1) defining a problem, (2) proposing hypotheses, (3) collecting data, (4) evaluating evidence, and (5) making a conclusion—have become institutionalized in the so-called "scientific method" of problem solving.

Often overlooked is the fact that the procedure, as proposed by Dewey, includes two thought processes. Defining the problem and proposing hypotheses involve *inductive discovery*. In gathering data and applying and testing solutions, one engages in *deductive proof*. It is clear that problem solving of this type makes use of both inductive and deductive thought processes.

When inquiry is conducted in such a way that learners find out the meanings of concepts and form conclusions and generalizations from data they themselves have gathered, we may refer to such an inquiry as a *discovery experience*. For example, in a science experiment dealing with the effect of light on a growing plant, children may have two plants of the same variety, of similar size, and grown under the same environmental conditions. One is left to grow as usual in sunlight, and the other is covered. All other conditions of heat, moisture, and exposure are the same for the two plants. In a few days, noticeable changes occur. From these observations, children conclude that sunlight is an essential component of plant growth. Throughout this process, their teacher tells them neither what will happen nor what to expect. The teacher may cue them with periodic thought questions to guide inquiry, but the children themselves discover the relationship. When educators refer to inquiry, they are usually referring to this kind of discovery learning. It is important to note that *discovery*, used in this sense, does not mean that children are uncovering new knowledge; they are discovering knowledge hitherto unknown to *them*.

Intrinsic to the effectiveness of both inquiry and discovery is the assumption that students would rather actively seek knowledge than receive it through traditional expository (i.e., information delivery) methods such as lectures, demonstrations, and textbook reading. Although inquiry and discovery are important teaching tools, there is sometimes confusion about exactly what inquiry teaching is and how it differs from discovery learning. The distinction should become clear as you study the following descriptions of these two important tools for teaching and learning.

Perhaps a major reason why inquiry and discovery are sometimes confused is that in both, students are actively engaged in problem solving. *Problem solving* is the ability to recognize, identify, define, or describe a problem, determine the preferred resolution, identify potential solutions, select strategies, test solutions, evaluate outcomes, and revise any of these steps as necessary.[2]

> *Before students can begin doing research and inquiry on their own, they need to experience nonfiction reading and writing and learn to generate questions and find resources.*
>
> —Cathy Tower
>
> *Source:* C. Tower, "Questions That Matter: Preparing Elementary Students for the Inquiry Process." *The Reading Teacher* 53(7): 550–557 (2000).

Inquiry Versus Discovery

Problem solving is not a teaching strategy but a high-order intellectual behavior that facilitates learning. What a teacher can and should do is to provide opportunities for students to identify and tentatively solve problems. Experiences in inquiry and discovery can provide those opportunities. With the processes involved in inquiry and discovery, teachers can help students develop the skills necessary for effective problem solving. Two major difference between discovery and inquiry are (a) who identifies the problem and (b) in the percentage of decisions that are made by the students. Table 8.1 shows three levels of inquiry, each level defined according to what the students does and decides.

It should be evident from Table 8.1 that what is called Level I inquiry is actually traditional, didactic, "cookbook" teaching, where both the problem and the process for resolving it are identified and defined for the student. The student then works through the process to its inevitable resolution. If the process is

TABLE 8.1
Levels of Inquiry

	Level I (not true Inquiry)	Level II	Level III
Problem identification	Identified by teacher or textbook	Identified by teacher or textbook	Identified by student
Process of solving problem	Decided by teacher or textbook	Decided by student	Decided by student
Identification of tentative solution to problem	Resolved by student	Resolved by student	Resolved by student

The levels of inquiry are adapted from "the three different levels of openness and permissiveness . . . for laboratory enquiry" by Joseph J. Schwab, *The Teaching of Science as Enquiry* (Cambridge, MA: Harvard University Press, 1962), 55.

well designed, the result is inevitable, because the student "discovers" what was intended by the writers of the program. This level is also called guided inquiry or discovery, because the students are carefully guided through the investigation to (the predicable) "discovery."

Level I is in reality a strategy within the delivery mode, the advantages of which were described earlier in this chapter. Because Level I "inquiry" is highly manageable and the learning outcome is predictable, it is probably best for teaching basic concepts and principles. Students who never experience learning beyond Level I are missing an opportunity to engage their highest mental operations, and they seldom (or never) get to experience more motivating, real-life problem solving. Furthermore, those students may come away with the false notion that problem solving is a linear process, which it is not. As illustrated by Figure 8.6, true inquiry is cyclical rather than linear. For

FIGURE 8.6
The inquiry cycle

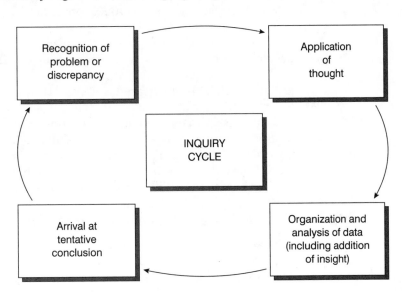

Activity 8.1: Does It Really Matter What It's Called?

From the time of her first brush with the classroom as a student teacher, it was clear that Ms. Marsh had a knack for asking questions that sparked children's thinking. And they loved it! She would rarely come right out and tell them much of anything. She would rephrase and clarify what they said and, in the process, would provide a cue or two that led them in the direction of what they wanted and needed to know. Now, in her seventh month as a contracted teacher, her classroom was something of a science laboratory, a museum, a "fix-it" shop, an art gallery, and a learning resources center all wrapped into one. Her students seemed always to be talking interestedly about what was going on in the classroom and would often ask each other questions about projects and activities. A colleague told her one day, "How lucky you are to have such a curious and interested group of children. They've changed so this past year."

"Yes, they do seem interested in what we are doing, and they learn a great deal on their own. But I must get back to school this summer and broaden my knowledge of inquiry teaching," replied Ms. Marsh.

1. Is there anything about this sketch that suggests that Ms. Marsh is already making effective use of the inquiry mode of teaching?
2. Are the terms *discovery learning* and *inquiry teaching* referring to the same thing? Explain why they are or are not.
3. What do you think of her colleague's comment that Ms. Marsh is "lucky to have such a curious and interested group of children"?

---

that reason, Level I is not true inquiry, because it is a linear process. Real-world problem solving is a cyclical rather than linear process. One enters the cycle whenever a discrepancy or problem is observed and recognized, and that can occur at any point in the cycle.

By the time students are in grade 5, they should be provided experiences for true inquiry, which begins with Level II, where students actually decide and design processes for their inquiry. In true inquiry there is an emphasis on the tentative nature of conclusions, which makes the activity more like real-life problem solving, where decisions are always subject to revision if and when new data so prescribe.

At Level III inquiry students recognize and identify the problem as well as decide the processes and reach a conclusion. In project-centered teaching, students are usually engaged at this level of inquiry. By the time students are in middle and upper grades, Level III inquiry should be a major strategy for instruction, which is often the case in schools that use cross-age teaching and interdisciplinary thematic instruction. But, it is not easy; like most good teaching practices it is a lot of work. But also like good teaching, the intrinsic rewards make the effort worthwhile. As exclaimed by one teacher using inter-disciplinary thematic instruction with student-centered inquiry, "I've never worked harder in my life, but I've never had this much fun, either."

The Critical Thinking Skills of Discovery and Inquiry

In true inquiry, students generate ideas and then design ways to test those ideas. The various processes used represent the many critical thinking skills. Some of those skills are concerned with generating and organizing data; others

FIGURE 8.7
Inquiry cycle processes

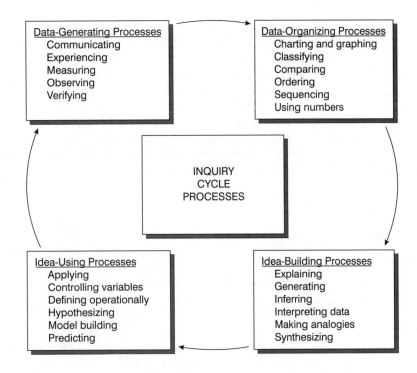

are concerned with building and using ideas. Figure 8.7 provides four main categories of these thinking processes and illustrates the place of each within the inquiry cycle.

Some processes in the cycle are discovery processes, and others are inquiry processes. Inquiry processes include the more complex mental operations (including all of those in the idea-using category). Project-centered teaching provides an avenue for doing that, as does problem-centered teaching.

Inquiry learning is a higher-level mental operation that introduces the concept of the discrepant event, something that establishes cognitive disequilibrium (using the element of surprise to challenge their prior notions) to help students develop skills in observing and being alert for discrepancies. Such a strategy provides opportunities for students to investigate their own ideas about explanations. Inquiry, like discovery, depends upon skill in problem solving; the difference between the two is in the amount of decision-making responsibility given to students. Experiences afforded by inquiry help students understand the importance of suspending judgment and also the tentativeness of answers and solutions. With those understandings, students eventually are better able to deal with life's ambiguities. When students are not provided these important educational experiences their education is incomplete.

One of the most effective ways of stimulating inquiry is to use materials that provoke students' interest. These materials should be presented in a non-threatening, noncompetitive context, so students think and hypothesize freely.

The teacher's role is to encourage students to form as many hypotheses as possible and then support their hypotheses with reasons. After the students suggest several ideas, the teacher should begin to move on to higher-order, more abstract questions that involve the development of generalizations and evaluations. True inquiry problems have a special advantage in that they can be used with almost any group of students. Members of a group approach the problem as an adventure in thinking and apply it to whatever background they can muster. Background experience may enrich a student's approach to the problem, but is not crucial to the use or understanding of the evidence presented to him or her.

Assumptions

It is assumed that when they are taught by inquiry, children benefit from being self-directed, critical thinkers and problem solvers. Inquiry is largely learner-centered, requiring that children be "actively involved" in learning, which means that they exercise initiative. Inquiry involves a search–surprise element, and this characteristic makes it highly motivating. The outcomes of learning are less predictable. When using inquiry, the *process* of learning (how children learn content) is perceived to be at least as important an outcome as is the *product* (what they learn). Learning should be kept open ended, the achievement of goals being simply an intermediate step to additional investigation. Teachers therefore encourage learners to wonder and imagine, and this curiosity leads to further inquiry. Learners have individual learning styles, and teachers can best accommodate these when learners are responsible for their own learning. There is less need to focus on a search for "right" answers because the conclusions are tentative in terms of the data available at the time.

Major Purposes

The major purpose of inquiry teaching is to provide a means for learners to learn and apply the intellectual skills related to critical thinking and problem solving. If thinking is to be the central purpose of U.S. education, as many believe it should be, then teachers must devise ways to help individuals develop that capability. Inquiry is intended to do this by focusing on developing such mental processes as identifying and analyzing problems, stating hypotheses, collecting and classifying relevant data, interpreting and verifying data, testing hypotheses, and coming to conclusions. It seeks to develop independence. Teachers encourage children to find things out for themselves by inquiring. Through inquiry, they should *learn how to learn*. Inquiry stresses discovering things for oneself.

As travel agencies advertise, "getting there is half the fun." This relates to the inquiry process in that the inquiry or the search is both the means and the end. Inquiry carries its own reward, quite apart from what students learn in the way of content and skills. It is important to understand this aspect of the inquiry mode, particularly if you are concerned to cover certain subject matter at certain grade levels. The purpose of inquiry is to provide training in the development of specific intellectual skills, not to master—or even to cover— specified elements of subject matter.

Role of the Teacher

Because inquiry is highly learner centered, the teacher's role is that of a facilitator who challenges learners by helping them identify questions and problems and who guides their inquiry. The teacher provides an atmosphere that ensures freedom of exploration and good human relations, along with needed psychological support. Insofar as possible, the teacher tries to encourage independent habits of work. As needed, the teacher helps children find appropriate sources of information and is responsible for ensuring an adequate number of appropriate instructional resources are available. The teacher restates and clarifies student responses and suggests alternative interpretations of data. The teacher structures the situation to the extent that inquiry can actually take place. That is, the children are not wholly free to wander about on their own "doing inquiry." The teacher does not stress seeking *the* right answer but helps children find and validate appropriate answers. The teacher must be particularly skillful in asking the kinds of questions that encourage critical thinking and problem solving.

For inquiry learning to proceed smoothly and effectively it is doubly important to ensure that children understand and follow procedures.

Role of the Learner

The use of inquiry requires learners to exercise considerable initiative in finding things out for themselves. They must be actively engaged in their own learning and, therefore, must be minimally self-directed. Naturally, it is not expected that teachers will leave them unguided in their inquiry searches, but it is expected that teachers will encourage them to ask questions, to challenge material presented to them, and to think about alternatives. Within limits, learners, with the teacher's help, set their own goals and convert those into specific learning objectives. They are free to explore broadly and are provided many opportunities to make choices. They are encouraged to range widely in their search for information. The learner's role is not to respond to questions the teacher poses but to ask questions and to discover the answers through quests and searches.

Use of Instructional Resources

Learners can use effectively any of the conventional resources (e.g., textbooks, supplementary books, films, pictures, field trips, computers, resource persons, and the library) for inquiry searches. Indeed, teachers encourage learners to use a range of data sources. In inquiry, as in good teaching in general, the question is not so much *what* instructional resources children use as *how* they use them. Inquiry necessitates getting data in order to make interpretations. Presumably, children (and their teacher) have raised questions and suggested hypotheses concerning the topic under study before commencing the information search. They then use the instructional resources to shed light on these queries.

Method of Assessment

Assessment of learning from inquiry focuses on the extent to which learners are able to use the intellectual skills associated with this method of learning. Because the major purpose of inquiry is to generate and verify propositions, learners should not be evaluated only on their ability to recall and reproduce information. Sometimes assessment is based on the extent to which knowledge has been transmitted. This is an obvious confusion of purposes in the instructional and evaluation phases of learning. Standardized tests that focus on assessing critical-thinking and problem-solving skills are generally more appropriate for evaluating inquiry-based instruction than are primarily subject-matter-based tests. Assessments that require students to perform tasks to demonstrate knowledge or skill, as well as those that use student-produced materials or portfolios that contain work samples, are all appropriate for use with inquiry.

Activity 8.2: But How Do You Do It, Really?

The National Council for the Social Studies was holding its annual convention in a nearby city, and Ms. Simmons, a first-year second-grade teacher, decided to attend. She found the experience both inspiring and instructive, but was confused about some of the things she heard. At the first general session, the opening speaker emphasized, "Teaching is not telling. Children have to experience firsthand the cultural world that surrounds them. They need to find things out for themselves. They need to inquire and to discover."

The next day Ms. Simmons attended another general session, where the speaker was just as eloquent, just as distinguished, and just as convincing as the first. He told the audience, "You must consider how a culture is passed on from one generation to another. Is it likely or even reasonable to expect that each individual as a part of the growing process will rediscover the whole of culture? I think not. Not even with the best schools and the most creative teachers could we reasonably expect that a child would discover all that she or he needs to know. We cannot rely on discovery as the means of transmitting the culture to children and youth. Culture cannot be discovered; it must be passed on or it is forgotten."*

1. How can Ms. Simmons reconcile these two points of view?
2. Are the speakers necessarily in disagreement?
3. What do these speakers tell you about the importance of being able to use more than one mode of teaching?

*Attributed to Jerome S. Bruner.

THE DEMONSTRATION

Ms. Giles is introducing cursive writing to her third-grade class. She finds it impossible to explain what is involved. Therefore, she makes use of the writing board. As she writes the letters on the board, she explains how each letter is formed. She points out to her students how they are to make specific curves and how best to overcome any difficulties they might encounter. Ms. Giles says, "Now watch carefully how I make the top part of the letter. I will do it a few more times." This teacher is *showing*, *doing*, and *telling*. These are the essential components of a demonstration.

Sometimes teachers develop demonstrations on the spur of the moment when they discover the limitations of a verbal explanation. Suddenly, writing board erasers become ships in a harbor to clarify a social studies concept; pencils in groups help students visualize a mathematics concept; playground balls illustrate the positions of the sun, the earth, and the moon in a solar eclipse. Such improvised demonstrations are common in teaching. Whether preplanned or improvised, demonstrations can be effective in communicating to learners.

Demonstrations can be and often are combined with other strategies such as exposition, inquiry, and questioning. For example, a teacher may be conducting an experiment on magnetism in a science lesson, using magnets and iron filings to illustrate certain magnetic principles. The teacher may conduct the experiment by asking questions: "If I place this magnet under the glass with the iron filings on it, what, if anything, will happen to the iron filings? Why do you think so? Shall we try it and see? . . . Now then, why do the filings take this particular shape? What would happen if I turned the magnet around?"

Here we see the teacher demonstrating while conducting a lesson that is basically inquiry oriented. Students are hypothesizing, applying prior knowledge to the present inquiry, and testing their hunches through the demonstration procedure.

The same demonstration setting could be used in an expository situation. Instead of asking questions, the teacher would be telling the class what to expect, what to look for, what is likely to happen, and why things happened as they did. Such demonstrations are usually used with more mature learners. With young children, most educators prefer a more inquiry-oriented procedure, with greater direct learner involvement.

Demonstrations, therefore, can serve at least two educational purposes. The first is that they can illustrate and dramatically present ideas, concepts, and principles in an engaging way. It is more interesting and provocative to see something happening than to listen to an explanation alone. Even professional actors depend on props and staging to get their ideas across to their audiences. The chances of misunderstanding are minimized if learners can see as well as hear what the teacher is explaining. Oral explanations used alone are necessarily more abstract than when combined with a relevant demonstration.

Demonstrations also provide value in addition to aiding in learning subject matter and content-related skills. They can develop critical-thinking skills. This is especially the case with some aspects of mathematics, science, and social studies. Demonstrations provide opportunity for learners to speculate on what will happen, how it will happen, and why it happens as it does. This is undoubtedly the greatest value in having young learners participate directly in demonstrations. By involving themselves in the demonstration, they are applying and practicing important thinking skills that should become a permanent part of their education.

Assumptions

The demonstration may accept portions of, or all of, the assumptions that apply to inquiry or expository strategies. Good teaching is perceived in part as good communication, and demonstration facilitates communication. It assumes that learning will be enhanced if children are exposed to a functioning model or guide. This exposure will shape learners' future behavior or attitudes because they will be inclined to imitate the demonstration model. Through observing a demonstration, learners engage in sympathetic behavior by visualizing, observing, and perhaps even verbalizing subvocally what is happening, and this strengthens achievement of the desired behavior. Even when the teacher is conducting the demonstration alone, without direct student involvement, children may be participating intellectually; conducting the demonstration mentally and following along with what the teacher is doing. Learning is further facilitated through demonstration by *focusing attention on the most critical aspects of what students are to learn*. That is, a well-conducted demonstration is one in which the key ideas stand out clearly.

Major Purposes

The major purpose of a demonstration is to show how something is to be done, how something happens or works, or how something should not be done. Demonstrations are used to improve communication. Many demonstrations are extensions of exposition, the only difference being that the demonstration stresses seeing in addition to hearing. Demonstration can help overcome difficulties where there is the expectation of failure to understand an oral explanation, where there are frequent errors in learning, and where the possibility of misunderstanding is high.

Role of the Teacher

The role of the teacher (or other demonstrator) is to plan, organize, and execute the demonstration in a way that makes clear the key ideas students are to learn. The demonstration must be factually and technically correct and must be presented in a step-by-step sequence. The teacher must be able to show, in conducting the demonstration, what is to be learned. If demonstrating a skill, the teacher must be able to perform it proficiently. If equipment is involved, such as a motion picture projector, maps and globes, or science laboratory materials, the teacher must have those ready and must know how to use them for the demonstration. It is the teacher's responsibility to ensure that everyone in the class will be able to see and hear the demonstration.

Role of the Learner

When using the demonstration, the learner's role is to observe, listen, and follow the presentation carefully and attentively in order to understand what is being communicated. In some instances, learners may be required to participate in the demonstration or to replicate it using duplicate materials or equipment. The teacher/demonstrator may ask children to respond to questions at critical points in the demonstration, to provide feedback, thereby showing the extent of their understanding.

Use of Instructional Resources

Instructional resources for a demonstration consist of whatever materials and equipment are needed to conduct that demonstration. Children may or may not need materials other than those used in the demonstration. Ordinarily, teachers design followup to a demonstration, and for this purpose may use conventional instructional resources such as textbook assignments or special readings. Appropriate use of these materials would be similar to those described in the discussions of expository and inquiry teaching.

Method of Assessment

Any assessment device is satisfactory that measures the extent to which students have achieved the purposes of the demonstration. Teachers may give written tests, but discussion is also useful in revealing understanding or misconceptions. Teachers may require learners to replicate the demonstration or to explain it to someone else. Teachers should observe students' behavior, noting whether they are omitting important points, whether they display misunderstanding or confusion, whether they follow proper sequences, or whether any other deficiency is apparent that will require further clarification or reteaching.

SKILLS INSTRUCTION

General principles and procedures for skills instruction are not applied in exactly the same way to all skills. Nevertheless, the same basic principles are present: meaningfulness, learner involvement, practice, feedback, application, and maintenance. In applying these principles, we caution you to not allow skills teaching to become routine and ritualized. Also, you must interpret the guidelines in ways consistent with the developmental and trait differences among learners. With these precautions in mind, let us examine what is involved in teaching a skill.

Meaningfulness

As is true of most learning, skills instruction is facilitated if learners understand what the skill is all about, what is involved in performing it, how to apply it, and "what it's good for." Demonstrations are effective for showing meaningfulness and for illustrating a good performance, and they are frequently used in teaching skills that involve physical movement. For example, the music teacher demonstrates how to move the bow in playing the cello, the physical education teacher shows how to dribble a basketball, and the primary-grade teacher demonstrates how to move the hand and fingers in handwriting. Not all skills are so easily demonstrated. In the case of skills that are mainly intellectual, it is necessary to show the *results* or *effects of skill use* rather than the skill itself. For example, teachers can show that one can arrive at a correct answer in mathematics, locate a place on a map, or find a specific book in the library by using certain skills.

Learner Involvement

If students are to learn skills at a high level of proficiency, they must involve themselves heavily in the process. Skills learning requires practice and application. When learners invest themselves thoroughly in learning a skill, they constantly seek ways to practice and apply it. Contrast this with other learners, ones who devote only a minimum effort to the skill and give that time grudgingly. One can take any skill as an example: reading, writing, playing a musical instrument, doing physical activities, and learning magic tricks. An individual who is self-directed and highly motivated to learn a skill will proceed much more rapidly and efficiently than one who is not. A key to good skills teaching, therefore, is to provide instruction in such an engaging way that learners are not only willing but are eager to involve themselves in it.

Practice

Practice, *with the intent to improve*, is an absolutely essential requirement in learning a skill. It does not matter how meaningful the teaching has been or how well learners understand what they are to do; they are not going to be able to perform a skill proficiently unless they practice it. Through practice, learners develop the ability to respond with ease and confidence. Students learn to perform essential academic skills so well that they apply them intuitively. There can be no question that lack of practice is a major factor in poorly developed skills. However, if practice is to be a productive exercise, it must take place under certain conditions. Poorly conducted or half-hearted practice sessions can be detrimental to a learner's performance. This would occur if the learner is allowed to practice incorrect responses or if the practice session encourages poor habits of work.

Although "practice makes perfect" is often used as a guideline for teaching and learning skills, *improvement* rather than perfection is the appropriate outcome of practice. Furthermore, the *desire to improve* is a very important condition of practice. Learners who go through the motions of a practice exercise but whose hearts are not in it will have a difficult time improving performance. It may even produce the reverse effect, a *dis*incentive, because the experience is generating bad feelings, or a *negative affect*, toward the skill. This means that learners not only will engage in practice in an unproductive way but will avoid situations in which they must use the skill. This obviously takes them further away from developing proficiency in performance. Thus, highly motivated short practice sessions, with a strong intent to improve, are usually more productive.

Improving a skill may mean performing it with greater ease and precision, or it may mean doing it with greater speed. If improvement is sought in the precision of the responses, learners must make a conscious effort to eliminate unnecessary movements and errors. The teacher would need, therefore, to show or tell in what ways a performance is faulty. Exact repetition of the skill is *not* a good format when seeking this type of improvement. Instead, learners must know how to improve their responses and must work on those specific deficiencies in practice sessions. But if the improvement sought is increased speed of response, it would be appropriate for learners to practice by repetition, trying to become ever faster. In either case, *having learners keep records of the improvement made in practice sessions will enhance their learning.*

In the early stages of skills learning, it is important to supervise the performance carefully. This is to ensure that learners will do it correctly. Left unguided, children may practice incorrect responses, which, of course, means that they must unlearn these errors before they can progress. Once they are able to do the skill, frequent, short practice sessions will promote improvement. When performance has reached an acceptable level, periodic practice, together with opportunities for application, should be enough to maintain proficiency.

Feedback

One of the most important elements in skills learning is *feedback:* learners must receive evaluative information concerning their performance. In skills learning, learners receive feedback on both successes and failures and therefore can make the adjustments necessary to improve performance. *Positive* feedback tells learners of successes, that what they are doing is correct. *Negative* feedback tells them what is incorrect, that their performance is faulty or is going in the wrong direction.

Generally speaking, positive feedback is more productive than negative feedback in maintaining a high level of motivation and promoting successful performance. Success experiences are positive and predictable in their effect on the individual, whereas individuals are more variable in their response to failure. Some regard failure as a challenge, others are crushed by it; however, almost everyone responds positively to success.

Finally, an important difference between the two types of feedback is the extent to which they guide learners' improvement. Because positive feedback emphasizes what is correct, students can replicate a performance to ensure continued success. With negative feedback, learners are simply told that they are performing incorrectly and are not provided direction in *how* to improve. This can result in a trial-and-error sequence of experiences unless the teacher provides additional guidance and direction. Negative feedback is necessary, but it should be coupled with specific suggestions about how to improve the performance.

Teachers are one of the most important sources of feedback. This is the strongest argument in favor of reduced class size. Teachers can supervise and provide feedback more easily to fewer children. Besides their teacher, learners often get feedback on their performances from each other. If handled sensitively, this can be an important means of facilitating skills attainment. By using self-correcting materials and by keeping careful records on trials, learners can obtain a considerable amount of performance feedback. In addition, electronic devices able to provide learner feedback (such as computers, pulse counters, or timers) may be available.

Application

Essential to skill development is the opportunity to use the skill in a practical setting. Without it, learning the skill will seem dissociated from its real-world context. For example, writing and spelling should not be thought of as being used, and useful, only during certain periods in the day or week. Students should apply writing, spelling, and reading skills frequently throughout the day in all other subjects—excellent settings in which to practice basic skills. One of the reasons holistic language learning methods have gained such widespread support in recent years is that they teach language competencies in authentic settings in which their interrelatedness is apparent.

The traditional attitude toward skills development might be described as "learn now, apply later." Great emphasis has been given to basic learning skills in the elementary grades, the idea being that children will use them in later grades or in later life. This attitude has a detrimental effect on skills improvement in two important ways. First, it separates skills teaching from practical application in the early stages; second, it shortens the length of time devoted to skills instruction. Learning and applying skills must go hand in hand. In reading, for example, we would say that children should learn to read and should read to learn at the same time. Teachers should not separate these two processes.

Whenever it is assumed that skills are taught in the lower grades and applied later, there is a tendency to discontinue prematurely the systematic instruction in skills. Consequently, many students complete school with their basic skills at a usable level of about the fifth or sixth grade. For example, there are many adults who can read maps no better than a fifth- or sixth-grade child, because that was the last time they received any instruction on that cluster of skills. If students are to improve and refine their skills, instruction in some skills should continue into and, in some cases, through high school. The application of skills should begin from the moment they are introduced in the primary grades. In this way, teachers can maintain a good balance between direct instruction and functional application throughout the entire program.

Maintenance

When students use and apply skills regularly, there will be little problem in maintaining them at a satisfactory level. Problems arise, however, when a skill is taught and then not used for a long time. Through disuse, children lose whatever proficiency they may have developed. This usually means that the next time children need a skill, they must be retaught before they can use it. In cases where skills are maintained through regular use, teachers should check from time to time to make sure that children are performing them correctly and reteach as needed. This will ensure that faulty habits will be corrected before they become a permanent part of children's response patterns.

BASIC SKILLS—THE THREE Rs

As we know, in the United States from colonial times to the present elementary schools have had the responsibility of teaching the basic skills of reading, writing, and arithmetic. Great importance is attached to these skills because they deal so fundamentally with basic literacy. A person who does not have a respectable command of basic literacy skills is greatly handicapped in doing schoolwork and will be limited in making choices in life outside school. Even though these skills are often dubbed "the three Rs," they involve a vast array of skills and subskills that make it possible for children to become fully communicating human beings. As a teacher, you must ensure your program meets the following requirements if you desire to have a strong program in the basic skills:

1. The program is structured, systematic, and sequential.
2. The program is interesting and stimulating to children.
3. You conduct frequent assessments to ensure continuous progress.
4. The program is personalized.
5. Methods and materials stress purposeful and functional uses of skills.
6. The program encourages habits of independence on the part of learners.

Developing a Structured, Systematic, and Sequential Program

In situations where we find casualties in learning basic skills, we often see what might be called a *nonprogram* in these skills. Instruction is entirely incidental to the informal activities of the classroom. Children write when there is a reason to write. They read when they have an interest in reading. They learn to write and spell because they want to communicate something in written language. All of this is commendable and should be encouraged. Certainly, we want children to use basic skills in purposeful ways, and no doubt some children can learn basic skills this way. But for most children, this approach is much too haphazard and opportunistic. It suggests that complex skills can be taught and learned catch-as-catch-can, with a disregard for the sequence in which learning occurs. The outcome of this approach, if widely applied, is predictable: Many children will not learn the basic skills well enough to meet the requirements of school, to say nothing of life outside school. This is not to say, however, that there are not a few especially talented teachers who, using this approach, can achieve remarkable results with children.

Individual teachers may choose to use some of the newer approaches to teaching communication skills, such as those based on the concepts of emergent literacy and holistic language learning. Others may elect a more conventional basal program. But in either case, they must plan a program of systematic instruction. This means that they will devote time to such instruction on a regular, planned basis, teaching the various components of the skills sequentially, progressing from simple to complex variations. They will use well-prepared instructional materials produced by reputable authors and publishers. They will clearly identify the specific skills to be developed and will appraise student achievement behaviorally. These are qualities that characterize a structured and organized program.

You have a right to expect your school district to provide curriculum documents that detail the structure and sequence of the basic skills program. Such documents should spell out specifically what skills are to be attended to and what level of attainment is expected. If such documents are not available, you should study the teacher's manuals that accompany the reading, language arts, and mathematics texts used in your school. These manuals will acquaint you with the organization and structure of the skills program developed in the material. Although you will probably not want to follow such a textbook program precisely, it will provide an organizing framework around which you can build your basic skills program.

Making the Program Interesting and Stimulating

Instruction in basic skills can easily fall into an uninspiring routine, one that varies little from day to day and that becomes mindless and dull. For example, each day at the prescribed time, children go to their places, and the lesson picks up where it was left the day before. This ritual repeats day after day.

Little wonder that children, and their teacher, too, find this type of program little short of drudgery. It would be unusual to expect any dramatic achievement to result from such uninspired teaching.

What is needed in effective skills instruction is the enthusiasm and interest that children bring with them in their early days of school—the time when learning to read, write, spell their names, and do a little simple arithmetic represents major success experiences for them. To maintain a consistently high level of interest, make use of a variety of practice formats. Instead of or in addition to the conventional practice exercises, make generous use of activities that involve practical applications of skills: contests and games, visual and auditory aids, mechanical and electronic devices, and other vehicles that children find interesting. Variety seems to pay big dividends in keeping the practice session spirited and intellectually vigorous.

Conducting Frequent Assessments

Progress in skills development (increased proficiency of performance) is a continuous, gradual, and cumulative process. The *rate of improvement*, however, is irregular, progressing rapidly for a while, then slowing to allow for integrating and consolidating skills. Skills development does not occur in stages marked off by grade level, birthdays, or levels of schooling. Because progress is continuous and gradual, it is often referred to as *developmental*.

The term *developmental*, however, is not meant to imply that progress in using a skill occurs as a natural unfolding process, similar to children's physical growth and development. For example, most children would learn to walk on their own without adult intervention by the time they are 2 years old. On the other hand, without instruction and/or a conscious intent to learn and improve, learning a complex psychological skill such as reading is not likely to occur at all. Skills development can be arrested at any point, for several reasons. It is essential, therefore, that you make frequent checks of children's progress and that you *record results for future reference*. Record keeping is critical. You need not be particularly concerned about the amount of improvement in a child's skill from day to day or week to week. But you should be *very* concerned if you see no progress over a period of a few months or in a school year. Nonetheless, frequent assessments—day-to-day and week-to-week—will alert you to any problems children might be having so you can correct them before they seriously impede children's progress.

Cases are frequently reported in which children have advanced to the third or fourth grade before it is discovered that they are having a reading or a writing problem or a problem with mathematics. There can be little excuse for this kind of oversight. Of course, there will be children in these grades and even several grades beyond who are deficient in basic skills, but they should have been detected early in their school life. When proper attention is given to assessment, difficulties are diagnosed early, and appropriate measures are taken to correct them. There are, of course, children with complex learning difficulties that require highly specialized corrective measures. But most learning problems of children are relatively simple to diagnose and to correct.

Personalizing the Program

There is much about the nature of the school setting that, when allowed, can discourage you from personalizing (individualizing) instruction in skills. You often have from 15 to 25 or more children with whom to work. Often, these children are of the same age and may not be very different from one another in physical size. This is especially the case in the primary grades. Moreover, tradition reinforces the idea that you are teaching a *class* rather than *individuals* who just happen to be grouped together. It is only when you begin to look at children individually that differences between and among them become apparent.

The range of individual differences between and among children who have been randomly selected for grade groups in the elementary school is well documented. Children of the same chronological age differ in their rate of learning, interest in learning, learning styles and capacities, motivation to learn, and almost every other relevant variable on which we have data. As you know, your challenge is to devise teaching methods that will accommodate the individual variations in children in group settings.

Individualizing instruction in skills does not mean that you are to shunt each child off to work alone on a workbook exercise. Individualized instruction can and most often does take place in dyads and small groups formed to meet specific needs. These pairs and groups are temporary and flexible. There is no particular procedure or formula to recommend, except to say that you probably cannot individualize instruction if you teach your class as a whole group day after day. You need to make a careful study of individual

---

Activity 8.3: What Went Wrong for Antoine?

In school, things went quite well for Antoine until he reached the fourth grade. He was a sensitive, quiet, well-behaved boy and enjoyed the relaxed and informal program in the primary grades. Now his teacher was asking him to read considerably more than his teacher had the year before, and Antoine was not a very good reader. Besides, he had to find things in the encyclopedia, on the Internet, and in the library, and he did not know how to find what he was supposed to be looking for. He couldn't pick out a main idea, nor could he write a summary sentence. It just seemed as though nothing in school made much sense to him anymore. He was so discouraged that

he would sometimes just sit and stare out the window. One day, his teacher said to him, "Antoine, you will just have to improve your work-study skills." He didn't even know what she was talking about.

1. How might the teacher have been more helpful to Antoine?
2. Why is the fourth grade such a critical year in terms of work-study skills?
3. If Antoine's problems are left unattended, what would you predict his future in school to be?
4. If you have ever known an "Antoine," how did things work out?

children. By so doing, you will get to know the achievement level of each one and will know what special help each requires. Then, by carefully grouping together children who are at similar levels in their performance of a skill, you and others (aides and other children) can instruct these small groups. Naturally, there will be many times when you will need to assist individual learners. Much of the time, however, you can productively conduct skills instruction in small groups (we discuss personalizing instruction and small-group instruction further in Chapter 9).

Using Methods and Materials That Stress Purposeful and Functional Use of Skills

This guideline is consistent with today's attention being given to the need to integrate more of the curriculum and to relate it more explicitly to life outside of school. As a general rule, children should practice and use skills in settings closely similar to those found in ordinary life. You cannot assume that your skills curriculum is complete simply by following the basic text that the school has adopted for the various skills areas. You must be continually sensitive to the reality that skills are interrelated and that they are practically applied in people's everyday lives.

Encouraging Habits of Independence

As soon as possible, children should be "on their own" in reading, writing, spelling, mathematics, and all of the subskill components that make up these basic skills. If this is to happen, you will need to present them with many opportunities to apply and use newly acquired skills. Children develop independence in skills use by *using* the skills. As children gain independence, they are constantly reinforcing and practicing their skills, thereby relying less on the school and on you, the teacher, to provide these enriching and extending experiences. The object or ultimate goal of any skills program is, of course, to make all children independent and truly "on their own" in using basic skills, and as early as possible.

SUMMARY

With this chapter you continued learning about building a strategy repertoire and about selecting instructional strategies. You continued to study the importance of learning modalities and their relationship to selecting instructional modes. In this chapter in particular, you learned about the importance of selecting strategies that enhance what is called *authentic learning*.

Throughout this book and especially in this chapter, rather than focus your attention on selecting a particular model of teaching, we prefer to emphasize

Activity 8.4: Is There a Preferred Way?

Mr. Barto sets aside specific time periods during the day when he teaches basic skills such as reading, writing, spelling, handwriting, and oral and written expression. He feels this is the best way to provide individual assistance to children and to keep track of their progress. Beyond that, he does not do much with skills teaching.

Ms. West takes a more holistic approach to teaching skills. She does not provide specific time periods for skills instruction but lengthens her science and social studies periods and teaches the basic skills as needed in connection with these subjects. She feels skills should be taught not in isolation but in situations where they are used.

Ms. Brookover combines what Mr. Barto and Ms. West do. She has specific periods of short duration for systematic and sequential instruction but also makes a big point of having children apply these skills in science, social studies, and, where appropriate, all areas of the school curriculum. She believes that both types of experiences are needed to ensure children's satisfactory development and maintenance of skills.

1. Why does Ms. Brookover's approach have advantages over those of Mr. Barto and Ms. West?
2. Which of the three methods is potentially most vulnerable to neglect of skills teaching? Which is most vulnerable to meaningless teaching? Why?
3. Assuming that all three teachers teach the same grade and that children in all three groups are roughly equivalent in their ability to learn, do you think that standardized skills test scores among the three groups would vary significantly?

the importance of an eclectic model—selecting the best from various models or approaches. For example, although there will be times when you want to use a direct, teacher-centered approach, perhaps by a minilecture and a demonstration, many other times you will want to use an indirect, student-centered approach such as small learning groups. And because of the diversity of your students it is likely that there will be even more times when you will be doing both at the same time, such as working with one small group of children while another group or several groups in various areas of the classroom are working at learning stations or on their project studies.

Finally, you are constantly assessing each child's developing skills and knowledge base and then restructuring and redirecting that child's learning activities on the basis of those individual assessments.

STUDY QUESTIONS AND ADDITIONAL ACTIVITIES

1. Which of the teaching modes discussed in this chapter do you believe presents the greatest potential for classroom management problems? Why? How could teachers prepare to avoid problems when using this mode?
2. Describe the meaning of *authentic learning*. What would you consider to be its antithesis?
3. It is often claimed that "teaching is *not* telling." If this is true, why do so many teachers continue to do a great deal of "telling"? For a specific grade level (K–6) describe with examples when telling by the teacher is okay and when it is not okay.

4. In discussions of teaching strategies, the learners' role is sometimes described as either "passive" or "active." List some things children do when they are "actively involved" in their learning. Does a child need to be doing something physical to be "actively involved"? Explain.

5. Are "hands-on learning" and "minds-on learning" inseparable? Explain.

6. Of the three teaching strategies discussed in this chapter—expository, inquiry, and demonstration—one is principally direct instruction, another is indirect instruction, and the third can be either. Describe which is which and reasons that make it so. Which, if any, strategy would you feel most comfortable using? Explain why?

7. Divide your class into grade-level groups, at least two groups, K–3 and 4–6. Have each group devise two separate lesson plans to teach the same topic to the same group of students (identified), one plan using direct instruction and the other using indirect. Have groups share the outcomes of this activity with one another.

8. It is said that when taught by access strategies, students learn less content but learn it more effectively. If this is accurate, could it be a problem for a teacher using strategies within this mode? Explain.

9. Do you believe the access or delivery mode better encourages high-level student thinking, or do you believe there is no difference? Explain. Can you find research evidence to support your belief? With current emphasis on standardized testing, is one or the other more appropriate in today's classroom? Explain why or why not.

10. Do you believe the access or delivery teaching mode does more to enhance the development of student self-esteem, or do you believe there is no difference? Explain. Can you find research evidence to support your belief?

NOTES

1. John Dewey, *How We Think* (Boston: D. C. Heath, 1933), 106.
2. A. L. Costa (Ed.), *Developing Minds: A Resource for Teaching Thinking* (Alexandria, VA: Association for Supervision and Curriculum Development, 1985), 312.

FOR FURTHER PROFESSIONAL STUDY

Amaral, L. M., Garrison, L., and Klentschy, M. "Helping English Learners Increase Achievement Through Inquiry-Based Science Instruction." *Bilingual Research Journal* 26(2): 213–239 (2002).

Beamon, G. W. "Guiding the Inquiry of Young Adolescents." *Middle School Journal* 33(3): 19–27 (2002).

Bell, L. I. "Strategies That Close the Gap." *Educational Leadership* 60(4): 32–34 (December 2002–January 2003).

Crawford, B. A. "Embracing the Essence of Inquiry: New Roles for Science Teachers." *Journal of Research in Science Teaching* 37(9): 916–937 (2000).

Fischer, P. "Wow! Kindergarten/First-Grade Inquiry." *Primary Voices K–6* 10(3): 9–15 (2002).

Freedman, M. P. "Using Effective Demonstrations for Motivation." *Science and Children* 38(1): 52–55 (2000).

Gray, E. N. "A Literacy Growth Spurt During Inquiry: Tommy's Story." *Language Arts* 78(4): 325–332 (2001).

Hamm, M., and Adams, D. "Collaborative Inquiry: Working Toward Shared Goals." *Kappa Delta Pi Record* 38(3): 115–118 (2002).

Harvey, S., and Goudvis, A. *Strategies That Work: Teaching Comprehension to Balance Understanding.* Portland, ME: Stenhouse, 2002.

Marzano, R. J. "Classroom Curriculum Design." Chapter 11 of *What Works in Schools: Translating Research into Action.* Alexandria, VA: Association for Supervision and Curriculum Development, 2003.

Marzano, R. J. "Instructional Strategies." Chapter 9 of *What Works in Schools: Translating Research into Action.* Alexandria, VA: Association for Supervision and Curriculum Development, 2003.

Marzano, R. J.; Pickering, D. J.; and Pollock, J. E. "Generating and Testing Hypotheses." Chapter 9 of *Classroom Instruction That Works: Research-Based Strategies for Increasing Student Achievement.* Alexandria, VA: Association for Supervision and Curriculum Development, 2001.

Owens, R. F.; Hester, J. L.; and Teale, W. H. "Where Do You Want to Go Today? Inquiry-Based Learning and Technology Integration." *Reading Teacher* 55(7): 616–625 (2002).

Pappas, M. L. "Managing the Inquiry Learning Environment." *School Library Media Activities Monthly* 16(7): 27–30, 36 (2000).

Roser, N. L., and Keehn, S. "Fostering Thought, Talk, and Inquiry: Linking Literature and Social Studies." *Reading Teacher* 55(5): 416–426 (2002).

Sears, S. *Introduction to Contextual Teaching and Learning.* Fastback 504. Bloomington, I Phi Delta Kappa Educational Foundation, 2003.

Searson, R., and Dunn, R. "The Learning-Style Teaching Model." *Science and Children* 38(5): 22–26 (2001).

Takahashi-Breines, H. "The Role of Teacher-Talk in a Dual Language Immersion Third Grade Classroom." *Bilingual Research Journal* 26(2): 461–483 (2002).

Tower, C. "Questions That Matter: Preparing Elementary Students for the Inquiry Process." *Reading Teacher* 53(7): 550–557 (2000).

Walberg, H. J., and Paik, S. J. *Effective Educational Practices.* Educational Practices Series 3. Brussels, Belgium: International Academy of Education, 2000.

Wolfe, P. Chapter 8, "Making Curriculum Meaningful Through Problems, Projects, and Simulations." In: *Brain Matters: Translating Research into Classroom Practice.* Alexandria, VA: Association for Supervision and Curriculum Development, 2001.

INTASC Principles	PRAXIS III Domains	NBPTS Standards
• The teacher uses an understanding of individual and group motivation and behavior to create a learning environment that encourages positive social interaction, active engagement in learning, and self-motivation. (Principle 5)	• Creating an Environment for Student Learning (Domain B)	• Multiple Paths to Knowledge

Rather than diluting standards and expectations, exemplary elementary schools and teachers, believing in the learning potential of each and every child, are able to effectively modify the key variables of time, methodology, and grouping to help individual children master the curriculum. One advantage of self-contained classrooms is that teachers are in control of the time spent on a given lesson or unit of study and basically are free to modify time however they deem necessary. One way that classroom teachers can modify time is by carefully grouping children to maximize learning. In their restructuring efforts schools have found other ways of modifying the time factor.[1] The possible variations are nearly limitless. Throughout this textbook we talk of ways of varying methodology, a topic you will continue learning more about throughout your program of teacher preparation and, indeed, throughout your teaching career. In this final chapter we discuss ways of grouping children to enhance positive interaction and quality learning.

ANTICIPATED OUTCOMES

After completing this chapter, you should be able to do the following:

1. Discuss the advantages and disadvantages of each of several ways of grouping children for learning.
2. Identify the process skills that children need to work successfully in groups. Describe ways of teaching them these skills.
3. Describe the concept of *quality learning* and its meaning for elementary school teaching.
4. Describe specific ways to personalize learning, even in a classroom of 15 or more children.
5. Describe situations when it would be advantageous to use paired learning.
6. Describe situations when it would be advantageous to use small-group learning.
7. Distinguish between *small-group learning* and the *cooperative learning group*.
8. Describe situations when it would be advantageous to use several types of learning groups simultaneously.
9. Describe situations when it would be advantageous to use whole-group instruction.
10. Describe the concept of "cooperative learning."
11. Discuss the strengths and limitations of cooperative learning.
12. Describe the teacher's role when children are learning alone, in dyads, in small groups, in cooperative learning groups, in large groups, and at classroom learning centers.
13. Describe the concept of the classroom "learning center" and how you would use it in your teaching.
14. Distinguish the learning center from the learning station.
15. Describe guidelines for using homework in elementary school instruction.

16. Express an opinion about the advantages and disadvantages of providing opportunity for "student recovery" as presented in this chapter.

17. Complete the development of the daily lessons for your unit plan that you began working on in Chapter 6. Share your completed unit plan with your classmates and instructor, for their feedback.

GROUP PROCESS SKILLS

Most likely you assume that people learn group-work skills by experience, that is, by participating in group efforts. Although this assumption, of course, is true, it overlooks the fact that instruction can greatly enhance learning group-work skills. It is not enough simply to provide the *opportunity* to work in small groups; you must also instruct children in how to function in the roles associated with group efforts. You may best accomplish this by demonstrating through role play how individuals function in small groups. From these demonstrations, you can generate standards you may then use in evaluating the performance of groups.

It is difficult to imagine how one could learn to work cooperatively with others by working in isolation. To develop children's group-work skills you must plan many classroom activities that involve their working together. Not all of these efforts will be successful; this is to be expected, because children will make mistakes while learning. The advantage of the school environment is that mistakes seldom result in disastrous consequences. Furthermore, you are there to help children learn from their mistakes. In this respect, in-school experiences are different from those outside school. Learning to work independently is important, too, but this is not the format in which group-work skills are developed.

The following skills need to be taught and learned in connection with group efforts:

1. Contributing to collaborative group planning (providing suggestions, evaluating proposals, suggesting alternatives, compromising on points of difference).

2. Defining problems (raising questions, suggesting which questions are relevant, listening to and respecting the views of others).

3. Organizing to achieve a defined task (deciding on a plan of action, suggesting subtasks and specific assignments, deciding what materials will be needed).

4. Working as a committee member (knowing and carrying out specific responsibilities, assisting with planning, cooperating and working with others rather than in isolation, supporting the leadership of the chairperson, working responsibly toward the achievement of group goals).

5. Assuming the leadership of groups (developing plans cooperatively with group members, respecting the suggestions and contributions of group members, moving the group toward the achievement of its goals, delegating

responsibility as needed, serving as spokesperson for the group, maintaining democratic rather than autocratic relationships with group members).

Instruction in group-work skills must occur over a period of time. You may single out one subskill and concentrate attention on it when it applies particularly well to the work of the class. Guidelines or standards for group work *should* be developed cooperatively with children. You may post these and use them as criteria for assessing group work.

When applying these skills, for young children it is usually a mistake to begin by dividing an entire class into several small subgroups. These children cannot handle this degree of independence; they have not developed the maturity to be entirely self-directed. It is better to begin with one small group to which you give a specific task with clear directions. You should closely supervise this group. The remainder of the class, the larger group, can be kept intact at this point. Gradually, all children can become members of such small groups, at which time two or more groups can be at work simultaneously. In time, you can have the entire class working productively in small groups. You must frequently assess group-work skills, and positively reinforce children generously when their efforts are successful. For older children, you will need to learn the extent to which they have already developed their ability to work in groups.

QUALITY LEARNING AND PERSONALIZED INSTRUCTION

Learning, as you know, is an individual or personal experience. Yet as a classroom teacher you will be expected to work effectively with students on other than an individual basis—perhaps with as many as 20 or more at a time. Much has been written of the importance of individualizing learners' instruction. Virtually all the research concerning better instructional practice emphasizes greater individualization, or personalization, of instruction.[2] We know of the individuality of the learning experience. And we know that while some children are primarily verbal learners, many more are primarily visual, tactile, or kinesthetic learners. As a teacher, you will find yourself in the difficult position of simultaneously "treating" many separate and individual learners with individual learning needs, capacities, styles, and preferences.

Elementary school teachers use exploratory learning, cooperative learning, project-based learning, classroom learning centers, and small-group learning to personalize instruction and to respond to the variety of individual student competencies, interests, needs, and abilities. They vary the length of time for instructional activities and the size of instructional groups, and also vary the learning strategies within a given time period.

Common sense tells us that student achievement in learning is related to both the quality of attention and the length of time given to learning tasks. Benjamin Bloom, building on a model developed earlier by John Carroll, developed the concept of individualized instruction called *mastery learning*, saying that students need sufficient time on task (i.e., engaged time) to master content before moving on to new content.[3] From that concept came the development of printed modules of instruction called *programmed instruction* (which, today, would likely be presented as computer software programs), which allow students to control their own learning pace. The instruction is mastery oriented; that is, students demonstrate mastery of the content of one module before proceeding to the next.

Today's Emphasis: Quality Learning for Each Child

As we emphasized at the start of this book, in Chapter 1, and again now in this final chapter, emphasis today is, or should be, on mastery of content, or *quality learning* as it is often called, rather than coverage of content, or quantity of learning. Because of this emphasis and research that indicates that quality learning programs positively affect achievement, mastery learning has resurfaced as an important concept. Today's efforts utilize a results-driven curriculum model with instruction that focuses on students' constructing individual knowledge through mastery and assessing student learning against anticipated learning target or outcome standards.

In some instances, unfortunately, attention may only be on the mastery of minimum competencies; thus, students are not encouraged to work and learn to the maximum of their talents and abilities. By mastery of content, we mean that students demonstrate their use of what they have learned. Periodic performance assessment apprises teachers of student's current level of mastery.

Assumptions About Quality Learning

Today's concept of quality, or mastery, learning is based on the following assumptions[4]:

1. Mastery learning can ensure that students experience success at each level of instruction—experiencing success at each level provides incentive and motivation for further learning.
2. Quality learning, or mastery of content, is possible for each student. It is no longer professionally or socially acceptable (if indeed it ever was) that a percentage of children will slip through the educational cracks and eventually drop out.
3. Although all students can achieve mastery, some children may require more time than others to master particular content.
4. For quality learning to occur, instruction must be modified and adapted, not students. For example, tracking and ability grouping do not fit with the concept of mastery learning.
5. Most learning is sequential and logical.
6. Most, if not all, desired learning outcome standards can be specified in terms of observable and measurable performance.

Components of Any Quality Learning Model

Any instructional model designed to teach toward quality (mastery) learning will contain the following five components:

1. Clearly stated learning outcome standards that can be translated into learning objectives
2. Preassessment of learners' present knowledge
3. An instructional component, with choices and options for students
4. Practice, reinforcement, frequent comprehension checks (both diagnostic and formative assessment), and corrective instruction at each step to keep learners on track
5. Postassessment to determine the extent of student mastery of the objectives

Students are informed of the learning expectations (target objectives) and then receive appropriate instruction. The essence of appropriate instruction is the cycle of teaching, testing, reteaching, and retesting.[5] The cycle continues until each child reaches some level of mastery and, depending on lesson content, this takes longer for some children than for others. In other words, exemplary schools and teachers are those who are able to effectively modify the key variables of time, methodology, and grouping to help each child achieve some acceptable and measurable level of mastery of the curriculum. In this final chapter, we are focusing on ways of grouping children to enhance positive interaction and quality learning for each and every child.

Selected Strategies for Personalizing Instruction for Quality Learning

Regardless of the number and diversity of children in your classroom, you can immediately provide an effective degree of personalized instruction by using the following techniques (and others):

• Begin study of a topic from where children are in terms of what they know (or think they know) and what they want to know about the topic. Strategies for doing this include "think–pair–share" (discussed in the next section) and KWL.[6] With the KWL strategy, you make three columns on a sheet of butcher paper or an overhead transparency. At the top write the topic. Then title the three columns *K* (for what we already *know*), *W* (for what we *want* to know about the topic), and *L* (for what we *learned* about the topic). Starting with the K column, solicit from children what they know or think they know about the topic and write those items in the column. When that is exhausted, move to the W column and solicit from children what they would like to learn about the topic. You fill in the L column later toward completion of the study as a means of review. See Figure 9.1 for variations of the KWL strategy.

• Provide students with choices from a rich variety of pathways and hands-on experiences to learn more about the topic.

- **KWLQ:** Students record what they already know about a topic (K), formulate questions about what they want to learn about the topic (W), search for answers to their questions (L), and ask questions for further study (Q).
- **POSSE:** *Predict* ideas, *organize* ideas, *search* for structure, *summarize* main ideas, and *evaluate* understanding.
- **PQRST:** *Preview, question, read, state* the main idea, *test* yourself by answering the questions you posed earlier.
- **QAR:** Helping children understand *question and answer* relationships.
- **RAP:** *Read* paragraphs, *ask* questions about what was read, and *put* in own words.
- **Reciprocal teaching:** Students are taught and practice the reading skills of summarizing, questioning, clarifying, and predicting.
- **SQ3R:** *Survey* the chapter, ask *questions* about what was read, *read, recite,* and *review.*
- **SQ4R:** *Survey* the chapter, ask *questions* about what was read, *read* to answer the questions, *recite* the answers, *record* important items from the chapter into their notebooks, then *review* it all.
- **SRQ2R:** *Survey, read, question, recite,* and *review.*

FIGURE 9.1
Methods for helping students develop their higher-level thinking skills and their comprehension of expository material[7]

- Provide multiple instructional approaches (that is, using multilevel instruction in a variety of settings, from learning alone to whole-class instruction).
- Empower students with responsibility for decision making, reflection, and self-assessment.

In the most effective elementary school learning environment, during any given day of school, an individual child might experience a succession of group settings. For the balance of this chapter we discuss ways of grouping children for learning: learning alone; working in pairs (dyads); working at learning centers; working in small groups, including cooperative learning groups (CLGs); and working in large groups.

LEARNING ALONE

Although some children learn well in pairs, and others learn well with their peers in groups—collaboratively, cooperatively, or competitively—or collaboratively with adults, and others learn well in combinations of these patterns, some students learn best alone. These students often are gifted, nonconforming, able to work at their own pace successfully, and comfortable using media. They may also be seemingly underachieving but potentially able students for whom the usual conventional instructional strategies don't work as well.

LEARNING IN PAIRS (PAIRED TEAM LEARNING)

Paired team learning is a strategy whereby students study and learn in *dyads* (teams of two). Specific uses for paired team learning include drill partners, paired reading, book report pairs, computer pairs, summary pairs, assignment partners, and elaborating and relating pairs. Other types of learning pairs include peer-assisted learning, cross-age coaching, and think-pair-share.

Peer-assisted learning (PAL) is a strategy whereby one classmate tutors another. It is useful, for example, when one student helps another who has limited proficiency in the English language or when a student skilled in math helps another who is less skilled. For many years, it has been demonstrated repeatedly that peer tutoring is a significant strategy for promoting active learning.[8]

Cross-age coaching is similar to peer tutoring, except that one student coaches another from a different, usually lower, grade or age level.[9] Many school districts have service learning projects that involve older students mentoring elementary school children. The "older students" might be from the upper elementary grades, or a middle school, high school, or college.

Think–pair–share is a strategy wherein students in dyads examine a new concept or topic about to be studied. After members of each dyad discuss what they already know or think they know about the concept, they present their perceptions to the whole group. This is an excellent technique for discovering students' misconceptions about a topic. You may introduce a writing step, a modification called *think–write–pair–share* and have dyad members think and write their ideas or conclusions before sharing with the larger group.

THE CLASSROOM LEARNING CENTER

Another significantly beneficial way of pairing students for instruction (as well as of individualizing the instruction and learning alone and integrating the learning) is by using the classroom learning center (LC) or learning station (LS). [*Note:* Whereas each learning center is distinct and unrelated to others, learning stations are sequenced or in some way linked to one another, as discussed in the TEAMS approach below.] The LC is a special station located in the classroom where one student (or two, if student interaction is necessary or preferred at the center, or as many as four or five students in the case of learning stations) can quietly work and learn at the student's own pace more about a special topic or to improve specific skills. All materials needed are provided at that center, including clear instructions for operation of the center.

The value of classroom learning centers as instructional devices undoubtedly lies in the following facts. LCs can provide instructional diversity. While working at a center, the student is giving time and quality attention to the learning task (learning toward mastery) and is likely to be engaging her most effective learning modality, or integrating several modalities or all of them.

Learning centers in the classroom are of three types. In the *direct-learning center*, performance expectations for cognitive learning are quite specific and the focus in on mastery of content. In the *open-learning center*, the goal is to provide opportunity for exploration, enrichment, motivation, and creative discovery. In the *skill center*, as in a direct-learning center, performance expectations are quite specific but the focus is on the development of a particular skill or process.

In all instances the primary reason for using a learning center is to individualize—that is, to provide collections of materials and activities adjusted to the various readiness levels, interests, and learning profiles of students. Other reasons to use an LC are to provide (a) a mechanism for learning that crosses discipline boundaries, (b) a special place for a student with exceptional needs, (c) opportunities for creative work, enrichment experiences, multisensory experiences, and (d) opportunity to learn from learning packages that utilize special equipment or media of which only one or a limited supply may be available for use in your classroom (e.g., science materials, a microscope, a computer, a videodisc player, or some combination of these). Classroom learning centers should always be used for educational purposes, never for punishment. [*Note:* What we are calling a classroom learning center is not to be confused with what in some schools in sometimes referred to as a Modified Learning Center, a place on the campus that is staffed by a paraprofessional, sometimes a social worker, where students may be sent from the regular classroom for a variety of reasons, such as to complete an assignment, as a place to calm down, because of inappropriate classroom behavior, for conflict resolution and problem solving, and as an on-campus suspension.]

To adapt instruction to the curriculum and to students' individual needs and preferences it is possible to design a learning environment that includes several learning stations, each of which uses a different medium and modality or focuses on a special aspect of the curriculum. Students then rotate through the various stations according to their needs and preferences.

To construct an LC you can be as elaborate and as creative as your time, imagination, and resources allow. Students can even help you plan and set up learning centers, which will relieve some of the burden from your busy schedule. The following paragraphs present guidelines for setting up and using this valuable instructional tool.

The center should be designed with a theme in mind, preferably one that integrates the student's learning by providing activities that cross discipline boundaries. Decide the purpose of the center and give the center a name, such as "our community," "the center for the study of wetlands," or "walking tour of Washington, DC," or "traveling to Mexico City," or "patterns in nature," or "the United Nations," or "our state capitol," or " center for our class newspaper," and so on. The purpose of the center should be clearly understood by the students.

The center should be designed so as to be attractive, purposeful, and uncluttered, and should be identified with an attractive sign. Learning centers should be activity-oriented (i.e., dependent on the student's manipulation of materials, not just paper-and-pencil tasks).

Topics for the center should be related to the instructional program—for review and reinforcement, remediation, or enrichment. The center should be self-directing (i.e., specific instructional objectives and procedures for using the center should be clearly posted and understandable to the student user). An audio- or videocassette or a computer program is sometimes used for this purpose. The center should also be self-correcting (i.e., student users should be able to tell by the way they have completed the task whether or not they have done it correctly and have learned).

The center should contain a variety of activities geared to the varying abilities and interest levels of the students. A choice of two or more activities at a center is one way to provide for this.

In the most effective elementary school learning environment, during any given school day, an individual child might experience a succession of settings, from whole groups and small groups to dyads and learning alone. Using small groups, as shown here, can enhance children's opportunities to learn group-work skills and assume greater control over their own learning.

Materials to be used at the center should be maintained at the center, with descriptions for use provided to the students. Materials should be safe for student use, and you or another adult should easily supervise the center. Some centers, as the suggested titles above suggest, may become more or less permanent centers, that is, remain for the school term or longer, whereas others may change according to what is being studied at the time.

LEARNING IN SMALL GROUPS

Small groups are those involving three to five children, in either a teacher- or student-directed setting. Using small groups for instruction, including the cooperative learning group (discussed in the next section), enhances the opportunities for children to (1) learn group-work skills and (2) assume greater control over their own learning, sometimes referred to as *empowerment*.[10]

Purposes for Using Small Groups

You may form small groups to serve a number of purposes. They might be useful for a specific learning activity (e.g., reciprocal reading groups, where students take turns asking questions, summarizing, making predictions about, and clarifying a story). Or you might form them to complete an activity requiring materials in short supply, or to complete a science experiment or a project, lasting only as long as the project does. You will have various rationales for assigning children to groups, and may group children according to (1) personality type (for example, sometimes you may want to team less assertive children together to give them the opportunity for greater management of their own learning), (2) social pattern (for example, sometimes it may be necessary to break up a group of rowdy friends, or it may be desirable to broaden associations among students), (3) common interest, (4) learning styles (for example, forming groups either of mixed styles or of styles in common), or (5) according to their abilities in a particular skill or their knowledge in a particular area. One specific type of small group is the cooperative learning group.

COOPERATIVE LEARNING

From his research on social interaction and learning, Lev Vygotsky (1896–1934) argued that learning is most effective when learners cooperate with one another in a supportive learning environment under a teacher's careful guidance.[11] Cooperative learning, group problem solving, problem-based learning, and cross-age tutoring all have grown in popularity as a result of research evolving from Vygotsky's work.

The Cooperative Learning Group (CLG)

The *cooperative learning group* is a *heterogeneous* group (that is, mixed according to one or more criteria, such as ability or skill level, ethnicity, learning style, learning capacity, gender, or language proficiency) of three to six students who work together in a teacher- or student-directed setting, emphasizing support for one another. Often, a CLG consists of four students of mixed ability, learning styles, gender, and ethnicity, with each member of the group assuming a particular role. Teachers usually change the membership of each group several to many times during the year.

The Theory and Use of Cooperative Learning

The theory of cooperative learning is that when small groups of students of mixed backgrounds and capabilities work together toward a common goal, members of the group increase their friendship and respect for one another. As a consequence, each individual's self-esteem is enhanced, students are more motivated to participate in higher-order thinking, and students achieve academically.[12]

Although there are several models of cooperative learning,[13] the primary purpose of each is for the groups to learn—which means, of course, that individuals within the groups must learn. Rather than competing for rewards for achievement, group members cooperate with one another by helping one another learn, so that the group will be rewarded.

Roles Within the Cooperative Learning Group

It is advisable to assign roles (specific functions) to each member of a CLG, rotating roles either during the activity or from one activity to the next. Although titles may vary, five typical roles are as follows:

- *Group facilitator,* whose role is to keep the group on task.
- *Materials manager,* whose role is to obtain, maintain, and return materials the group needs to function.
- *Recorder,* whose role is to record all group activities and processes, and perhaps to periodically assess how the group is doing.
- *Reporter,* whose role is to report group processes and accomplishments to the teacher and/or the entire class (you may combine the roles of recorder and reporter when using groups of four members).
- *Thinking monitor,* whose role is to identify and record the sequence and processes of the group's thinking. This role encourages metacognition and the development of thinking skills. Research has demonstrated that students who talk about how they and others think become better learners.[14]

It is important that students understand and perform their individual roles, and that all group members perform their tasks as expected. No student should be allowed to ride on the coattails of the group.

What Students and the Teacher Do When Using Cooperative Learning Groups

Actually, for learning by CLGs to work, each member must understand and assume two roles or responsibilities—as a member of the group, and that of seeing that all others in the group are performing their roles. Sometimes this requires interpersonal skills that children have yet to learn or to learn well. This is where you must assume some responsibility. Simply placing children into CLGs and expecting each member and each group to function and to learn the expected outcomes may not work. In other words, children must learn the skills of cooperation, and if all your students have not yet learned these skills (and they probably have not), then you will have to teach them. This doesn't mean that if a group is not functioning you immediately break it up and reassign members to new groups. Part of group learning is learning the process of how to work out conflict, which may require your assistance. With your guidance the group should be able to identify the problem that is causing the conflict, then brainstorm some options and mediate at least a temporary solution. If a particular skill is needed, then with your guidance students can identify and learn that skill.

When to Use Cooperative Learning Groups

You may use CLGs for problem solving, investigations, opinion surveys, experiments, review, project work, test making, or almost any other instructional purpose. Just as with small-group work in general, you can use CLGs for most any purpose at any time, but as with any other type of instructional strategy, you must be careful not to overuse it.

Outcomes of Using Cooperative Learning Groups

When you have planned and managed the process well, the outcomes of cooperative learning include (1) improved communication and relationships of acceptance among students, (2) quality learning with fewer off-task behaviors, and (3) increased academic achievement. In the words of Good and Brophy,

> Cooperative learning arrangements promote friendships and prosocial interaction among students who differ in achievement, sex, race, or ethnicity, and they promote the acceptance of mainstreamed handicapped students by their non-handicapped classmates. Cooperative methods also frequently have positive effects, and rarely have negative effects, on affective outcomes such as self-esteem, academic self-confidence, liking for the class, liking and feeling liked by classmates, and so forth.[15]

Cooperative Group Learning, Assessment, and Grading

Normally, the CLG is rewarded on the basis of group achievement, though individual members within the group can later be rewarded for individual contributions. Because of peer pressure, when using CLGs you must be cautious about using group grading.[16] Some teachers give bonus points to all members of a group to add to their individual scores when everyone in the group has reached preset criteria. In establishing preset standards, the standards can be different for individuals within a group, depending on each member's ability and past performance. It is important that each member of a group feel rewarded and successful. For determination of students' report card grades, individual student achievement is measured later through individual results on tests and other sources of data.

Why Some Teachers Have Difficulty Using CLGs

Sometimes, teachers have difficulty using CLGs and either give up trying to use the strategy or simply tell students to divide into groups for an activity and call it cooperative learning. For CLGs to work well, you must plan in advance and manage effectively. Each student must be given training in and have acquired basic skills in interaction and group processing and must realize that individual achievement rests with that of their group. Each student must be assigned a responsible role within the group and be held accountable for fulfilling that responsibility. And, while a CLG activity is in process, you must continually monitor groups for possible breakdown of the group process. When you notice a potential breakdown, quickly intervene to help the group get back on track.

LARGE-GROUP INSTRUCTION

Used frequently by most or all teachers, *large groups* are those that involve more than five students, and usually the entire class. Direct whole-class instruction is teacher centered, and although inefficient for meeting children's individual needs and interests, it is convenient for teaching the same skill or subject to an entire group, making assignments, administering tests, setting group expectations, and making announcements.[17]

In ordinary conversation, the term *group* means simply an aggregate of individuals. This term has a more specialized meaning in the context of the classroom, where the reference is to a collection of task-oriented individuals who are mutually dependent on each other for the purpose of successfully achieving a common goal. To be a group, children must have a psychological identity with one another. They also must have an esprit de corps that binds them together. A classroom of children does not inherently have these characteristics. As teacher, you will need to make the necessary provisions for your classroom of children to become a group. These provisions are based primarily on establishing a group atmosphere in the classroom, making provisions for individual differences, and teaching the skills needed for effective group participation.

EXAMPLES OF LARGE- AND SMALL-GROUP INSTRUCTION

We here present vignettes featuring Ms. Baxter and Mr. Bond as illustrations of how two teachers developed group management plans for their classrooms. As you read the vignettes, we suggest that you and your classmates do the following: (1) identify the techniques that Ms. Baxter and Mr. Bond used in teaching children in small groups; (2) identify the learner outcomes that resulted from instruction in small groups that would have been difficult to achieve had they been taught in a whole-class setting; and (3) list and share ideas that you gain from your reading.

Large- and Small-Group Instruction: Primary Grades

Ms. Baxter recognized that children need to develop effective group skills early in their school life. She also knew the importance of teaching the skills that are basic to effective group participation. She knew the importance of preparing learners for small-group work by making certain they possessed the skills necessary to perform group tasks. She decided to begin small-group work slowly by first building group spirit and effective social behavior in the whole class.

Ms. Baxter began on the first day of school to include children in the performance of certain duties related to classroom upkeep. She wanted them to acquire a feeling of responsibility for developing and maintaining the learning environment. She spent considerable time during planning period each morning in helping children establish good speaking and listening habits and accept each other's points of view. These experiences convinced her that her students were capable of beginning to work in small groups.

Ms. Baxter's First Group Discussion

Ms. Baxter discovered during her first lesson, designed to introduce the unit of study, "Learning About Communities," that variability in children's ability to carry on a group discussion was far greater than she had anticipated. She found that many children insisted on talking at the same time and that their responses to her questions were inclined to be irrelevant. She realized that she would have to structure group discussions more carefully to enable learners to accomplish the planned objectives. Ms. Baxter concluded that this group had the potential for participating in group discussion when the topic was limited in scope. She closed the lesson by having them suggest ways in which they might improve their discussion. After everyone agreed on the rules, she wrote them on the class chart shown here.

Ms. Baxter decided to ask the more mature children to help her assess how well the class observed their rules. The idea worked very well, and she felt she would continue having individual children assist in the assessment. She handled this situation as a language learning as well as a social learning experience. Through discussion, children learn to listen to others, to express their own ideas orally, and in some instances to summarize their conclusions in writing, as was the case here.

Activity 9.1: Laughter and Love in the Classroom

Children should have an opportunity to work in groups organized on the basis of criteria other than reading ability. They need to get acquainted with children they would not get to know well if groups were based entirely on success in reading.

Teachers who make provisions for multibased groups for their students experience the rewards that come from hearing and seeing laughter and love in the classroom. This is because children are free to accept each other on new terms. They begin to appreciate one another because they are free from the pressure of always having to compete.

1. After you have read these vignettes on classroom group management, decide whether Ellen Baxter and Jim Bond provided their children with this kind of atmosphere.
2. Determine what additional provisions you would make to create an atmosphere of laughter and love.

Making Provisions for Variability in Reading Levels

In a prior lesson, Ms. Baxter had followed a picture-study activity by asking children to read silently to find answers to questions she had included in her lesson plan. In doing so she discovered that the children differed widely in their skimming skills and in their ability to identify the main idea. She realized that she would need to consider these differences carefully in the very near future, when she expected children to gather information from other sources related to the unit of study.

In a second lesson, Ms. Baxter decided that she would provide variety in the way children could gather additional information, and at the same time, would vary the level of conceptualization required (Figure 9.2). She planned two types of activities to accomplish this goal, one based on reading and another on picture study. A search of the school library produced several copies of a reference book containing a section on "Community Life." She decided to make an assignment from it for one small group; this would include a teacher-directed learning activity based on picture study, followed by an art activity designed to produce illustrations. Children would discuss pictures of community life and then draw their own pictures of community activities. Another small group, composed of learners capable of reading independently, would be assigned a silent reading in the

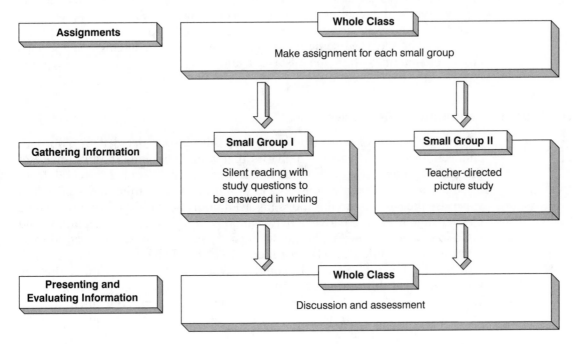

FIGURE 9.2
Ms. Baxter's reading group plan

textbook based on "Meeting Needs in Communities." She would provide these children with a short list of study questions to guide their reading, and would call on them to share their answers with the class at the close of the information-gathering period.

Ms. Baxter learned a great deal about group management skills as a result of the lesson. She had suggested that the small group with the independent reading assignment spend 15 minutes on it. In her concern that children develop habits of self-direction, she had reminded them to observe the time by referring to the clock and to pace their reading by it. But she had become so engrossed in the picture-study activity in the second small group that she herself had failed to watch the time. She suddenly became aware that the children in the other small group either had completed their reading assignment or had completely lost interest in it.

She managed to get the members of the reading group together again, and they sat quietly. But by that time, several children in the small group with whom she had spent her time had also become restless and noisy. It was obvious that many of them had not prepared the assigned illustration. She decided to not have children present their information. Instead, she conducted a whole-class discussion and assessment, during which everyone made suggestions for improvement.

That evening, Ms. Baxter reflected on what had happened. She realized that her procedure had been faulty. In the first place, she had not provided adequate supervision for the small group of independent readers. She had also failed to pace the lesson well. From this reflection and self-appraisal, it is clear that Ms. Baxter had learned some important lessons about managing small groups and would not make the same mistakes again.

Ms. Baxter's Culminating Activities

After several days of work-study activities, Ms. Baxter decided to plan with children for creative learning activities that would conclude the first phase of the unit of study, "Learning About Communities." She decided to schedule 40 to 50 minutes for these lessons, as she would need more time to organize and supervise the various small groups involved in the activities. Having the whole class engage in each creative activity would be too time consuming and would not allow children to concentrate on the activities that most appealed to their interests and abilities. Ms. Baxter recognized the challenge of managing several small groups, all of which would be working at the same time. But she recognized that this approach would permit her to assess individual children on such criteria as skill development and personal–social adjustment as they participated in small-group activities. It would also give her an opportunity to observe which children worked well together.

She referred to her sketch plan (presented in Chapter 6) for the concluding activities she had anticipated using. With these ideas as guidelines, Ms. Baxter and her students planned the following performance exhibits as a culmination of the first phase of the unit:

1. Prepare a bulletin board display of "Communities Across Our Country."
2. Create illustrated stories of people working together in a community.
3. Paint a mural showing how our community provides for the four basic needs of its citizens.
4. Make wall charts with short explanatory statements on major inventions that have changed communities.
5. Develop dramatizations about a family preparing to move to a new community.
6. Plan a quiz program based on answering the following questions:
   What streets, parks, schools, and public buildings are named for community people?
   Who were some of the most famous persons who ever visited our town?
   How did the people who first settled here earn their living?
   Do people still do these things for a living today?
   Who were the most unusual and most interesting early settlers in our community? Why?

Figure 9.3 presents Ms. Baxter's management plan for lessons based on these concluding activities.

Ms. Baxter's management plan worked satisfactorily. Ms. Ginsburg, the school principal, observed several of the activities and praised Ms. Baxter for her careful plan. She also encouraged Ms. Baxter to participate in an upcoming staff development workshop on cooperative learning. Ms. Ginsburg suggested that Ms. Baxter read an article on this approach to learning prior to the workshop, providing her with a copy of the article.

Large- and Small-Group Instruction: Intermediate Grades

At the intermediate-grade level, students should be accustomed to working in small groups to accomplish various learning tasks. However, it would be dangerous for you to make the assumption that they necessarily are skillful at working in small groups. Before attempting small-group work, you should assess carefully students' ability to perform well in a situation in which more than one instructional group is working at the same time. Your assessment may indicate that they need some skill training in this area before you can successfully expect to use multilevel instruction.

Although there has been much criticism of "textbook teaching," it is often true that instruction at the intermediate-grade level is highly oriented to textbooks. Children enter the middle grades with a range of reading abilities, but textbooks are geared to the average reader. Furthermore, there is heavier reliance than in the primary grades on printed material as a means of learning subject matter and related skills in social studies, literature, science, and mathematics. Thus, students must be able to read to be able to

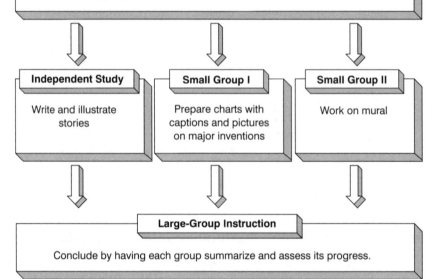

First Day

Large-Group Instruction

1. Organize whole class for activities.
2. Conduct discussion on learning activities that will help us conclude our study. Review information gathered from previous reading, picture study, interviews, and previous class discussion.
3. Teacher records children's suggestions in appropriate categories.
4. Final story contains summary statements on topic.
5. Record on unit chart.
6. Assess work and plan for tomorrow's activities.

Second Day

Small-Group Instruction

1. Organize as a whole class. Have children locate in their assigned small group to begin work.
2. Three small groups will work as follows:

Independent Study

Write and illustrate stories

Small Group I

Prepare charts with captions and pictures on major inventions

Small Group II

Work on mural

Large-Group Instruction

Conclude by having each group summarize and assess its progress.

Second-day management plan followed until small-group activities are completed. These activities interspersed with the following plan:

On Following Days

Modified Large-Group Instruction

1. Keep large group together.
2. Have children in groups of 3–5 dramatize a scene of a family preparing to move to a new community with other children as an audience.
3. Conduct a small-group TV quiz.

FIGURE 9.3
Ms. Baxter's group management plan

learn. It is fair to say that reading is the predominant learning mode for students at this and subsequent grade levels. This is a concern to those educators who know that children's interest in school begins to decline appreciably during the intermediate grades. We return to an earlier observation (Chapter 8): Student interest is directly related to the teacher's skill in providing a variety of motivating and engaging learning activities. Teachers who rely entirely on reading as a learning mode are restricting the avenues of learning available to students.

Mr. Bond knew this, and therefore was determined to provide his class with a variety of learning activities, even in the face of the school principal's admonition that children must learn the essentials set forth in their textbooks. He also appreciated the difficulty inherent in the fact that problems, topics, and themes presented in the intermediate-grade curriculum are far more abstract than those at the primary-grade level. This, he knew, is as typical in mathematics as it is in the social studies. He concluded that, under these constraints, the best way for him to proceed would be to base his program on information learning and to attempt to provide students with extended learning activities in language and creative experiences—activities offering concrete, personalized learning opportunities. Let us return to his earlier planning for his social studies unit (presented in Chapter 6) to learn how well he succeeded.

Mr. Bond's First Social Studies Lesson

Mr. Bond began by explaining to his students that he was interested in learning about their experiences in social studies during the previous year. Then he proceeded with questions he had planned for this assessment. He learned several important facts as a result of the discussion:

1. The children were fairly skilled in group discussion. They talked in turn, listened attentively, and seemed to respect each other's responses. He concluded that part of this might be because, almost without exception, the class was intact from last year. He also surmised that their teacher had been somewhat successful in building a feeling of group spirit.

2. He concluded that children had been largely restricted to assign–read–discuss–write learning activities. Some students said they enjoyed reading about the history and geography of their region, but they disliked "always having to discuss it and then write it out." Several others said they "got tired of taking so many tests" on it. Others said they were "tired of always having to read something."

3. Their responses to his question, "Why do you think it is important for us to study the United States and the other Americas?" were highly diversified, but most children had a strong degree of interest in the topic. Mr. Bond considered this to be a positive factor. It would be largely up to him to find ways to sustain their interest.

The activities he used to introduce the children to the basic textbook convinced him that they had received very little instruction in *study skills*. Their former teachers had likely made teacher-directed study assignments. Students' reference skills seemed weak. There were, however, five or six children who always had the correct responses to his directions and questions. The majority of the group made serious efforts to respond and seemed to be interested in what he was asking them to do. He observed an unresponsive group of four children who spent most of the time whispering to each other.

Mr. Bond learned that he had planned too many activities for a single lesson. He did not have time for the last part of the lesson, when he had hoped to ask the class to match pictures of landforms with their probable locations on the regional map. Nor did he arrive at the place in the lesson at which he had planned an assignment for the next day. Instead, he asked children for their comments about their textbook. He concluded that they were impressed by its colorful layout and study aids. He decided to continue where he had left off in the plan the following day. During the next few days, he would assess children's ability to read in the social studies, a content field that would introduce many new terms and concepts and that would require them to develop a number of map and study skills.

Making Provisions for Variability in Reading Levels

Mr. Bond realized the importance of teaching reading in a content field such as social studies. He knew that although students had learned certain skills during regular reading instruction, he must review these skills—and reteach them, if needed—in the social studies unit. His plan for meeting the reading needs of the students follows and is diagrammed in Figure 9.4.

1. Continue with the whole class in directed study of the textbook. His purpose was to have students acquire selected map and study skills while introducing them to a few major concepts about the geography, climate, and resources of the Americas.

2. Children with the reading skills needed for independent study of the basic textbook would be assigned to one large reading group. This included three fourths of the class. He would follow the excellent suggestions contained in the teacher's manual for helping children to read effectively. The remainder of the class would be assigned to a second group, which would occasionally do directed reading of the basic textbook and at other times would read in selected reference books. These books would treat parallel topics, written at a less sophisticated conceptual level and with a simpler vocabulary. Because the range of reading ability in the second group clustered around an early second- to a late third-grade level, he would need to change his approach and to adjust materials for them.

Because Mr. Bond had limited experience in actually managing children in small groups, he determined to proceed carefully and to avoid a large number of small groups, at least until he established his management of the whole

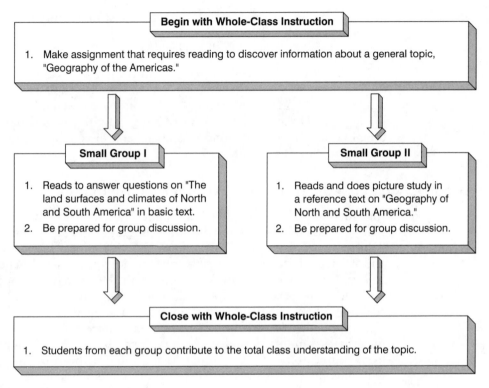

FIGURE 9.4
Mr. Bond's group plan for social studies

class. With this model in mind, Mr. Bond tentatively identified other approaches to provide meaningful reading experiences for the class:

For Small Group I

To individualize learning:

1. Have students use research references, encyclopedias, the Internet, etc., to enrich reading in their textbook.
2. Suggest picture study by individual children.
3. Have class read selected fiction related to topic.
4. Have children read newspapers and other journals.

For Small Group II

To provide variety in learning:

1. Use teacher-directed oral reading of the textbook.
2. Encourage picture study on a group basis.

3. Have children read silently in references that contain suitable concept and vocabulary load.
4. Teacher should read orally to group.

Mr. Bond felt the need to provide individualized reading experiences for the children in Small Group I especially, because their reading differences ranged from a late fourth-grade level to a few who could read at the tenth-grade level. His guidance during reading activities would have to focus on Small Group II, but Mr. Bond was aware that he could not neglect the other small group in this respect.

Providing Additional Opportunities to Gather Information

Intermediate-grade-level teachers sometimes tend to equate research with reading, but children may gather information in numerous other ways, using field trips, the Internet, films, filmstrips, videotapes, interviews, television, and related photographs. At the intermediate-grade level, where children's ability to read varies more widely than in the primary grades, these additional learning resources offer children from the lowest to the highest level of reading achievement opportunities to work together in a small group assigned to gather information. Some children may not read very well but can, nonetheless, interpret and make inferences based on information obtained from sources other than reading. Using multimedia provides these learners with the opportunity to become contributing members of the group.

Mr. Bond planned to vary the membership of Small Groups I and II from time to time. This made it possible for children who had difficulty reading to gather information through learning resources not dependent on reading ability. He could still apply his basic model for group management—he only needed to change the membership of the subgroups. This provision is important for the psychological support of the less capable reader.

Mr. Bond's Culminating Activities

Mr. Bond's sketch plan included activities that were to occur in the language arts and creative arts classes. They were intended to personalize instruction for children and to make social studies more meaningful to them. Mr. Bond decided to have children engage in the following variety of extended learning activities:

1. Visit the school library and locate information (reading materials and other media) on the geography of the Americas.
2. Prepare artwork illustrating landforms and vegetation types that are characteristic of the natural regions of the Americas.
3. Prepare oral reports to present basic learning. These will include results of interviews on how physical features affect how people live and work in the community.
4. Use artwork to illustrate major learning, including illustrations and maps of the regions studied.

LEARNING FROM ASSIGNMENTS AND HOMEWORK

An *assignment* is a statement of *what* the student is to accomplish—to do. Assignments, whether completed at home or at school, can ease student learning in many ways, but when poorly planned they can be discouraging to students as well as upsetting to an entire family. *Homework* can be defined as any out-of-class task assigned students as an extension of classroom learning. Like all else that you do as a professional teacher, it is your professional responsibility to think about and plan carefully any and all homework assignments that you give to children. This includes thinking about how you would feel were you given the assignment and about how much out-of-class time you expect the assignment to take.[18]

Plan early and thoughtfully the types of assignments you will give (e.g., daily and long-range; minor and major; in class or at home, or both; individual, paired, or group), and prepare assignment specifications. Assignments must correlate with specific instructional objectives. *Never* give assignments as busy-work or as punishment. Let students know the purpose of each assignment. The purpose, for example, might be to prepare them for what is to come in class, or to practice what they have learned in class, or to extend the learning of class activities and perhaps even to involve family members.[19]

Avoid assignments that could pose a safety hazard for children. Use caution in giving assignments that could be controversial. If you think an assignment might be controversial it is probably best to avoid giving it. At least, talk it over with your colleagues or principal before deciding. Further, avoid any assignment you would not be willing to do yourself. Think carefully before making *any* assignment. For example, one third-grade teacher planned a lesson to study flowers. In preparation, and as children's assignment for the next day, she told each child to bring a flower to class. As you might expect, several children got their flowers the next morning by "borrowing them" from the garden of a home adjacent to the school. The angry homeowner phoned the principal with a loud and not uncertain complaint about the children's behavior. You must always think carefully *before* giving children any assignment, and this thinking should occur during the preactive phase of instruction, rather than during the active phase.

Provide differentiated, tiered, or optional assignments—assignment variations you give to students or that they select on the basis of their interests and learning capacities.[20] Students can select or be assigned different activities to accomplish the same objective, such as read and discuss, or they can participate with others in a more direct learning experience. After their study, as a portion of the assignment, students share what they have learned. This is an example of *multilevel instruction*.

The time beyond school students need to complete assignments will vary according to grade level and school policy. There is always debate about the value of homework, especially for the elementary grades.[21] A generally accepted rule of thumb for the time a homework assignment is to take a child to do is what is often referred to as the *Ten Minute Rule*, about 10 minutes per grade level: that is, 10 minutes for a first grader, 20 minutes for a second grader, 30 minutes for a third grader, 40 minutes for a fourth grader, and so forth.

Teachers have found it beneficial to prepare individualized study guides with questions students may answer and activities they may do while reading textbook chapters as homework. One advantage of a study guide is that it can make reading a more than visual experience. Study guides can help to organize student learning by accenting instructional objectives, emphasizing important points to learn, providing a study guide for tests, and encouraging students to read homework assignments.

As a general rule, homework assignments should stimulate thinking by arousing children's curiosity, raising questions for further study, and encouraging and supporting the self-discipline required for independent study.

Determine the resources that students will need to complete assignments, and check the availability of these resources. This is important; you cannot expect students to use that which is unavailable to them. Many will not use any materials that are not readily available.

Avoid yelling out assignments as students are leaving your classroom. When giving assignments in class, you should write them on a special place on the writing board or give a copy to each student, or require students to write the assignment into their assignment folder, taking extra care to be sure that assignment specifications are clear and allowing time for students to ask questions about an assignment. It is important that your procedure for giving and collecting assignments be consistent throughout the school year. Try to avoid changing assignment specifications after students have received them; especially avoid changing them at the last minute. Last-minute changes frustrate students who have already completed the assignment and show little respect for these students.

Allow time in class for students to begin work on homework assignments, so you can give them individual attention (guided or coached practice). The benefits of this coached practice include being able to (1) monitor student work so that children do not go too far in a wrong direction, (2) help students reflect on their thinking, (3) assess the progress of individual students, and (4) discover or create a "teachable moment." For example, while monitoring students doing their work, you might discover a commonly shared student misconception. Taking advantage of this teachable moment, you then stop and talk about the misconception and attempt to clarify it.

It is well known from research studies that timely, constructive, and corrective feedback on homework—and the teacher's grading of homework—increases student achievement. If the assignment is important for children to do, then you must give your full and immediate attention to the product of their efforts. Read almost everything that your students write. Students are much more willing to do homework when they believe it is useful, when you treat it as an integral part of instruction, when you read and evaluate it, and when it counts as part of their grade.

Provide feedback about each student's work, and be positive and constructive in your comments. Always think about your written comments and try to ensure that they convey your intended message, rather than an unwanted, hidden one. When writing comments on student papers, consider using a color other than red, such as green or blue. Although to you this may sound unimportant, to many people, red carries a host of negative connotations (e.g., blood, hurt, danger, stop), and students often perceive its use as punitive.

Since not all children have the advantage of having home computers with printers, you must avoid the temptation of awarding higher grades to students who turn in homework papers that have been printed at home.

Rather than grading by giving a percentage or numerical grade, with its negative connotations, many teachers sometimes prefer to score assignments with constructive and reinforcing comments and symbols they have created for this purpose.

You must attend to the development of students' reading, listening, speaking, and writing skills. Attention to these skills must also be obvious in your assignment specifications and your assignment grading policy. Reading is crucial to the development of a person's ability to write. For example, to foster high-order thinking, students in any subject can and should be encouraged to write, or draw representations of, their thoughts and feelings about material they have read.

Strategies for Student Recovery

Although it is important to encourage students to make good initial efforts sometimes, for a multitude of reasons, a student's first effort is inadequate or is lacking entirely. Perhaps the student is absent from school without legitimate excuse, or the student does poorly on an assignment or fails to turn in an assignment on time or at all. Although accepting late work from students is extra work for you, and although allowing the resubmission of a marked or tentatively graded paper increases your paperwork, many teachers report that it is worthwhile to give students opportunity for recovery and a day or so to make corrections and resubmit an assignment for an improved score. However, out of regard for students who do well from the start we advise you to think carefully and thoughtfully before allowing a resubmitted paper to receive a top mark (unless, of course, it was of top quality originally).

Some teachers and schools provide recovery methods that encourage students by recognizing both achievement and improvement on achievement reports and by providing students with second opportunities for success on assignments, although at some cost to encourage a good first effort.

Students sometimes have legitimate reasons for not completing an assignment by the due date. You should listen and exercise professional judgment in each instance. As someone once said, there is nothing democratic about treating unequals as equals. The provision of recovery options seems a sensible scholastic tactic.

A downfall for some beginning teachers is that they become buried under mounds of student homework to read and mark, leaving them less and less time for effective planning. To keep this from happening to you, consider the following suggestions. Although you should read almost everything that students write, you can read papers with varying degrees of intensity and scrutiny depending on the purpose of the assignment. For assignments that are designed for learning, understanding, and practice, you can allow students to check them themselves using either self-checking or peer-checking, during which you can walk around the room, monitor activity, and record whether a student did the assignment or not, or, after the checking, you can collect the papers and do your recording. Besides reducing the amount of paperwork for you, student self- or peer-checking provides other advantages: (1) it allows students to see and understand their errors, (2) it encourages productive peer dialogue, and (3) it helps them develop self-assessment techniques and standards. If the purpose of the assignment is to assess mastery competence, then only you should read, mark, and grade the papers.

SUMMARY

This chapter has continued the development of your repertoire of teaching strategies. As you know, children can be quite peer conscious, can have relatively short attention spans for experiences they are uninterested in, and prefer active experiences that engage many or all of their senses. Most are intensely curious about things of interest to them. Cooperative learning, student-centered projects, and teaching strategies that emphasize shared discovery and inquiry within a psychologically safe environment encourage the most positive aspects of thinking and learning. Central to your strategy selection should be those that encourage children to become independent thinkers and skilled learners who can help in planning, structuring, regulating, and assessing their own learning and learning activities.

The experiences of Ms. Baxter and Mr. Bond can provide us with useful insights in how to deploy children for classroom instruction. It is significant to note that both of these teachers were constantly alert to the dynamics going on around them and adjusted their instructional plans accordingly. This reinforces the teacher's role as a *decision maker*. Once again, we stress the importance of the teacher's *judgment* in making those decisions. A decision resulting from the exercise of poor professional judgment could have long-lasting adverse consequences.

These examples also dramatically illustrate how pervasive language and communication skills are in the elementary school curriculum. As we see the curriculum emerge in Ms. Baxter's and Mr. Bond's classrooms, we are reminded of the holistic nature of language. Children listen to their teacher's oral instruction. They read material to gain information. They share ideas with their classmates. They write responses or reactions to assignments.

Perhaps they read what they or their classmates have written. There is a constant reliance on language use in these classrooms, and Ms. Baxter and Mr. Bond use these language-rich settings to help children refine, sharpen, and use their language skills and abilities with even greater clarity and precision.

Finally, we call attention to the social context of learning in these classrooms. The social setting of the classroom provides teachers with marvelous opportunities to teach the social and group skills required for social life. It is not only that children learn cooperatively but that they also *live* cooperatively. Nearly all of their lives will be spent with other human beings. Whatever problems, frustrations, pleasures, satisfactions, or stresses they experience in life will doubtless flow from their ability (or inability) to relate in satisfactory ways to other human beings. Thus, the lessons children learn about social relationships not only contribute to their effectiveness as democratic citizens but also to their own mental health and happiness as effective human beings.

You have reached the end of this text. We, the authors of this book, wish you the very best in your new career.

STUDY QUESTIONS AND ADDITIONAL ACTIVITIES

1. Why did Ms. Baxter and Mr. Bond change their classes from whole group to small-group instruction over a period of several days rather than on a single day?

2. What classroom activities are particularly well suited to a whole-class configuration? Which ones are best for small groups? In both, explain why.

3. What criteria did Ms. Baxter and Mr. Bond apply in evaluating the effectiveness of their small-group instructional endeavors?

4. When assessing products of group work, presumably a cooperative effort, teachers may want to give the same grade to all participants or may grade each one's contribution separately. Which method is likely to encourage improved study habits? Which method are students likely to perceive as being fairer? What do the cooperative learning specialists have to say about this issue?

5. What would you consider an "unwise grouping" of children? What ill effects might result from such an unwise grouping?

6. It is an aphorism that to learn something well students need time to practice it. There is a difference, however, between solitary practice and coached or guided practice. Describe the difference and the conditions where you would use each.

7. Divide into teams of four, and have each team develop one learning center. Set up and share the learning centers in your classroom.

8. Does saying that a student is "on task" necessarily imply that the student is mentally engaged? Is it possible for a student to be mentally engaged

although not on task? If so, explain ways the teacher might help the child become on task and mentally engaged. Explain your answers.

9. Identify and describe instructional strategies that encourage students to become independent thinkers and skilled learners. How, specifically, can teachers determine when children have for their age become such thinkers and learners?

10. Find out and report to others in your class what guidelines for homework are used by schools in your local area for each grade level, kindergarten through sixth grade.

NOTES

1. See, for example, R. L. Canady and M. D. Rettig, "Block Scheduling: The Key to Quality Learning Time," *Principal* 80(3): 30–34 (2001).

2. J. M. Carroll, "The Copernican Plan Evaluated," *Phi Delta Kappan* 76(2): 105–113 (1994).

3. See B. Bloom, *Human Characteristics and School Learning* (New York: McGraw-Hill, 1987), and J. Carroll, "A Model of School Learning," *Teachers College Record* 64(8): 723–733 (1963).

4. See J. Battistini, *From Theory to Practice: Classroom Application of Outcome-Based Education* (Bloomington, IN: ERIC Clearinghouse on Reading, English, and Communication, 1995).

5. T. L. Good and J. E. Brophy, *Looking in Classrooms*, 9th ed. (New York: Addison Wesley Longman, 2003), 318.

6. See D. M. Ogle, "K-W-L: A Teaching Model That Develops Active Reading of Expository Text," *The Reading Teacher* 39(6): 564–570 (1986). See also J. Bryan, "K-W-L: Questioning the Known," *The Reading Teacher* 51(7): 618–620 (1998).

7. Source of POSSE: C. S. Englert and T. V. Mariage, "Making Students Partners in the Comprehension Process: Organizing the Reading 'POSSE'," *Learning Disability Quarterly* 14(1): 23–138 (1991). Source of PQRST: E. B. Kelly, *Memory Enhancement for Educators*, Fastback 365 (Bloomington, IN: Phi Delta Kappa Educational Foundation, 1994), 18. Source of QAR: H. A. E.

Mesmer and E. J. Hutchins, "Using QARs with Charts and Graphs," *Reading Teacher* 56(1): 21–27 (2002). Source of RAP: J. B. Schumaker et al., *The Paraphrasing Strategy* (Lawrence, KS: Edge Enterprises, 1984). Source of SQ3R: F. P. Robinson, *Effective Study* (rev. ed.), New York: Harper & Brothers, 1961). The original source of SQ4R is unknown. For SRQ2R, see M. L. Walker, "Help for the 'Fourth-Grade Slump'—SRQ2R plus Instruction in Text Structure or Main Idea," *Reading Horizons* 36(1): 38–58 (1995). About reciprocal teaching, T. L. Good and J. E. Brophy, *Looking in Classrooms*, 9th ed. (New York: Addison Wesley Longman, 2003), 426–429.

8. See, for example, D. Fuchs et al., "K-Pals: Helping Kindergartners with Reading Readiness," *Teaching Exceptional Children* 33(4): 76–80 (2001).

9. See, for example, R. B. Schneider and D. Barone, "Cross-Age Tutoring," *Childhood Education* 73(3): 136–143 (1997) and D. Krueger and B. Braun, "Books and Buddies: Peers Tutoring Peers," *The Reading Teacher* 52(4): 410–414 (December 1998–January 1999).

10. See, for example, K. H. Barclay and C. Breheny, "Letting the Children Take Over More of Their Own Learning: Collaborative Research in the Kindergarten Classroom," *Young Children* 49(6): 33–39 (1994).

11. L. Vygotsky, *Thought and Language* (Cambridge, MA: MIT Press, 1926).

12. See, for example, J. D. Laney et al., "The Effect of Cooperative and Mastery Learning Methods on Primary Grade Students' Learning and Retention of Economic Concepts," *Early Education and Development* 7(3): 253–274 (1996), and J. R. Lampe et al., "Effects of Cooperative Learning Among Hispanic Students in Elementary Social Studies," *Journal of Educational Research* 89(3): 187–191 (1996).

13. See L. S. Walters, "Four Leading Models," *Harvard Education Letter* 16(3): 5 (2000).

14. J. W. Astington, "Theory of Mind Goes to School," *Educational Leadership* 56(3): 46–48 (November 1998).

15. Good and Brophy, *Looking in Classrooms*, 284.

16. See S. Kagan, "Group Grades Miss the Mark," *Educational Leadership* 52(8): 68–71 (1995), and D. W. Johnson and R. T. Johnson, "The Role of Cooperative Learning in Assessing and Communicating Student Learning," Chapter 4 in T. R. Guskey (Ed.), *Communicating Student Learning*, ASCD Yearbook (Alexandria, VA: Association for Supervision and Curriculum Development, 1996).

17. A. C. Ornstein, "Synthesis of Research: Teaching Whole-Group Classrooms," *Peabody Journal of Education* 70(2): 104–116 (1995).

18. See the several articles about the pros and cons of homework in the April 2001 issue of *Educational Leadership* (volume 58, number 7). See also J. Franklin, "Enough Already? Questioning Homework for Young Children," *Curriculum Update* 5 (2001).

19. A useful reference for teachers and parents/guardians is M. C. Radencich and J. S. Schumm, *How to Help Your Child with Homework: Every Caring Parents' Guide to Encouraging Good Study Habits and Ending the Homework Wars (for Parents of Children Ages 6–13)*, rev. ed. (Minneapolis, MN: Free Spirit, 1997).

20. See, for example, M. H. Sullivan and P. V. Sequeira, "The Impact of Purposeful Homework on Learning," *Clearing House* 69(6): 346–348 (1996).

21. See, for example, S. Black, "The Truth About Homework," *American School Board Journal* 183(10): 48–51 (1996).

FOR FURTHER PROFESSIONAL STUDY

Bergen, D. "Differentiating Curriculum with Technology-Enhanced Class Projects." *Childhood Education* 78(2): 117–118 (Winter 2001–2002).

Cavazos, L. F. "Emphasizing Performance Goals and High-Quality Education for All Students." *Phi Delta Kappan* 83(9): 690–697 (2002).

Curtis, D. "The Power of Projects." *Educational Leadership* 60(1): 50–53 (2002).

Diffily, D. "Project-Based Learning: Meeting Social Studies Standards and the Needs of Gifted Learners." *Gifted Child Today Magazine* 25(3): 4–43, 59 (2002).

Ford, M. P. and Opitz, M. F. "Using Centers To Engage Children During Guided Reading Time: Intensifying Learning Time Away from the Teacher." *The Reading Teacher* 55(8): 710–717 (2002).

Franklin, J. "The Art of Differentiation." *Education Update* 44(2): 1, 3, 8 (2002).

Fredrick, L. D., Keel, M. C., and Neel, J. H. "Making the Most of Instructional Time: Teaching Reading at an Accelerated Rate to Students at Risk." *Journal of Direct Instruction* 2(1): 57–63 (2002).

Griffin, M. L. "Why Don't You Use Your Finger? Paired Reading in First Grade." *Reading Teacher* 55(8): 766–774 (2002).

Hamm, M. and Adams, D. "Collaborative Inquiry: Working Toward Shared Goals." *Kappa Delta Pi Record* 38(3): 115–118 (2002).

Hart, T. "From Mediocrity to Mastery: Finding the Patterns of Knowledge." *Educational Horizons* 80(2): 77–82 (2002).

Hoeck-Buehler, S. "Let's Play Tag! A Technique for Successful Mixed-Ability Group Reading." *Reading Teacher* 54(5): 477–478 (2001).

King, C. M., and Parent Johnson, L. M. "Constructing Meaning via Reciprocal Teaching." *Reading Research and Instruction* 38(3): 169–186 (1999).

Laney, J. D. "A Sample Lesson in Economics for Primary Students: How Cooperative and Mastery Learning Methods Can Enhance Social Studies Teaching." *Social Studies* 90(4): 152–158 (1999).

Lederhouse, J. N. "The Power of One-on-One." *Educational Leadership* 60(7): 69–71 (2003).

Leonard, J., and McElroy, K. "What One Middle School Teacher Learned About Cooperative Learning." *Journal of Research in Childhood Education* 14(2): 239–245 (2000).

Lotan, R. A. "Group-Worthy Tasks." *Educational Leadership* 60(6): 72–75 (2003).

Marzano, R. J.; Pickering, D. J., and Pollock, J. E. "Cooperative Learning." In: *Classroom Instruction That Works*, pp. 84–91. Alexandria, VA: Association for Supervision and Curriculum Development, 2001.

Motamedi, V., and Sumrall, W. J. "Mastery Learning and Contemporary Issues in Education." *Action in Teacher Education* 22(1): 32–42 (2000).

Nussbaum, E. M. "The Process of Becoming a Participant in Small-Group Critical Discussions: A Case Study." *Journal of Adolescent & Adult Literacy* 45(6): 488–497 (2002).

O'Day, S. "Creative Drama Through Scaffolded Plays in the Language Arts Classroom." *Primary Voices K–6* 9(4): 20–25 (2001).

Pilger, M. A. *Multicultural Projects Index: Things to Make and Do To Celebrate Festivals, Cultures, and Holidays Around the World*, 2nd ed. Englewood, CO: Libraries Unlimited, 1998.

Rillero, P.; Gonzalez-Jensen, M.; and Moy, T. "Moon Watch: A Parental-Involvement Homework Activity." *Science Activities* 36(4): 11–15 (2000).

Rothberg, M. "Re-Enactment of the Ellis Island Experience with Sugartown Elementary School." *School Library Media Activities Monthly* 14(5): 27–28 (1998).

Schniedewind, N., and Davidson, E. "Differentiating Cooperative Learning." *Educational Leadership* 59(1): 24–27 (2000).

Smutny, J. F. *Differentiated Instruction*. Fastback 506. Bloomington, IN: Phi Delta Kappa Educational Foundation, 2003.

Stevens, B. A. and Tollafield, A. "Creating Comfortable and Productive Parent/Teacher Conferences." *Phi Delta Kappan* 84(7): 521–524 (2003).

Stright, A. D. and Supplee, L. H. "Children's Self-Regulatory Behaviors During Teacher-Directed, Seat-Work, and Small-Group Instructional Contexts." *Journal of Educational Research* 95(4): 235–244 (2002).

Vail, K. "Homework Problems: How Much Is Too Much?" *American School Board Journal* 188(4): 24–29 (2001).

Walberg, H. J., and Paik, S. J. *Effective Educational Practices*. Educational Practices Series 3. Brussels, Belgium: International Academy of Education, 2000.

Walters, L. S. "Putting Cooperative Learning to the Test." *Harvard Education Letter* 16(3): 1–5 (2000).

Williams, K. R. "Clean Chemistry: Entertaining and Educational Activities with Soap Bubbles." *Journal of Chemical Education* 79(10): 1168–1169 (2002). Note: This article is useful for teaching young children as well as older children and adults.

Zimmerman, J. "How Much Does Time Affect Learning?" *Principal* 80(3): 6–11 (2001).

Glossary

ability grouping The assignment of students to separate classrooms or to separate activities within a classroom according to their perceived academic abilities. *Homogeneous grouping* is the grouping of students of similar abilities, while *heterogeneous grouping* is the grouping of students of mixed abilities. See also *tracking*.

accommodation The cognitive process of modifying a schema or creating new schemata.

accountability Reference to the concept that an individual is responsible for his or her behaviors and should be able to demonstrate publicly the worth of the activities carried out.

active learning See *hands-on learning*.

adolescence the period of life from the onset of puberty to maturity terminating legally at the age of majority, generally the ages of 12 to 20, although young or early adolescence may start as soon as age 9.

advance organizer Preinstructional cues that encourage a mental set, used to enhance retention of materials to be studied.

affective domain The area of learning related to interests, attitudes, feelings, values, and personal adjustment.

alternative assessment Assessment of learning in ways that are different from traditional paper-and-pencil objective testing, such as a portfolio, project, or self-assessment. See *authentic assessment*.

anticipatory set See *advance organizer*.

articulation Term used when referring to the connectedness of the various components of the formal curriculum. *Vertical articulation* is used when referring to the connectedness of the curriculum K–12; *horizontal articulation* refers to the connectedness across a grade level.

assessment The relatively neutral process of finding out what students are learning or have learned as a result of instruction. See also *evaluation*.

assignment A statement telling the student what he or she is to accomplish.

assimilation The cognitive process by which a learner integrates new information into an existing schema.

at risk General term given to a student who shows a high potential for not completing school.

authentic assessment The use of evaluation procedures (usually portfolios and projects) that are highly compatible with the instructional objectives. Also referred to as *accurate, active, aligned, alternative, direct,* and *performance assessment*.

behavioral objective A statement of expectation describing what the learner should be able to do upon completion of the instruction. See also *curriculum standards*.

behaviorism A theory that equates learning with changes in observable behavior.

block scheduling The school programming procedure that provides large blocks of time (e.g., 2 hours) in which individual teachers or teacher teams can organize and arrange groupings of students for varied periods of time, thereby more effectively individualizing the instruction for students with various needs and abilities.

brainstorming An instructional strategy used to create a flow of new ideas, during which judgments of the ideas of others are forbidden.

CD-ROM (compact disc-read only memory) Digitally encoded information (up to 650 MB of data that can include animation, audio, graphics, text, and video) permanently recorded on a compact (4.72 inch or 12 cm in diameter) disc.

character education Focuses on the development of the values of honesty, kindness, respect, and responsibility.

classroom control The process of influencing student behavior in the classroom.

classroom management The teacher's system of establishing a climate for learning, including techniques for preventing and handling student misbehavior.

closure In a lesson, the means by which a teacher brings the lesson to an end.

coaching   See *mentoring*.

cognition   The process of thinking.

cognitive disequilibrium   The mental state of not yet having made sense out of a perplexing (discrepant) situation.

cognitive domain   The area of learning related to intellectual skills, such as retention and assimilation of knowledge.

cognitive psychology   A branch of psychology devoted to the study of how individuals acquire, process, and use information.

cognitivism   A theory that holds that learning entails the construction or reshaping of mental schemata and that mental processes mediate learning. Also known as *constructivism*.

common planning time   A regularly scheduled time during the school day when teachers who teach the same students meet for joint planning, parent conferences, materials preparation, and student evaluation.

competency-based instruction   See *performance-based instruction*.

comprehension   A level of cognition that refers to the skill of understanding.

computer-assisted instruction (CAI)   Instruction received by a student when interacting with lessons programmed into a computer system. Known also as *computer-assisted learning* (CAL).

computer literacy   The ability at some level on a continuum to understand and use computers.

computer-managed instruction (CMI)   The use of a computer system to manage information about learner performance and learning-resources options in order to prescribe and control individual lessons.

constructivism   See *cognitivism*.

continuous progress   An instructional procedure that allows students to progress at their own pace through a sequenced curriculum.

convergent thinking   Thinking that is directed to a preset conclusion.

cooperative learning   A genre of instructional strategies that use small groups of students working together and helping each other on learning tasks, stressing support for one another rather than competition.

core curriculum   Subject or discipline components of the curriculum considered as being absolutely necessary. Traditionally these are English/language arts, mathematics, science, and social science.

covert behavior   A learner behavior that is not outwardly observable.

criterion   A standard by which behavioral performance is judged.

criterion-referenced assessment   Assessment in which standards are established and behaviors are judged against the preset guidelines, rather than against the behaviors of others.

critical thinking   The ability to recognize and identify problems and discrepancies, to propose and to test solutions, and to arrive at tentative conclusions based on the data collected.

curriculum   Originally derived from a Latin term referring to a race course for the chariots, the term still has no widely accepted definition. As used in this text, curriculum is that which is planned and encouraged for teaching and learning. This includes both school and nonschool environments, overt (formal) and hidden (informal) curriculums, and broad as well as narrow notions of content—its development, acquisition, and consequences.

curriculum standards   Statements of the essential knowledge, skills, and attitudes to be learned.

deductive learning   Learning that proceeds from the general to the specific. See also *expository learning*.

detracking   An effort to minimize or eliminate separate classes or programs for students according to their differing abilities.

developmental characteristics   A set of common intellectual, psychological, physical, and social characteristics that, when considered as a whole, indicate an individual's development relative to others during a particular age span.

developmental needs   A set of needs unique and appropriate to the developmental characteristics of a particular age span.

diagnostic assessment   See *preassessment*.

didactic teaching   See *direct instruction*.

differentiated instruction   The modification of curriculum content, process, or product based on formal or informal assessment of a student's readiness, interests, and personal profile. See also *individualized learning*.

direct experience   Learning by doing (applying) that which is being learned.

direct instruction   Teacher-centered instruction, typically with the entire class, and where the teacher controls student attention and behaviors as opposed to permitting students greater control over their own learning and behaviors.

direct intervention   Teacher use of verbal reminders or verbal commands to redirect student behavior, as opposed to nonverbal gestures or cues.

direct teaching See *direct instruction*.

discipline The process of controlling student behavior in the classroom. The term has been largely replaced by the terms *classroom control* or *classroom management*. It is also used in reference to the subject taught (e.g., language arts, science, mathematics, and so forth).

discovery learning Learning that proceeds from identification of a problem, through the development of hypotheses, the testing of the hypotheses, and the arrival at a conclusion. See also *critical thinking*.

divergent thinking Thinking that expands beyond original thought.

downshifting Reverting to earlier learned, lower cognitive level behaviors.

DVD (digital versatile disc) Like CD-ROMS but with a much greater storage capacity.

early adolescence The developmental stage of young people as they approach and begin to experience puberty. This stage usually occurs between 10 and 14 years of age and deals with the successful attainment of the developmental characteristics typical for this age span.

eclectic Using the best from a variety of sources.

effective school A school where students master basic skills, seek academic excellence in all subjects, demonstrate achievement, and display good behavior and attendance. Known also as *exemplary school*.

elective High-interest or special-needs courses that are based on student selection from various options.

elementary school Any school that has been planned and organized especially for children of some combination of grades kindergarten through 6. There are many variations, though; for example, a school might house children of preschool through grade 7 or 8 and still be called an elementary school.

empathy The ability to understand the feelings of another person.

equality Considered to be same in status or competency level.

equilibration The mental process of moving from disequilibrium to equilibrium.

equilibrium The balance between assimilation and accommodation.

equity Fairness and justice, with impartiality.

evaluation Like assessment, but includes making sense out of the assessment results, usually based on criteria or a rubric. Evaluation is more subjective than is assessment.

exemplary school See *effective school*.

exceptional child A child who deviates from the average in any of the following ways: mental characteristics, sensory ability, neuromotor or physical characteristics, social behavior, communication ability, or multiple handicaps. Also known as a *special-needs child* and *special education student*.

exploratory course A course designed to help students explore curriculum experiences based on their felt needs, interests, and abilities.

expository learning The traditional classroom instructional approach that proceeds as follows: presentation of information to the learners, reference to particular examples, and application of the information to the learner's experiences.

extended-year school Schools that have extended the school year calendar from the traditional 180 day to a longer period such as 200 days.

extrinsic motivators Motivation of learning by rewards outside of the learner, such as parent and teacher expectations, gifts, certificates, and grades.

facilitating behavior Teacher behavior that makes it possible for students to learn.

facilitative teaching See *indirect teaching*.

family See *school-within-a-school*.

feedback Information sent from the receiver to the originator that provides disclosure about the reception of the intended message.

formative assessment Evaluation of learning in progress.

goal, course A broad generalized statement about the expected outcomes of a course.

goal, educational A desired instructional outcome that is broad in scope.

goal, teacher A statement about what the teacher hopes to accomplish.

hands-on learning Learning by doing, or active learning.

heterogeneous grouping A grouping pattern that does not separate students into groups based on their intelligence, learning achievement, or physical characteristics.

high-stakes assessment An assessment is called *high stakes* if use of the assessment's results carry serious consequences, such as when a student's grade promotion rests on the student's performance on one test.

holistic learning Learning that incorporates emotions with thinking.

homogeneous grouping A grouping pattern that usually separates students into groups based on their intelligence, school achievement, or physical characteristics.

house See *school-within-a-school*.

inclusion The commitment to the education of each special-needs learner, to the maximum extent appropriate, in the school and classroom he or she would otherwise attend.

independent study An instructional strategy that allows a student to select a topic, set the goals, and work alone to attain them.

indirect teaching Student-centered teaching using discovery and inquiry instructional strategies.

individualized instruction See *individualized learning* and *differentiated instruction*.

individualized learning The self-paced process whereby individual students assume responsibility for learning through study, practice, feedback, and reinforcement with appropriately designed instructional packages or modules.

inductive learning Learning that proceeds from specifics to the general. See also *discovery learning*.

inquiry learning Like discovery learning, except here the learner designs the processes to be used in resolving the problem, thereby requiring higher levels of cognition.

instruction Planned arrangement of experiences to help a learner develop understanding and to achieve a desirable change in behavior.

instructional module Any freestanding instructional unit that includes these components: rationale, objectives, pretest, learning activities, comprehension checks with instructive feedback, and posttest.

integrated (interdisciplinary) curriculum Curriculum organization that combines subject matter traditionally taught separately.

interdisciplinary team An organizational pattern of two or more teachers representing different subject areas. The team shares the same students, schedule, areas of the school, and the opportunity for teaching more than one subject.

interdisciplinary thematic unit (ITU) A thematic unit that crosses boundaries of two or more disciplines.

intermediate grades Term sometimes used to refer to grades 4–6. An intermediate school, for example, is an elementary school that houses children of grades 4–6.

internalization The extent to which an attitude or value becomes a part of the learner. That is, without having to think about it, the learner's behavior reflects the attitude or value.

intervention A teacher's interruption to redirect a student's behavior, either by direct intervention (e.g., by a verbal command) or by indirect intervention (e.g., by eye contact or physical proximity).

intrinsic motivation Motivation of learning through the student's internal sense of accomplishment.

intuition Knowing without conscious reasoning.

leadership team A group of teachers and administrators, and sometimes students, designated by the principal or elected by the faculty (and student body) to assist in the leadership of the school.

lead teacher The member of a teaching team who is designated to facilitate the work and planning of that team.

learning The development of understandings and the change in behavior resulting from experiences. For different interpretations of learning, see *behaviorism* and *cognitivism*.

learning center (LC) An instructional strategy that utilizes activities and materials located at a special place in the classroom and that is designed to allow a student to work independently at his or her own pace to learn one area of content. See also *learning station*.

learning station Like a learning center, except that whereas each learning center is distinct and unrelated to others, learning stations are sequenced or in some way linked to one another.

learning modality The way a person receives information. Four modalities are recognized: visual, auditory, tactile (touch), and kinesthetic (movement).

learning resource center The central location in the school where instructional materials and media are stored, organized, and accessed by students and staff.

learning style The way a person learns best in a given situation.

looping An arrangement in which the cohort of students and teachers remain together as a group for several or for all the years a child is at a particular school. Also referred to as *multiyear grouping, multiyear instruction, multiyear placement,* and *teacher-student progression*.

magnet school A school that specializes in a particular academic area, such as science, mathematics and technology, the arts, or international relations. Also referred to as a *theme school*.

mainstreaming Placing an exceptional child in regular education classrooms for all (inclusion) or part (partial inclusion) of the school day.

mastery learning The concept that a student should master the content of one lesson before moving on to the content of the next.

measurement The process of collecting and interpreting data.

mentoring One-on-one coaching, tutoring, or guidance to facilitate learning.

metacognition The ability to plan, monitor, and evaluate one's own thinking.

middle grades Grades 5–8.

middle school A school that has been planned and organized especially for students of ages 10–14, and that generally has grades 5–8, with grades 6–8 being the most popular grade-span organization, although many varied patterns exist. For example, a school might include only grades 7 and 8 and still be called a middle school.

minds-on learning Learning in which the learner is intellectually active, thinking about what is being learned.

misconception Faulty understanding of a major idea or concept. Also known as a *naïve theory* and *conceptual misunderstanding*.

modeling The teacher's direct and indirect demonstration, by actions and by words, of the behaviors expected of students.

multicultural education A deliberate attempt to help students understand facts, generalizations, attitudes, and behaviors derived from their own ethnic roots as well as others. In this process students unlearn racism and biases and recognize the interdependent fabric of society, giving due acknowledgment for contributions made by its members.

multilevel teaching See *multitasking*.

multimedia The combined use of sound, video, and graphics for instruction.

multiple intelligences A theory of several different intelligences, as opposed to just one general intelligence; other intelligences that have been described are verbal/linguistic, musical, logical/mathematical, naturalist, visual/spatial, bodily/kinesthetic, interpersonal, and intrapersonal.

multipurpose board A writing board with a smooth plastic surface used with special marking pens rather than chalk. Sometimes called a *visual aid panel*, the board may have a steel backing and then can be used as a magnetic board as well as a screen for projecting visuals.

multitasking The simultaneous use of several levels of teaching and learning in the same classroom, with students working on different objectives or different tasks leading to the same objective. Also called *multilevel teaching*.

naïve theory See *misconception*.

norm-referenced Individual performance is judged relative to overall performance of the group (e.g., grading on a curve), as opposed to being criterion-referenced.

orientation set See *advance organizer*.

overlapping A teacher behavior where the teacher is able to attend to more than one matter at once.

overt behavior A learner behavior that is outwardly observable.

peer tutoring An instructional strategy that places students in a tutorial role in which one student helps another learn.

performance assessment See *authentic assessment*.

performance-based instruction Instruction designed around the instruction and assessment of student achievement against specified and predetermined objectives.

performance objective See *behavioral objective*.

phonemic awareness The ability to identify, isolate, and manipulate the individual sounds, or phonemes, in words.

phonics The application of letter-sound knowledge to decoding words.

phonological awareness The knowledge of the sounds in language, including the ability to hear syllables in words, hear the parts of words, hear individual sounds in words, and to identify and make rhymes.

portfolio assessment An alternative approach to evaluation that assembles representative samples of a student's work over time as a basis for assessment.

positive reinforcer A means of encouraging desired student behaviors by rewarding those behaviors when they occur.

preassessment Diagnostic assessment of what students know or think they know prior to the instruction.

procedure A statement telling the student how to accomplish a task.

psychomotor domain The domain of learning that involves locomotor behaviors.

reciprocal teaching A form of collaborative teaching where the teacher and the students share the teaching responsibility and all are involved in asking questions, clarifying, predicting, and summarizing.

reflection The conscious process of mentally replaying experiences.

reflective abstraction See *metacognition*.

reliability In measurement, the consistency with which an item or instrument is measured over time.

rubric An outline of the criteria used to guide the assessment of a student's work.

rules In classroom management, rules are the standards of expectation for classroom behavior.

schema (plural: schemata) A mental construct by which the learner organizes his or her perceptions of situations and knowledge.

school-within-a-school Sometimes referred to as a *house, cluster, village, pod,* or *family*, it is a teaching arrangement where one team of teachers is assigned to work with the same group of about 125 students for a common block of time, for the entire school day, or, in some instances, for all the years those students are at that school.

self-contained classroom Commonly used in the primary grades, it is a grouping pattern where one teacher teaches all or most all subjects to one group of children.

self-paced learning See *individualized learning*.

sequencing Arranging ideas in logical order.

simulation An abstraction or simplification of a real-life situation.

special-needs student See *exceptional child*.

standards See *curriculum standards*.

student teaching A field experience component of teacher preparation, traditionally the culminating experience, where the teacher candidate practices teaching children while under the supervision of a credentialed teacher and a university supervisor.

summative assessment Assessment of learning after instruction is completed.

teacher leader See *lead teacher*.

teaching See *instruction*.

teaching style The way teachers teach; their distinctive mannerisms complemented by their choices of teaching behaviors and strategies.

teaching team A team of two or more teachers who work together to provide instruction to the same group of students, either alternating the instruction or team teaching simultaneously.

team teaching Two or more teachers working together to provide instruction to a group of students.

terminal behavior That which has been learned as a direct result of instruction.

thematic unit A unit of instruction built on a central theme or concept.

theme school See *magnet school*.

think time See *wait time*.

tracking The practice of the voluntary or involuntary placement of students in different programs or courses according to their ability and prior academic performance. See also *ability grouping*.

traditional teaching Teacher-centered direct instruction, typically using lectures, discussions, textbooks, and worksheets.

transition In a lesson, the planned procedures that move student thinking from one idea to the next or that move their actions from one activity to the next.

untracking See *detracking*.

validity In measurement, the degree to which an item or instrument measures that which it is intended to measure.

village See *school-within-a-school*.

wait time In the use of questioning, the period of silence between the time a question is asked and the inquirer (teacher) does something, such as repeats the question, rephrases the question, calls on a particular student, answers the question him- or herself, or asks another question.

whole-language learning A point of view with a focus on seeking or creating meaning that encourages language production, risk-taking, independence in producing language, and the use of a wide variety of print materials in authentic reading and writing situations.

withitness The teacher's timely ability to intervene and redirect a student's inappropriate behavior.

year-round school A school that operates as is tradiational, that is with 180 school days, but the days are spread out over 12 months rather than the more traditional 10. Most common is a 9 weeks on, 3 weeks off format. Although not truly "year-round," at least as defined here, sometimes the term is used by a school or district when the school year is extended just 1 or 2 weeks in either the spring or in the fall, or both, but still with a month or more summer break.

young adolescent The 10- to 14-year-old experiencing the developmental stage of early adolescence.

Index

Abuse
  child, 32
  drug, 31–32
Academic failure, 214
Access mode, 283, 285
Accomplishment
  defined, 265
Accountability, 60, 202
Accuracy, 82
Accurate assessment, 245–247
Achievement
  defined, 265
  reporting student progress,
      267–272
Achievement testing, 29–30
  preparing students for, 29–30
Acquired immune deficiency
      syndrome (AIDS), 31
Active assessment, 245–247
Activities
  providing a variety of, 54–55
Activity reinforcers, 109
Adair, J., 42
Adams, A. H., 100
Adams, D., 100, 312, 345
Adams, J. M., 189
Adams, T. L., 239
Adams-Bullock, A., 133
Adler, S. A., 41, 44
*Affective and Cognitive Domains,
  The*, 192
Affective domain, 174, 178
  education in, 182–183
Affective domain hierarchy,
      181–182
After school
  unsupervised, 13
Airasian, P. W., 274
Albert, L., 110, 132
Algorithms, 150
Aligned assessment, 245–247
Aligned curriculum, 170
Allen, R., 73, 274
Allington, R. L., 191
Alternative assessment, 245–247
Alternative response tests, 254
Alternative schools, 8

*Alternatives to Retention and Social
      Promotion*, 275
America's Children, 31, 42, 190
Amral, L. M., 311
Amrein, A. L., 30
Analysis, 180
Anderson, G. E., 275
Anderson, W., 40
Andrade, H. G., 274
Anecdotal records, 252
Anticipated outcomes, 173, 224
Antisocial students, 213
Application, 180
Approximation, 150
Aristotle, 2
Armbruster, B., 191
Armstrong, T., 99, 239, 240
Arter, J., 274
Arts
  curriculum standards, 168
Asp, E., 274
Assertive discipline, 106, 109
Assertive Discipline, 132
*Assessing Young Children's Social
      Competence*, 192
Assessment, 224. *See also*
      Evaluation; Grading; Tests
  accurate, 245–247
  basic skills, 307–308
  classroom, 254–256
  in contest of instruction, 250
  cooperative learning, 328
  demonstration, 301
  diagnostic, 249
    learner characteristics,
      224
    procedure, 260–265
  direct, 245–247
  expository style, 290–291
  vs. grading, 267
  inquiry, 298
  language, 245–250
  oral report
    checklist, 258
  performance, 245–247
  portfolio guidelines, 260
  preassessment, 249

  procedure
    student progress, 251–253
    student participation, 256–260
Assignments. *See also* Homework
  learning from, 339–342
Astington, J. W., 100, 345
At-risk children, 14, 82, 214, 239
Attainment
  acceptable level, 173
Attendance
  compulsory school, 27
Attention deficit hyperactivity
      disorder (ADHD), 211
Audio-Visual Market Place, 67
Augmented decoding, 143
Authentic assessment, 245–247
Authentic learning, 284, 285
Avery, L. D., 241
Awakening Genius in the Classroom,
      99

Bailey, J. M., 274
Baker, R. A., 134
Baker, W. P., 133
Bakunas, B., 191
Banks, J. A., 43, 73
Barclay, K. H., 344
Barker, V., 43
Barone, D., 344
Barrow, L. H., 100
Bartek, M. M., 100
Basal reading program, 143
Basic School, The, 6, 40
Basic skills, 221–222, 305–309
  assessment, 307–308
  independence habits, 309
  methods and materials, 309
  program personalization,
      308–309
  stimulating program, 306–307
  structured, systematic, sequential
      program, 306
Battistini, J., 344
Beamon, G. W., 311
Beck, I. L., 100
Becker, R. R., 100

Becoming a Multiple Intelligences School, 238
Behavior modification, 106
Behaviors
  expected learner, 173
  facilitating, 52
  inappropriate
    consequences, 123
  intelligent, 83, 106
    characteristics, 79–83
    cognitive view, 83
  modeling appropriate, 55, 60
Bell, L. I., 50, 100, 311
Bergen, D., 191, 345
Berkowitz, R., 203
Berliner, D. C., 30
Berman, P., 239
Beyond Behaviorism, 133
Biancarosa, G., 191
Bicultural programs, 24
Bierlein, L. A., 41
Bilingual education, 23
Bilingual programs, 24
Bizar, M., 189
Black, S., 42, 43, 100, 191, 240, 345
Blackwelder, B. B., 133
Bloom, B. S., 190, 191, 318, 344
Bluffing, 98
Bodily learning style
  defined, 205
Bodrova, E., 191
Boers, D., 274
Bond, B., 274
Bower, B., 275
Boyer, Ernest L., 6, 40
Bracey, G. W., 274
Brain Compatible Assessments, 275
Brand, S., 240
Braun, B., 344
Breheny, C., 344
Brice, A., 43
Briggs, L. J., 190, 192
Brighton, C. M., 191
Brogan, B. R., 100, 344
Brogan, W. A., 100
Bromfield, R., 133
Brookhart, S. M., 274
Brophy, J. E., 57, 73, 107, 132, 133, 345
Brown, D. E., 100
Brown, J., 240
Bruce, B. C., 100
Bruner, J. S., 286
Brunn, M., 189
Brunner, P. M., 42
Bryan, J., 344
Bucher, K. T., 133
Bullying, 33–35
Burgoon, J. D., 42
Burns, M. T., 133

Burrett, K., 40
Bursuck, W. D., 275

Cade, T., 240
Cadwallader, T. W., 42
Cairney, T. H., 38
Cairns, R. B., 42
Callahan, C. M., 240
Canady, R. L., 344
Canter, Lee, 109, 132
Canter, Marlene, 109, 132
Career portfolio, 257
Carnegie Foundation for the
  Advancement of Teaching, 6
Carr, J. F., 274
Carr, S. C., 274
Carroll, John, 318, 344
Caskey, M., 240
Cassel, P., 132
Cavazos, L. F., 191, 345
CD-ROM, 69
Cermak, S., 189
Chamberlain, E., 73
Chancellor, D., 101
Chappuis, S., 274
Character, 2
Character education, 5
  Internet resources, 6
Charney, R., 133
Charter school, 25
Cheating, 118
Checkley, K., 191
Checklists, 252, 258–259
Chen, Y., 274
Cheney, D., 203
Child, The, 41
Child abuse, 32
Child neglect, 32
Childs, K. M., 101
Chin, C., 100
Chollas Elementary School (San
  Diego, CA), 25
Ciardiello, A. V., 100
Citizenship education, 4–5
Civics
  curriculum standards, 168
Clarification, 58, 88
Clark, G., 239
Classifying, 83
Classroom
  assessment, 254–256
  atmosphere, 108
  *Awakening Genius in the
    Classroom*, 99
  climate, 108
  Control Theory in the Classroom,
    132
  *Creating an Inviting Classroom
    Environment*, 133

*Discipline and Group Management
  in Classrooms*, 73
diversity, 8–11
environment, 108
experience
  social psychology view, 83
learning center, 322–325
Looking in Classrooms, 73
management, 108–111
  organizational aspects,
    122–129
  principles, 112–113
multiage, 8
*Multiple Intelligences in the
  Classroom*, 239
Natural Classroom Assessment,
  276
organization, 60
person-centered, 110–111
Positive Classroom Discipline, 133
Positive Classroom Instruction,
  133
*Positive Discipline in the
  Classroom*, 132
Praise in the Classroom, 73
question-driven, 96
Scoring Rubrics in the Classroom,
  274
self-contained, 8
*Student-Involved Classroom
  Assessment*, 74
*Classroom Applications of
  Educational Measurement*,
  275
Classroom Assessment, 274
Classroom Management, 73
Classroom Spaces that Work, 133
Clayton, M. K., 133
Cleland, J. V., 274
Clement, R., 43
Closure, 224
Clough, J. B., 42
Cognitive domain, 174, 177
  hierarchy, 179–181
Coker, D., 191
Collaborative Decision Making,
  41, 239
Collaborative group planning, 317
Collier, V. P., 41
Collins, K. M., 240
Collins, V. D., 192
Columbine High School (Littleton,
  Colorado), 35
Combs, A. W., 133
Commitment, 51
Committee members, 317
Communicating, 185
Communicating Student Learning,
  274
Communication, 61

Communication model, 111
Community, 35–37
Comparing, 83
Competency-based grading, 265
Competent classroom teacher
   characteristics, 59–64
Completion tests, 254
Comprehension, 180
Compulsory school attendance, 27
Computer-assisted instruction
      (CAI), 65, 67
Computer-assisted learning
      (CAL), 67
Computer-based instructional
      tools, 67–70
Computer-managed instruction
      (CMI), 67
Computers, 64–65, 67–70
Concluding, 83
Conduct. *See also* Discipline
   unprofessional, 17
Cone, S. L., 190
Cone, T. P., 190
Conferences, 252
Confidence, 62
Conflict
   immediate resolution, 120
   instruction on, 120–121
   long-range solutions, 120
   minimizing, 119–122
   resolution, 119–122
Conley, D. T., 40
Conn, K., 73
Consequences
   vs. punishment, 115
Content areas
   reading comprehension, 144
Control
   defined, 106–107
Control theory, 106
Control Theory in the Classroom, 132
Controversy
   preparing for and dealing with,
      235–237
Conventional unit, 232
Cookson, P., 43, 73
Cooper, J. D., 191
Cooperative learning, 325–328
   assessment, 328
   grading, 328
   small groups, 208
   theory and use, 326
Cooperative learning groups (CLG),
      326
   difficulty using, 328
   outcomes, 327
   roles within, 326–327
   when to use, 327
Cooperative thinking, 80
Copyright, 67

Coray, G., 274
Corbett, D., 73
Corbin, L., 43
Corrective instruction
   procedure, 260–265
Corrective reading, 145
Costa, A. L., 72, 73, 99, 311
Costante, C. C., 191
Cotton, K., 43
Coy, D. R., 16
Craig, J., 42
Craig, W. M., 42
Crawford, B. A., 311
Creating, 185
*Creating an Inviting Classroom
      Environment*, 133
Creating Partnerships with Parents,
      203
Creative dramatics, 159
Creative thinking, 162–163
Creativity, 80
   and high-achieving students,
      213
Criterion-referenced grading, 265
Criterion-referenced measurement,
      246
Criterion-referenced tests, 247–249
Critical thinking, 294–296
   questioning, 96–98
Critical thinking skills, 162–163
Cross-age coaching, 322
Cruickshank, D. R., 72
Cueing, 89
Cultural Foundations of Education,
      41
Cultural identity, 18
Current, L., 125
Curriculum
   documents influencing, 167–169
   elementary classroom, 140–141
   Internet resources on, 167
   learning objectives, 174
   national standards, 167–168
   skill areas, 160–162
   skills in, 160–166
   standards, 29–30
      arts, 168
      civics, 168
      economics, 168
      English/language arts, 168
      foreign language, 168
      geography, 168
      health and physical education,
         168
      history, 168
      Massachusetts, 169
      mathematics, 168
      Montana, 169
      North Carolina, 169
      physical education, 168

      reading, 168
      science, 168
      social studies, 168
      technology, 168
      Texas, 169
   state standards, 168–169
*Curriculum and Evaluation
      Standards*, 150, 189
Curtis, D., 240
Cutter, J., 240

Daily schedule, 221
   planning, 216–217, 220
Dale, E., 286
Dance, 158
Daniels, D. C., 73
Daniels, H., 189
Data
   facilitating student acquisition,
      55–56
Davidson, E., 346
Davidson, G., 73
Davies, D., 43
Davis, G. A., 133
de Jong, E. J., 41
De Lisi, R., 276
Deasy, R. J., 191
DeCesare, D., 43
Decision making, 61
   Collaborative Decision Making, 41,
      239
   phases, 50–51
      interactive, 50
      preactive, 50
      reflective, 50
Deductive proof, 291
Deffes, R., 191
Defiance, 118
Deiro, J. A., 73
DeJong, W. S., 42
Delivery mode, 283, 284
Demers, C., 274
Demonstration, 299–301
   assessment, 301
   assumptions, 300
   instructional resources, 301
   learner's role, 301
   purpose, 300
   teacher's role, 300–301
Developing Minds, 311
Devona, H., 239
Dewey, J., 291, 311
Diagnostic assessment, 249
   learner characteristics, 224
   procedure, 260–265
Diaries, 252
Didactic style, 283
Differentiation in Practice, 192
Diffily, D., 191, 345

Direct assessment, 245–247
Direct experiences, 286, 287
Direct instruction
   defined, 280–281
Direct-learning center, 323
Direct measurement, 246
Directions
   clarity, 127
Directness
   degrees, 283
Discipline
   assertive, 106, 109
   Assertive Discipline, 132
   defined, 106
   judicious, 111
   Judicious Discipline, 133
   Positive Classroom Discipline,
      133
   Positive Discipline, 73
   *Positive Discipline in the
      Classroom*, 132
   self-discipline, 106
   *Teacher's Guide to Cooperative
      Discipline, A*, 132
*Discipline and Group Management
   in Classrooms*, 73
Discipline that Works, 133
Discipline Without Tears, 132
Discovery, 294–296
   vs. inquiry, 292–294
Discovery experience, 291
Discovery learning, 162–163
Divergent-thinking students, 213
Diversity
   classroom, 8–11
Dixson, C., 239
Domenech, D. A., 40
Douglass, S. L., 191
Doyle, W., 133
Dreikurs, Rudolph, 110, 132
Driscoll, A., 73
Drug abuse, 31–32
Dryfoos, J. G., 41
Dual-immersion, 24
Dual-language, 24
Duck, J., 43
Duffy, G. G., 143, 189
Duffy-Hester, A. M., 189, 238
Duhaney, L. M. G., 276
Dunn, R., 74, 239, 240, 241, 312
Duration, 234–235
Dyads, 322

Earhart, A., 82
Economics
   curriculum standards, 168
Edison, T., 65
*Educating Americans for the 21st
   Century*, 151, 189

Education Act Amendments of 1972
   (PL 92-318)
   Title IX, 16
Education for All Handicapped
   Children Act (EAHCA)
   (PL 94-142), 21–22, 210–211
Educational Assessment of Students,
   275
Educational broker, 59
Educational opportunity
   equality, 15–29
Educational spending
   variations, 15
Edwards, J. A., 100
Effective Educational Practices, 312
Efficiency, 26
Eidson, C. C., 192
Eisner, E., 96
Elementary classroom curriculum,
   140–141
Elementary education
   fundamental purposes, 3–8
Elementary schools
   key practices, 26
   trends, 26
Elliott, S. N., 190
Emotional Intelligence, 99
Empathy, 80
Empowerment, 116
Encouragement, 111
   vs. praise, 57
Englert, C. S., 344
English, L., 238
English as a second language
   (ESL), 23
English language
   newcomers to, 22–24
English/language arts, 140, 141–149
   curriculum standards, 168
English language learners (ELL),
   23, 206–208
Environment
   creating psychologically safe,
   56–58
Estimation, 150
Ethnic minorities, 11
Ethnicity, 18
Evaluation, 181, 245. *See also*
   Assessment
   *Curriculum and Evaluation
      Standards*, 150
   formative, 231, 247
   summative, 247
Evaluative (judgmental) responses,
   87
Expectations of Excellence, 190
Expected learner behavior, 173
Explaining, 287–288
Expository style, 283, 287–291
   assessment, 290–291

assumptions, 288–289
instructional resources, 290
learner's role, 289–290
purposes, 289
teacher's role, 289
Expressive arts, 141, 158–159
   planning learning activities for,
      218–219, 222
Extended families, 13

Fagan, H., 191, 240
Family instability, 214
Family life, 11–14
Family socioeconomic situation,
   214
Family tragedy, 214
Farenga, S., 274
Farr, B., 276
Farrell, A. D., 42
Fasko, D., 240
Feedback
   homework, 340–341
Feldhusen, J. F., 239
Ferrell, R., 276
Filcheck, H. A., 133, 275
Finn, J. D., 43
Finn, K. V., 43
Fischer, P., 100, 312
Folk songs, 159
Ford, M. P., 345
Foreign language, 166–167
   curriculum standards, 168
Foreign language experience
   (FLEX), 166
Foreign language in the elementary
   school (FLES), 166
Formative evaluation, 231, 247
Forrest, L., 134, 241
Forton, M. B., 133
Foss, K., 74
Foster-Harrison, E. S., 133
Franklin, J., 240, 274, 345
Franks, L., 191, 240
Fredericks, A. D., 191
Fredrick, L. D., 240, 345
Freedman, M. P., 312
Freedom to Learn, 111
Freeland, K., 239
Freiberg, H. J., 74, 110–111, 133
Froyen, L. A., 73
Frykholm, J. A., 240
Fuchs, D., 344
Full-day kindergarten, 14
Full inclusion, 21, 210
Full-service schools, 14, 156

Gagne, R. M., 190
Galbraith, P., 99

Garcia, J. A., 36
Gardner, H., 238
Garrison, L., 311
Garthwait, A., 275
Gathercoal, F., 133
Gathercoal, P., 111
Gauthier, L. R., 100
Gay, G., 43, 73
Gender
  vs. sex, 41
Gender bias, 19
Gender discrimination, 16
Gender equity, 19–20
  questioning, 91
Generalizing, 83
Genesee, F., 239
Geography
  curriculum standards, 168
Georgiady, N. P., 275
Gersten, R., 191
Geva, E., 191
Gifted and At Risk, 239
Gil, D. G., 42
Giles, H., 43
Ginott, H. G., 111, 133
Glasser, W., 110, 132
Glassner, S. S., 190
Glenn, H. S., 132
Glossary, 347–353
Goals. *See also* Objectives
  clarity, 127
  expectations, 224
  instructional
    facilitating achievement,
      113–116
  and objectives, 169–178
  *Taxonomy of Educational Goals
    Handbook*, 191
Goals 2000, 29
Goleman, D., 99
Gonzalez-Jensen, M., 346
Good, T. L., 57, 73, 107, 132, 133,
  344, 345
Goofing off, 116–117
Goos, M., 99
Gordon, E. W., 43
Gordon, T., 111, 133
Goudvis, A., 312
Gould, F., 43
Grade-level organization, 27–28
Graded school concept, 28–29
Grading, 265–266. *See also*
  Assessment
  vs. assessment, 267
  competency-based, 265
  cooperative learning, 328
  criterion-referenced, 265
  determining, 266
  norm-referenced, 265
Grading, 274

*Grading and Reporting Student
  Progress in an Age of
  Standards*, 276
Grant, J., 40, 240
Graphic reinforcers, 109
Gray, E. N., 312
Greb, F., 240
Greco, L. A., 133, 275
Greene, L., 192
Greer-Chase, M., 133
Griffin, M. L., 191, 345
Grigorenko, E. L., 238
Grossman, P. L., 276
Group discussion, 251
Group facilitator, 326
Group leadership, 317
Group learning, 316–353
Group process skills, 317–318
Growth portfolios, 257
Grunwald, B. B., 132
Guardians, 35–37. *See also* Parent(s)
  conference preparation, 260–272
  establishing contact with, 268
  involvement
    reference items, 203
*Guide for Developing an
  Interdisciplinary Thematic
  Unit, A*, 241
Guided oral reading, 145
Gunter, P. L., 240
Guskey, T. R., 274, 275
Gustafson, C., 43, 203
Gut, G. M., 190

Haertel, G. D., 132
Hamm, M., 100, 312, 345
Hands-on/minds-on learning, 285
Handwriting, 146–147. *See also*
  Writing
Hardin, B., 43
Hardin, M., 43
Harpaz, Y., 100
Harris, D. E., 274
Harris, J. R., 41
Harris, R., 35
Harris, R. L., 100
Harrow, A. J., 191
Hart, T., 345
Hartnell, M., 100
Harvey, S., 312
Hauslein, C. M., 191
Hawley, W. D., 43, 73
Health and physical education, 141,
  154–158
  curriculum standards, 168
  planning learning activities for,
    219, 222
Hecht, M., 43
Henk, W. A., 275

Herschell, A. D., 133, 275
Hester, J. L., 312
Hewit, J. S., 41
Hickenbottom, S., 228
High-achieving students
  and creativity, 213
History
  curriculum standards, 168
Hitz, R., 73
Hoban, C. F., Sr., 286
Hoeck-Buehler, S., 345
Hoerr, T. R., 238
Hofferth, S. L., 43
Hoffman, J. V., 43, 143, 189
Holley, W., 191
Home–school partnerships, 38
Homeless, 11
Homework
  feedback, 340–341
  *How to Help Your Child with
    Homework*, 38
  learning from, 339–342
  student recovery, 341–342
*How to Help Your Child with
  Homework*, 38, 345
How We Think, 311
Hugging, 17
*Human Characteristics and School
  Learning*, 344
Human relations
  working toward warm, 116
Humor, 63, 82
Hunkins, F. P., 99
Hunsader, P. D., 74, 134
Hutchins, E. J., 344
Hymowitz, K. S., 43

Illicit drug use, 31–32
Immersion, 23
Implementation phase
  of instruction, 227–231
*Implementing Student-Led
  Conferences*, 274
Improvement, 302–303
Impulse writing, 149
Impulsiveness, 80
Inappropriate behavior
  consequences, 123
Inclusion, 21–22, 210
Inclusive elements, 234–235
Indirect instruction
  defined, 280–281
Individualized Educational Program
  (IEP), 22, 210
Individuals with Disabilities
  Education Act (IDEA)
  (PL 101-476), 21, 210–211
Inductive discovery, 291
Inferring, 83

Influence, 2
Information processing
  perspective, 83
Information technology, 64–65
Inlay, L., 191
Inquiry, 294–296
  assessment, 298
  assumptions, 296
  cycle, 293, 295
  instructional resources, 297–298
  learner's role, 297
  levels, 293
  purpose, 296–297
  teacher's role, 297
  vs. discovery, 292–294
Inquiry skills, 162–163
Inquiry teaching, 291–298
Instruction
  beginning organization, 199,
    203–204
  decision-making phases of, 50–51
  direct *vs.* indirect, 283–284
  organizing, 225–227
  planning for, 203–204
Instructional accountability
  accepting and sharing, 53–54
Instructional competencies
  identifying and building, 51–59
Instructional goals
  facilitating achievement, 113–116
Instructional material, 224
Instructional media, 65–70
Instructional objectives, 170,
    171–173
  formulating, 225
Instructional planning
  importance, 196–241
Instructional strategies
  facilitating, 52
  selection, 280–312
    theoretical considerations,
      280–287
Instructional units, 231–235
  types of, 232–233
Integrated Character Education, 40
Integrated thematic unit (ITU), 233
Intellectual freedom
  providing boundaries, 114–115
Intelligent behavior, 83, 106
  characteristics, 79–83
  cognitive view, 83
Interactive phase
  of decision making, 50
Interdisciplinary thematic unit
    (ITU), 233
Interests, 63
Intermediate grades
  large-group instruction, 333–335
  small-group instruction, 333–335
Internalizing, 182

Internet, 64–65, 66–67
Internet and the Law, 73
Interpersonal learning style
  defined, 205
Intrapersonal learning style
  defined, 205
*Introduction to Contextual Teaching
    and Learning*, 312
Irvine, J. J., 43, 73

Jackson, A. W., 133
James, P., 74
Jankuniene, Z., 43
Jarvin, L., 238
Jensen, E., 208
Jimerson, S. R., 275
Johns, K. M., 240
Johnson, D. W., 42, 274, 345
Johnson, F. R., 191
Johnson, H., 54
Johnson, L. M., 346
Johnson, R. T., 42, 274, 345
Joiner, L. L., 240
Jones, F., 111, 133
Jones, R., 203
Jones Model, 111
Jonsberg, S. D., 43
Joyce, B., 274
Judgment, 245
Judicious discipline, 111
Judicious Discipline, 133
Juel, C., 191

K-W-L strategy, 320
Kafka, K., 273, 274
Kagan, S., 345
Kaplan, L. S., 275
Kapusnick, R. A., 191
Kasten, W. C., 40
Katsiyannis, A., 16
Katz, L. G., 192
Kaufman, A. M., 275
Kazemek, F. E., 74
Keehn, S., 241, 312
Keel, M. C., 240, 345
Kellam, S. G., 133
Keller, C. L., 240
Kellough, N. G., 71, 175
Kellough, R. D., 71, 73, 74, 175,
    192, 240, 241, 286
Kelly, E. B., 189, 344
Kelly, K., 43, 240
Kim, E. C., 286
Kim, Y., 44
Kinesthetic learning style
  defined, 205
King, C. M., 346
Kinsey, S. J., 40

Kirk, B. V., 41
Klentschy, M., 311
Knowledge, 179–180
  applying to new situations, 80
Knowledge-based tests, 255
Kohlberg, I., 82, 100
Koskinen, P. S., 189
Kosmoski, G. J., 275
Koufetta-Menicou, C., 100
Kounin, J., 54, 73, 111
Krank, H. M., 41
Krashen, S., 191
Krathwohl, D. R., 191
Kreider, H. M., 42, 203
Krueger, D., 344

Labeling
  avoid, 261
Lake, K., 273, 274
Lampe, J. R., 345
Laney, J. D., 345, 346
Lang, M., 133
Language arts. *See also* English/
    language arts; Foreign
    language
  planning learning activities for,
    217–218, 222
Language conventions, 147–149
Language-minority children
  guidelines for working with,
    207–208
Lantieri, L., 43
Large-group instruction, 328–329
  examples, 329–338
  intermediate grades, 333–335
  primary grades, 329
Larrivee, B., 74
Lathrop, A., 74
Lawrence, K. M., 275
Lawson, A. E., 133
Lead-up activities, 249
Learner performance, 250
Learning, 62. *See also* Quality
    learning
  alone, 321
  assessing, 62
  from assignments, 339–342
  constructivist approach, 83
  disruptions to, 117
  from homework, 339–342
  organization, 212
  in pairs, 322
  personalized instruction, 318–321
  small groups, 325
  understanding process, 60
Learning achievement
  student(s), 255
Learning activities
  for expressive arts, 218–219, 222

planning, 217–219, 220–222
  selecting developmentally
    appropriate, 285
Learning center
  classroom, 322–325
Learning difficulty
  student(s), 263
Learning environment
  planning, 217, 220
  structuring, 53
Learning experiences ladder,
  285–287
Learning objectives
  curriculum, 174
  measurable, 173–174
Learning problem
  evidence, 262–263
Learning styles, 17, 205–214
  defined, 205
Least restrictive environment (LRE),
  21, 210
Lederhouse, J. N., 275, 346
Lee, C., 99
Lee, E., 15
Lefstein, A., 100
Left-Handed Students, 189
Lehr, F., 191
Leland, C. H., 40
Leonard, J., 346
Leong, D. J., 191
Lesson plans, 60–61, 223–231
  components, 223–231
  defined, 223
  examples, 225–230
  form, 223
  level of specificity, 223
  sample, 175–176
  written
    adjustment, 198–199
    purpose, 197–198
    rationale, 197–199
Lessow-Hurley, J., 191
Leu, D. J., 74
Leuder, D. C., 203
Levenson, W., 65
Lewis, D. W., 43
Liebert, R. M., 41
Lifto, D., 74
Limited English proficiency (LEP),
  206–208
Limited English speaking (LES), 23
Lindeman, B., 43
Linguistic learning style
  defined, 205
Lipnickey, S. C., 275
Lipton, G. C., 192
Literacy, 3–4, 140
Literacy Leadership for Grades 5–12,
  192
Literacy Market Place, 67

Literal comprehension
  questioning, 93
Literature, 159
  planning learning activities for,
    222
Little, C. A., 241
Little, L. P., 40, 240
Little, T. S., 40, 240
Logical consequences, 106, 110
Logical/mathematical learning style
  defined, 205
Logs, 252
Looking in Classrooms, 73, 132, 133,
  344, 345
Looping, 8
Looping, 40, 240
Lopez, M. E., 42, 203
Lotan, R. A., 346
Lott, L., 132
Low-income students, 25
Lumsden, L., 42
Lying, 118

Magnet schools, 25
Magnusson, S. J., 240
Magoon, C., 228
Mains, L., 239
Mainstreaming, 22
*Maintaining Sanity in the
  Classroom*, 132
Maintenance programs, 24
Maldonado-Colon, E., 189
Malecki, C. K., 190
Mallen, L. P., 133
Management
  *Responsible Classroom
    Management for Teachers and
    Students*, 133
Manipulating, 185
Manning, B., 203
Manning, M. L., 133
Marchand-Martella, N. E., 192
Mariage, T. V., 344
Marinak, B. A., 275
Marking, 265–266
Marr, D., 189
Marriott, D. M., 43
Martella, R. C., 192
Martin, B. L., 192
Martin, M. A., 274
Martin, R., 100
Marzano, R. J., 43, 73, 74, 134, 190,
  192, 240, 274, 275, 312, 346
Masia, B. B., 191
Massachusetts
  curriculum standards, 169
Mastery learning, 318–319
Matching tests, 254
Materials manager, 326

Math anxiety, 150
*Math Wonders to Inspire Teachers
  and Students*, 240
Mathematical learning style
  defined, 205
Mathematics, 141, 149–150
  curriculum standards, 168
  planning learning activities for,
    218, 221
Matkins, J. J., 275
Matson, B., 189
Maurer, M. M., 73
McAndrews, T., 40
McCarthy, M. H., 43
McClellan, D. E., 192
McClung, M. S., 43
McCown, C., 40
McDonald, J. A., 43
McElroy, K., 346
McGoogan, G., 74
McKeown, M. G., 100
McLaughlin, V. L., 41
McNeil, C. B., 133, 275
McTighe, J., 274
Meaning, 144
*Meaning and Measurement of Moral
  Development, The*, 100
Measurement, 245
Measuring instrument
  reliability, 249–250
*Meeting the Needs of Second
  Language Learners*, 191
Mental arithmetic, 150
Mental development
  enhancing, 113
Mesmer, H. A. E., 344
Met, M., 166, 190, 192
Metacognition, 81, 256
Metzger, M., 134
Meyer, A., 239
Meyer, M. R., 240
Miller, H. M., 192, 203
Minds-on learning, 285
Minicucci, C., 239
Minority children
  language guidelines, 207–208
Moats, L. C., 192
Moir, E., 49
Montana
  curriculum standards, 169
Montgomery, K., 275
Montgomery, W., 43, 134, 240
Moon, C. E., 41
Moon, T. R., 275
Moore, J. C., 275
Moore, J. N., 240
Moral education, 5
Morrow, L. M., 238
Moskal, B. M., 275
Motamedi, V., 346

Moustafa, M., 189
Moving, 184
Moy, T., 346
Mulholland, L. A., 41
Multiage classrooms, 8
Multicultural Projects Index, 346
Multicultural Teaching, 239
Multilevel instruction, 339
Multiple choice tests, 254
*Multiple Intelligences in the
  Classroom*, 239
*Multiple Intelligences of Reading and
  Writing*, 240
Multiracial children, 12
Multiyear grouping, 8
Multiyear instruction, 8
Multiyear placement, 8
Munk, D. D., 275
Music, 158
Musical learning style
  defined, 205

Natale, J. A., 43, 192
National Charter School Directory,
  42
National Council for the Social
  Studies (NCSS), 153
National Council of Teachers of
  Mathematics (NCTM), 150
National Council on Education
  Standards and Testing, 29
National Governors Association, 29
National Network of Partnership
  2000 Schools, 36
*National Science Education
  Standards*, 152, 190
*National Standards for Parent/Family
  Involvement Programs*, 36,
  203
Natural Classroom Assessment, 276
Naturalist learning style
  defined, 205
Neel, J. H., 240, 345
Neighborhood violence, 36
Nelsen, J., 73, 110, 132
Nelson, L. L., 226
New Skills for New Schools, 203
New York Elementary School
  (Lawrence, KS), 139
Newton, L. D., 101
Nieto, S., 43, 73
Nitko, A. J., 275
No Child Left Behind Act of 2001, 7
Noels, K., 43
Non-English-speaking (NES), 23
Nonprejudiced, 60
Norm-referenced grading, 265
Norm-referenced tests, 247
North Carolina

curriculum standards, 169
North Dade Center for Modern
  Languages (Miami, FL), 25
Nussbaum, E. M., 346
Nuthall, G., 240

Objectives. *See also* Goals
  and goals, 169–178
  instructional, 170–173
    formulating, 225
  learning
    curriculum, 174
    measurable, 173–174
  sequencing, 185–186
  *Taxonomy of Educational
    Objectives*, 190
Observation, 251
O'Day, S., 346
Ogle, D. M., 344
Olweus, D., 44
One-parent family, 13, 41
Oosterhof, A., 275
Open-learning center, 323
Opitz, M. F., 345
Optimism, 62
Oral reading, 145
Oral report assessment
  checklist, 258
Organizational changes, 6–7,
  24–28
Organizing, 182
Ornelas, V., 36
Ornstein, A. C., 345
Osborn, J., 191
O'Sullivan, S., 44
Outcome-based education (OBE),
  170
Outcome-based measurement, 246
Overlapping, 54, 111
Owens, R. F., 312
Owings, W. A., 275
Ownbey, M., 240
Ownership, 116

Pai, Y., 41, 44
Paik, S. J., 312, 346
Paired team learning, 322
Palincsar, A. S., 240
Pappas, M. L., 312
Paraphrasing Strategy, The, 344
Pardini, P., 42
Parent(s), 35–37. *See also* Guardians
  conference preparation, 260–272
  establishing contact with, 268
Parent/guardian involvement
  reference items, 203
Parent–student–teacher
  organizations (PSTO), 36

Parent–teacher associations (PTA),
  36
Parent–teacher organizations (PTO),
  36
Partial inclusion, 21, 210
Partnership, 36
Passive acceptance responses, 87
Pastor, P., 44
Paterno, J., 189
Paul Revere Charter/LEARN Middle
  School (Los Angeles, CA), 25
Payne, R. K., 241
Paynter, D. E., 191
Pearson, P. D., 44
Pedagogical opposites, 282
Peer-assisted learning (PAL), 322
Pepper, F. C., 132
Perceiving, Behaving, Becoming, 133
Perfectionists, 213–214
Performance assessment, 245–247
  setting up, 247
Performance-based measurement,
  246
Performance standards, 170
Performance testing, 246–247
Permanent records, 204
Persistence, 82
Person-centered classroom, 110–111
Personal development, 5–6
Personal pain, 214
Personal reading, 144–145
Personalized instruction
  quality learning, 318–321
  strategies, 320–321
Physical activity, 208
Physical arrangements, 127–128
Physical contact, 17
Physical education, 141, 154–158
  curriculum standards, 168
  planning learning activities for,
    219, 222
Physical freedom
  providing boundaries, 114–115
Piaget, J., 82, 100
Pickering, D. J., 312, 346
Pilger, M. A., 346
Place, W. A., 100
Plan(s). *See also* Lesson plans
  details, 196–241
  preparation time, 196
Planning
  daily schedule, 216–217, 220
  instructional
    importance, 196–241
    personal example, 215–222
  and teaching
    sequential procedures, 232
  weekly, 222–223
Poetry, 159
Polite, V. C., 100

Pollack, D. R., 275
Pollock, J. E., 312, 346
Popham, W. J., 44
Portes, A., 44
Portfolio(s), 250, 252, 256–259
    career, 257
    growth, 257
    for instruction and assessment
        guidelines, 260
    proficiency, 257
    showcase, 257
Portfolio Organizer, 275
Posamentier, A. S., 240
Positive Classroom Discipline, 133
Positive Classroom Instruction, 133
Positive Discipline, 73, 132
Positive Discipline in the Classroom,
    132
Poverty, 10
Praise
    vs. encouragement, 57
Praise in the Classroom, 73
Prater, M. A., 192
Preactive phase
    of decision making, 50
Preassessment, 249
Precision, 82
Preferred activity time (PAT), 111
Pressley, M., 238
Primary grades
    large-group instruction, 329
    small groups, 329
Priorities
    establishing, 215–216, 220
Privilege reinforcers, 109
Probing, 88
Problem(s)
    defining, 317
    learning
        evidence, 262–263
    posing, 82
    seriousness, 116–118
    solving, 292
        questioning, 96–98
Procedures, 111, 224
    vs. rules, 115
Professional associations, 59
    guidelines for dealing with
        controversial topics, 236
Professional responsibilities, 48,
    62–63
Professionalism, 51
Proficiency portfolios, 257
Programmed instruction, 319
Protheroe, N., 192
Psychology of Intelligence, The, 100
Psychomotor domain, 174, 178,
    184–185
Pullout approach, 206
Punishment

vs. consequences, 115
Purkey, W. W., 134
Put Reading First, 191

Quackenbush, M., 42
Quality education, 6–8
Quality learning, 319
    assumptions, 319
    components, 320
    personalized instruction,
        318–321
    personalizing instruction
        strategies, 320–321
Quality School, The, 132
Queen, J. A., 133
Question-driven classroom, 96
Questioning, 58, 78–101
    all students, 90
    critical thinking, 96–98
    developing skill in, 83–86
    framing and stating, 84–85
    gender equity, 91
    literal comprehension, 93
    pacing, 86
    plan, 212
    procedural, 92–93
    raise hands, 91
    real-world problem solving,
        96–98
    reflective (thought), 94
    sequencing, 85–86
    specific purposes, 90–94
    student responses to, 86–89
    from students, 94–98
    wait time, 91
Questioning Skills for Teachers, 73
Quinn, A. E., 44

Races, 17–19
Racism, 12, 17–19
Radencich, M. C., 38, 345
Radziewicz, C., 41, 239
Rakow, S. J., 273
Rasmussen, K., 44, 190
Ratcliff, N. J., 275
Ravitch, D., 44, 275
Rea, P. J., 41
Readiness testing, 249
Reading, 142–143
    basal reading program, 143
    comprehension
        content areas, 144
    corrective reading, 145
    curriculum standards, 168
    levels
        variability, 331–332, 336–338
    oral, 145
    personal, 144–145

planning learning activities for,
    217–218, 221
Put Reading First, 191
Reading Horizons, 344
Real-world problem solving
    questioning, 96–98
Reality therapy, 110
Reality Therapy, 132
Reasoning, 162–163
Receiving, 181
Reclaiming Our Schools, 40
Recorder, 326
Reeves, M. J., 239
Reflections, 224
Reflective decisions
    written lesson plans, 197
Reflective phase
    of decision making, 50
Reflective thinking, 162–163
Reid, J., 241
Reinemann, D., 275
Reinoso, M., 134
Reliability, 63
    measuring instrument, 249–250
Religion
    Internet source, 190
Render, G. F., 41
Reporter, 326
Resource Guide for Teaching, A,
    73, 240
Responding, 182
*Responsible Classroom Management
    for Teachers and Students*,
    133
Responsible involvement
    developing skills, 115–116
Restating, 88
Results-driven education (RDE),
    170–173
Rettig, M. D., 344
Rhodes, W. A., 133
Ricci, B. J., 203
Ridenour, C. S., 100
Ridgway, E., 192
Rillero, P., 346
Ripple effect, 111
Risks, 14, 82, 214, 239
Roberts, P. L., 241
Roberts, T., 101
Rodgers, C., 74
Roe, M. F., 273
Rogers, C., 110–111
Rolheiser, C., 275
Romano, L. G., 275
Ronis, D., 275
Room citizenship
    planning learning activities for,
        219–220
Rose, D. H., 239
Roseberry-McKibbin, C., 43

Rosenbusch, M. H., 190
Roser, N. L., 241, 312
Rothberg, M., 346
Routines, 125–126
Rowe, M. B., 73
Rubado, K., 241
Rubrics
  numerical reporting
    sample, 266
  scoring, 258–259
    sample, 259
  Scoring Rubrics in the Classroom,
    274
Rudolph, W., 82
Rules, 111
  vs. procedures, 115
Rumberger, R. W., 41
Rusnak, T., 40
Ryan, K., 40

Safe schools
  Internet resources, 121
Safety, 62
  planning learning activities for,
    219
Safran, S. P., 190
Salcido, R. M., 36
Salend, S. J., 276
Samples, K., 42
Sanders, T., 44
Sapna, V., 44
Scaffolded instruction, 212
Scaife, J., 100
Schaeffer, E. F., 44
Schedule, 125–126. *See also* Plan(s)
Schieffer, C., 192
Schielack, J. F., 101
Schiller, L., 239
Schneider, R. B., 344
Schniedewind, N., 346
Schofield, J. W., 43, 73
Schon, D., 72
Schon, I., 192
Schonfeld, D. J., 42
School(s)
  alternative, 8
  attendance, 27
  charter, 25
  elementary
    key practices, 26
    trends, 26
  full-service, 14, 156
  getting acquainted, 200
  magnet, 25
  National Charter School Directory,
    42
  National Network of Partnership
    2000 Schools, 36
  New Skills for New Schools, 203

onsite visit, 200–202
  planning new beginning, 199–203
  Quality School, The, 132
  Reclaiming Our Schools, 40
  Study of Charter Schools, A, 25
  *Teaching Methods for Today's
    Schools*, 41
  Understanding Charter Schools, 41
School as a Home for the Mind, 72,
    73, 99
School Begins at Two, 54
School choice, 24–28
School nurse, 155–156
School restructuring, 6–7
School term
  starting well, 122–124
School-within-a-school (SWAS), 8
Schools Without Failure, 132
Schumaker, J. B., 344
Schumm, J. S., 38, 345
Schwab, J. J., 293
Schwartz, S., 239
Schwartz, W., 12, 16, 42
Science, 141, 151–153
  curriculum standards, 168
  planning learning activities for,
    218, 222
Science: An Integrated Approach, 192
Science for All Americans (SFAA),
    151, 152, 189
Science K–8, 241
Scientific literacy, 151
Scientific thinking, 162–163
Scoring rubrics, 258–259
  sample, 259
Scoring Rubrics in the Classroom,
    274
Sears, S., 312
Searson, R., 74, 241, 312
Security
  written lesson plans, 197
Seeds University Elementary School
    (Los Angeles), 35
Selected response tests, 254
Self-concept, 164
Self-contained classrooms, 8
Self-control, 106
Self-direction
  developing skills, 115–116
Self-discipline, 106
Self-esteem, 164, 259
Self-image, 164
Sensale, L. M., 44
Senses, 82
Sensitive students, 214
Sequeira, P. V., 345
Serafini, F., 74, 276
Sex
  vs. gender, 41
Sexism, 19

Sexual harassment, 16, 17
Shapiro, J. P., 42
Shartrand, A. M., 42, 203
Shaunessy, E., 101
Shearer, C., 192
Sherman, L., 99, 191, 240
Sherman, S., 40
Short answer tests, 254
Showcase portfolios, 257
Sidelnick, M. A., 192
Silence, 58
Sileo, N. M., 192
Silgo Creek Elementary School
    (Silver Springs, MD), 190
Simon, K. G., 101
Simonsen, F. L., 192
Simpson, C., 74
Simulated experiences, 286, 287
Singh, N., 44
Single parents, 10
Sketch plan, 222–223
Skill center, 323
Skillings, M. J., 276
Skills instruction, 301–305
  application, 304–305
  feedback, 303–304
  learner involvement, 302
  maintenance, 305
  meaningfulness, 302
  practice, 302–303
Skinner, B. F., 65, 132, 198
Slocumb, P. D., 241
Small groups
  cooperative learning, 208
  examples, 329–338
  intermediate grades, 333–335
  learning, 325
  primary grades, 329
Smith, A. F., 192
Smith, J. K., 276
Smith, K., 239
Smith, L. F., 276
Smith, P. H., 41
Smutny, J. F., 346
Social development
  enhancing, 113
Social intelligence, 80
Social reinforcers, 109
Social relations
  encouraging harmonious,
    119–122
Social skills, 163–166
Social studies, 141, 153–154
  curriculum standards, 168
  defined, 153
  planning learning activities for,
    218, 222
Social tragedies, 31–35
Socioeconomic influences, 14–15
Socratic questioning, 89–90

Sosniak, L., 30, 42
Spatial learning style
    defined, 205
Special attention, 63
Special needs, 209–211, 214
Special-needs students
    guidelines for working with,
        211–212
Spelling, 145–146
    conscience, 146
Standard unit, 232
Standardization, 26
Standardized tests, 247
Stealing, 118
Stephan, W. G., 43, 73
Sterling, D. R., 275
Sternberg, R. J., 238
Stevahn, L., 275
Stevens, B. A., 346
Stevens-Smith, D. A., 192
Stiggins, R. J., 74, 273, 274, 276
Stodolsky, S. S., 276
Strahan, D. B., 134
Strategies
    instructional
        facilitating, 52
        selection, 280–312
    K-W-L strategy, 320
Strecker, S. K., 192
Stright, A. D., 134, 346
Student(s)
    corrective work, 263–265
    and creativity, 213
    diversity and differences
        guidelines for working
            with, 209
        recognizing and working with,
            206–207
    gifted
        working with, 213–214
    individual differences, 10
    learning achievement, 255
    learning difficulty, 263
    mobility, 13
    questioning from, 94–98
    rights, 16–17
    at risk
        working with, 14, 82, 214, 239
    special-needs, 209–211
        guidelines for working with,
            211–212
    values, 6
*Student Cheating and Plagiarism in
    the Internet Era*, 74
*Student-Involved Classroom
    Assessment*, 74, 273, 274,
    276
Student progress
    elementary teachers
        assessment procedure, 251–253

report
    planning for first, 268
    preparation, 270–271
Study of Charter Schools, A, 25
Study skills, 162
Styles
    learning, 17, 205–214
Subject matter content, 59
    relating to students' lives, 63
Substance drug abuse, 31–32
Succeeding with Standards, 274
Sullivan, M. H., 345
Sullivan, P., 43
Summative evaluation, 247
Sumrall, W. J., 346
Supplee, L. H., 134, 346
Surviving Your First Year of Teaching,
    74
Svoboda, M. L., 192
Sylwester, R., 273
Synthesis, 180–181
Systematic discrimination, 18

Takahashi-Breines, H., 312
Tangible reinforcers, 109
Task
    organizing to achieve defined, 317
Tax credits, 24–25
*Taxonomy of Educational Goals
    Handbook*, 191
Taxonomy of Educational Objectives,
    190
*Taxonomy of the Psychomotor
    Domain*, 191
Taylor, J. A., 134
Taylor, R., 192
Taylors Elementary School (Taylors,
    SC), 139
Teachable moments, 198, 207
Teacher
    competent classroom
        characteristics, 59–64
Teacher and Child, 133
Teacher-made tests, 253
Teacher–student progression, 8
*Teacher's Guide to Cooperative
    Discipline, A*, 132
Teaching
    and planning
        sequential procedures, 232
    realities, 215–220
Teaching Children to Care, 133
*Teaching Methods for Today's
    Schools*, 41
*Teaching Thinking Through Effective
    Questioning*, 99
Teale, W. H., 312
Technology
    curriculum standards, 168

Technology of Teaching, The, 132
Telling, 287–288
Ten Minute Rule, 339–340
Terms, 347–353
    clarification, 106–111
Testing
    achievement, 29–30
    National Council on Education
        Standards and Testing, 29
    performance, 246–247
    readiness, 249
Tests. *See also* Assessment
    alternative response, 254
    completion, 254
    criterion-referenced, 247–249
    knowledge-based, 255
    matching, 254
    multiple choice, 254
    norm-referenced, 247
    preparation, 254
    selected response, 254
    short answer, 254
    standardized, 247
    teacher-made, 253
Texas
    curriculum standards, 169
Thames, D. G., 192
Theater, 158
Thematic unit, 232
Think–pair–share, 320, 322
Think–write–pair–share, 322
Thinking, 79–83, 90
    flexibility, 80
    monitor, 326
Thomas, J., 275
Thomas, K., 100
Thomas, W. P., 41
Thomas J. Pappas School
    Web site, 41
Thompson, M., 240
Thought and Language, 344
Three Rs, 305–309
Tiedt, I. M., 239
Tiedt, P. L., 239
Tiegerman-Farber, E., 41, 239
Title IX
    Education Act Amendments of
        1972 (PL 92-318), 16
Token reinforcers, 109
Tollafield, A., 346
Tomal, D. R., 134
Tomasetti, B. W., 275
Tomlinson, C. A., 30, 42, 104, 134,
    192, 241
Torrez, N., 240
Tower, C., 101, 292, 312
Tracey, D. H., 238
Traditional style, 283
Traditional unit, 232
Transitional bilingual education, 23

Transitions, 128–129
Trumbull, E., 276
Trump, K. S., 42
Tuition costs, 25
Turning Points 2000, 133
Two-way programs, 24

*Ulrich's International Periodicals
    Directory*, 67
Underachieving students, 214
Understanding, 80
Understanding Charter Schools, 41
Unit
    format, 234–235
    instructional, 231–235
        planning and developing,
            233–234
        standard, 232
    teaching, 154
    thematic, 232
    traditional, 232
Unprofessional conduct, 17
Unsupervised
    after school, 13
Upham, D. A., 203

Vacca, D. M., 241
Vail, K., 190, 346
Validity
    measuring instrument, 249–250
Valued Voices, 192
Values-based management plan,
    106
Valuing, 182
Vandergrift, L., 99
VanTassel-Baska, J., 241
Verbal experiences, 286
Verbal/linguistic learning style
    defined, 205
Verrill, J., 275

Vicarious experiences, 286, 287
Victor, E., 192, 241
Violence, 33–35, 118
Violence Against Children, 42
Visual arts, 158
Visual experiences, 286
Visual/spatial learning style
    defined, 205
Volger, K. E., 241
Vouchers, 25
Vukelich, C., 273
Vygotsky, L., 325, 344

Wager, W. W., 190
Walberg, H. J., 132, 312, 346
Waldron-Soler, K. M., 192
Walling, D. R., 239
Walters, L. S., 345, 346
Walther-Thomas, C., 41
Wang, C., 276
Want, M. C., 132
Warger, C., 241, 276
Wassermann, S., 73
Weast, J. D., 41
Web sites, 66–67
Weekly plan, 222–223
Weertz, M., 40
Weiss, H. B., 42, 203
Weissbourd, R., 74
Welker, C. J., 42
Wells, H. G., 2
Wessler, S. L., 16
Wherry, J. H., 44, 203
Whipple, A. D., 275
Whiteford, T., 43
Whitehead, D., 101
Whittier, K. S., 41
Whole language, 144
Wilen, W., 73, 101
Willard-Holt, C., 41, 239
Willey, R., 73

Williams, K. R., 346
Wilmer, J. W., 100
Wilson, B., 73
Wimbey, A., 100
Windsor, M., 189
Winebrenner, S., 241
Withitness, 54, 111
Witt, V., 192
Wolfe, P., 312
Woo, M., 238
Wooten, D. A., 192
Work samples, 252
Writing, 148
    board, 299
    handwriting, 146–147
    impulse, 149
    *Multiple Intelligences of Reading
        and Writing, The*, 240
    think–write–pair–share, 322
Written lesson plans
    adjustment, 198–199
    purpose, 197–198
    rationale, 197–199
Wynne, E. A., 40

Xin, J. F., 134, 241

Yell, M. L., 16, 41, 239
Yopp, H. K., 192
Yopp, R. H., 192
York, K. C., 192
Young, J. C., 192
Young, P. G., 192
Youth gangs, 32–33

Zemelman, S., 189
Zimmerman, E., 239
Zimmerman, J., 346
Zirkel, P. A., 134